MW00826236

GCN
GLOBAL CYCLING NETWORK

This publication was made by, and is published by, the *Global Cycling Network* ("GCN"). The GCN brand is owned by and associated logos are the registered trademarks of Play Sports Network Limited, a company registered in the United Kingdom at Chiswick Park Building 2, 566 Chiswick High Road, London W4 5YB United Kingdom.

First published in Great Britain in 2020

Studio and lifestyle photography by Joby Sessions
Additional photography by Stephen Mckay
Cover bike courtesy of Specialized
Pages 15 and 17 bikes courtesy of Canyon
Pages 15 and 20 bikes courtesy of Pinarello

Rest easy: no bikes were harmed in the making of this book.

ISBN: 978-1-8382353-1-4

Printed and bound in Great Britain by Hampton Printing Ltd, Bristol.

This book is printed on recyclable FSC (Forestry Stewardship Council) certified paper, which is sourced from sustainably managed forests, produced at a mill and printed by a printer that has been certified to the ISO 14001 environmental standard using vegetable oil based inks, and aqueous based coatings.

www.playsportsnetwork.com

PRESENTS

ESSENTIAL ROAD BIKE MAINTENANCE

all you need to know to fix your bike

BEGINNER BASICS - TOP TOPS - SET-UP SECRETS - ESSENTIAL REPAIRS - TECH EXPLAINED - PROBLEMS SOLVED

GCN
GLOBAL CYCLING NETWORK
PINARELLO
QUARQ
"But do, test and learn.
Try stuff. Don't be afraid"

FILLING A BICYCLE-SHAPED HOLE

Welcome to the Essential Road Bike Maintenance *guide!*

If you follow us regularly on GCN, I'm pretty sure you'll have already come across some of our other books, such as *The Plant-Based Cyclist* or *Endurance: How To Cycle Further*, which are all great but they do leave an obvious bicycle-shaped hole on the bookshelf. As in, they're not actually about the bike. So of course, we needed to fix that. Which is where this book comes in: a proper bike-focused bible to all those essential bike maintenance, repairs, and set-up tasks that we all need to know. I'm talking everything from basic bike set-up, how to get your wheels on and off, through setting up gears, bleeding brakes, and beyond. Basically, pretty much everything you would want to tackle on your bike (or bikes, plural) yourself. And then some.

Our idea was to not only fill it with all the essential workshop walkthroughs you'll need to take on most projects, but also to add in a huge amount of tips, hacks, and know-how to help improve both your workshop skills and your ride. What you won't find, however, is really, *really* advanced, pro-level topics such as how to build a wheel, facing frames or tapping threads, and so on; in part because they could easily fill an entire book themselves, partly because if you're at that level there are already some great books that cover them really well (and that no-doubt already grace your shelves), but mostly – for the rest of us – these are where a good local bike shop is worth their weight in gold.

But do, test and learn. Try stuff. Don't be afraid. Welcome to the world of bike maintenance!

Ollie Bridgewood – **GCN Tech Presenter**

How To Watch The Videos

So you can get both 'show-how' and 'know-how', every walkthrough has a companion video which you can watch for free from your computer, tablet or smartphone. To watch, either type in the short-link URL – e.g. *https://gcn.eu/GetPerfectShifting* – into your browser, or scan the QR code with your phone. Most will scan the code automatically with their camera, but if you need a QR code reader there are plenty of good, free ones to choose from across both the Apple and Android app stores.

"We've an ever-growing list of videos on virtually every conceivable bike repair, upgrade, hack or know-how topic"

WHAT IS GCN?

Celebrating everything that's great about cycling

The *Global Cycling Network* (GCN) is the world's largest and fastest growing online cycling channel in the world, bringing together a global community of road cyclists all bound together by daily entertaining, inspiring and informative videos, presented by ex-pro riders – from World Champions and Grand Tour finishers to Olympic medalists – across YouTube, Facebook, Instagram, the GCN app and beyond.

Every day of every week we create unique, informative and entertaining stories from all over the world of cycling to fuel your passion and knowledge for everything two-wheeled – all with the aim of helping you become a better rider: from tech advice and know-how, riding skills, entertaining features, riding inspiration, racing, and more, you can find it and watch them all for free on GCN.

We also have our sister channel, *GCN Tech*, which is dedicated to everything and anything to do with road bike tech: news, previews, know-how, workshop 'how-tos', pro bike checks, the latest and greatest innovations in bike technology, and much, much more. We've also got an ever-growing list of even more videos on virtually every conceivable bike repair, upgrade, hack or know-how topic for you to browse, watch and enjoy.

Across both channels, and on top of our daily new video releases, we also have thousands of videos already published for you to discover, browse and watch – including all of those featured in this book and many more – whenever and however you want. Videos as varied as how to fix your bike, what not to do on your first ever sportive or gravel race, and even the weird world of recumbent racing. Yeah, we even have that.

Need something to inspire you and get your blood pumping, like epic adventures around the world? We've got a lot of that. Want to know what life is like as a pro racer? Yes, we've got that – and more. Much, much more.

All our videos are presented by ex-pro riders-turned-presenters to offer you a uniquely qualified look into the world of cycling, inspiring through their passion, humour and insight, and placing you at the heart of everything we do.

Did we mention that you can also ride with us at our own events and festivals? That we have our own club delivering members exclusive sock designs every month? And our very own GCN app especially for our global community of cycling enthusiasts? Or that you can also find our content in Spanish, Italian, Japanese, French and German as well as English? We didn't? Well, we do, and yes you can.

And if you're into racing, we've also created the world's best place to watch and experience pro racing with the GCN Race Pass: 100% live and interactive racing, all season-long; the best analysis; no more adverts; by fans, for fans – all in the GCN app. You can find out more at **https://racepass.globalcyclingnetwork.com**.

So if you like the sound of all that why not saddle up to discover more about us at: **www.youtube.com/gcn** and **www.youtube.com/gcntech?**

 /gcn  /globalcyclingnetwork  /globalcyclingnetwork  @gcntweet  gcnclub.com

CONTENTS

INTRODUCTION

1 QUICK-START

2 TRANSMISSION

3 BRAKING

CONTENTS

KNOWLEDGE

ROAD BIKE TYPES

A road bike isn't just a road bike not anymore – there are now three broad categories: lightweight bikes, aero bikes, and endurance bikes

Lightweight Road Bikes

The lightweight road bike is most well-known as simply a road racing bike. But whereas aero road and endurance road bikes have characteristic geometries, the geometry of lightweight road bikes can vary considerably from brand to brand, so you might be as low and as stretched out as an aero bike, or even verging on as upright and as comfortable as an endurance bike. However, they're all typically stiff and comfortable, with classic frame silhouettes and generally round tube profiles. Of course, they're lightweight – around 250g lighter than even the lightest aero bike – and the majority of pro racers opt for a lightweight road bike most of the time.

Aero Road Bikes

In pure performance terms, aero bikes are the fastest types of bike you can buy. As well as being designed to be aerodynamic there are other things that set an aero bike apart from a lightweight road bike. For example, to help make you more aerodynamic, these tend to have the lowest front ends out there; so if you've got the flexibility in your hamstrings and your glutes then you'll be able to adopt a super aerodynamic position. However, this means they're not actually going to be suitable for every type of rider; many people are going to struggle to find a comfortable position on them. But if you're a proper racer with good flexibility, you can make them more comfortable on the road by running wider tyres and reap the benefits of both speed and comfort.

Endurance Road Bikes

Endurance bikes are a much broader category: generally speaking, they're road bikes which are built for comfort over long long distances, rather than for out-and-out racing speed – so perfect for long-distance rides, sportives and so on. They do give you a more upright and taller position than a race bike because they've got taller front ends and, as the reach from the handlebars to the saddle is also a little bit shorter coupled with slightly more relaxed geometry, they tend to be a little bit more stable and less twitchy to handle out on the road. As comfort is key, they also tend to have clearance for bigger tyres – up to and over 28c in width – and the frames are less vertically stiff than a normal road bike to help take even more sting out of the road.

KNOWLEDGE

ALL-ROAD BIKES

All-road is a new category that covers any road-derived bike that can ride on-and off-road

Gravel Bikes

Some gravel riding is basically just road riding, but a little dirtier on smooth non-Tarmac road, whereas some gravel riding is essentially mountain biking on rooty and rocky trails, so the spectrum of gravel riding – and gravel bikes – is the spread of terrains and surfaces from road to mountain bike. While a gravel bike is truly a 'do-it-all' bike some perform better at one end of the spectrum than the other, and vice-versa. Happily, most fall somewhere in the middle: with grippy tyres ranging from 35mm to 50mm (bigger tyres mean better versatility across a mix of off-road terrains); hydraulic disc brakes ensure consistent and powerful braking (and don't place any restrictions on tyre clearances), and slightly lower gear ratios than road bikes ensure the ability to ride up and down most things on- and off-road. Fittingly, many gravel bikes also get pressed into bike-packing duties.

Cyclo-Cross Bikes

The original off-road bike that's focused on performing for cyclo-cross (CX) racing through the winter season. Still a drop-bar bike derived from road racing but adapted for off-road CX races with narrower tyres than a gravel bike, and a more race focused and aggressive geometry. Pure-race bred CX bikes are out-and-out race machines and can lack any practical extras, including bottle bosses.

COMMUTER & URBAN BIKES

Getting you from home to work, and back again; and to the shops or to the cafe to meet with friends

Although commuter and urban bikes can look incredibly varied they all serve the purpose of being practical for the job in hand: getting from A to B, day in, day out. Some commuters are old road bikes pressed into commuting duties; some are drop-bar road-bike style but designed for the rigors of commuting in all weathers; others being hybrid-style flat bar bikes with a more upright riding position; some with gears; some with only one (aka a singlespeed), and some being fixed-wheel (aka fixie) upon which you can't freewheel or coast (as the pedals don't stop going around), and many more. For the most part, their brakes, gears, wheels and tyres all work in the same way as those seen on other road bike types, so the walkthroughs you find in this book will help keep them running smoothly, too. That said, there are a few notable exceptions, such as singelspeeds, fixies and bikes with hub gears and/ or belt drives as they need different servicing and set-up to traditional derailleur-style gears.

KNOWLEDGE

ROAD BIKE ANATOMY

Find your way away your bike confidently with the names of its key parts and components

5 Transmission (Gears)

Head over to page 20 for all the info

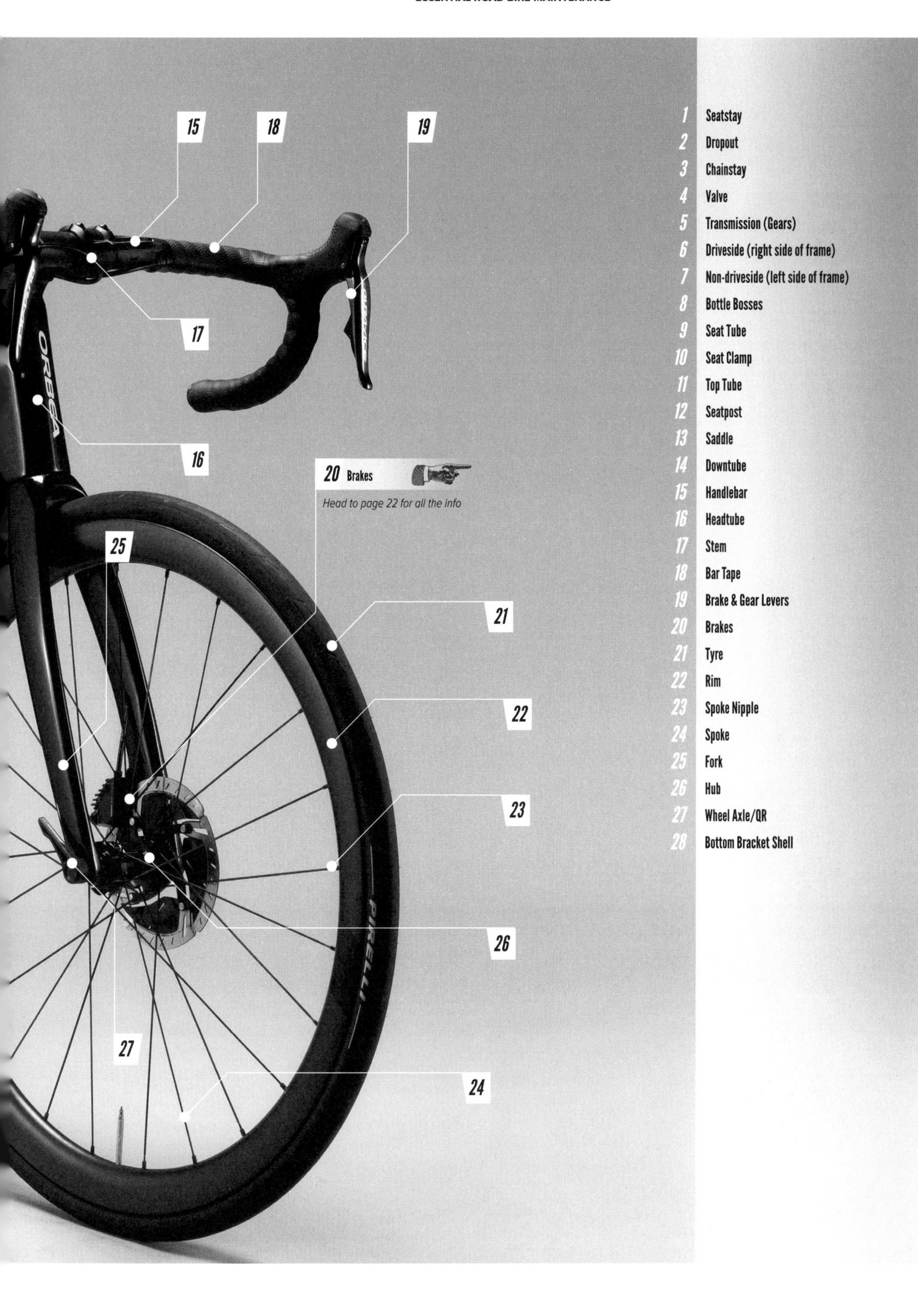
15
18
19
17
16
20 Brakes
Head to page 22 for all the info
25
21
22
23
26
27
24
1 Seatstay
2 Dropout
3 Chainstay
4 Valve
5 Transmission (Gears)
6 Driveside (right side of frame)
7 Non-driveside (left side of frame)
8 Bottle Bosses
9 Seat Tube
10 Seat Clamp
11 Top Tube
12 Seatpost
13 Saddle
14 Downtube
15 Handlebar
16 Headtube
17 Stem
18 Bar Tape
19 Brake & Gear Levers
20 Brakes
21 Tyre
22 Rim
23 Spoke Nipple
24 Spoke
25 Fork
26 Hub
27 Wheel Axle/QR
28 Bottom Bracket Shell

KNOWLEDGE

DRIVETRAIN

Find your way away your bike confidently with the names of its key parts and components

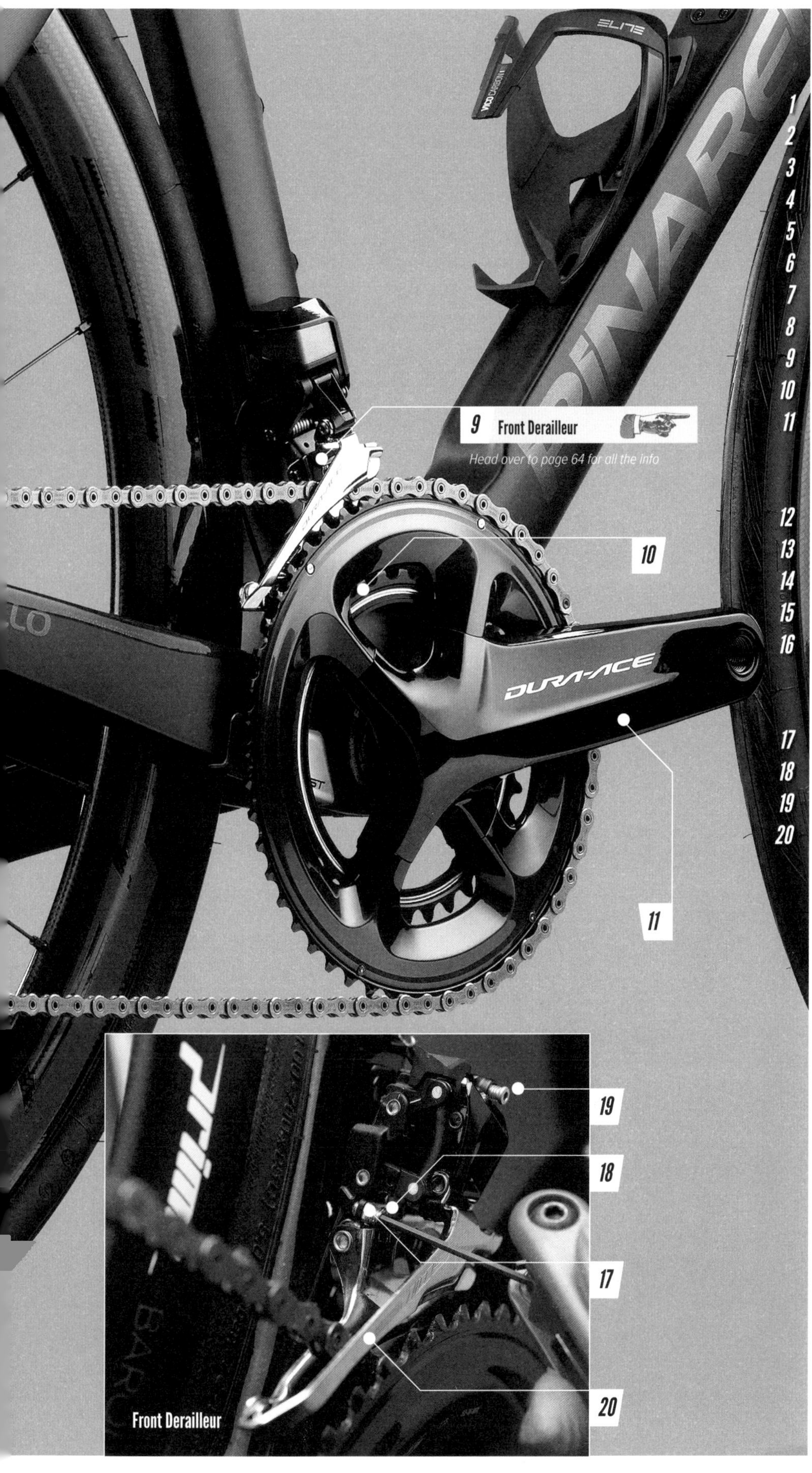

1 Cassette
2 Mech Hanger
3 B-link
4 Rear Derailleur/Mech
5 Upper Jockey Wheel
6 Lower Jockey Wheel
7 Pulley Cage
8 Chain
9 Front Derailleur/Mech
10 Chainring
11 Crankset

Rear Mech Inset

12 High (H) Limit Screw
13 Low (L) Limit Screw
14 B-Tension Screw
15 Cable Pinch Bolt
16 Cable Inner

Front Mech Inset

17 High (H) Limit Screw
18 Low (L) Limit Screw
19 Cable Tension Screw
20 Mech Cage

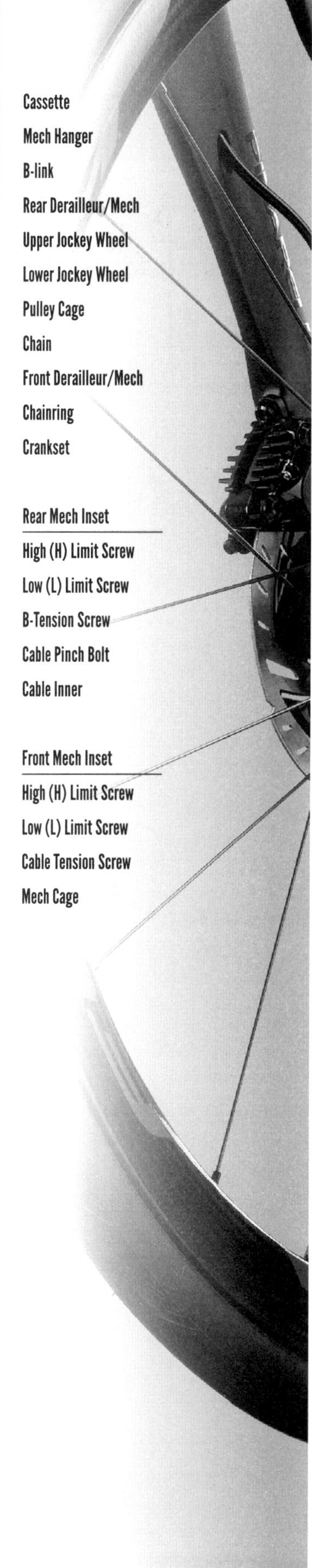

KNOWLEDGE

BRAKES

Scrubs your speed by pushing the brake pads either against the wheel rim's sidewall braking surface, or against a disc brake rotor

RIM BRAKE

Traditional road bike brakes use a cable to actuate a caliper brake pushing traditional rubber brake pads against the wheel rim

1. Inner Brake Cable
2. Cable Clamp
3. Cable End Cap
4. Pad Bolt
5. Pad Screw
6. Outer Cable
7. Barrel Adjuster
8. Brake Arm
9. Quick Release (QR) Cam
10. Pad Holder
11. Brake Pad

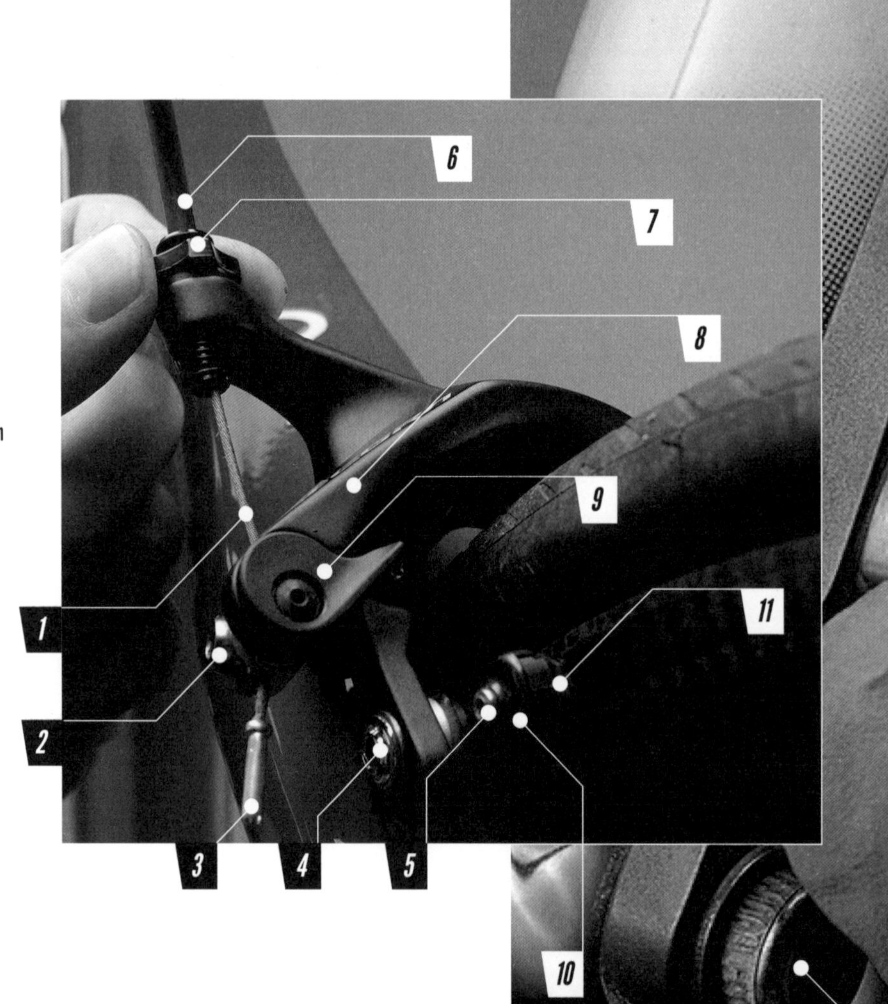

DISC BRAKE

Modern disc brakes have become more prevalent to deliver better, more consistent all-weather braking performance. Available in both cable and hydraulic types

1 Caliper Mounting Bolts (Upper and Lower)
2 Mounting Plate (For Direct Mount Brakes)
3 Hose
4 Connector Nut/Collar
5 Calliper Body
6 Bleed Nipple
7 Brake Pads

ESSENTIAL TOOLS & EQUIPMENT

1. Allen Keys
Most jobs on your bike will require an Allen key or two (or three!). Get a set ranging from 2 to 12mm, ideally with ball-ends on one end.

2. Tyre Levers
Another puncture repair essential is a pair of tyre levers. Avoid the metal ones as they can easily damage your inner tube, tyre and even your rim.

3. Cassette Lockring Tool
One of the essential tools you'll need to remove or fit a cassette onto your rear wheel. SRAM and Shimano can use the same tool, but you'll need a specific one for Campagnolo cassettes.

4. Chain Whip
Used in conjunction with the cassette lockring tool, the chain whip holds your cassette in place (preventing it from turning) while you loosen the locknut.

5. Pump
Without a pump, you won't be able to keep your tyres inflated or fix a puncture. Ideally you want two – a mini-pump to carry on rides and a track pump with a gauge for your workshop.

6. Adjustable Spanner
This has a huge number of potential uses, but it is often used to turn the cassette locking tool when removing a cassette. One is always worth having to hand.

7. Screwdrivers
Phillips and flat-head screwdrivers are useful for all kinds of jobs such as setting the limit screws on your derailleurs, fitting cleats and loads more.

8. Chain Tool
If you want to remove, shorten or fit a new chain to your bike, then you'll need a good chain tool. Go for the best quality one you can afford.

Great To Have

9. Workstand
So handy, it's almost an essential. A workstand will hold your bike upright and secure at a nice height for you to work on.

10. Torque Wrench
Similarly, a torque wrench is so useful it probably should be in the 'essential' category. Use it to ensure all your bolts are done up correctly and you don't damage components by over-tightening. It eliminates all doubt.

11. Long Nose Pliers
Handy for pulling cables taught and generally holding things in place while you tighten something up.

12. Cable Cutters
To cut brake and gear inners without causing them to fray, you'll need a dedicated cable cutter. If you've got hydraulic brakes, you'll also need a hose cutter.

13. Torx Keys
If your bike has lots of Torx bolts (also called hex wrenches) instead of Allen key bolts, then a set of Torx keys are an essential. If not, it's handy to have a set just in case.

KNOWLEDGE

GREASE, LUBRICANT, ANTI-SEIZE & THREADLOCK

Which ones to use on your bike and where best to use them

Grease

What Is It?

Grease is a lubricant made mostly from oil and an added thickener which turns it into a semi-fluid kind of substance. As well as lubricating moving parts, grease provides a level of water resistance and can also contain additives that resist corrosion and reduce friction too.

Where Should I Use It?

Grease is mostly used on moving parts of your bike that don't get taken apart that often, such as bottom bracket threads, bearings, brake lever assemblies and seat posts.

Which Type Is Best?

There are loads of bike-specific greases available, but basically you should go for a medium viscosity grease on all your bolts and bearings. Thick greases will prevent your bearings from moving properly while thinner greases will need replacing more often. During winter, or if you're doing a lot of riding in nasty conditions, you could try using marine grease which is super-sticky and extremely water repellent.

Anti-seize

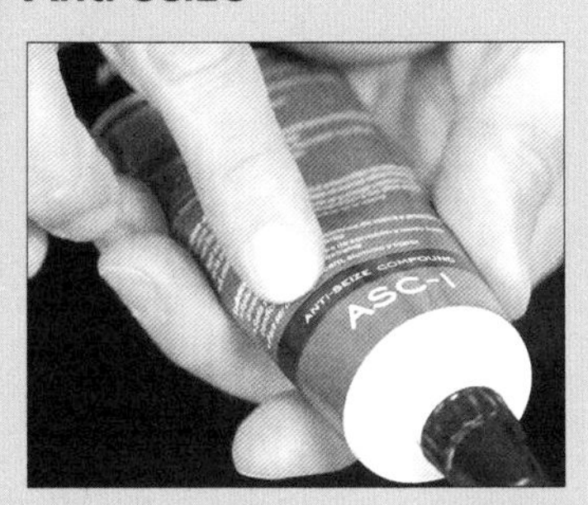

What Is It?
Basically anti-seize is a specialist grease that contains ground up bits of either nickel or copper. It's designed to stop components from seizing together, particularly when those components are made from reactive metals, such as aluminium and titanium.

Where Should I Use It?
Bottle cage bolts, stem bolts, aluminium bottom brackets or pedal threads.

Which Type Is Best?
Nickel and copper anti-seizes essentially have the same properties as each other, so either one is fine.

Carbon Assembly Paste

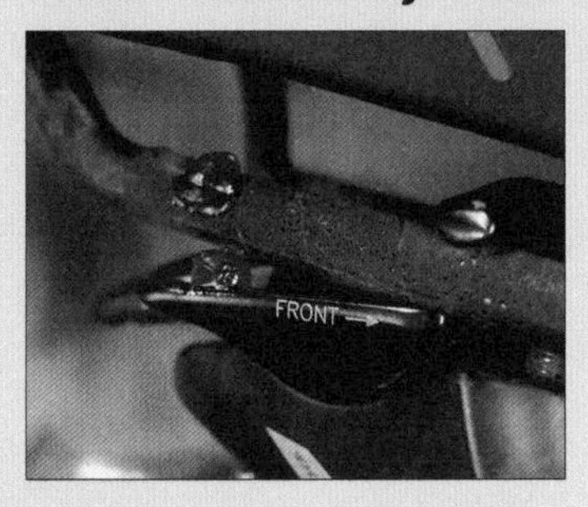

What Is It?
Carbon assembly paste is a paste that's slightly tacky to the touch and contains, in most cases, tiny granules of plastic to create more friction when applied to components that have been clamped together. This friction improves grip which means you need less torque when tightening and reduces the risk of damaging more fragile carbon components from over-tightening.

Where Should I Use It?
When you're clamping carbon parts or carbon and alloy parts together, such as fitting seatposts in frames, stems and bar, and saddle rails in seatpost heads.

Which Type Is Best?
Be sure to check the specific instructions on the product, but all carbon assembly pastes essentially provide the same basic function.

Threadlock

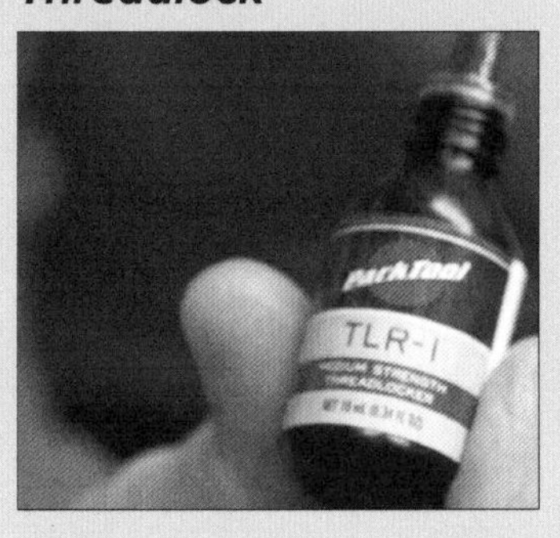

What Is It?
Threadlock is essentially a glue that does exactly what it says on the label – it locks your threads ensuring that components won't work loose while you ride. It's best to also use an adhesive primer to prevent components from bonding permanently.

Where Should I Use It?
On small, safety-critical components such as chainring bolts, disc brake rotors fixings, derailleur jockey wheel bolts, or any bolts that have a tendency to work themselves loose over time.

Which Type Is Best?
Threadlock usually comes in medium and high strength formulas. We'd recommend using medium strength for road bike use. Higher strength threadlock is better suited to bike fixings that get put under a lot of load, such as rear suspension systems on mountain bikes.

Lubricant

What Is It?
There are loads of different lubricants out there, but essentially they are all designed to reduce, wear and corrosion of your moving components.

Where Should I Use It?
On your chain, which will then lubricate your cassette, jockey wheels and chainrings as you pedal.

Which Type Is Best?
This depends on the conditions you're riding in. Wet lubes are designed to stay on your chain and drivetrain in wet weather, though its sticky nature means it easily picks up dirt, grime and dust as you ride. Dry lubes are designed for dry conditions and, though wet when applied, dry leaving a film-like covering which attracts a lot less dirt or dust than wet lube. The drawback is that dry lube washes off easily, which can happen if you get caught in the rain.

KNOWLEDGE

COMMON WORKSHOP MISTAKES

It's easy to make mistakes when DIY workshopping and they can end up expensive too. Here's how to avoid the most common wrenching wrongs

With impatience, slight lapses of concentration, ill advised short cuts or tool improvisation, we're not too proud to say we've made all the mess ups listed here – often more than once. Luckily for you we're not so ashamed we don't want to admit our mistakes and let you learn from them rather than repeating them yourself. So here's our unlucky twelve workshop fails that you should definitely avoid.

Screwing The Wrong Way

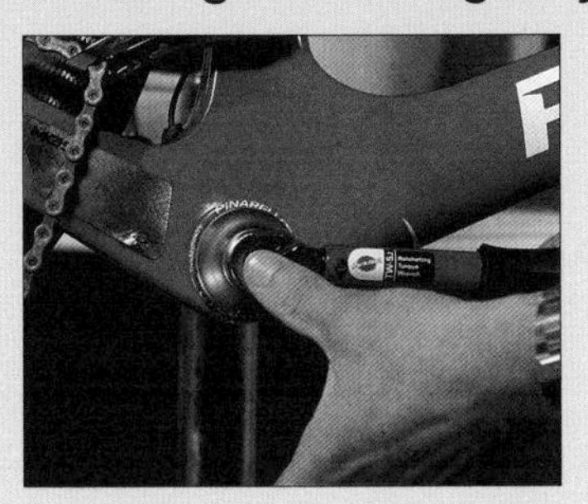

Because the bolts and other things that tighten on bikes are often presented at an odd angle it can be really confusing to work out which way to loosen or tighten them.

The Fix

In most cases it's 'righty-tighty, lefty-loosey'. So if the bolt is facing you then turning right/clockwise from the top will tighten it, but turning it left/anti-clockwise will loosen it. Bottom bracket cups are often reverse thread on the left hand side though.

THE HACK

If you manage to damage the opening section of threads in a component it's sometimes possible to re-cut them by screwing the bolt in from the back of the component. This works particularly well with pedals, but always be aware that the re-cut threads won't be as secure as the originals.

Don't Use The Wrong/Damaged Tools

Using the wrong tools (or the right tool wrongly) might even be more common than using them in the wrong direction. You might not even realise you're doing anything wrong either as an adjustable spanner or a slightly damaged Allen key might seem a snug fit to start and only slip and ruin the bolt when you apply more pressure.

The Fix

Always use fixed size spanners not adjustable ones wherever possible. Don't be tempted to use slightly damaged/rounded or cheap Allen keys either.

Don't Cross-Thread

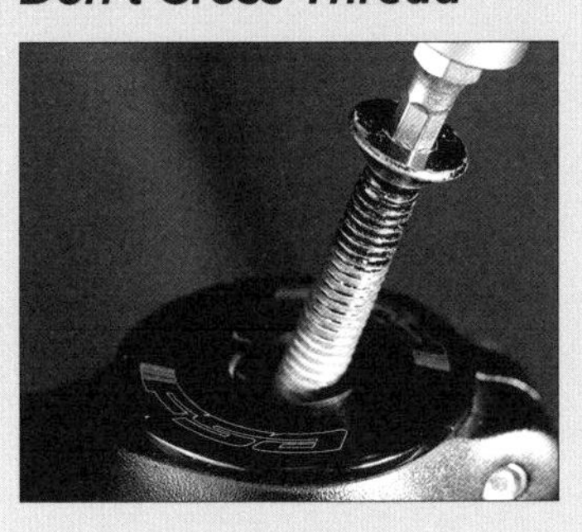

Another common mistake we've all made is to screw something – a bolt, or often a pedal – in at the wrong angle so that the screw threads cross. It doesn't have to be wrong by much to potentially destroy the threads in a lightweight alloy component and ruin it completely either.

The Fix

The best fix is to make sure the bolt is lined up perfectly straight by checking from as many angles as possible as you start to engage the thread. If in doubt go really carefully and continually re-check for the first few turns until you're sure but stop immediately if it starts looking wrong. Sometimes deliberately turning the bolt backwards to check that it stays in line as you spin it rather than twisting to one side can help you line up accurately too. Threads should also engage smoothly and easily with minimal resistance.

Don't Under/Over Tighten

Always tighten bolts up to the right tension. Too loose and the component can slip or rattle free which can be really dangerous with bars and stems etc. Too tight and you can strip the threads of the component or crush whatever it's clamping, effectively destroying them.

The Fix

The best fix for this is to use a torque wrench that tells you exactly how tight each fastening is and refer that to the torque marked on the component or in the instructions. However, as a general rule, the smaller the bolt or Allen key you're working with, the lower the torque it needs. So hold the key/wrench near the bolt end on a 2 or 3mm Allen/Hex bolt only using full leverage on a long key/wrench on a 6, 8 or 10mm bolt.

▶▶ COMMON WORKSHOP MISTAKES

Don't Clamp Components Unevenly

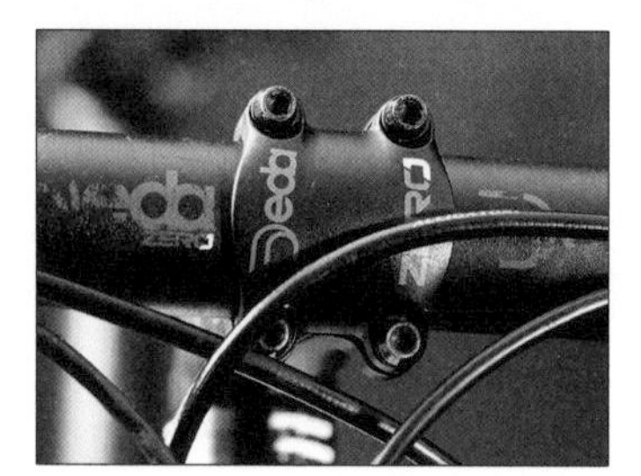

If there are two or more bolts clamping a component in place then make sure all the bolts are at the same tension. Otherwise you risk crush damage, or all the bolts gradually creeping towards the lowest tension of the team and coming loose.

The Fix

Do the first bolt up till it just nips slightly tight. Now do the second (and third and fourth) up as tight. Now tighten the first a little more and repeat until they're all at the required torque. On four-bolt (stem face plate) patterns do the diagonally opposite bolts in sequence to spread the load and unless the instructions say otherwise make sure the clamping gap is the same top to bottom and side to side.

Never Clamp Your Frame

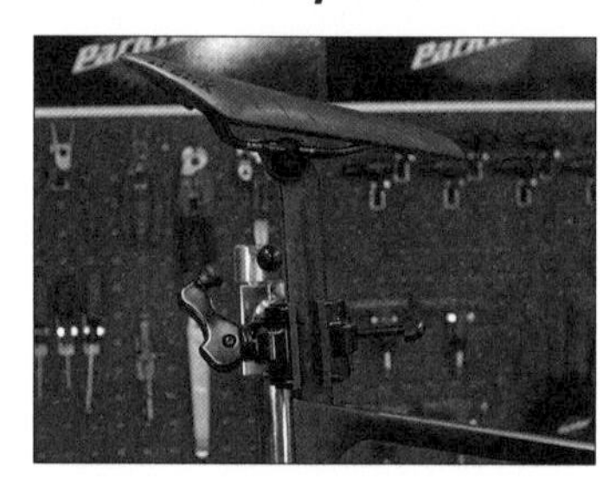

The number one howler we see in 'how to' videos and books is frames clamped into work stands by a frame tube, such as the top tube or the seat tube. The walls of frame tubes – in metal or carbon – are only fractions of a mm thick so it's very easy to crush them. You won't always be able to tell either as the damage can be internal so you'll know it's happened when your frame suddenly collapses. Not good. At all.

The Fix

Clamp the frame by the seat post, ideally using a cheap, thick alloy seat post rather than your fancy lightweight alloy or carbon one. This is so that if you do damage it by over-tightening the clamp, it's not the end of the world.

Don't Degrease Your Bearings

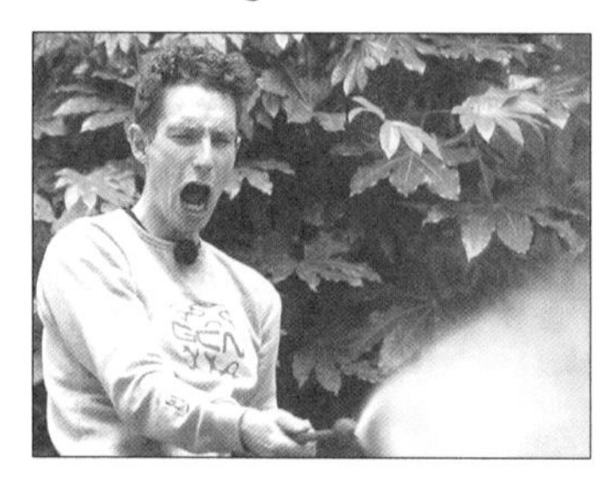

Accidentally spraying degreaser, a jet washer, or penetrating lubricant into your bearings will destroy the grease that keeps them running smooth.

The Fix

Avoid using a spray degreaser/light lube wherever possible. If you must then make sure you don't spray directly onto the seals by keeping the spray perpendicular to the faces of the bearings. Ditto with a jet wash.

"Accidentally spraying degreaser, a jet washer, or penetrating lubricant into your bearingss will destroy the grease"

Don't Lube Your Discs

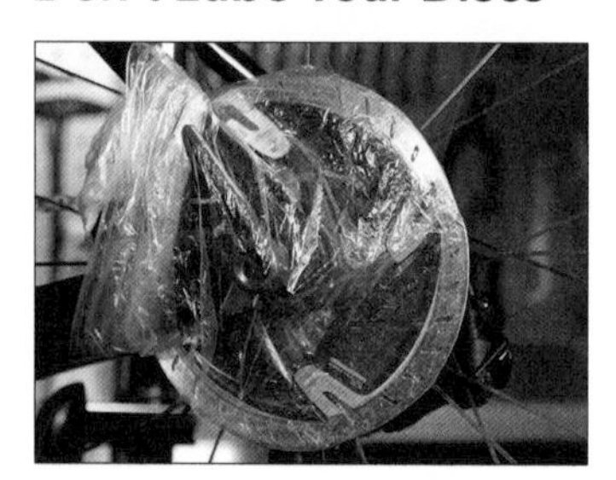

You only need to get a tiny amount of spray lube or polish onto your disc brake rotors or pads to make them dangerously useless. Cleaning off this contamination is almost impossible too.

The Fix

Ideally don't use a spray lube or polish at all, but if you do make sure you cover the rotors completely with a clean cloth or paper towel (you can even get specific rotor covers if you're fancy). Also, never touch the rotors or brake pad braking surfaces by hand – always wear gloves to protect the surfaces from contamination that can reduce their braking performance.

Don't Use The Wrong Disc Brake Fluid

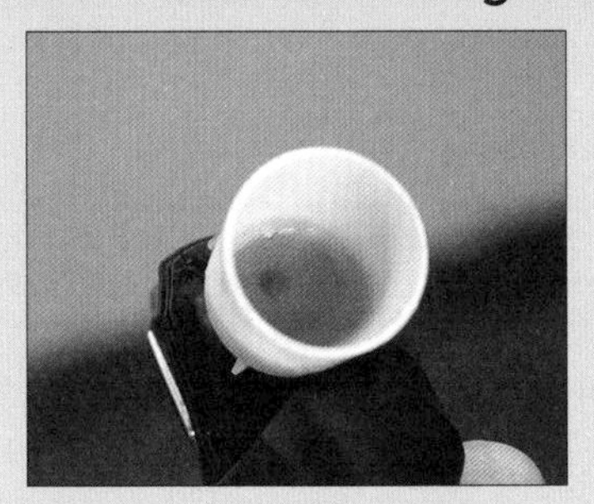

Using the wrong fluid in your brakes is even worse than sticking petrol in a diesel or vice-versa. Shimano, Campagnolo and TRP systems use mineral oil, while SRAM brakes use automotive style DOT 4.1 or 5.1 fluid.

The Fix

There isn't one. Using the wrong fluid will immediately damage the seals in your braking system so even if you flush it out immediately the damage is almost certainly done and the brakes will be dangerously unreliable. If that happens, then it's new brake time.

THE HACK

If you can't find mineral oil to re-bleed your system, you can use cooking oil in an emergency. The heat tolerance will be far lower though so it will only work to limp home carefully on the flat, not get you down an Alp. Make sure you fully flush out and re-bleed the system as soon as possible too.

Don't Cut Your Outer Cables Too Short

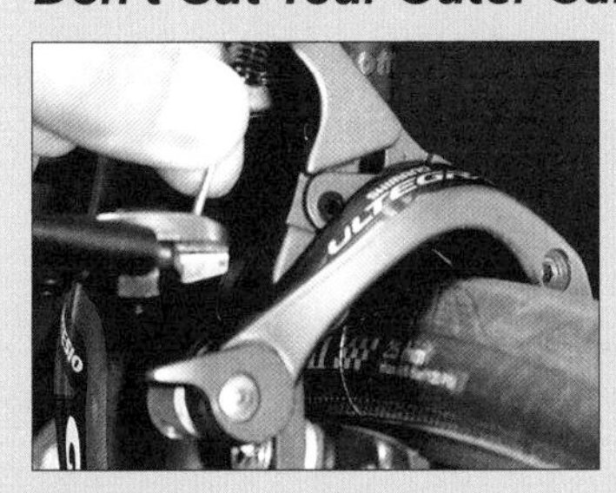

Having big loops of cable can look untidy, but always make sure you cut them long enough so that your bars can turn fully without them getting pulled tight. Otherwise you can potentially shift when you steer or rip them out if you turn too far. Cutting rear gear cable loops too short can compromise shifting too.

The Fix

Always double-check the length of outer when installing. Don't forget to allow for taping the bars pulling cables tighter and if in doubt leave a bit of extra length as you can always trim them later.

Don't Use Too Little Sealant

If you're using tubeless tyres it's sometimes tempting to skimp on the amount of sealant you use. Often this is because (A) it's expensive and (B) it's tempting to save weight. However, you need to remember that a standard tube weighs 120-150g, so even with a slightly heavier tyre you're still saving weight using 60g of sealant. You also need enough sealant to fully coat the tyre as some tubeless tyres are still slightly porous without it.

The Fix

If you're installing new tyres then we always add roughly double the width of the tyre. Or to put it another way, 50ml in a 25mm tyres, 60ml in a 28mm and 80mm in a 40mm tyre.

Don't Trap Your Inner Tubes

Trapping inner tubes between tyre and rim or tyre lever or rim can split them open before you've even finished fitting the tyre.

The Fix

Always partially inflate the inner tube and push it right up inside the tyre as you fit the bead carefully into place. If possible don't use levers at all – just work the tyre round to give you enough slack to use your thumbs to roll the bead on.

Also, be super-vigilante for any bits of inner tube peeping out over the tyre/rim gap too.

"Trapping inner tubes between tyre and rim can split them open before you've even finished fitting the tyre"

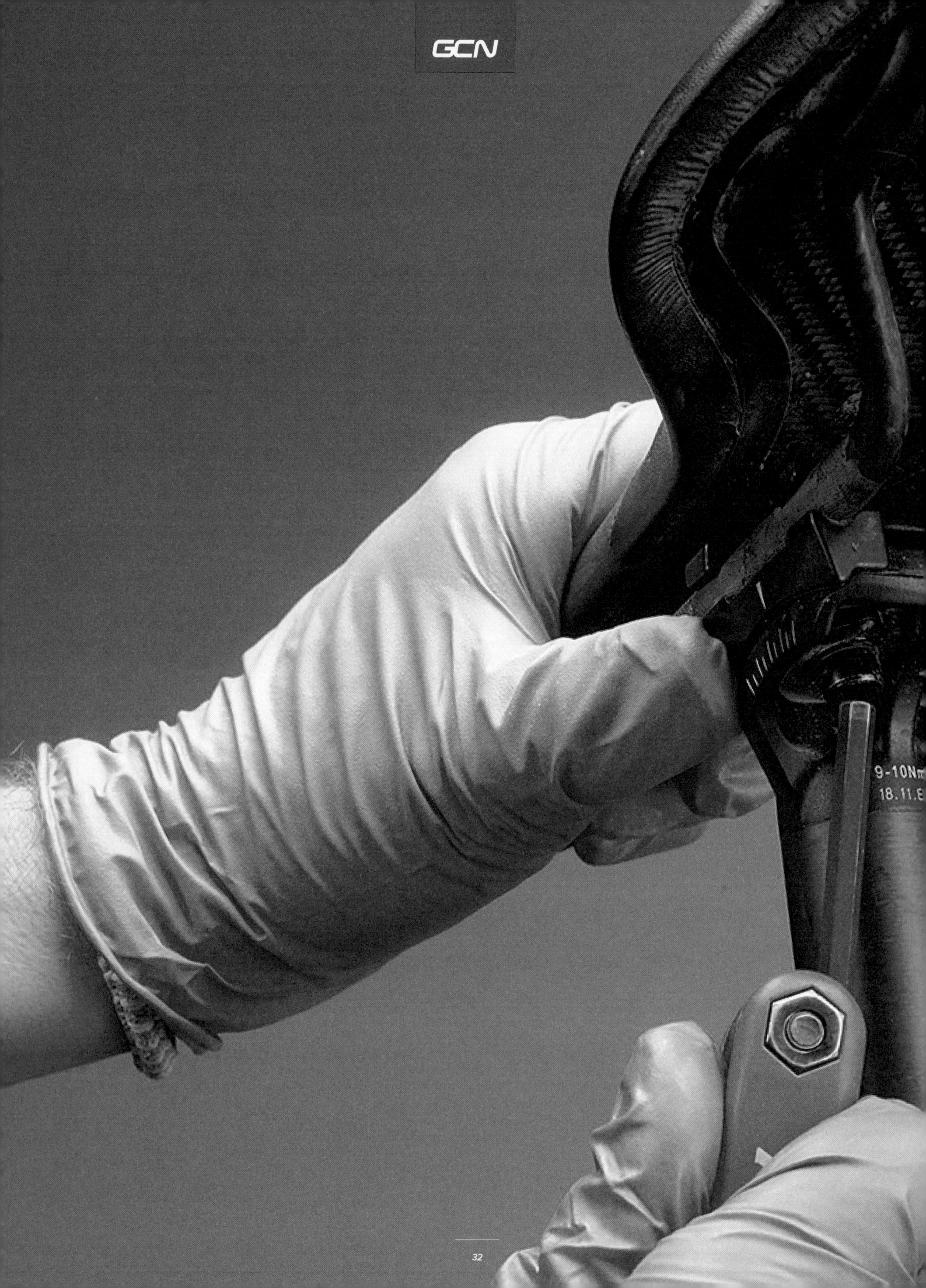

SECTION 1

QUICK START

All the basic workshop techniques you need to safely set up a new or used bike and get it ready to ride

BEGINNER BASICS

HOW TO CHOOSE THE CORRECT SIZE BIKE

When it comes to buying a new bike it's absolutely paramount that you pick the right size. Here's how to do it, whatever shape of rider you are

DIFFICULTY 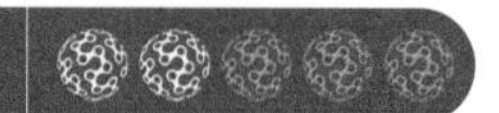

TIME 30 - 60 Minutes

TOOLS
- *Allen keys*
- *Plumb line*
- *Tape measure*

WHEN
- *You want to ensure you get a bike that fits you perfectly*

TECH EXPLAINED

Bike Sizing

Manufacturers will either label their bike in 't-shirt' sizes (small, medium, large, etc), or with a number. These generally range from 48 to 62, and that corresponds to the measurement in centimetres from the bottom bracket to the top of the seat tube. But just because you fit a 54 from one brand, it doesn't necessarily mean a 54 from another will fit you too.

1

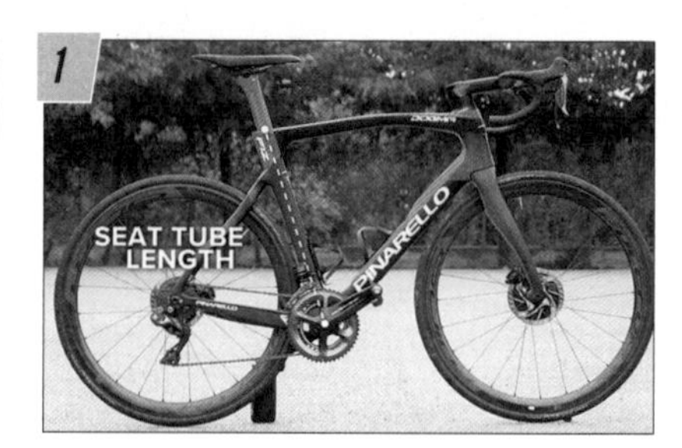

The effective seat tube length is just one of three really important ways of measuring a bike. The other two measurements are known as reach and stack – these are all international standards and should be listed by the manufacturer.

> *"The effective seat tube length is just one of three really important ways of measuring a bike. The other two measurements are known as reach and stack"*

WATCH THE VIDEO

Free show-how and know-how

https://gcn.eu/CorrectBikeSize

2

Reach refers to a horizontal line taken from the centre of the bottom bracket and measured to the centre of the head tube. This gives you the length of the bike from a fit point of view.

3

Stack is the vertical measurement of a line taken from the centre of the bottom bracket to the top of the head tube, giving you the height of the bike from a fit point of view.

It might sound slightly complicated, but it's kind of like buying a pair of trousers. Trousers come with a waist size, but they also come with a leg length. And much like buying trousers, you might have to try on several pairs, or ride several different bikes, to find the perfect fit for you.

Before getting onto that though, there's a simple but fundamental question to deal with first. What is your saddle height and how can you find it? An easy way to find it is to get onto your bike with the pedal at six o'clock. Set your saddle height so that when put your heel on the pedal your leg is straight.

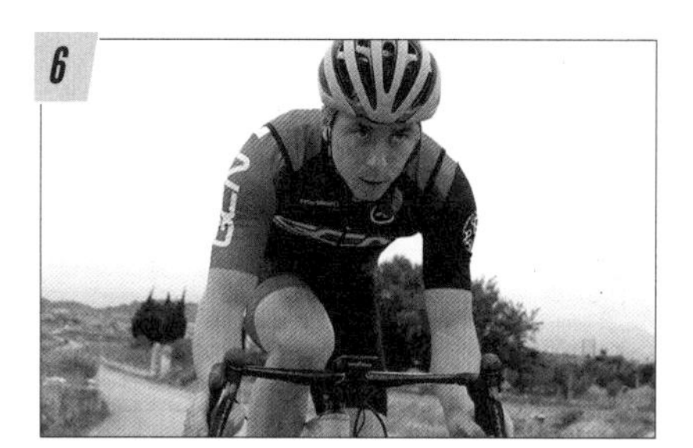

With your saddle height set, you can now start looking at your reach. However, you're restricted in the adjustments that you can make to the reach (see step 10, below), so it's crucial that you check it is right for you on a potential new bike before parting with your cash.

The reach of different bikes will vary depending on the model of bike as well as from brand to brand. It also depends on the type of riding the bike is designed for. Racing bikes are generally really long and low. Whereas a sportive or gravel bike will be a little bit shorter and higher.

If you're new to cycling or are a little bit less flexible than most, you'll probably favour a reach that's shorter and higher. Whereas if you're into going fast and don't mind holding a more aggressive position, you'll probably favour something that's longer and lower.

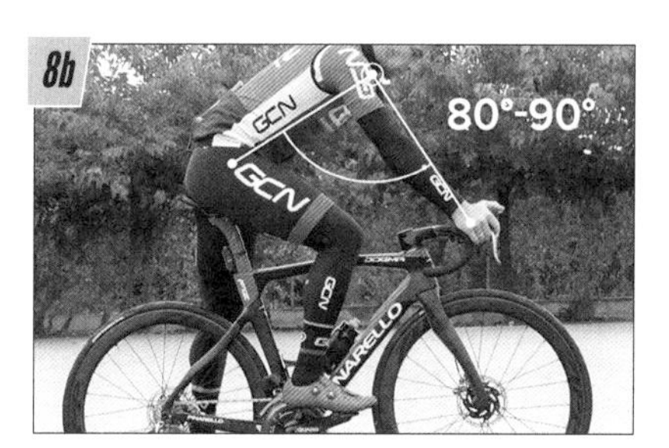

Generally speaking though, with your saddle in the correct position, the relationship from your shoulder to hip angle should be 40 to 45 degrees with your foot at the 3-o'clock pedal position and your arms should be 80 to 90 degrees from your shoulder when on the brake hoods.

If you need to adjust the height of your bars, this is relatively quick and easy to do so by adjusting your stem and spacers. Move spacers from above your stem to beneath it to raise your bars, or vice-versa to lower them. Head over to page 202 for full details on how to do this.

If you need to adjust the reach, you'll need to buy a new stem or bars – never try to adjust reach by moving your saddle. If you need to change your stem for one that's more than 2 to 3cm different in length, you probably need a different size frame as too long or short a stem can ruin the handling.

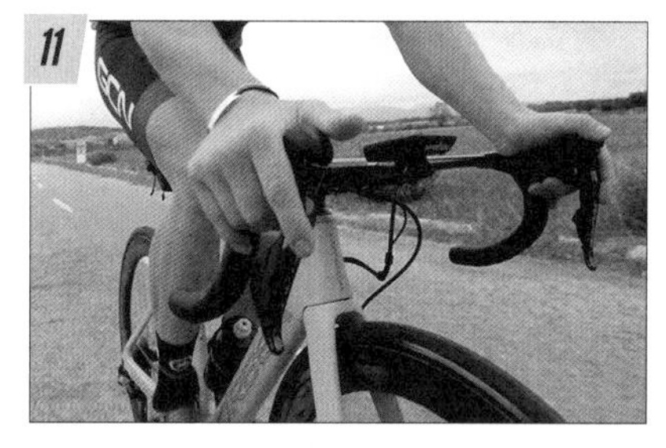

If you find a bike you absolutely love but you're kind of inbetween sizes, make your decision based on your riding style. If you prefer a more racier feel, go for a smaller bike and add a longer stem. If you want a more stable and upright position on the bike, go for the larger bike with a higher stack.

Need To Set Up Your New Bike?
Check out our guide on page 48

BEGINNER BASICS

HOW TO ASSEMBLE YOUR NEW BIKE

It's finally arrived, that big, bike-shaped box you've been awaiting for! Here's how to safely set up your new steed so you can get riding in confidence

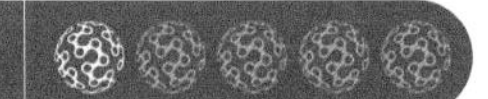

DIFFICULTY

TIME 20 - 40 Minutes

TOOLS
- *Allen keys*
- *Torque wrench*
- *Grease*
- *Tape measure*
- *Scissors*

WHEN
- *A bike-shaped box arrives on your doorstep!*

WATCH THE VIDEO

Free show-how and know-how

HOW TO ASSEMBLE A BIKE FROM A BOX

https://gcn.eu/BuildABike

SCAN CODE TO WATCH THE VIDEO

Whether you're new to cycling and are buying your first road bike, or if you're an experienced rider who's looking for an upgrade, it's not unlikely that your next bike purchase will be made online. Online bike shops and brands ship thousands of bikes across the globe directly to the consumer.

When your bike arrives, you can typically expect to find it in a semi-assembled state. Usually this means it will have been fully built and serviced by a mechanic and then partially disassembled to fit into a box for shipping. Here we go through what you need to do from unpacking your bike to getting it ready to ride.

> **"Online bike shops and brands ship thousands of bikes across the globe directly to the consumer"**

REMOVE THE PACKAGING

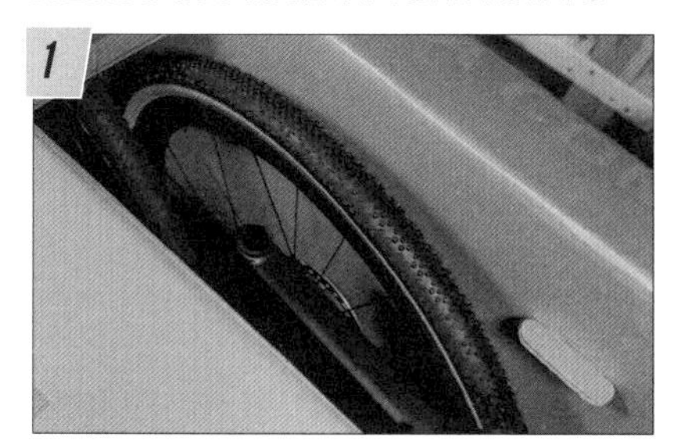

First things first – open up the box and remove your bike. Be careful of the industrial staples that tend to be used on the lid of the box – they are very sharp.

Remove the bike from its box, you'll usually find it with the rear wheel fitted, bars and stem removed and strapped to the side of the frame, and the front wheel stored in the box separately.

Rest the bike on the back wheel and the tips of the fork and set about taking the packaging off the frame. When you're snipping off the zip-ties around the bike, be careful not to scratch the frame.

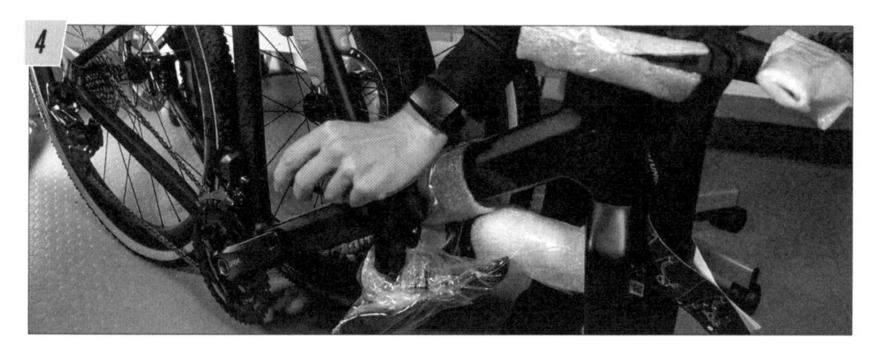

Take a minute to sort out all the packaging. Brands are getting better at packing bikes in a more environmentally sound manner, but you'll probably find you're left with a lot of zip-ties and plastic, so recycle or reuse what you can.

INSTALL THE SEATPOST

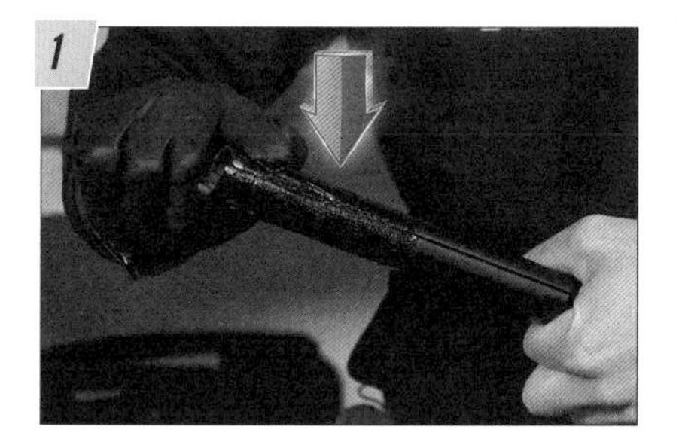

Before you fit it into the frame you need to prime your seatpost with some grease or assembly paste. If the frame and post are made of alloy use regular grease. If either part is made of carbon fibre, use a carbon assembly paste – which will add a bit more friction to the mix and help stop the post slipping.

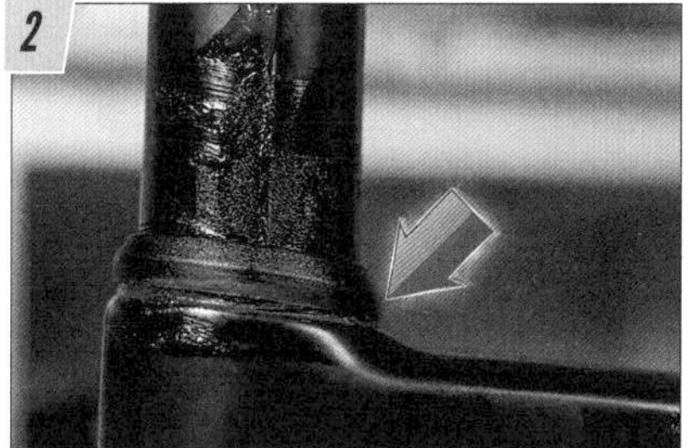

Some bikes have an external seatpost collar, which needs to be fitted to the frame before installing the post. If your frame has a more modern internal wedge type of seatpost clamp, make sure you add a touch of grease (not fibre grip) to this too. Just nip up the seatpost clamp up for now to stop it slipping.

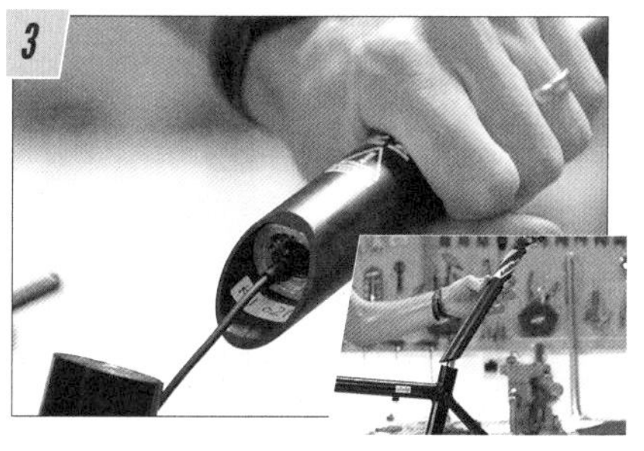

If your new bike has Di2, it's likely the battery will be housed inside the seat tube and the cable will be poking out from the top – usually taped to the frame. Simply plug this cable into the battery before fitting the seatpost and ensure not to pinch the cable between the seatpost and the frame.

HOW TO ASSEMBLE YOUR NEW BIKE

FIT THE STEM & BARS

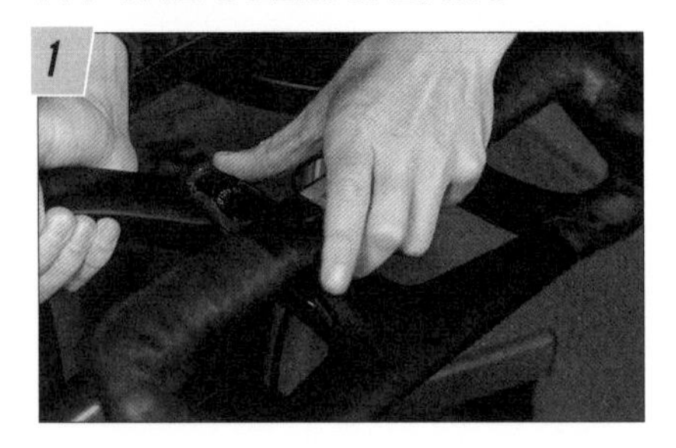

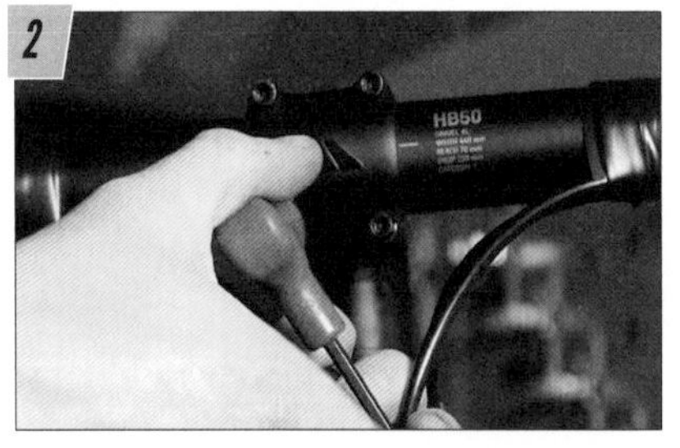

The stem will likely be loosely fitted to the steerer tube to stop the fork dropping out, so you just need to line it up and tension the headset. You may wish to lower it once you've ridden the bike.

Line the stem up roughly with the front of the bike, remove the faceplate, and be careful not to lose any of the bolts. Usually the shifters are already fitted to the bars along with the bar tape.

Offer the bars up to the stem, being careful not to trap any cables or hoses between the bar and stem. Reinstall the faceplate and tighten up the bolts just enough to stop the bars from slipping around.

INSTALL THE FRONT WHEEL

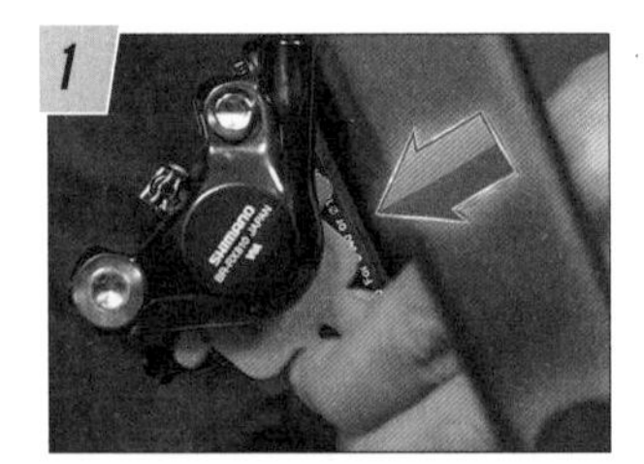

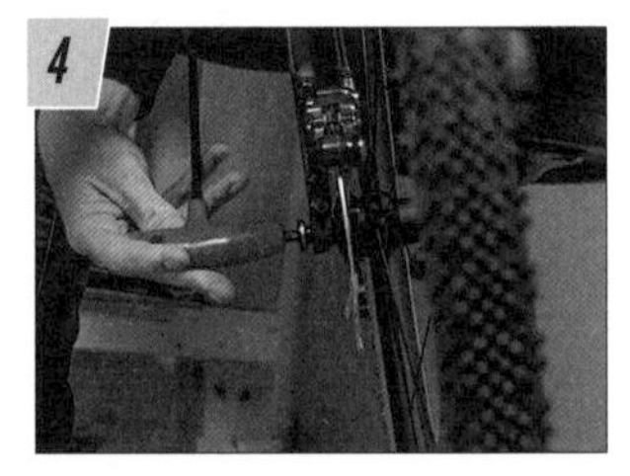

If your new bike has disc brakes, check there isn't a pad spacer in the calliper to stop the pads being pushed together during transit. If there is one, remove that and keep it – they're quite handy to have around.

If the bike has rim brakes, ensure the quick-release lever on the calliper is open to make sure it's as easy as possible to slot the wheel in.

When you've done that, simply lift the front of the bike up and slot the wheel in place. It's easier to do it on the floor rather than in a workstand, as you then know the wheel will sit centrally. See the page 40 for more.

Whether you've got a quick-release or a through-axle, it's important to apply a small amount of grease to stop it seizing in place or squeaking/creaking. For through-axles, pay particular attention to the threads.

FINISHING TOUCHES

Start with the stem, just tighten the top cap to remove any play from the headset, while still allowing the bars to turn without any resistance – and then tighten the stem bolts up to the recommended torque setting, usually about 5Nm.

Swing a leg over the bike and grab the shifters. You should be able to move the bars to make sure they're at the right angle for you. Tighten the faceplate bolts in sequence (working on opposite corners in an X-pattern) and ensure they all have an equal gap. See page 202 for more detail.

Then it's just a case of setting the seatpost to the right height. You can follow the steps on page 50, compare it to a previous bike or find your ideal height through a bit of trial and error on a test ride – or your turbo, if you have one.

FINISHING TOUCHES (CONTINUED)

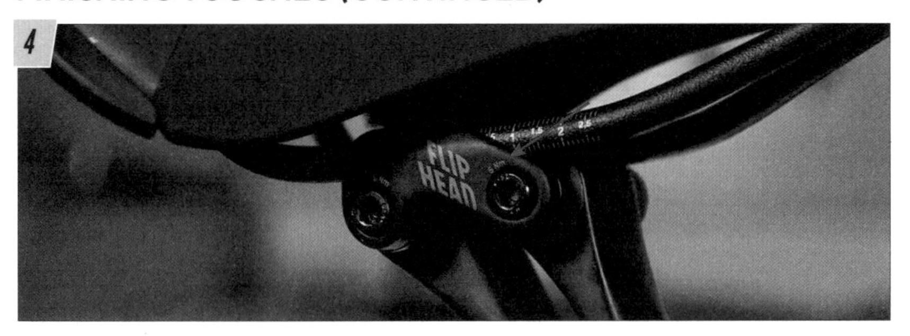

Once you're happy with that, make sure the clamp is appropriately torqued up and also check the actual saddle clamp bolt, too - these usually have a higher torque of around 10 to 12Nm – but do check the exact torque on the saddle rails and the saddle clamp itself.

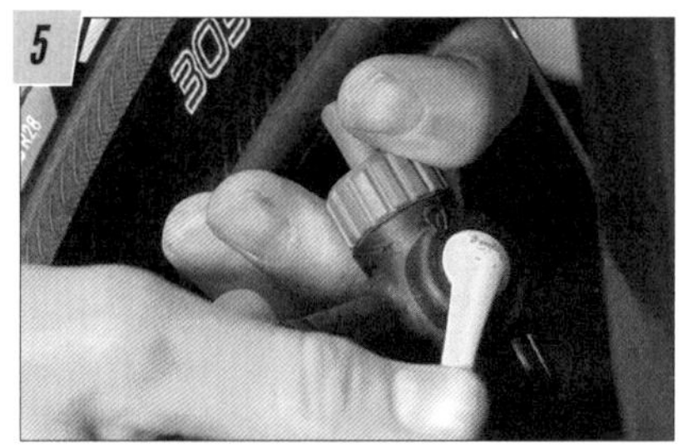

Pump up your tyres, fit your pedals (see pages 44 and 46 for more on these) and you're almost ready to ride!

PRE-RIDE CHECKS

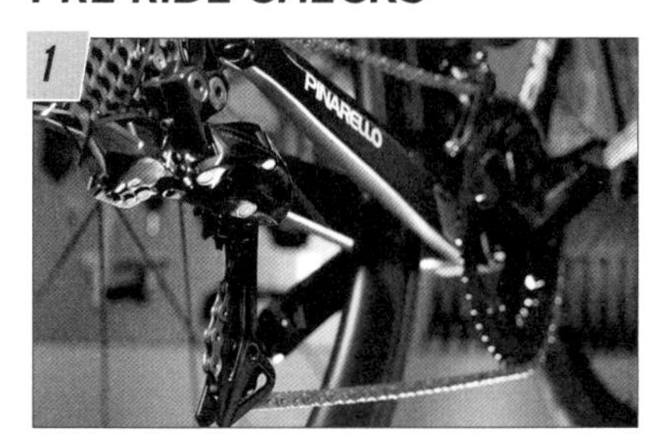

We're assuming the bike you've just built was serviced by the company you bought it from before shipping – but things can get knocked about in transit, so it's worth checking the gears, and especially the brakes, before you head out for your first ride.

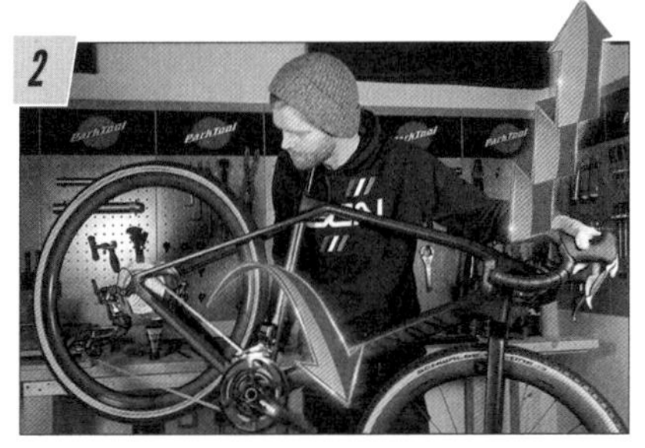

To check the gears, you can either mount the bike in a workstand, lift the rear wheel off the ground by hooking the saddle behind your neck, or ask a friend to hold it for you. Then simply keep the cranks turning and shift through the whole cassette in each chainring.

If you find the gears around the middle of the cassette shifting slowly or not at all, you may have a bent mech hanger. If so, while straightening is sometimes possible it's usually better to order a replacement. Fitting is usually one bolt to the frame with the derailleur removed.

Brakes are important to check before your first ride. Grab each brake lever and roll the bike forwards – your wheels should lock up, and not spin. If you have rim brakes, just make sure the pads don't rub on the tyre and that they hit the rim nice and squarely.

One last safety check before you ride – go back over every bolt on the bike and make sure they're all torqued appropriately. This is a simple process, but it's easy to miss a bolt or forget to tighten something up – and it's much better to discover them in your garage than out on the road.

Fitting Pedals For The First Time?
See page 44 for how to do it correctly

BEGINNER BASICS

HOW TO REMOVE & REPLACE WHEELS

Being able to take your wheels off and put them back is an essential skill to master. Here's how to do it quickly and easily

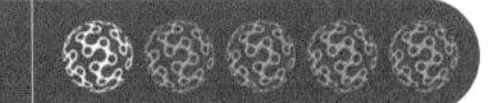

TIME 5 - 10 Minutes

TOOLS
- *Allen keys*
- *Wheel spanners*

WHEN
- *Packing your bike, fixing a puncture, changing a tyre, or other maintenance*

Being able to correctly remove and refit your wheels is a crucial skill that you'll need in order to fix a puncture by the side of the road, or pack your bike into a car.

While it's a very straightforward thing to do, it's possible to make some rookie mistakes which can damage your bike. But follow our method of correctly removing and refitting your wheels and you can't go wrong.

We'll go through quick-release skewers, through-axles, and rim and disc brakes. You won't need any tools unless you have through-axles that require Allen keys to be removed, or old-fashioned wheel nuts – in which case you'll need a pair of spanners.

TOP TIP

You will likely be tempted to remove and refit your wheels when your bike is upside down. However, being in contact with tarmac roads or gravelly car parks can easily damage your saddle, brake hoods, bar tape or GPS device (if you have one), and your bike can easily get knocked over – so don't do it!

"While it's a very straightforward thing to do, it's possible to make some rookie mistakes which can damage your bike"

WATCH THE VIDEO

Free show-how and know-how

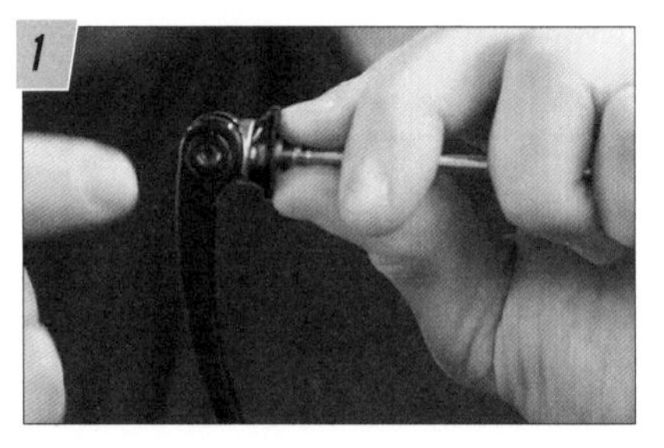

Before removing the wheels from your bike, you'll need to check your brake type and look at what kind of axle system is used to attach the wheels to your bike.

There are various different combinations of brake and axle types found on road bikes these days, so once you know which ones your bike is running, ensure to check the relevant steps in this walkthrough.

RIM BRAKES

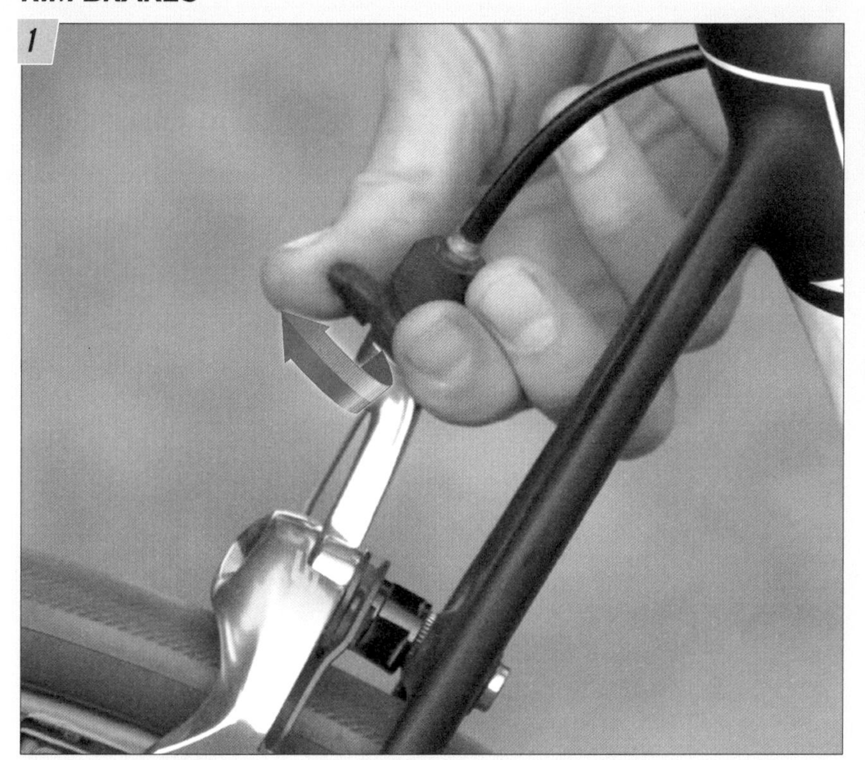

On rim brakes the pads sit too near the rims to allow the tyre to pass through them. To give the tyre enough space to pass easily, the calliper will need to be released. Look for a small quick-release lever on the side of the calliper, then push it upwards or outwards to move the brake pads away from the rim.

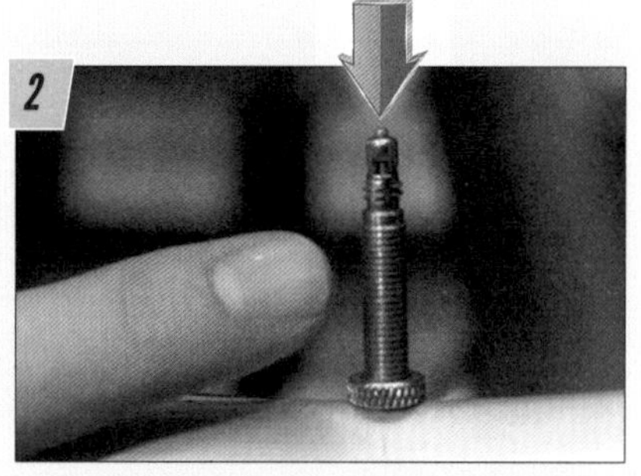

If your rim brakes are older and don't have a lever, the easiest way to remove the wheel is to partially deflate the tyre so it can fit through the brake calliper. You'll likely have Presta valves (as shown here), unscrew the very top part and then push it in to release some air.

DISC BRAKES

If you have disc brakes, the brake rotors (discs) will just slide out from between the pads without any adjustment to the brake calliper.

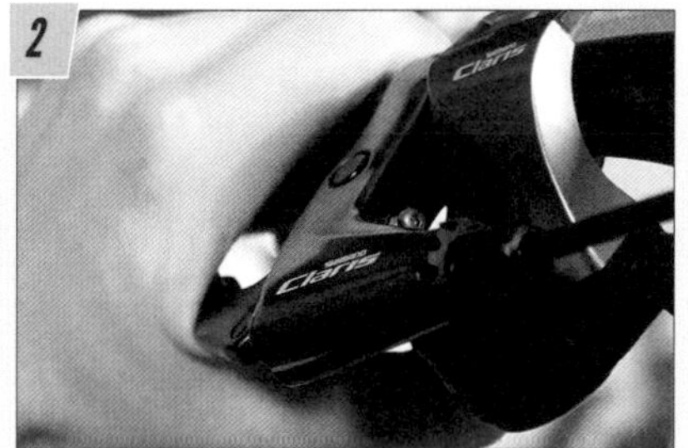

Once your wheel has been removed from the bike, do not pull the brake lever as this will push the pads together and it will be tough to get them apart again.

If your wheels have been removed for travelling, use either a specially designed pad spacer or a bit of folded card to put between the pads to guard against any accidental presses.

HOW TO REMOVE & REPLACE WHEELS

TYPES OF AXLE

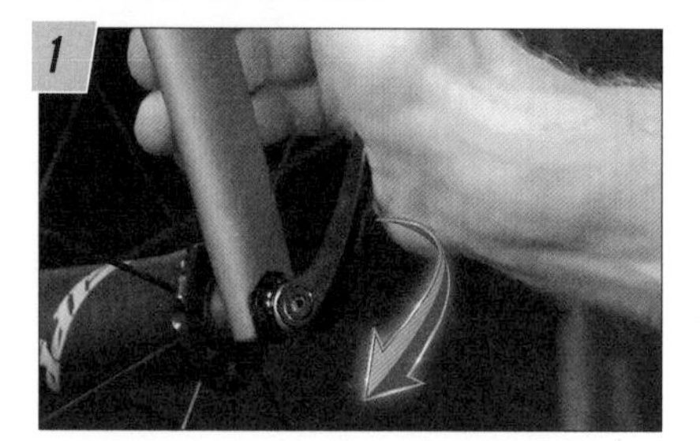

Quick-Release Axles To release the axle, simply pull the lever down. You might need to hold the lever and undo the nut on the other side to release the wheel, but only give it a few turns so you don't undo it all the way. You can now remove the wheel.

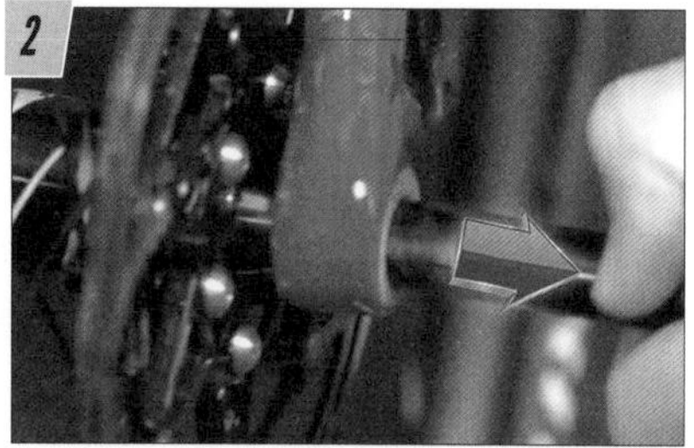

Through-Axles If your wheel has a through-axle, then it will need to be unscrewed to remove it. This is either done using an Allen key, or a built-in handle on the axle. Turn the axle counter-clockwise and then pull it out, this will allow the wheel to be removed.

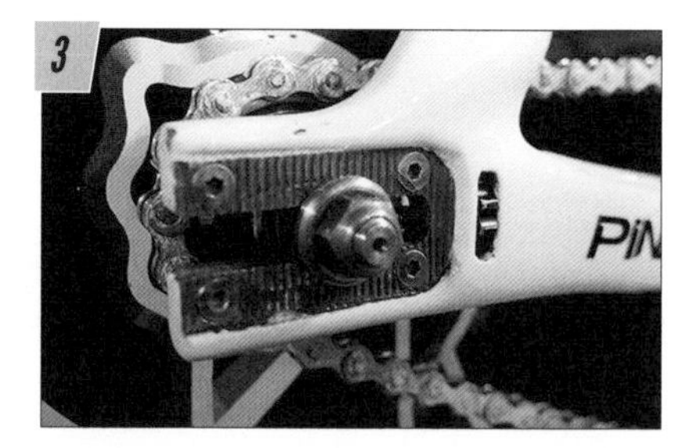

Wheel Nuts The third type of axle is a little less common and is usually only found on older bikes. A nutted axle will need to be loosened with a spanner. Loosen the nuts on either side just enough for them to pass the dropouts.

REMOVING THE FRONT WHEEL

Once you've released the axle and brakes (if necessary), your front wheel will easily slide out of your dropouts.

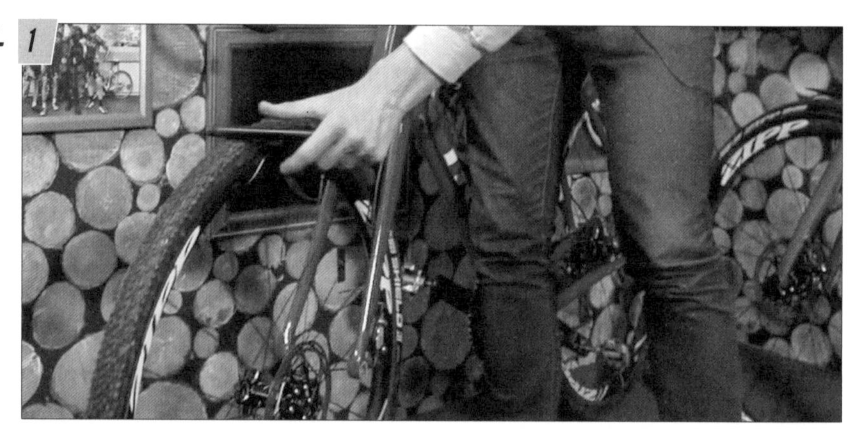

REFITTING THE FRONT WHEEL

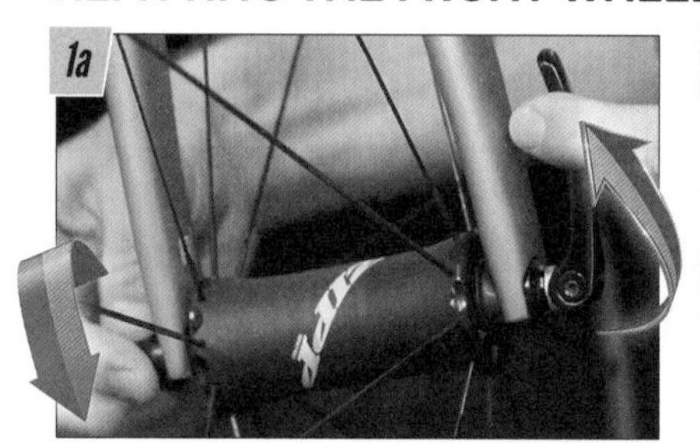

For a wheel with quick-release axle, slide the wheel back into place, making sure it is located correctly in the dropouts. With the lever open, hold the nut and turn the lever clockwise a few turns, and flip the lever inwards to close it.

You want to make sure the lever is tight enough that it won't spring open, but not so tight that it will be difficult to remove it again. Ensure that you locate the lever facing upwards, where it's less likely to snag on anything.

For wheels with through-axles, line up the wheel with the dropouts and slide the axle back in, turn it clockwise to engage the thread. Tighten the axle a touch more than finger tight, so that there is no chance of it loosening as you ride.

With nutted wheels, it is easiest to use two spanners – one on each side to tighten the wheel. Once tight, double-check that the wheel is sitting nice and straight in the dropouts, as tightening can cause it to shift.

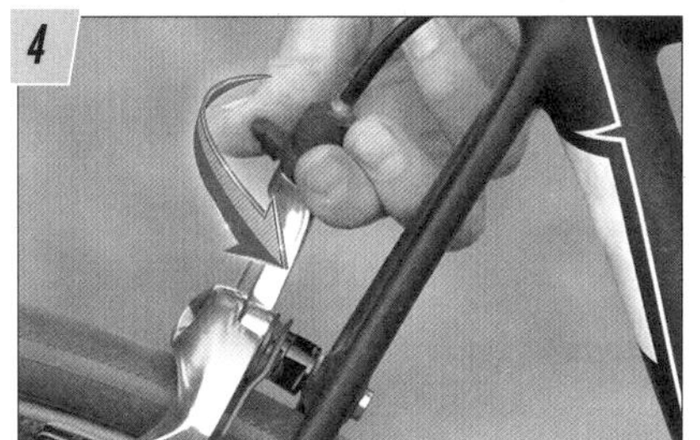

If you have rim brakes, push the quick-release lever down to push the pads back in position, or re-inflate the tyre if you have older style brakes.

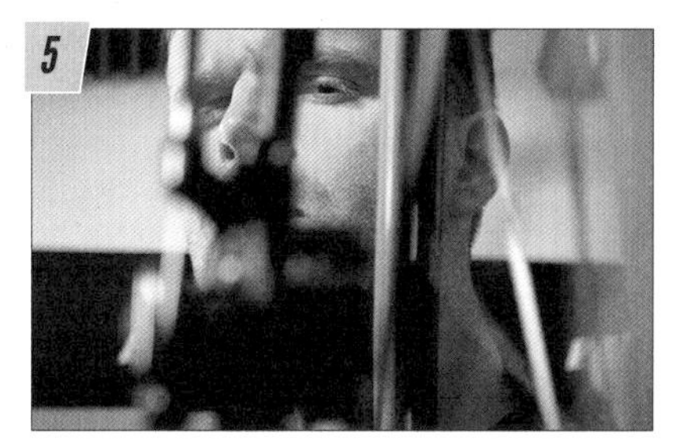

If you have disc brakes, be sure to carefully line up the brake rotor between the pads as you refit the wheel. Be aware that the rotor can knock the braking compound clean off the pad if it hits it.

REMOVING THE REAR WHEEL

Change into the smallest cog on the cassette. This will enable the rear wheel to come out more easily as the chain is less likely to snag on anything as the wheel comes out.

Hold onto the top tube and then with your other hand reach down and just pull the rear derailleur backwards ever so slightly and then lift it up to provide enough space for the back wheel to drop straight out.

REFITTING THE REAR WHEEL

Keep your rear wheel upright with the tyre on the ground, while holding the frame with your other. Guide the lower loop of chain underneath the cassette and rest the derailleur on a small sprocket. Push the derailleur back around the sprocket and the frame will drop onto the wheel.

If you have disc brakes, you will also need to ensure the rotors are correctly positioned between the brake pads before the wheel will sit back within frame dropouts.

Retighten your axle in the same way as described above for the front wheel and reposition your pads if you have rim brakes.

Before You Head Out On A Ride
Perform the pre-ride checks on page 60

BEGINNER BASICS

HOW TO FIT & REMOVE PEDALS

Replacing bicycle pedals can be confusing at first, but it doesn't have to be. Follow our guide to easily removing and installing any type of pedal

DIFFICULTY

TIME 5 - 10 Minutes

TOOLS
- *Pedal spanner or*
- *6 or 8mm Allen keys*
- *Cleaning rag*
- *Grease*

WHEN
- *Servicing pedals or fitting new ones*

1

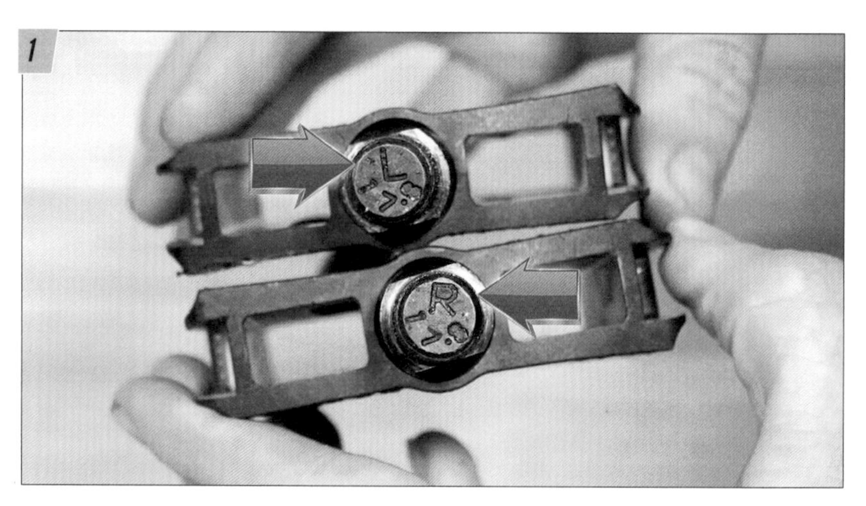

Pedals are left and right specific, so you need to ensure you're installing the right-hand pedal on the drive side (chainring side) of your crank arm and the left-hand pedal on the non-drive side. Handily, pedals often have a L and R printed on them to indicate which one is which.

WATCH THE VIDEO

Free show-how and know-how

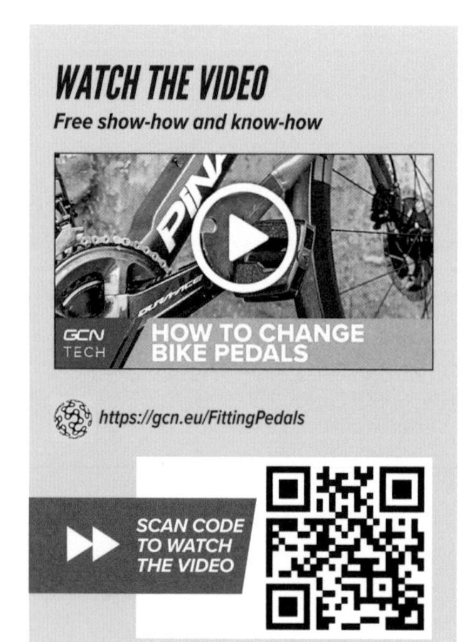

2

Left and right pedals have opposite threads, so a right-hand pedal has a clockwise thread and a left-hand pedal has an anti-clockwise thread. The reason for this is to stop the left pedal unwinding as you pedal along.

TOP TIP

An easy way to remember which direction to tighten and loosen each pedal is to put the crank arm in the forward position and then think about the direction in which you pedal. This forward direction will indicate which way to tighten the pedal and if you're unsure which pedal is which, take a look at the thread and apply the same thinking.

When fitting or removing pedals, it's easier to do it with the bike leaning on a wall rather than in a workshop stand. Having your bike on the ground means you can put your weight through the bike if you need to when removing pedals.

Rotate the crank arm into the forward position and, if you're able, start to thread in the pedal into the crank by hand, as this way you're less likely to strip the threads on the pedal should you accidentally cross-thread it.

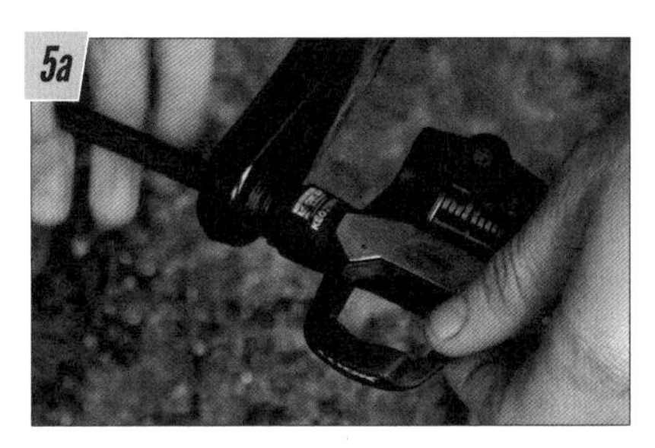

The pedal should thread on smoothly, then, once it's hand-tight, use your Allen key to tighten the pedal up. Push down on your Allen key while pulling up on the pedal to tighten – it doesn't need to be super-tight though.

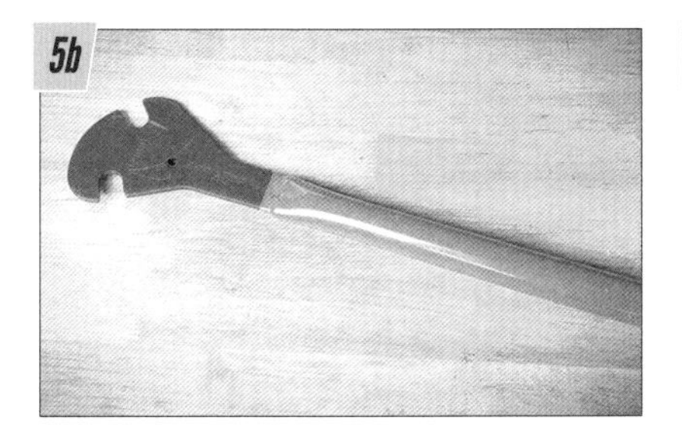

If using a pedal spanner instead of an Allen key, attach the spanner to the pedal via the little notch at the end of the pedal threads. If you don't have a pedal spanner, a regular 15mm spanner should fit if it's not too thick.

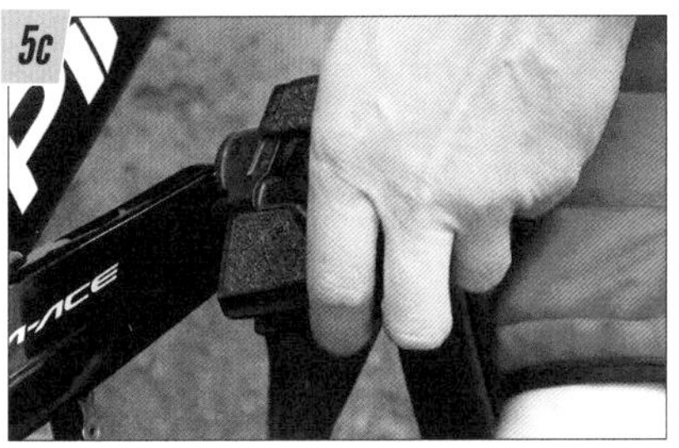

The fitting process is the same when using the spanner, so once the pedal is hand-tight just fully tighten it using your spanner.

TOP TIP

If you're installing used pedals onto a used crank, it's a good idea to wipe off the old grease from both parts and apply some fresh grease before fitting the pedals. This will stop them seizing together over time.

If you've got a really tight pedal and you're struggling to get it off with the Allen key, a tube or a piece of pipe can be very useful.

Slip the pipe over open the end of your Allen key to create a longer lever. This additional leverage should hopefully remove the pedal more easily.

TECH EXPLAINED

Reverse Threads

Particularly when removing stiff pedals, it can get a little tricky to remember which direction loosens off each side. To save any confusion, on the non-drive side, turn clockwise to loosen the pedal and anti-clockwise to tighten it, while on the drive side, turn anti-clockwise to loosen and clockwise to tighten.

Want To Service Your Pedals?
See page 210 for how to do just that

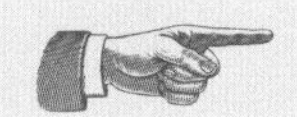

BEGINNER BASICS

HOW TO INFLATE YOUR TYRES

Keeping your tyres inflated to the correct pressure will help you ride faster and avoid getting pinch flats. Here's how to pump them up

DIFFICULTY

TIME	2 - 5 Minutes
TOOLS	• Track pump • Mini pump
WHEN	• Before you set off for a ride or need to re-inflate your tyres

When choosing a bike pump, ideally you want to get two – a small pump to carry when you're out riding and a proper track pump with a gauge to keep at home. It's loads easier to keep your tyres properly inflated with a track pump and it's always a good idea to check your pressures before setting off on a ride. To start, unscrew the plastic dust caps on the valves and keep them somewhere safe so they don't get lost.

WATCH THE VIDEO

Free show-how and know-how

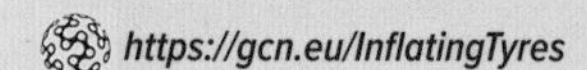

Figure out which valve type you have. You'll most likely be running Presta valves, easily identified by a little knurled pip in the top – which you undo to inflate and tighten down to seal. But if you're riding an older town bike, for example, you may have Schrader valves, as used on car tyres, pictured above.

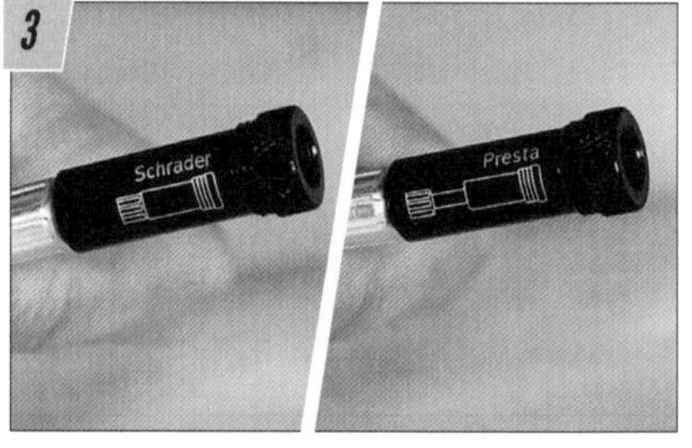

Pumps will almost always have an attachment for both of these valves types, so make sure you use the correct connection for yours. If you're not sure, a Presta valve will fit in the connector that is deeper and thinner, while a Schrader valve connector will be shallower and wider.

4

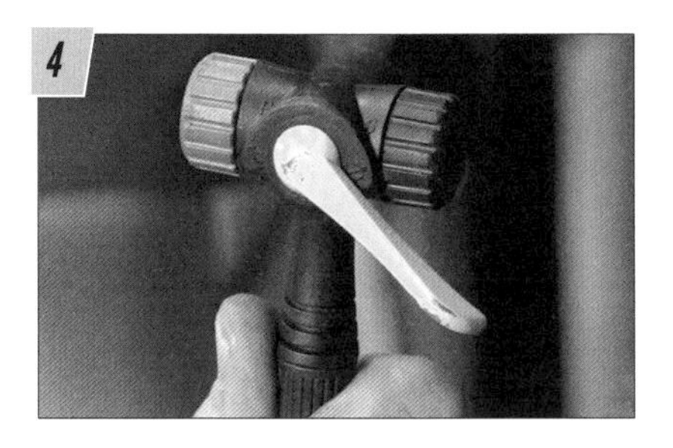

The heads on some track pumps have a fitting on either side for Schrader and Presta valves, while on others you have to unscrew and flip over the valve connector to change the type of valve it fits. On mini pumps, the threaded connecting hose usually has a different valve fitting at either end.

TECH EXPLAINED

Tubeless Tyres & Deep Section Wheels

If you have tubeless tyres, the valve that sits in the rim doesn't attach to an inner tube, it inflates the tyres from the rim itself. If you're running deep section wheels, you may also need valve extenders – which must be threaded onto the valve of your inner tube. They must be long enough to reach through the rims. Though these systems differ slightly from standard inner tubes, the method of adding more air is the same process as described here.

"Though these systems differ slightly from standard inner tubes, the method of adding more air is the same"

5a

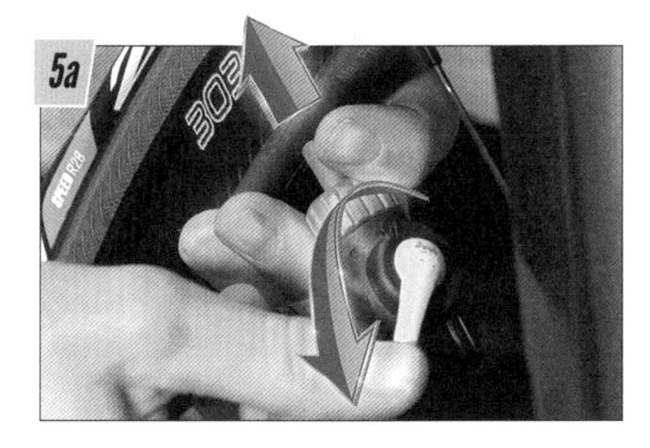

It's important not to damage the valve when connecting your pump. Place the head on the valve, and push it down – you may need to also press on the tyre to apply enough pressure. Once fully inserted, pull the lever towards you.

5b

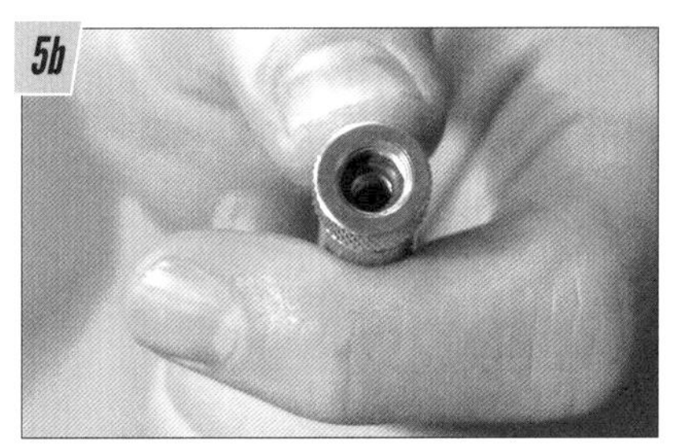

On the road you're likely to be using a pump with a threaded hose connector. If it's detachable, it's easier to connect the hose to the valve first, then connect the hose to the pump. If not, just thread it onto the valve, applying a little pressure to ensure the threads engage properly past the rubber seal.

6

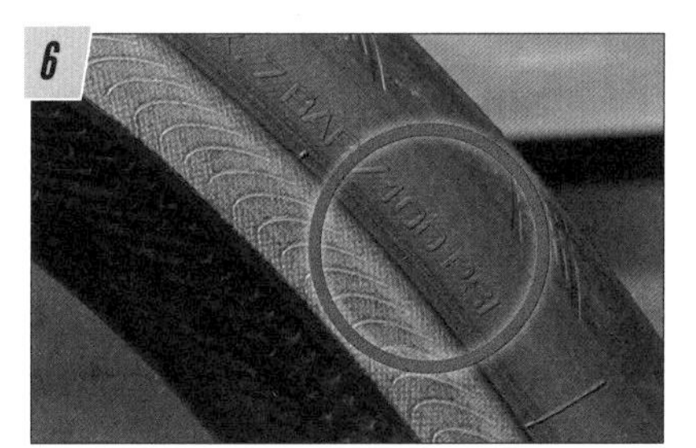

The best pressure to run your tyres at depends on all sorts of things – tyre size, rim width, rider weight, terrain and more. If you're unsure, a good starting point is to look at the recommended psi stated on the walls of your tyres (see Top Tip), or speak to more experienced riders.

TOP TIP

Run your tyres too hard and you'll feel every single bump in the road – no matter how small they may be. Too soft and your bike may feel less precise when cornering and you run the risk of getting pinch flats (aka snakebite punctures) when riding over potholes, etc. The best way to find the tyre pressure that suits you is to start around the manufacturer's maximum setting, see how that feels and work your way down 5psi or so until you find your sweet spot. Bear in mind that the bigger the tyre, the lower you can go with your minimum pressures.

7a

Once up to pressure, you need to disconnect the pump. If it's a track pump, return the lever to its original position and carefully pull off the head. Then, if running Presta valves, tighten down the little knurled pip to seal. Replace the dust caps.

7b

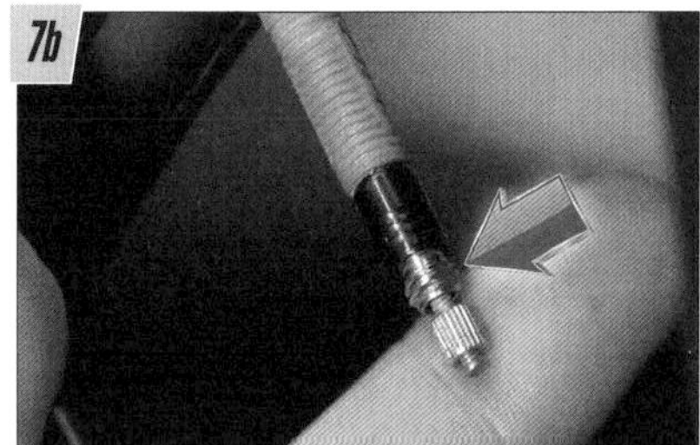

If using a threaded mini pump, take care not to remove the valve core as you wind the pump off – as all the air will come out in one great gush. If this happens, re-insert the valve core and carefully tighten it with pliers or a tyre lever – some brands of lever have a built-in valve core tool.

Fed Up With Punctures?
See page 156 for how to go tubeless

SET-UP SECRETS

HOW TO SET UP YOUR NEW BIKE

The arrival of a new bike is always a very special day, but how do you get your fresh bike fitting right and ready to ride?

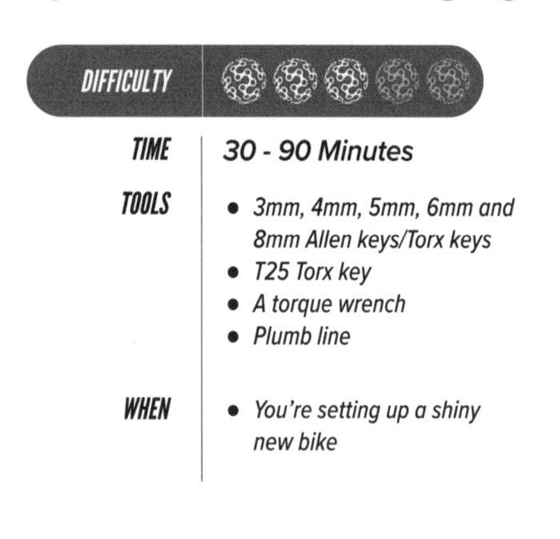

DIFFICULTY

TIME: 30 - 90 Minutes

TOOLS:
- 3mm, 4mm, 5mm, 6mm and 8mm Allen keys/Torx keys
- T25 Torx key
- A torque wrench
- Plumb line

WHEN:
- You're setting up a shiny new bike

WATCH THE VIDEO

Free show-how and know-how

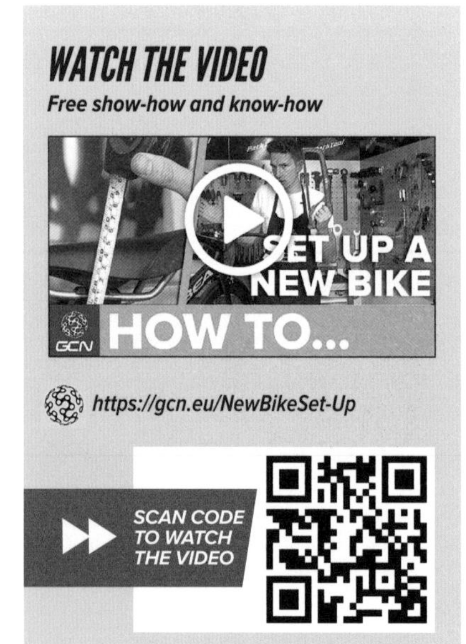

https://gcn.eu/NewBikeSet-Up

SCAN CODE TO WATCH THE VIDEO

It doesn't get much better than new bike day and we all want to get out riding our new whip as soon as possible. But if you don't check that it fits properly before you head off, then that first ride can end up really uncomfortable, disappointing and maybe even dangerous.

As long as your bike is roughly the right size then making it fit and ride comfortably, safely and efficiently won't take long at all, and only regular tools are required. So read through this guide to guarantee your first ride is a good one.

PERSONAL OR PRO BIKE FIT?

To get you a reasonable ready-to-ride fit we've included some simple but effective measuring strategies using just your legs and arms/hands. If you start from these as ballpark measurements you can then make adjustments to any aspects that don't feel quite right until you find your sweet spot. Keep any changes very small, as even a few millimetres or a degree or two can make a difference. Only make one change at a time too so you can be sure which

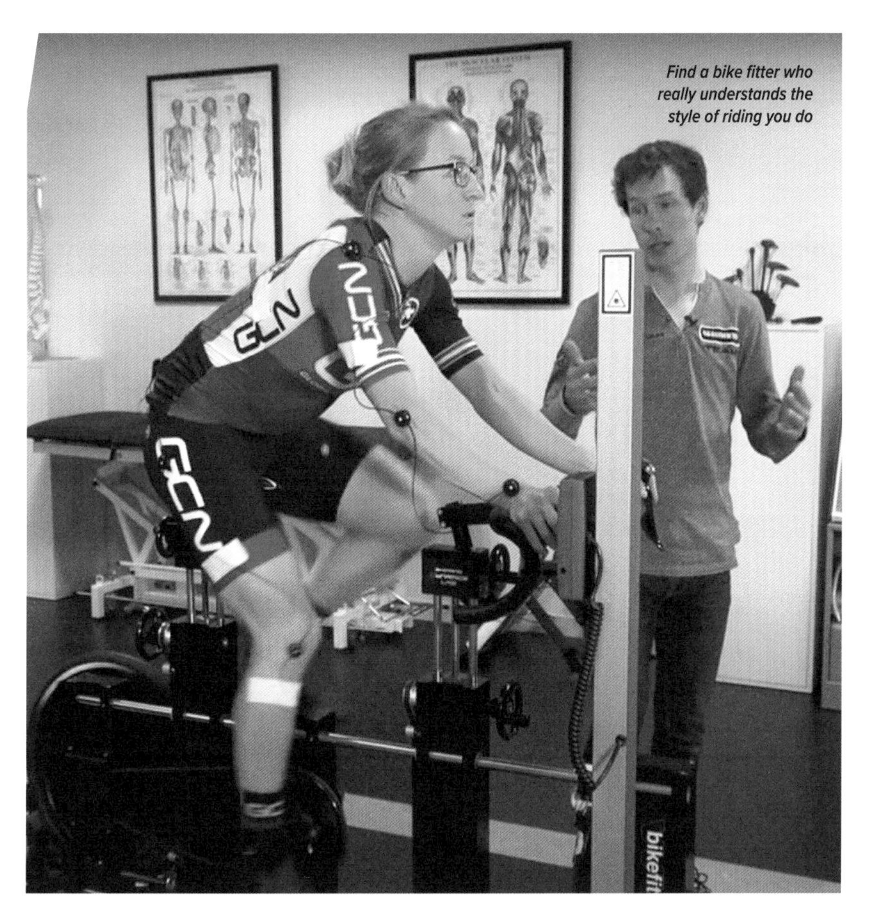
Find a bike fitter who really understands the style of riding you do

alterations have helped. Writing down the measurements and the tweaks you try as you go along will also help you track the process in case you need to rewind if subsequent adjustments give poor results. Be sure to write down the dimensions and angles once you find your sweet spot so you can easily restore them if something slips or you ever need to dismantle the bike for travelling.

If you're not confident to work towards a comfortable, efficient fit on your own then there are lots of shops and independent specialists that offer professional, in-depth bike fitting services.

These can be particularly useful if you have a specific fit issue or an injury to work around, but just like buying a bike do some research before choosing who is going to fit you to that bike. Ideally you want a fitter with a lot of experience and/or personal recommendations and positive reviews.

Select a fitter who understands the kind of riding you want to do, as an aero/triathlon specialist is less likely to appreciate exactly what works for bike packing as well as someone whose walls are covered with pictures of their bike on remote passes and peaks. In terms of telltale equipment, a fully adjustable bike rig means they can assess you and make functional changes while riding. It also shows they've invested in the right tools for the job. As is having a range of different components on-hand for swapping contact points (bars, saddle, stems, pedals and so on) to find which works best for you.

That said, beware of the 'all the gear and no idea' syndrome. Look for personal recommendations: one of the best bike fits we've ever experienced was from a coach with decades in elite level track racing who sized us up perfectly without even touching a tape measure.

"Keep any changes very small though as even a few millimetres or a degree or two can make a difference"

RECOMMENDED COMPONENTS

Lots of the fit-related components (stems, seatposts, seatpost clamps) use small bolts which have a specific tightening torque rate (normally 5Nm) marked next to them. That makes using a torque wrench that's set not to exceed that rating a sensible way to protect the components while still tightening them enough.

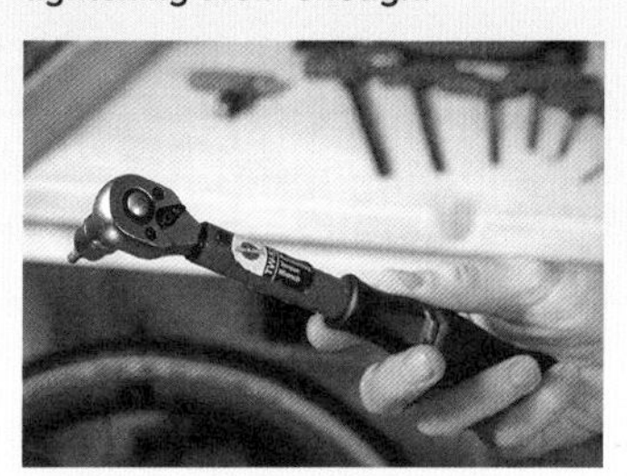

Carbon Assembly Paste

There are loads of names for this product, but they all use a grease like jelly full of small particles of a gritty feeling substance. While not always necessary, it comes in very handy if you have two shiny carbon components (bar and stem or seatpost and frame) that won't stop moving unless you use excessive clamping force.

HOW TO SET UP YOUR NEW BIKE

SADDLE HEIGHT

First set your saddle height. Loosen the bolt on the seatpost clamp on the frame enough to move the post without scratching it, but not so loose that it drops right into the frame. Position it so the saddle is roughly at hip height while you're standing next to the bike and then retighten.

Sit on the saddle with one pedal at the lowest point of the stroke. With your barefoot heel on the pedal your leg should be dead straight at full extension. If wearing shoes, adjust accordingly for their stack height.

TOP TIP

Gravel and mountain bike shoes have a thicker tread that will mean the effective saddle height is slightly lower than with a road shoe and cleats. Don't adjust to compensate this though, as it's better to run saddle height slightly lower off-road to increase control anyway.

If your leg is bent, loosen the seatpost clamp and raise the saddle slightly. If your leg is overextended or your hips are tilted, then lower the saddle slightly. Repeat with small adjustments until your saddle height is just right. Take the tape measure, check the distance between the centre of the crank axle and the top of the saddle and write it down for future reference.

SADDLE SET-BACK

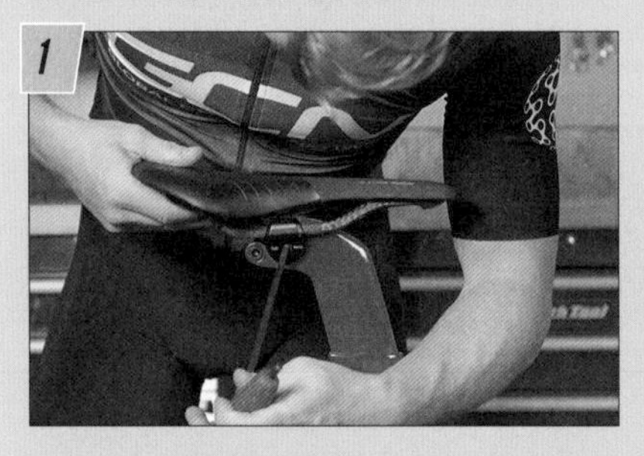

Sit on the saddle with your foot on the pedal in the forward level position. Run your plumb line exactly in line with the centre of your knee joint. The string should line up with the centre of the pedal axle.

If it doesn't line up with the pedal axle then undo the saddle clamp and slide the saddle backwards or forwards until it does. Once it's sorted make sure you check the saddle is level using the spirit level.

If you're running a low bar position or aero bar extensions, a more forward saddle position will help your breathing and reduce pressure on the front of the saddle.

HANDLEBAR REACH

1a

The next measurement to check is reach. That's the distance from centre of the bottom bracket to the centre of the handlebars. One measure of a good fit is to put your elbow against the nose of the saddle with your fingers running along the stem.

1b

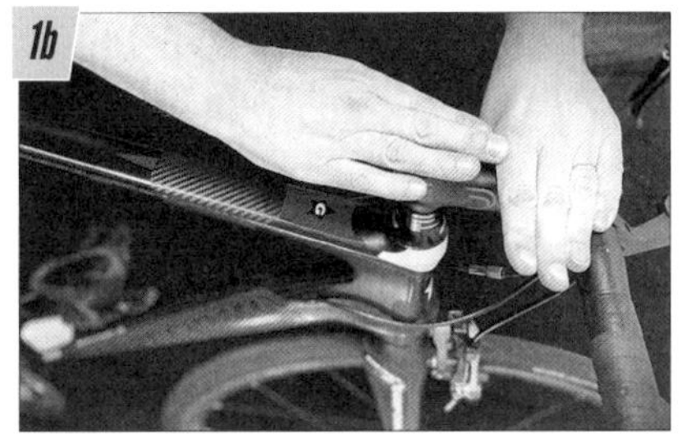

Put your other hand crossways so the widest part across your knuckles touches the index finger tip of the hand on the stem. The outer edge of your crossways hand should now be on the forward edge of the bar.

TOP TIP

A shorter reach to the bars will naturally create a more upright position that reduces strain on your arms and back. It can make it awkward to pedal when you're out of the saddle though and a longer stretch will make you lower and more aero for speed.

2

As saddle position is fixed, the only way to adjust the reach is to buy a new stem in a different length. But before you rush out and order one, check your bar set-up. That's because certain bars have much longer forward reach to the hoods and drops which is where your hands will be most of the time.

TECH EXPLAINED

Stem Length

While changing the length of a stem by 10mm or so won't affect handling too much, a big change will really alter steering feel. A longer stem will make the bike feel more stubborn to turn while a shorter stem will make it more twitchy.

BAR SET-UP

1

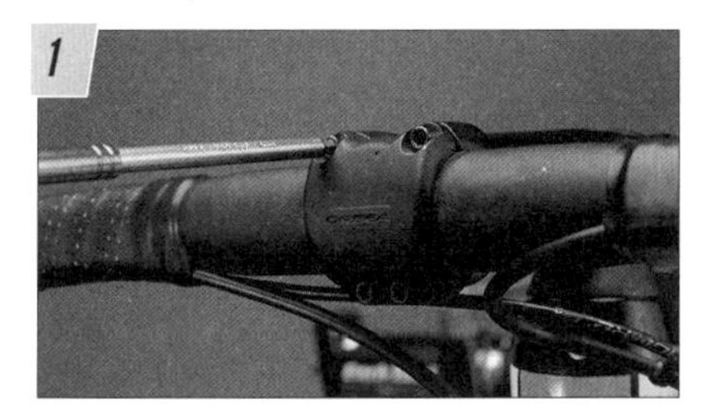

If you're building a bike up from a box then make sure that the stem is correctly aligned with the front wheel. Always check the stem and bar bolts are properly tightened up too, no matter who put the bike together.

2

There are loads of different shapes of bar but most are designed to work best with the lower part of the bend level and parallel to the floor. Loosen the stem bolts and use the spirit level (or your eyes) to get the correct rotation and then re-tighten.

3

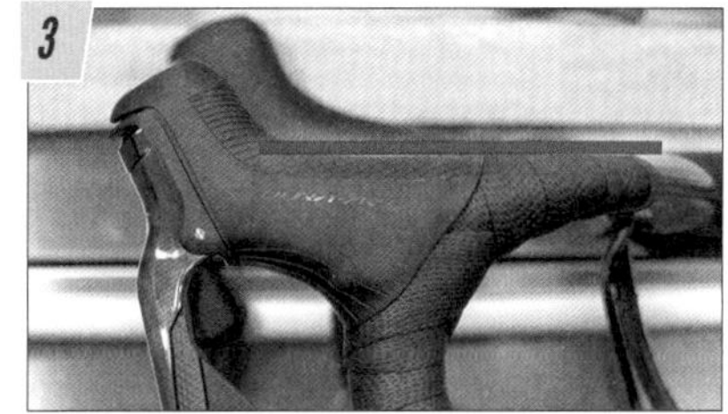

Most riders prefer the lever hoods to be horizontally aligned with the forward projecting section of the bars. If that is not how you like them (or how they've come set up on the bike) then you'll need to adjust them – see page 110 for more.

BAR SET-UP CONTINUED

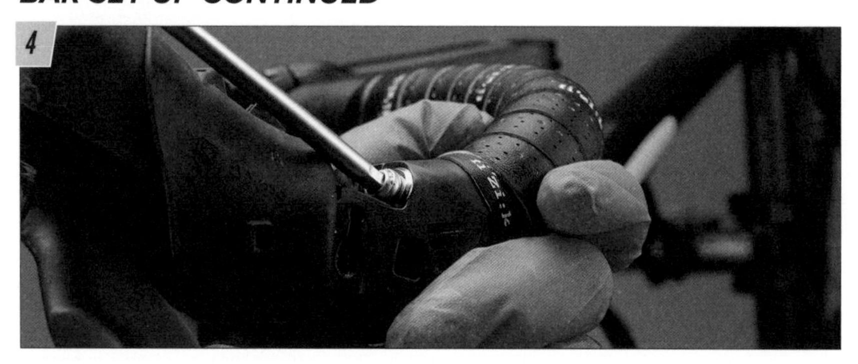

If it's not a big movement, then peel back the rubber hoods and find the clamp bolt underneath. Loosen it and then twist the levers slightly back and forth to shift them round the curve of that bar until they're right. Check the alignment from above and then tighten up.

TOP TIP

Use a long spirit level resting across the brake hoods to check that they're level with each other. Make sure you check the bike/bars themselves are vertical too though or they'll end up wonky.

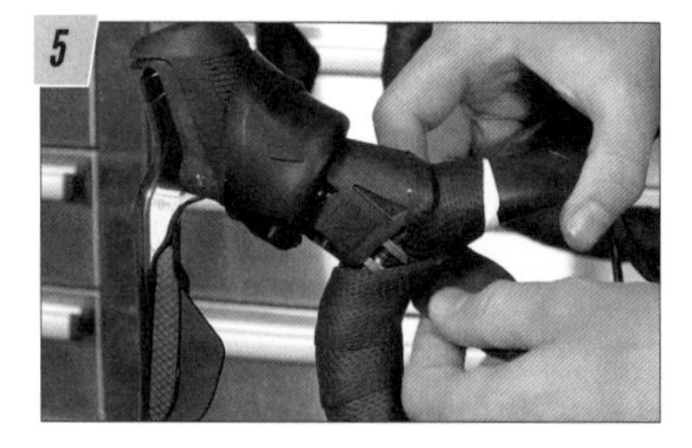

If they require more significant movement then you'll need to unwrap the bar tape to allow the levers to move further. Make sure you unwrap very carefully to avoid ripping or wrinkling the tape. You might also have to undo/replace the tape holding the cables/brake hose to the bar.

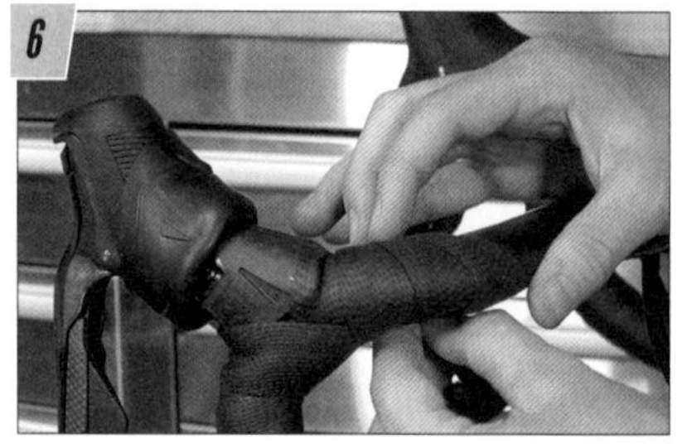

Once the levers are re-positioned, tighten them securely and then re-wrap the tape using the marks from the previous overlap as a guide. Fix fresh finishing tape to make sure it doesn't unravel. See page 200 for more on wrapping your bars.

BAR HEIGHT

TECH EXPLAINED

Internally Routed Cables

If you have a bike with hidden cables and hoses they'll be routed inside the stem and down into the frame through the spacers. That makes changing bar height a really complicated job involving splitting or removing and refitting the cables/hoses. If unsure, leave it to your local shop. If you're up for doing it yourself though, turn to page 204 for further advice.

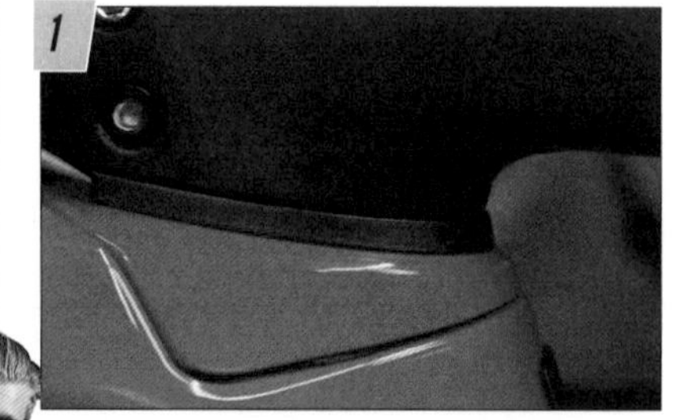

How high your bars are in relation to your saddle is personal preference. Most new bikes come with spacers underneath the stem. Moving one or more of these above the stem lets you experiment with a lower position.

TOP TIP

The higher your bars are the less weight you are putting on them – and the less you are potentially straining wrists, shoulders and back. However, the lower you are the more aerodynamic you will be and the faster you will go for a given effort. That's why you see pros using slammed stems, but gravel riders and tourers sitting upright.

BRAKE BALANCING

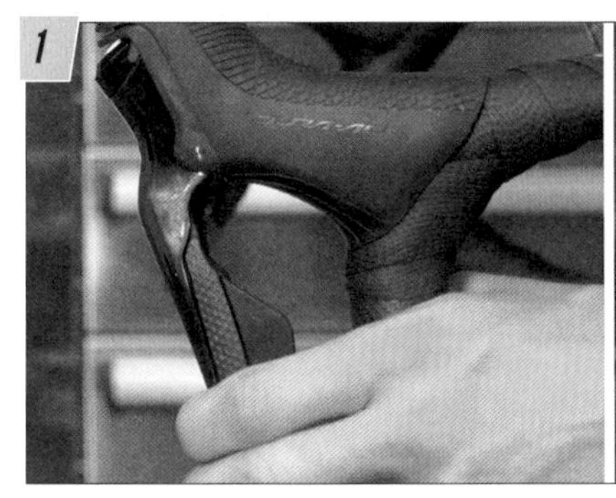

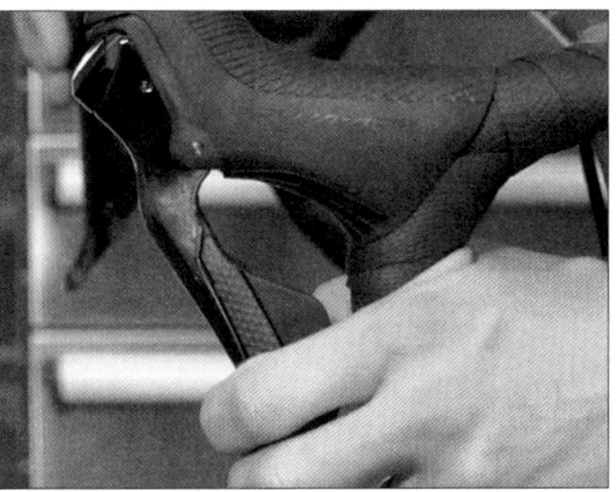

Some riders like their brakes to come on as soon as they pull the levers. Others prefer to have them engaging almost at the bars. Whichever you prefer, make sure you set your anchors up the way you want them before you ride and give yourself a fright.

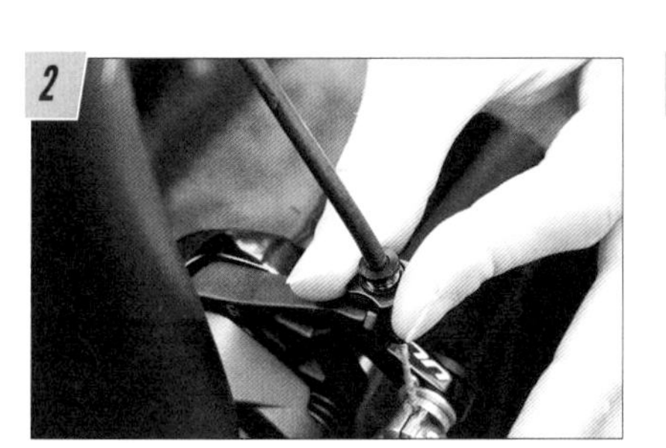

Cable brakes are easy to adjust. Small tweaks can be made by turning the barrel adjuster on the brake to open up or close the gap between brake pad and rotor/rim itself, or by releasing/tightening the cable to suit.

Hydraulic brakes are harder to balance, but premium sets have contact point adjusters in the lever. If not, you can reset the bite point by letting some fluid out of the reservoir and/or manually pushing the pads back into the calliper.

"It might seem weird to clean and lube a totally new chain on a totally new bike"

TOP TIP

If you have small hands and the levers are too far from the bars then you can reduce reach by fixing a small spacer onto the top of the lever blade where it contacts the brake lever body. Check you've made the spacer the right thickness for the reach you need before gluing it into place permanently though.

CLEANING & LUBING YOUR CHAIN

It might seem weird to clean and lube a totally new chain on a totally new bike. However, if you touch it you'll realise that shiny transmission is covered in grease to stop it corroding while it's in storage.

Before you put lube on you need to get the grease off. This is easiest to do with a degreaser spray or foaming chain cleaner. Ensure you don't get this near your hub bearings or your brake rotors.

Once the degreaser has soaked in, run the chain through a rag to clean it and dry it. Now take your lube of choice and apply according to the instructions to enjoy a clean and efficient first ride.

Don't Forget Your Safety Check
Make your bike is safe to ride on page 60

SET-UP SECRETS

HOW TO SET UP A BIKE FOR TALLER RIDERS

Getting a good bike fit if you're taller than average can be really hard. Here's what to look for when shopping and sizing

DIFFICULTY 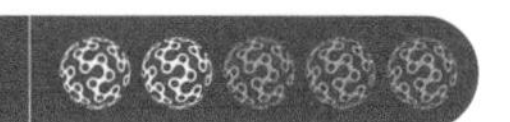

TIME 15 - 30 Minutes

TOOLS
- *Allen keys/Torx keys*
- *T25 Torx wrench*

WHEN
- *You're a taller than average rider*

FRAME CHOICE

1a

Not all brands offer really big sizes and even those that do can be very different in their actual dimensions. The key measurements to check are the top tube length and the head tube height. Top tube length defines the reach to the bars and head tube length the height potential of the bars.

1b

Choose a 'traditional' frame with a horizontal top tube frame rather than a 'compact' frame. That's because a long seat tube means less exposed seatpost with more inside the frame. This reduces stress and leverage on the frame and increases the overlap for more support and durability.

WATCH THE VIDEO

Free show-how and know-how

 *https://gcn.eu/TallRiderSet-Up*

SCAN CODE TO WATCH THE VIDEO

"Key measurements to check are the top tube length and head tube height"

1a

A bigger frame also needs to be stiffer so as not feel like a noodle. That means carbon fibre and alloy frames are generally a better choice than steel or titanium. Look for frames with a reputation of being rigid rather than comfortable as all those long pipes will always soften the ride slightly anyway.

TOP TIP

It might be tempting to just buy a longer seatpost to make a smaller frame 'fit'. Too much leverage through your frame can easily snap the whole top end of your bike though and if it's not the original post your warranty is void. Don't be tempted to run your original seatpost above the minimum insert line either.

WHEELS & TYRES

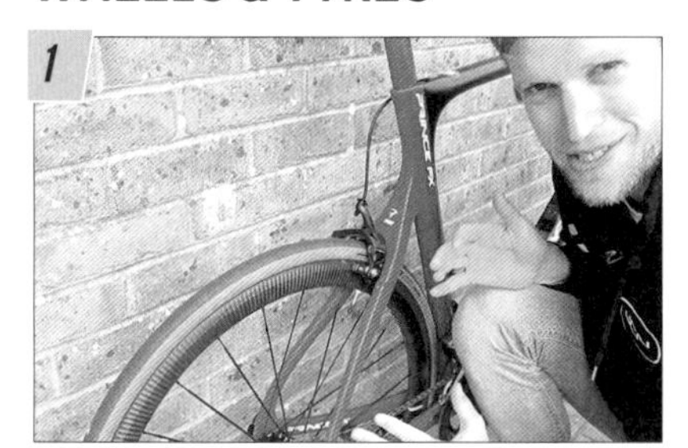

If you're a heavier rider you'll need wheels that are up to the job, so give super-light sets a miss. Avoid low spoke counts (24 or less) and pick wheels which are laced three-cross for extra strength.

The current trend for wider wheels and tyres is definitely good news for bigger riders as it puts more air between you and the road/track. Tubeless set-ups and/or heavy duty 'training' tyres also reduce the chance of getting a pinch puncture on a pothole or sharp stone. See page 156 for how to install tubeless tyres.

CRANKS & PEDALS

If you have long legs then you need long cranks to get the most from those big levers. Unfortunately cranks longer than 180cm are almost impossible to find and even 180mm cranks will often only be available on the most expensive models.

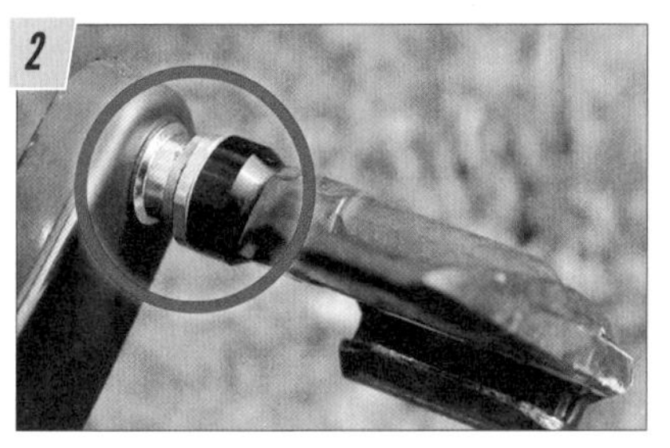

Shimano pedals have the biggest platform and the biggest cleats so give the best support for big feet. They're also available in a version with longer axles and more clearance so your shoes won't rub on the cranks or clip the chain stays at the back.

CONTACT POINTS

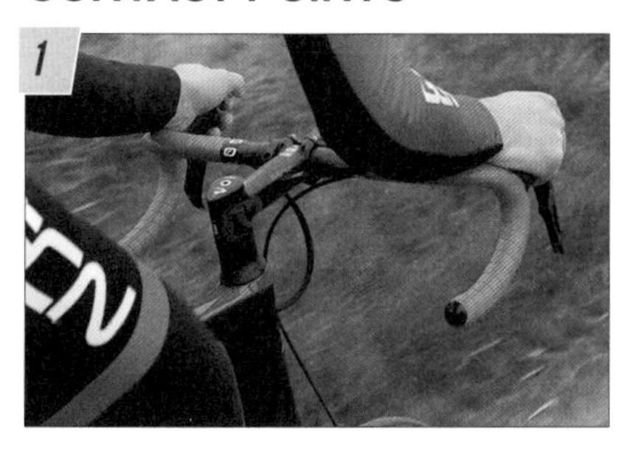

Wider shoulders need wider bars to match them. While anything over 46cm used to be rare, gravel riding trends have made wider bars up to 50cm easier to find.

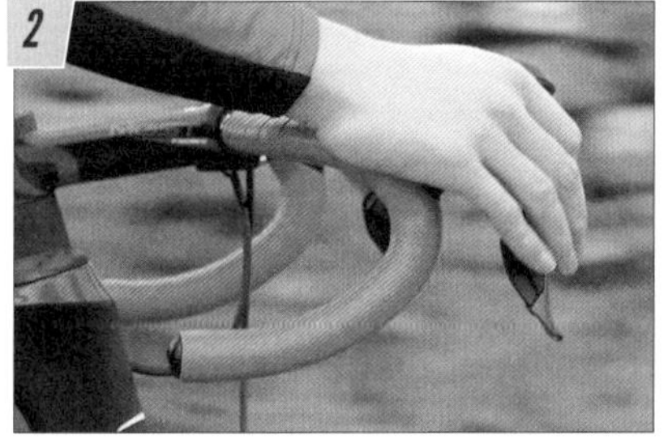

Big hands can feel cramped when wrapped around relatively skinny bars. Using thicker bar tape can add a bit of girth, or double-wrap to really bulk them up.

Taller and heavier riders obviously put more stress on saddles than lighter riders. So avoid super-light seats that are more likely to sag rather than properly support you.

For How To Fit Bar Tape
Head over to page 200

HOW TO SET UP A BIKE FOR SMALLER RIDERS

Getting a good bike fit if you're smaller than average can be really hard. Here's what to look for when shopping and sizing

DIFFICULTY
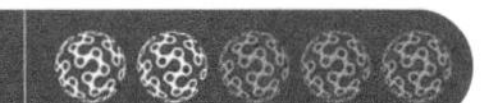

TIME 30 - 60 Minutes

TOOLS
- *Allen keys/Torx keys*
- *T25 Torx wrench*

WHEN
- *You're smaller than the average rider*

The most important parameter for smaller cyclists is reach. Being able to just about hold the handlebars does not mean that the reach is okay. If you're stretched out and your hips are rocked forward that's going to give you lower back, shoulder and neck pain.

Smaller riders need to look for a bike where the top tube is genuinely short. The actual sizes and reach of the smallest frames from different manufacturers can vary significantly, so research them carefully. You also really want to be able to try sitting on a bike before buying.

WATCH THE VIDEO

Free show-how and know-how

https://gcn.eu/SmallRiderSet-Up

TOE OVERLAP

Reducing the top tube length automatically brings the front and back wheels closer together. That can increase toe crossover – where your toes can literally hit the front wheel when you're turning. In the worst cases overlap can happen when your front foot is anywhere from one o'clock to five o'clock. This is obviously a real handling issue – particularly when track standing or riding at slow speeds.

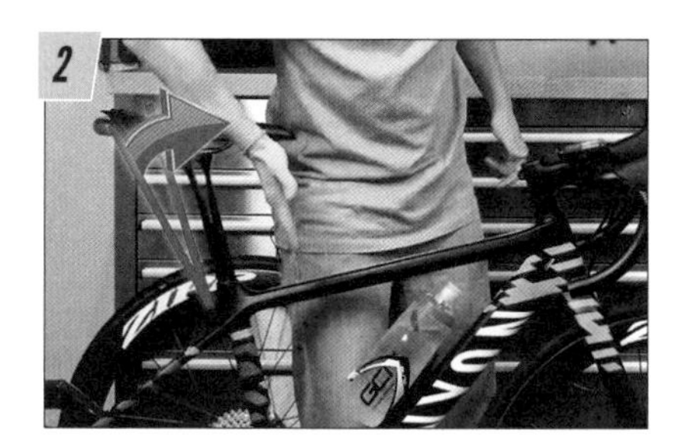

Some manufacturers reduce overlap by making the seat tube angle steeper which moves your upper body further forward in relation to your feet. That can affect the feel of the entire bike though.

Other brands increase the fork offset which puts the front wheel further from the frame. However, that reduces the stability of the steering, making the bike more twitchy through the bars. If you combine that with a shorter stem then things can get really nervous.

That means the best solution is smaller wheels, specifically 650B and 650C. Because the wheels are smaller, there's more space between them and your toes so overlap isn't an issue. Smaller wheels also feel more balanced and don't catch the wind as much which is always an issue for lighter riders.

COCKPIT SET-UP

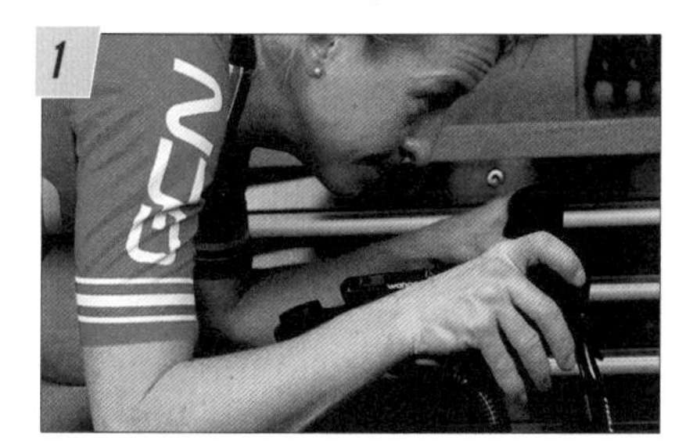

Small frames should have a small head tube but sometimes your bars can still be too high. Remove any spacers from under the stem to see if that drops them enough. If you still need to go lower, try a slightly shorter, downward sloping stem.

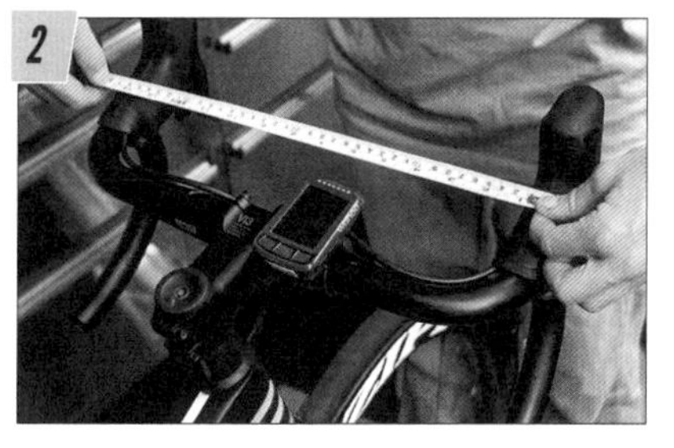

If you've got slim shoulders you don't need a wide bar either. Look for a 38 or even 36cm wide bar, but you will have to look hard as they're very rare. Try to find one with a shallow drop so you're not reaching so far in the lower position.

Smaller riders typically have small hands too. That means you'll need to keep the levers close to the bar so you can brake easily. Some levers have reach adjusters built-in or you can bring them closer with a wedge between the lever and the body.

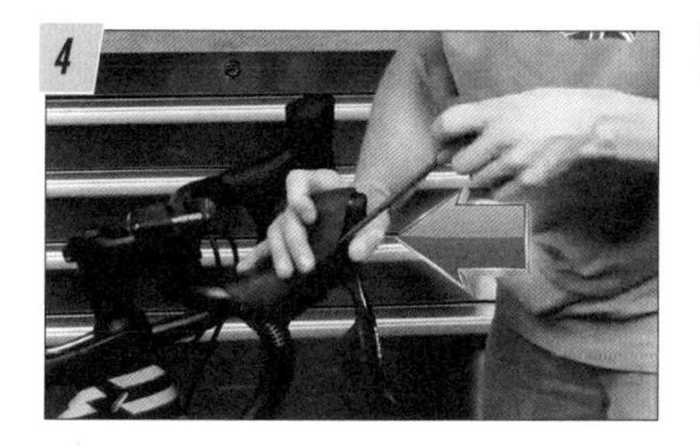

The position of the levers on the bar makes a big difference to how easily you can shift and brake. Experiment with what works for you by taking off the tape and moving the levers around until you're comfortable and can reach the controls easily.

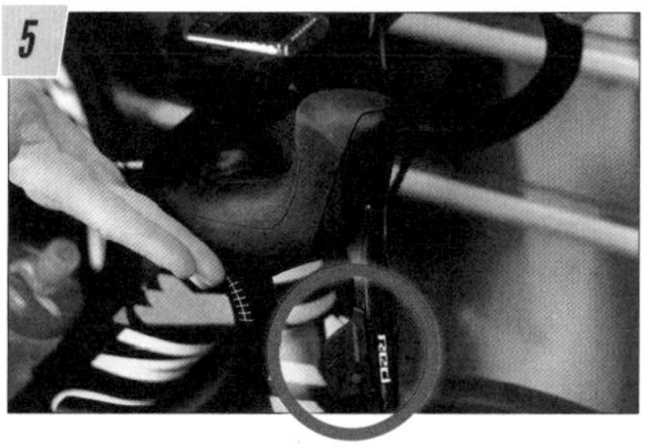

Some gear levers swing a long way across for each shift – which can be really awkward if you have small hands. Fatter hoods of mechanical shifters can also be hard to hold. That makes electronic shifting a real help if you can afford it.

Smaller frames can lack the space for a conventional bottle and cage to work well. Luckily there are lots of side loading cages now where the bottle can be twisted out to the side rather than pulled out forwards.

Gears Not Shifting Properly?
Head to page 64 and get them sorted

SET-UP SECRETS

10 PRO BIKE SET-UP HACKS

Want a bike that feels as near as you can get to a pro's? Then read on for our tuning and set-up tips

GRIP TAPE

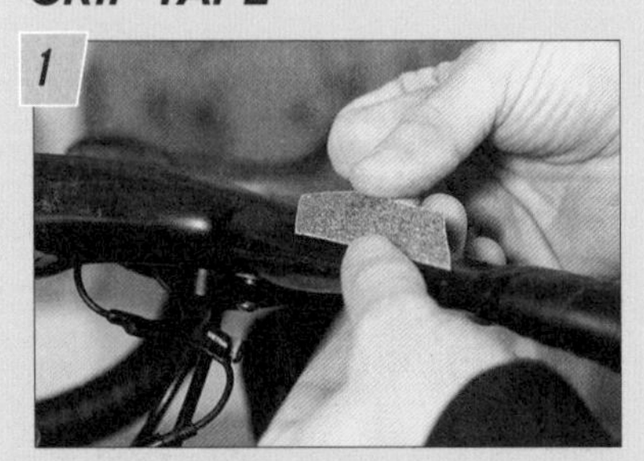

To help prevent bike components from getting slippery when they're wet or you're on rough roads, take some skateboard grip tape and cut it to fit onto your shifters, brake levers and the tops of carbon bars. The extra grip you'll get can really increase your confidence.

TYRE PRESSURES

Ensuring that you're running the correct tyre pressures on your bike is a must. While a track pump is great for ballpark pressure, nothing is as accurate as a digital gauge. It can be your best friend, especially when changing tyre brands or making small adjustments.

TAKE MEASUREMENTS

Pros go through a set-up regime and then use those measurements on whatever they ride. While the measurements don't always totally translate, they are still a great place to start when you move to a different bike. So get all of your set-up measurements and note them down.

QUICK-RELEASE

Tighten up your quick-releases so that the lever sits against the frame or fork up as much as possible. When riding in close proximity to other riders in a race or event, if another wheel was to go in between the quick-release and the wheel, it could flick it open, so you'd have to stop and adjust – or the outcome could also be far worse! Keeping them tucked into the frame also looks neat.

TIDY CABLES

Keep your bike looking tidy by joining cables and wires together where possible. You can do this using black electrical tape. Doing this will also give you some aero advantages too.

SADDLE ADJUSTMENTS

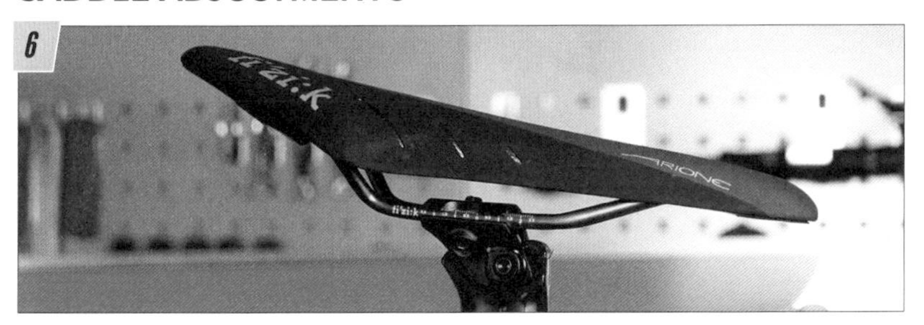

Not all races or events make the same demands. Subtle changes to saddle tilt or saddle height can really work wonders for your comfort and power output , depending on their nature and terrain. You might want your saddle higher if you're riding an event that's on smooth roads, for example, or to run it slightly lower on rougher terrain. Just a couple of millimetres could be enough to make a difference.

PEDAL TENSION

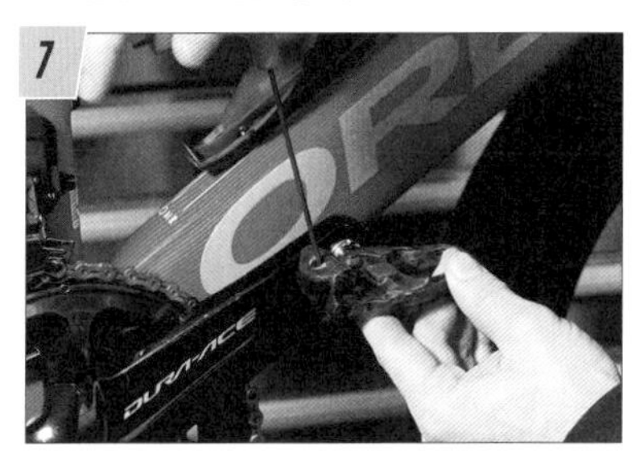

Tune your pedal spring tension to suit your riding. If you're into sprints, go super-tight to lock in the cleats. If you do long rides, you may well feel more comfortable with a lower tension.

LEVER PULL & BITE

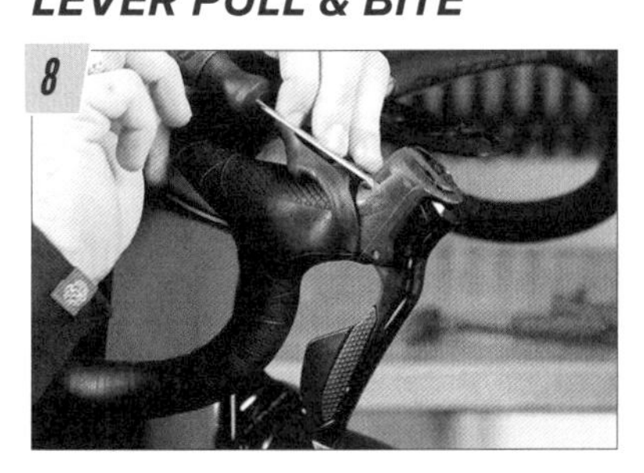

Not all brake levers fit all hands, so it's worth playing around with the reach adjustment to find a position that fits. Similarly, adjust your callipers and levers to get a bite point that suits you.

REDUCED FRICTION

For a pro feel, reduce the friction in every moving part by running a lightweight oil in the cables, derailleurs and all your bearings. You'll need to strip and relube after every ride though!

FIT A NEW CHAIN

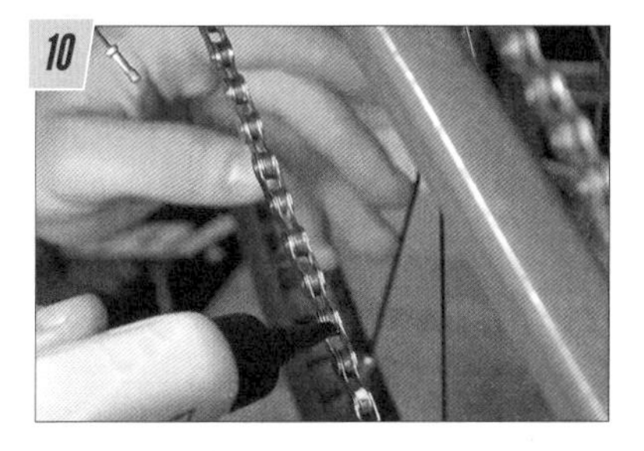

Nothign beats fitting a brand new chain: your drivetrain will immediately feel smoother and faster. Completely degrease it, then carefully re-lube each roller.

BEGINNER BASICS

HOW TO DO ESSENTIAL PRE-RIDE CHECKS

Before hitting the road with your bike it's a very good idea to do some quick checks on your bike. Here's what to look at

DIFFICULTY 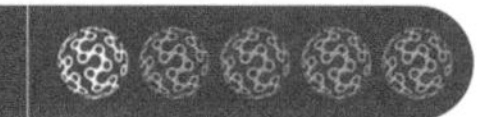

TIME 5 - 15 Minutes

TOOLS
- Pump
- Allen keys
- Small pick
- Glue
- Chain lube

WHEN
- Before every ride

Inspect the tyres for any cuts, slices and little bits of glass or any other debris that might have become embedded in the rubber.

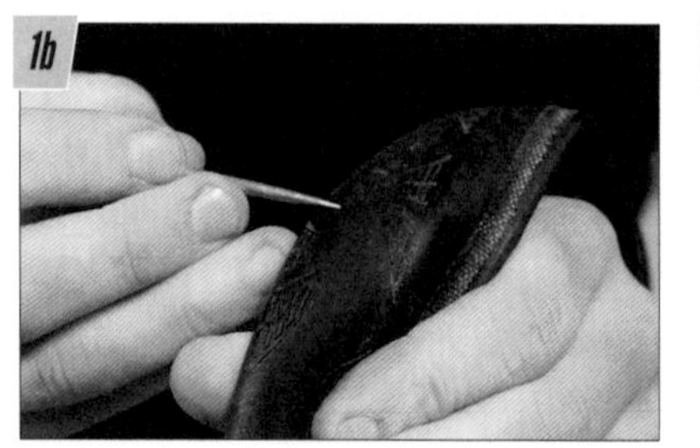

Should you find anything embedded, carefully prise it out with a pick or a thin bladed screwdriver, then use superglue or the glue from a puncture repair kit to seal up the cuts.

If the slice or cut is fairly large, don't risk riding your bike as you could end up having a blowout and a potentially serious crash. Unfortunately, the damaged tyre will need replacing.

WATCH THE VIDEO

Free show-how and know-how

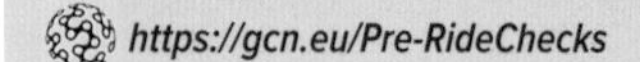

https://gcn.eu/Pre-RideChecks

Next, check you have the correct air pressure in your tyres. If you're unsure what it should be, the maximum pressure is usually printed on the walls of your tyre, so make sure you're somewhere close to but below that figure.

While checking your tyres, ensure your wheels skewers or through-axles are done up correctly. A partially undone skewer can become completely undone over the course of a ride and obviously you don't want that to happen!

Grab both brake levers and rock your bike backwards and forwards to check for anything loose or knocking. If there's any rocking at the front end, your headset may need adjusting (see page 192 for how to do that).

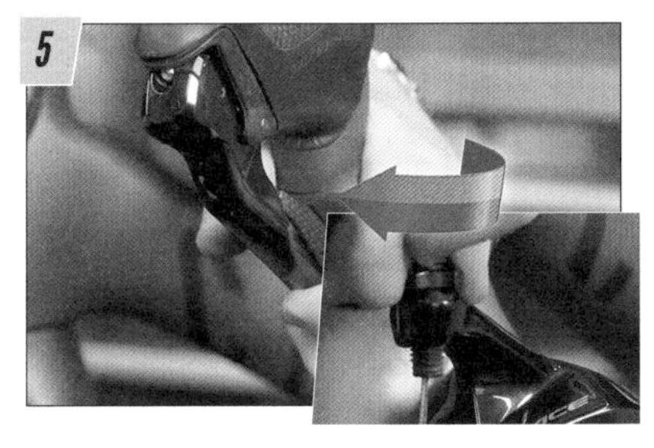

If you need to pull your levers right into the bar before the brakes fully engage, you may need to adjust your cable tension if you're using rim brakes. If so, on each brake calliper is a barrel adjuster. Give each one a few turns as necessary to add some more tension to the cables.

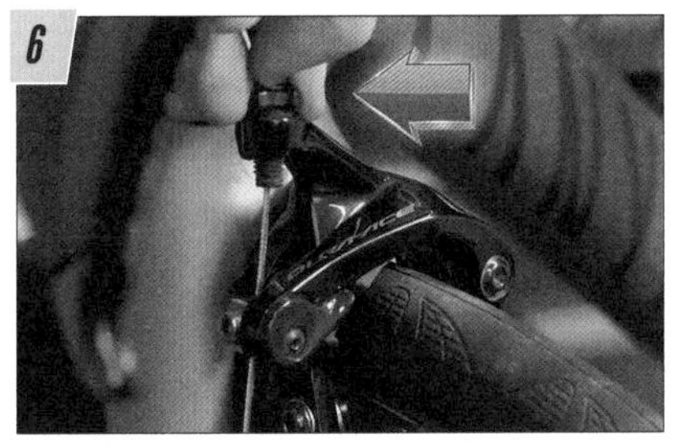

If the barrel adjuster is at its limit, screw it all the way in. Loosen off the brake cable clamp, squeeze the calliper so the pads are almost on the rim and tighten the cable up again. Check out page 118 for more on setting up your rim brakes.

Check to see how much wear is left on your brake pads. If they are almost at the wear indicators, you'll need to fit some new pads. See page 112 for details on how to do that.

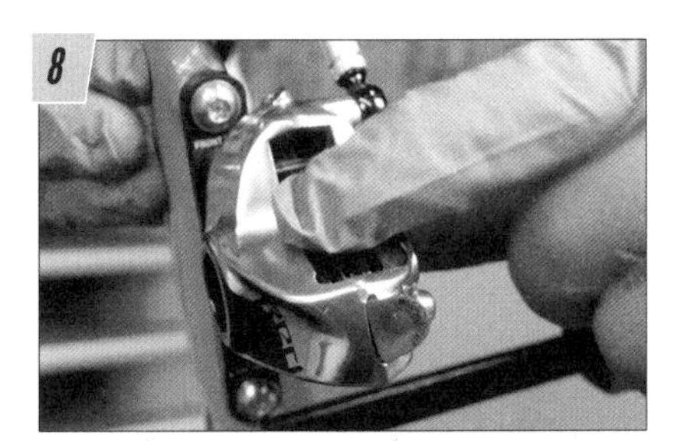

If you're pulling the brake levers into the bar and you're running hydraulic disc brakes, you'll either need to bleed the hydraulic system or replace worn brake pads – see page 132 for more on both of these procedures.

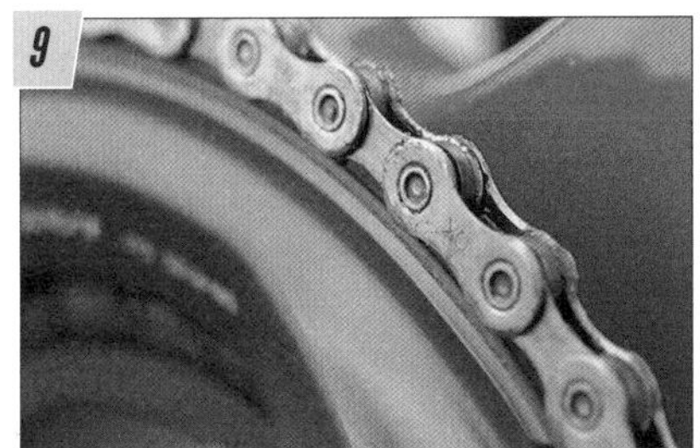

Check the chain. If it's looking really filthy, now is not the time for a full degrease, so quickly grab an old rag, grip the chain with it and turn the cranks until the chain runs through the rag a few times to remove the worst of the gunk.

However, if your chain looks bone dry, you'll need to give it a good lubing before you ride. Don't forget to wipe off any excess with a rag before you head out. Use the lube type that is best suited to the riding conditions. Head to page 222 for more chain cleaning and lubing tips.

Want A Showroom Clean Bike?
See page 214 for our cleaning guide

SECTION 2

TRANSMISSION

From indexing your gears to installing a brand new drivetrain, you'll find everything you need to know about road bike gears and transmission in this section

SET-UP SECRETS

HOW TO GET PERFECT SHIFTING

Grinding gears and imprecise changes can turn a bike ride into a frustrating experience. Follow our tips and soon your shifts will super-smooth once again

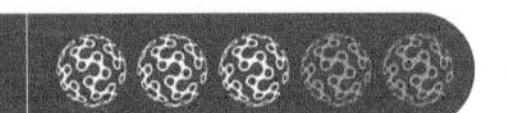

DIFFICULTY

TIME 20 - 60 Minutes

TOOLS

- Water displacer or silicone spray
- Spray lubricant
- Cable cutters
- File
- Chain checker
- Allen key set
- Torque wrench

WHEN

- Your gear shifts are noisy and imprecise

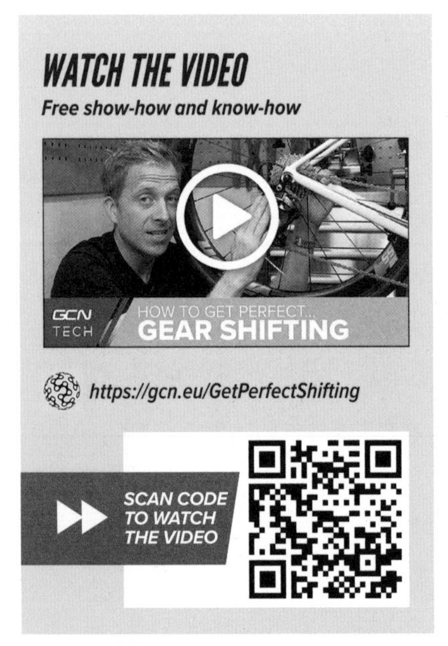

Badly shifting gears are a particular issue for new bike owners, not least because gear cables stretch after the first few rides causing vague and imprecise gear changes. While getting smooth running gears can seem like a bit of dark art at first, it's actually pretty simple once you understand the basics. Over the new few pages we'll explain everything you need to know to achieve ultra-smooth shifting.

DE-GUNK YOUR LEVER MECHANISM

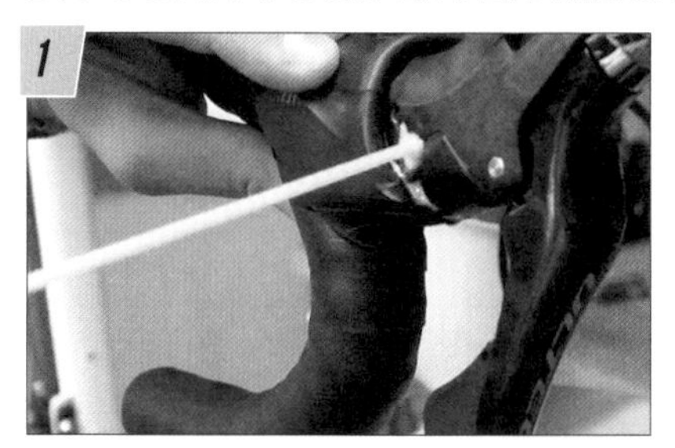

It's not uncommon for iffy shifting to be caused by your shifters themselves as the intricate inner parts can get gummed up from time to time. In cases like this, a blast from an air hose, or a can of water displacer or silicone lubricant can do the trick.

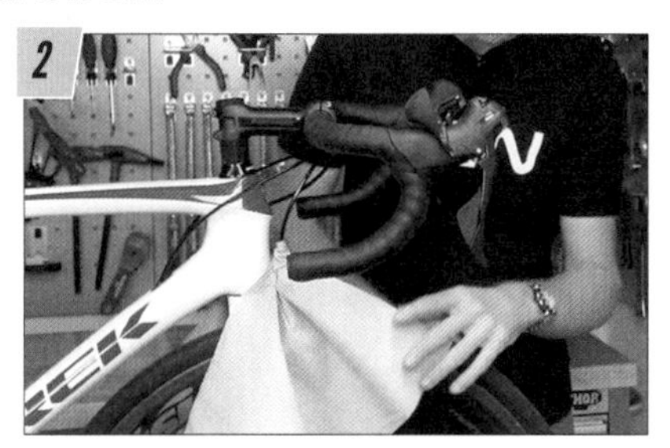

Particularly if you've used a water displacer, it's a good idea to now use some spray lube on the inners of your shifters. Take care not to get it onto the handlebar tape or the hoods and it's essential to cover your brakes and your wheel rims before doing any spraying to avoid contaminating them.

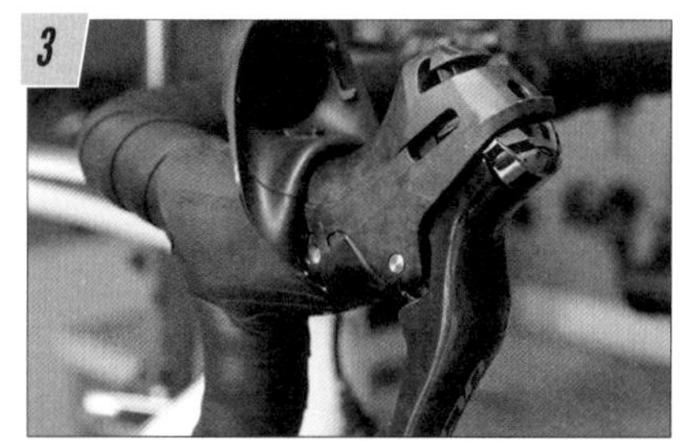

Roll down the top of your brake hoods to expose the shifters and give the mechanism a good blast. This is unlikely to be a permanent solution, but it should buy you a few more rides before you need to fit new cables.

OUTER CABLES

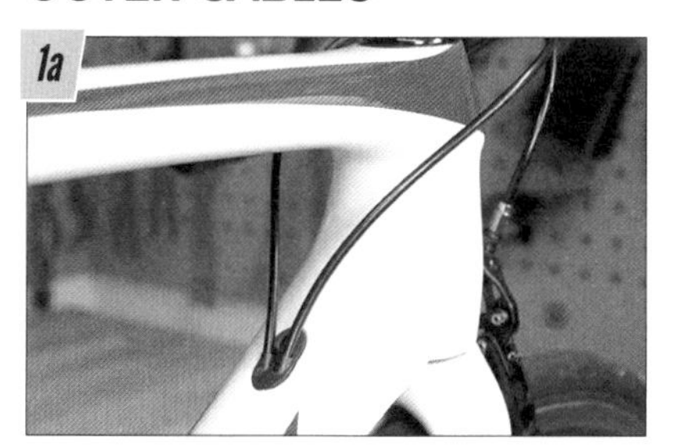

Check that your outer cables are taking as direct route as possible back to your derailleurs and do not have any sharp curves or bends in them which would add friction to the gear system.

Ensure that your cables are not getting snagged or pulled too much when you turn the bars, as this will add friction and restrict your shifting.

Have a look at where your cable loops around and into your rear derailleur. You want a nice loop that's not so long that it's likely to snag on anything, but not too tight so that it impairs shifting.

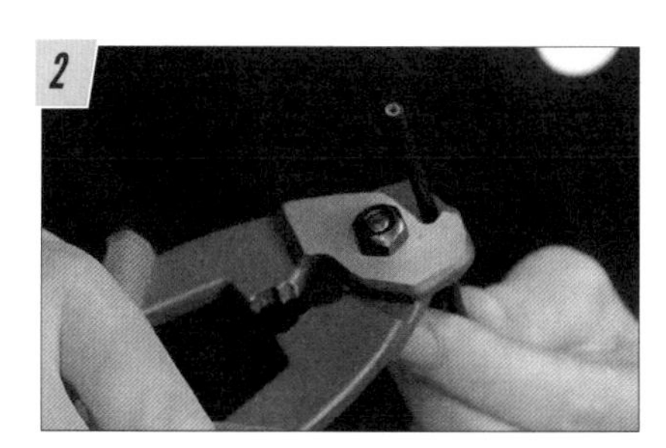

Check that your outer cable ends are as flat as possible. If they aren't, chop the end off with a dedicated cable cutter (rather than using pliers), ensuring you cut at a right angle to the cable, then use a file to get the ends super-flat.

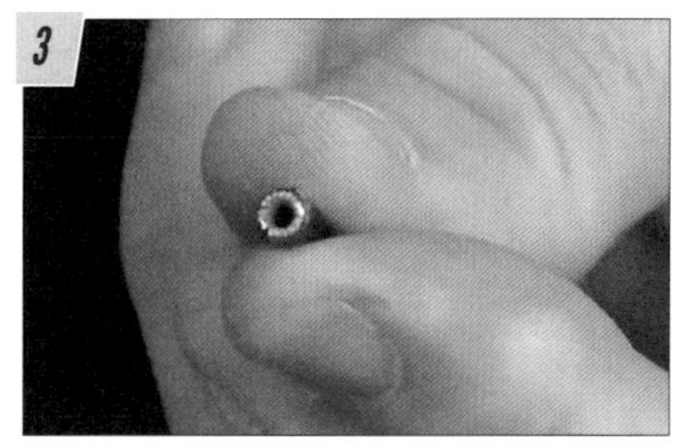

Make sure the ends of the inner sleeve of the cable outer are fully open (they can get compressed while cutting), then spray a water displacer or a very thin lightweight oil inside it before installing the cable ends and then finally inserting the inner cable once in position on your bike.

TOP TIP

If bare cables are visible underneath your bike's bottom bracket, get yourself some water displacer or lubricant spray and use it to clean out any dirt, mud or other gunge that tends to accumulate there as it can really affect your gear shifting.

HOW TO GET PERFECT SHIFTING

CHAIN AND CASSETTE

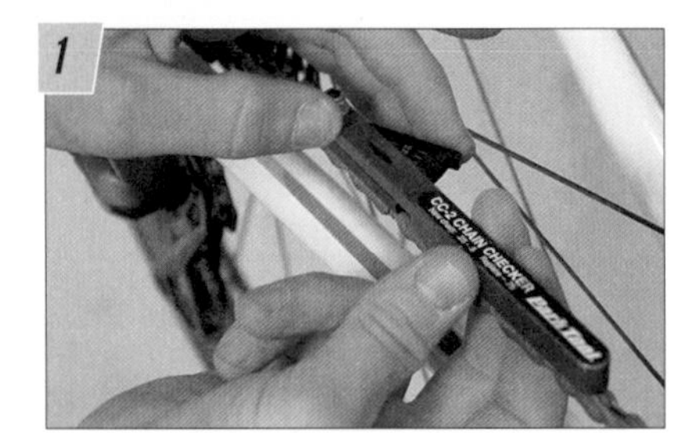

If your bike has seen plenty of miles, a worn out chain could be the source of your shifting problems. Use a chain-checker to see if your chain has stretched too much over time and needs to be replaced. See page 68 for more.

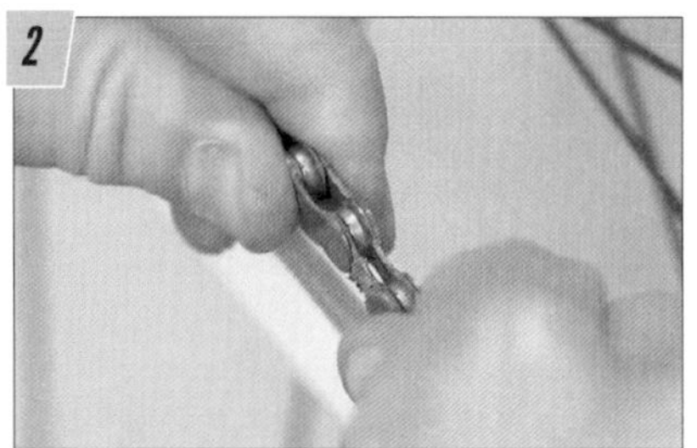

Stiff links can also cause poor shifting. To check for them, turn your cranks backwards while you keep a close eye on the chain. If you spot a link that doesn't move like the others, flex it backwards and forwards between your hands to loosen it up.

Inspect your cassette to see if everything looks as it should. You'll see that at least one or two teeth per sprocket have a different shape from the rest, but that is totally normal. However, any pointy looking teeth means they have been damaged.

REAR DERAILLEUR

Check your derailleur hanger bolts are tight as any movement here can result in sloppy shifting. Ensure only to tighten to around 2Nm so as not to break these fragile bolts. Check that the hanger is straight. If it's bent, it's much safer to replace it.

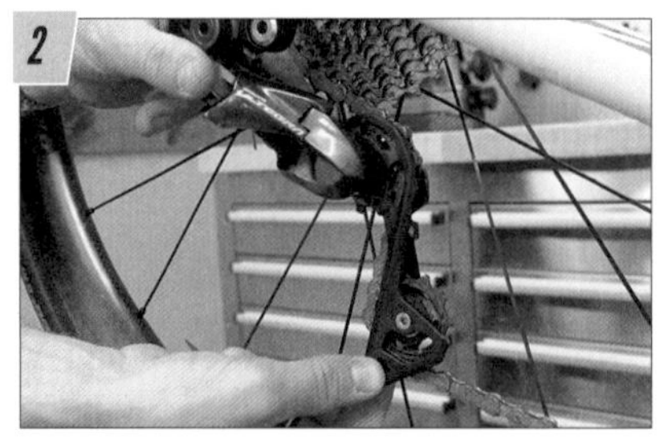

Have a look to check that your rear derailleur cage isn't super-sloppy from years of abuse. There's always going to be some sideways movement because there is a pivot point here, but if there's a lot, it's time to buy a new derailleur.

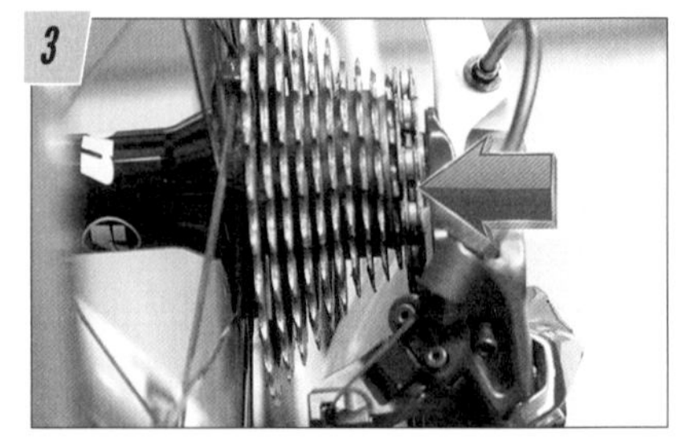

With your chain in the highest gear, check that the top upper jockey wheel is in line with the sprocket. If it's a little to the right, adjust the H (high) limit screw a quarter turn at a time until it lines up – or in the other direction if it's too far to the left.

Check the position of the L (low) limit screw on the derailleur by pedalling around with your cranks and then moving the derailleur body across by hand to see if it goes into the lowest (easiest) sprocket. If it goes any further, you'll need to adjust the low limit screw in the same manner as the high limit screw.

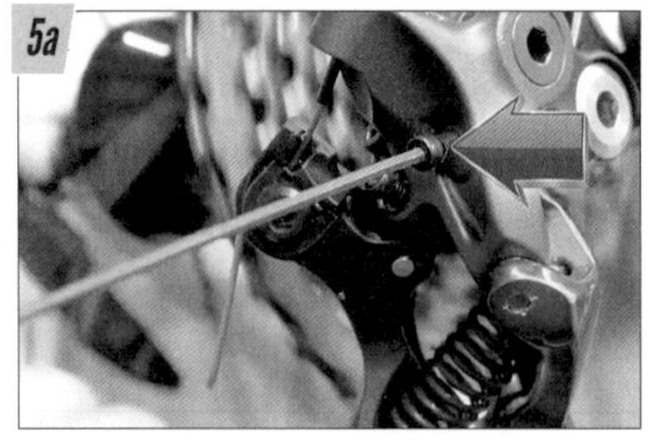

The third adjustment screw on the derailleur is the B-tension screw. It enables you to adjust the distance between your upper jockey wheel and the lowest sprocket on the cassette.

The gap between the jockey wheel and sprocket should be around 5 to 6mm in most cases. To make it easier to measure the distance, place an Allen key of the required thickness in the gap as you adjust the screw.

FRONT DERAILLEUR

Check that the front derailleur (if you have one, 1x systems don't) has been set up to the correct height. In the correct position, there should be about one to two millimetres gap between the teeth of the biggest chainring and front derailleur.

To adjust the front derailleur plate, put the chain in the easiest gear at the rear and the smallest chainring at the front. Then adjust the L (low) limit screw so that the inner of the front derailleur plate is about 1 to 2mm away from the inside of the chain.

The same adjustment technique can be applied when in the biggest chainring using the H (high) limit screw; you also want to have about 1mm between the outside edge of the chain and the inside of the derailleur cage.

INDEXING YOUR GEARS

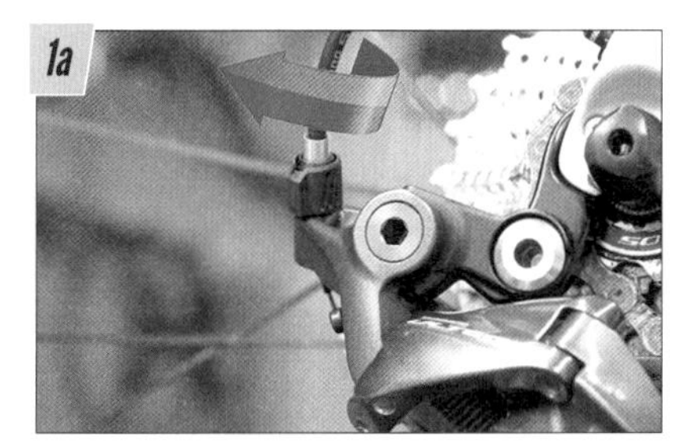

Put the chain on the biggest chainring and smallest sprocket on the cassette. Undo the cable clamp and wind in the barrel adjuster all the way in, then a full turn out again. Pull the cable fairly tight (but not too tight) and do up the cable clamp.

Start turning the cranks as if peddling and shift a gear. If the chain doesn't move to the next cog, increase the cable tension by unwinding the barrel adjuster a quarter turn at a time until the chain shifts without rattling around on the sprocket.

Once the chain is running silently, move through the other gears and repeat the tuning process until your chain moves smoothly up and down your cassette.

To adjust the front derailleur, put the chain on the smallest chainring, then release and retighten the cable to ensure you have enough tension. Rather than a barrel adjuster to make the necessary adjustments, some derailleurs have a micro-adjustment screw.

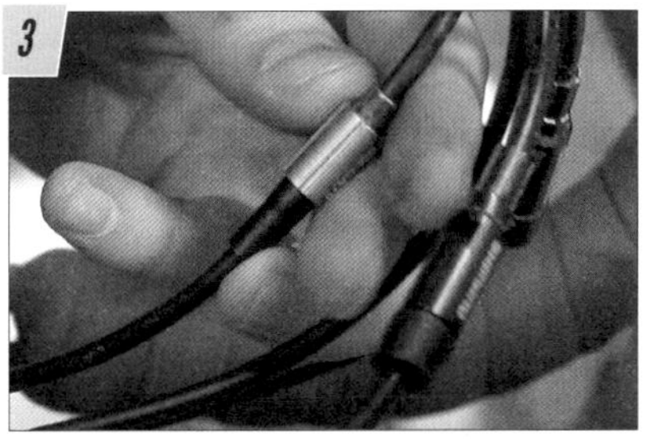

If your derailleur doesn't have an adjustment screw, we suggest adding an inline cable tension adjuster onto your front derailleur outer cable so you can simply take up or remove any of those fine cable adjustments.

TOP TIP

If you suspect that your rear derailleur hanger has taken a bash and is no longer straight, ask your local bike shop if they have a derailleur hanger alignment gauge and get your derailleur checked out.

Want Get a Perfectly Lubed Chain?
Head over to page 222 for all the info

ESSENTIAL REPAIRS

HOW TO TO REPLACE YOUR CHAIN

The easiest way to install a new chain on your bike, and how to check if your chain needs replacing

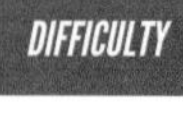

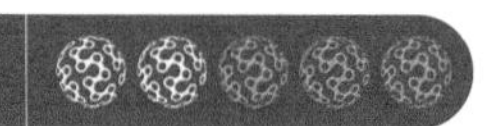

TIME 10 - 20 Minutes

TOOLS
- *Chain checker*
- *Chain tool*
- *Pliers*
- *Chain*

WHEN
- *When your chain becomes worn or unstable*

TECH EXPLAINED

Chain Wear

A common misconception is that chains actually stretch, however it's not strictly true unless you're putting an incredible amount of watts through the pedals. So how does the chain wear? Well, as it's moving around the cassette and chainrings dirt and oil inside the rivets and the rollers acts like a cutting paste and wears them away. This is why it is a very good idea to keep your chain clean as it's likely to to increase its lifespan. A chain that has excessive wear is not going to give good gear shifting as it won't sit perfectly on your cassette sprockets or chainrings, it will also wear out those components a lot faster too.

"Dirt and oil inside the rivets and rollers acts like a cutting paste and wears them away"

WATCH THE VIDEO

Free show-how and know-how

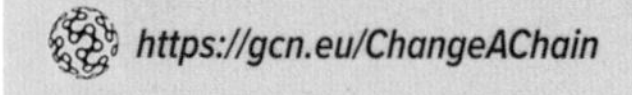

CHECKING YOUR CHAIN

Put your chain in the biggest chainring and the smallest sprocket on the cassette. With the cranks positioned vertically, pinch the chain at the three-o'clock position on the chainring and pull it away from the teeth. If you can see light between the chain and three or four teeth, it needs replacing.

A more accurate method of measuring chain wear is to use a chain-checker. The exact method for checking your chain will depend on the type checker you're using. But essentially, you're measuring the gap between links on your chain to see whether or not your chain needs replacing.

INSTALLING A NEW CHAIN

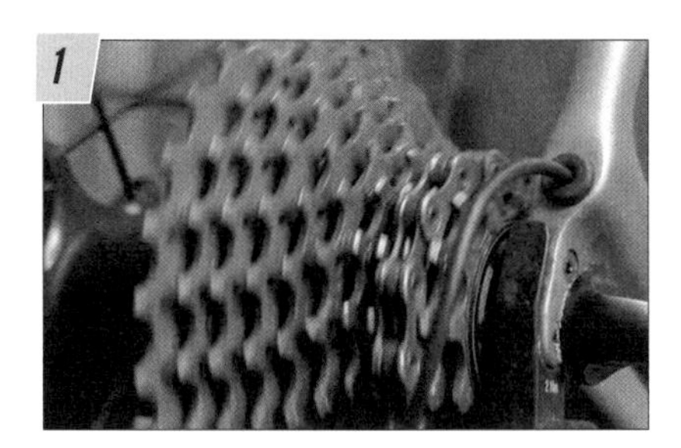

1

When buying a new chain, ensure you get one that is the right speed for your drivetrain. If you're unsure what that is, count the number of sprockets on your cassette. For example, if you have 11, then you need a 11-speed chain.

2

To get your new chain to the right length, hang it next to your existing chain and count the number of excess links. Keep in mind that you will need narrower links at each of the chain in order to join it if using a master link, or one narrow and one wide end if your new chain has a pin to join it.

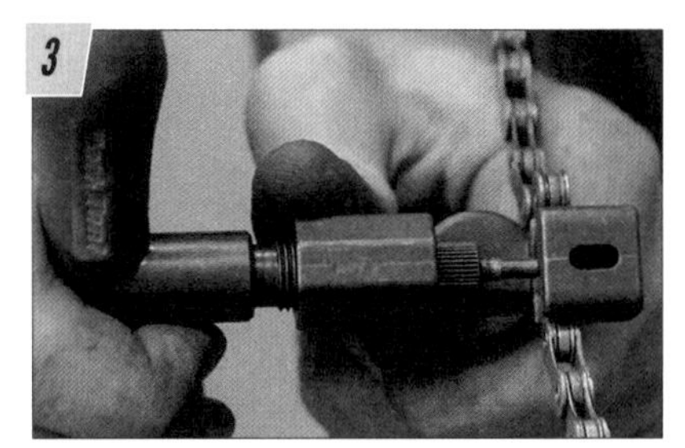

3

Unwind the threaded side of your chain-tool, then fit your chain onto the slotted part, ensuring the pin you need to remove to get your chain to the correct length sits in the centre of the slots. Then wind in the threaded side so the pin of your chain-tool pushes the chain's pin right out of the link.

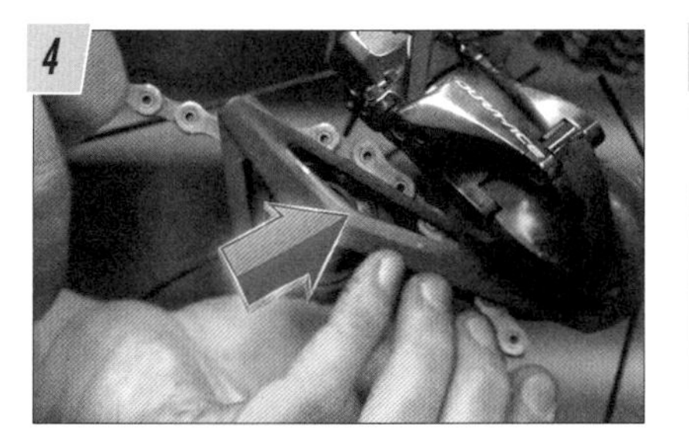

4

Before feeding in your new chain, use your shifters to set your derailleurs so that the rear is positioned by the biggest sprocket and the front is sitting above the biggest chainring. Feed your chain into the rear derailleur, ensuring to position it on the correct side of the tabs inside the derailleur cage.

5

Once you're through the rear derailleur, thread the chain around the biggest sprocket on your cassette, then around the biggest chainring, so the two loose ends of your chain meet at the lower position near the cranks.

6

If you don't have your old chain, here's how to work out the correct chain length. Install the chain as before, then tension it so that the rear derailleur is around the four o'clock position. Offer up both ends of the chain and shorten it by the number of links needed to keep the derailleur in this position.

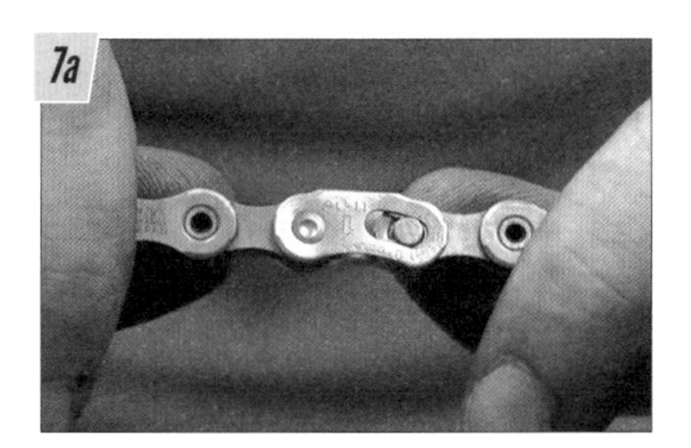

7a

As mentioned in step 2, chains either come with a pin, or a master link to join them. If using a master link, ensure you're joining it the right way up (usually marked by an arrow), then insert the pins into the chain one side at a time and slide them in against each other to click into place.

7b

If using a pin, put the internal link inside the external one, then take the pointy end of your pin and push it in by hand. Grab your chain-tool and use it to carefully push the pin into place, ensuring the indented mark on the pin has been pushed all the way through the link.

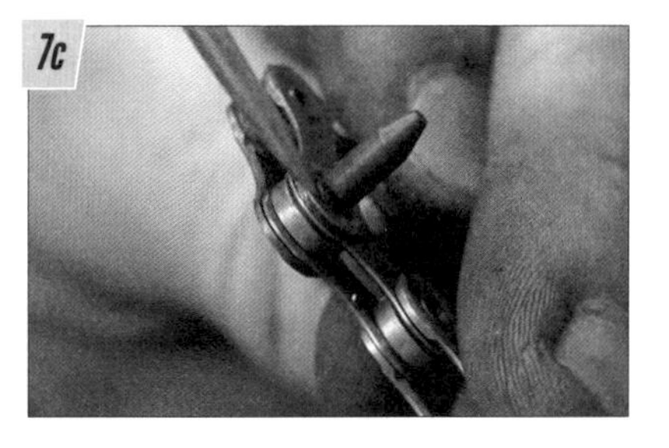

7c

Using your pliers, firmly grab hold of the end of the pin protruding from the chain. Holding the chain in one hand, twist the pliers to snap off the end of the pin. If the joined link is a little stiff, hold the chain either side of it and flex the link back and forth to free it up.

Need To Change Your Cassette?
Turn over the page for how to do that

ESSENTIAL REPAIRS

HOW TO REPLACE YOUR CASSETTE

It's a straightforward job to remove your cassette. Here's the best way to do it and how to tell when it should be replaced

DIFFICULTY

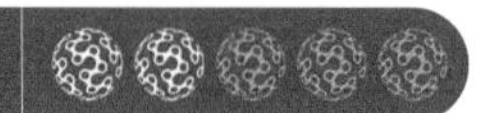

TIME 5 - 10 Minutes

TOOLS
- *Chain whip*
- *Adjustable spanner*
- *Lockring removal tool*

WHEN
- *Deep cleaning your bike, fitting new wheels, or changing a worn out cassette*

1

First, you'll need to remove the back wheel from your bike and the skewer – or through-axle – from the wheel itself (see page 40 for more info on this). This will allow you to access the lockring in the centre of your cassette.

TOP TIP

If a new chain skips and slips when pedalling hard, this is a sign that you need to fit a new cassette too. Inspect the cassette for any teeth that might have got damaged, they will usually look pointed like a shark's tooth. When fitting a new cassette, always ensure you fit a new chain too. Take a photo of your replacement cassette when brand new. This will help you check for wear at a later date – if you suspect it has got too worn to run properly after clocking lots of miles.

"If a new chain skips and slips when pedalling hard, this is a sign that you need to fit a new cassette too"

WATCH THE VIDEO

Free show-how and know-how

https://gcn.eu/ChangeACassette

SCAN CODE TO WATCH THE VIDEO

2

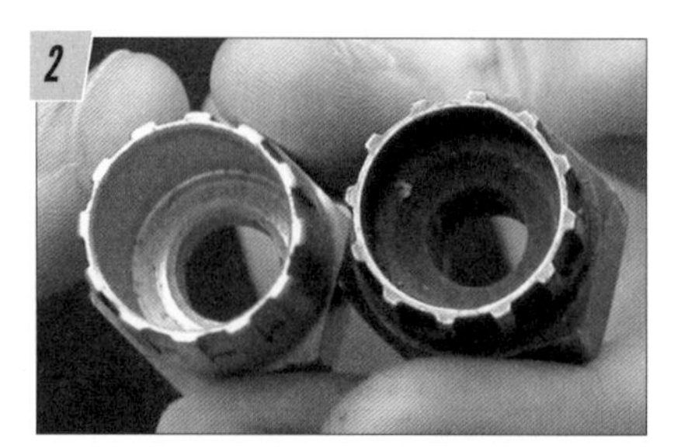

Before you grab your lockring removal tool, it's worth noting that there are two types – one for SRAM and Shimano and another for Campagnolo. They may look very similar, but the two different types are incompatible with each other.

3

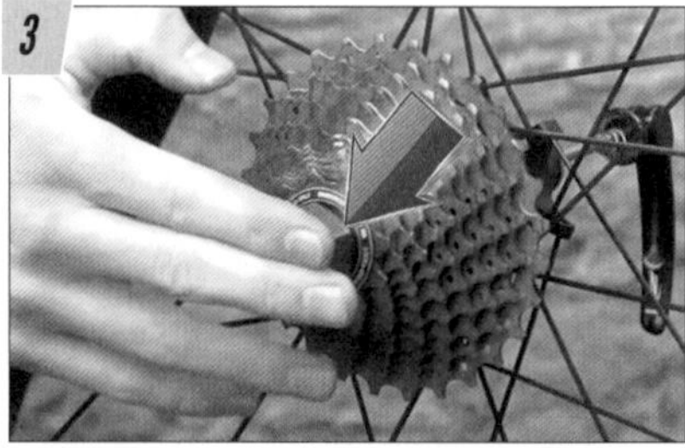

Fit the lockring removal tool in position on the lockring at the centre of the cassette and place the wheel at your feet.

TOP TIP

If you have a fairly shallow lockring removal tool, to stop it falling out of place when you're trying to loosen it, thread your wheel skewer back through the hub and the lockring removal tool, then do up the skewer to hold the removal tool in place.

Grab your chainwhip and drape the loose length of chain around one of the larger sprockets ensuring the chain whip handle is to the right hand side of the cassette. Give yourself enough room around the spokes as you don't want to skin your knuckles when the lockring comes loose.

Fit your adjustable spanner onto the lockring removal tool, then firmly push down with your right hand on the spanner while bracing the wheel and holding the chain whip in your left hand, this will loosen off the lockring.

If the lockring is stubbornly refusing to come loose you can try and jolt it free. Keep your hands on the tools but relax your arms, then suddenly apply pressure downwards with both arms and this should free it up.

Once you've loosened the lockring, remove the spanner, chain whip and quick-release skewer (or through-axle) as you should now be able to turn the lockring by turning the removal tool by hand. Without the lockring you should find that the cassette slides smoothly off.

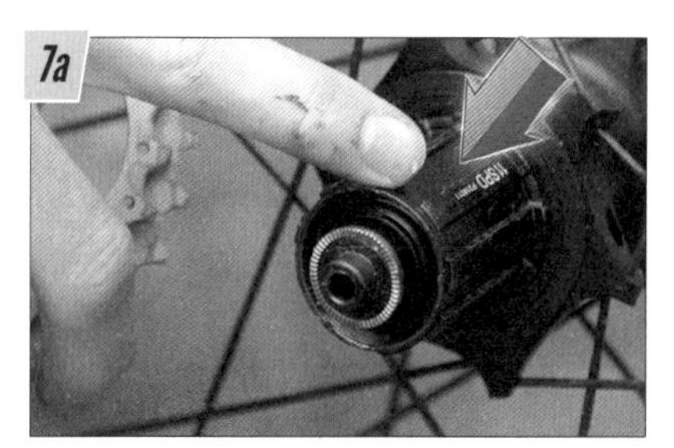

When re-fitting your cassette or installing a new one, apply some grease to the freehub body, then locate the place where one of the splines is slightly narrower with much wider gaps either side of it than the rest.

Look at your sprocket's internals and find the shaped section which matches up with the freehub body, then slide each section of the cassette on. Reattach your lockring by hand then finish off with the lockring tool and adjustable spanner and tighten until you hear a few loud creaks.

TECH EXPLAINED

Different Freehub Standards

Most road cassettes fit onto standard Shimano HG type freehub drivers, but there are various different options out there. In addition to cassettes that are compatible with Shimano type freehubs up to 11-speed (Shimano 12-speed uses their new Microspline system), SRAM also offer XD and XDR freehub drivers which work slightly differently. XD is primarily designed for mountain bike use and XDR is the road-specific variant – both have a threaded section near the spokes. To remove the cassette, use exactly the same process as we've described here, but the only difference is that you might need to use the adjustable spanner for a few more turns to loosen off the lockring and don't use your quick-release wheel skewer to hold it in place.

Want To Fit New Chainrings?
Then head over to page 74

HOW TO REPLACE & FIT GEAR CABLES

If your gear shifts have got sluggish and inaccurate, fitting new gear cables will give you months of super-slick shifting

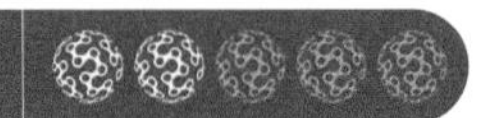

TIME 10 - 20 Minutes

TOOLS
- *New cables*
- *Cable cutters*
- *Pick*
- *File*
- *Inner sheath*
- *Grease*

WHEN
- *Your shifting feels slow or gritty*

TECH EXPLAINED

Gear Cable Upgrades

Fitting new gear cables is one of the best things you can do to improve the performance of your shifting. If you upgrade to better quality cable inners and outers, this will improve the accuracy of your gear changes and make your shifting action lighter – particularly on troublesome downshifts, i.e. going from the big ring to the little ring, or changing to harder gears at the cassette.

"Upgrading to better quality cable inners and outers will improve the accuracy of your gear changes"

WATCH THE VIDEO

Free show-how and know-how

REMOVING OLD CABLES

The first step is to remove your old cables, so loosen off the Allen key clamp bolt on the derailleur (it's the same for either the front or the rear derailleur), and then snip off the cable end cap using your cable cutters.

Before yanking the old cable out, check if your cables are routed internally. If they are, grab the inner sheath, thread it over the old cable and into the frame. When you start pulling the old cable out, the sheath gets dragged all the way through the frame and will act as a guide for the new cable.

Want To Index Your Gears?
See page 64 for how to do that

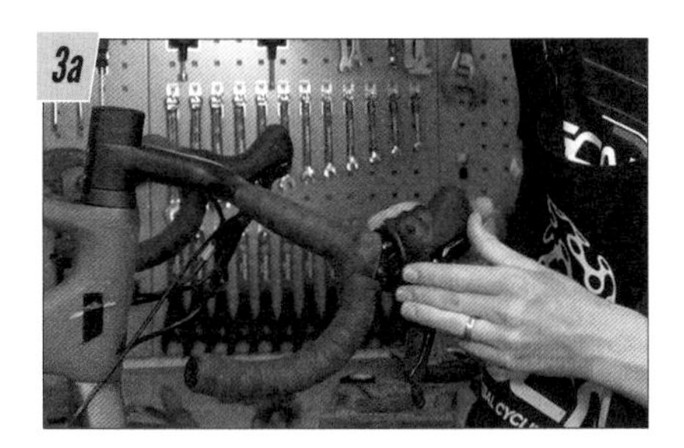

If you're replacing your cable outers as well as the inners, it will mean that you have to unwind your bar tape. However, if it's in good condition and not glued down, then you should be able to reuse it. See page 200 for more on taping bars.

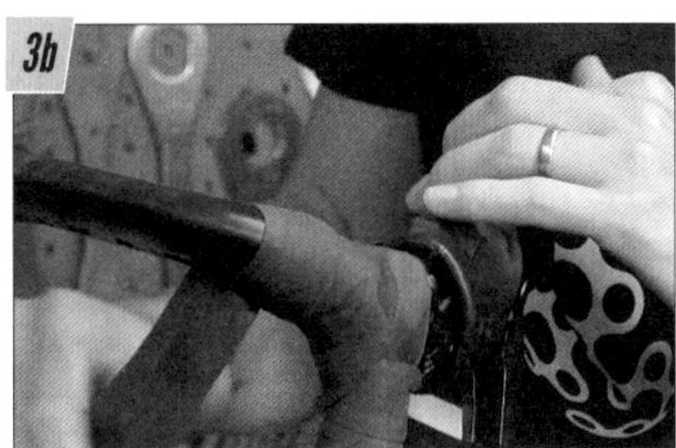

Pull back the lever hoods, then starting on the stem side of your bars, unwind your bar tape to just past the lever clamps.

PREPARING NEW CABLES

Hang onto the cable outers as once you've removed them as they will act as templates for the new ones. Hold the new cable next to the old one to match the lengths, then where the old one finishes, use your cable cutters to make a nice firm snip at 90 degrees.

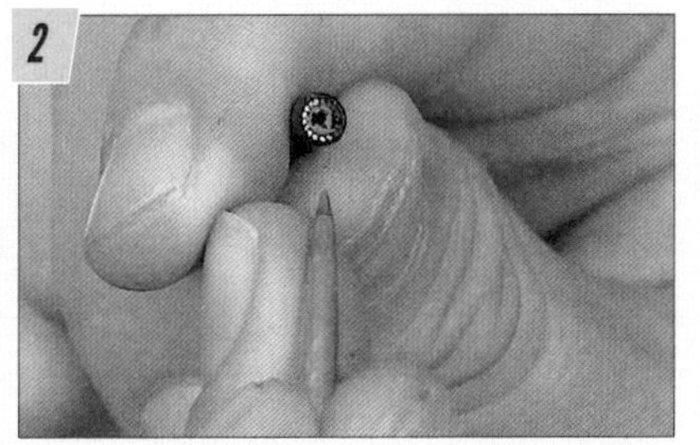

Once cut, you're likely to have to squeeze the end of the cable outer together to make it round again. The inner sheath is also likely to be a bit compressed, so take your pick and open it back up again.

Next, grab your file and use it on the cable end you've just cut to ensure it is super-flat. This will help keep the friction to a minimum as the cable inner moves past it during shifting.

FITTING NEW CABLES

Before threading your new cable into the shifter, make sure that it is positioned for the hardest (smallest) gear on your cassette. If working on the front shifter, position it as if it was on the easiest (smallest) chainring.

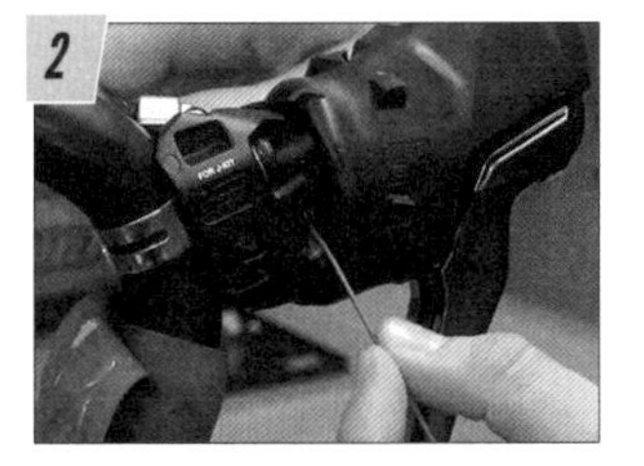

Thread your cable inner through the shifter. Next, add a cable ferrule to the first section of outer cable and slide the ferrule and outer cable along the inner cable into the bottom of the shifter.

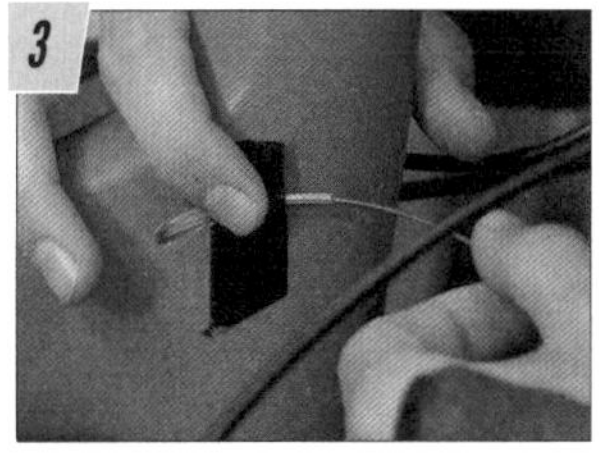

Fit a second ferrule to the first section of outer cable, then slide the inner cable into the sheath running through your frame. It's a good idea to give the inner a thin smear of grease to prevent water penetration.

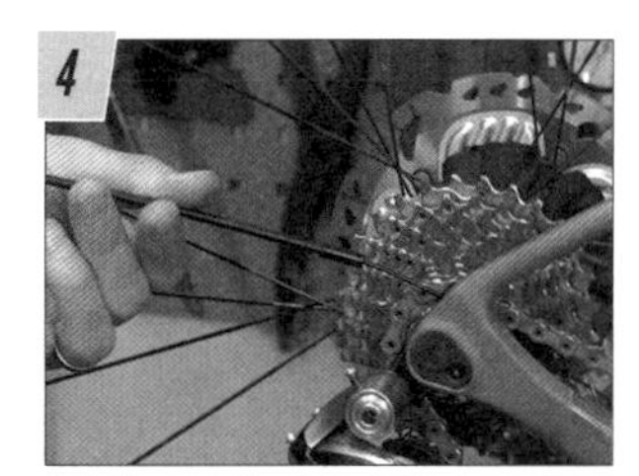

Where the inner cable exits your frame, run another piece of outer cable and ferrules in the same way as you did with the first (not required on a front derailleur), then run the inner through the clamp bolt and nip it up.

ESSENTIAL REPAIRS

HOW TO REPLACE YOUR CHAINRINGS

Worn or damaged chainring teeth will give you poor shifting and possibly much worse. Here's how to tell if they need changing and how to do it

DIFFICULTY 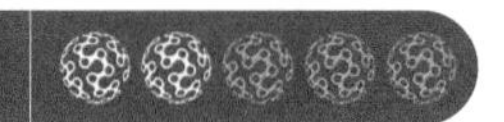

TIME 15 - 30 Minutes

TOOLS
- *5mm and 6mm Allen keys*
- *Torx keys*
- *Chainring peg spanner*
- *Torque wrench*
- *Grease*

WHEN
- *The teeth on your chainrings look misshapen and your chain is unstable*

TECH EXPLAINED

Why You Should Change Your Chainrings

Worn or damaged chainrings are not only inefficient, they can also be dangerous. Broken or degraded teeth could result in your chain becoming dislodged just as you're putting down some serious watts and cause you to crash.

Chainrings are usually the last drivetrain parts to wear down though, so if the rings have had it, your chain and cassette will definitely need replacing too (unless you've recently changed them that is).

> "Broken or degraded teeth could result in your chain becoming dislodged just as you're putting down some serious watts"

When examining your chainring for worn teeth, keep in mind though that your biggest chainring is designed with some teeth that have a different shape from the others – don't mistake their shape with being worn. The teeth on your inner ring should be a lot more regular in shape though.

If fitting a new chain onto a worn or damaged chainring, you may be able to feel that the chain is not engaging properly with the teeth of a chainring. While this can be an indicator that it needs replacing, it could just be a bedding-in process as the chain fully meshes with the chainring.

TECH EXPLAINED

Chainring Standards

Chainrings come in a variety of sizes, with different numbers of teeth, varying widths and are designed to fit different types of crank. They can also come with different BCDs (bolt circle diameter), which is the distance between the chainring bolts. Given the huge number of differing standards, it can be a bit of a minefield to choose a replacement. If you're totally happy with your current gear set-up, the easiest thing to do is go like-for-like and choose an identical chainring to the worn out one you're replacing. If perhaps though, you'd like to make some adjustments to your gearing, you could opt for a different sized chainring, but be sure to check it is completely compatible with your current drivetrain before trying to fit it. Most chainrings have their speed, number of teeth and BCD written on one side of them.

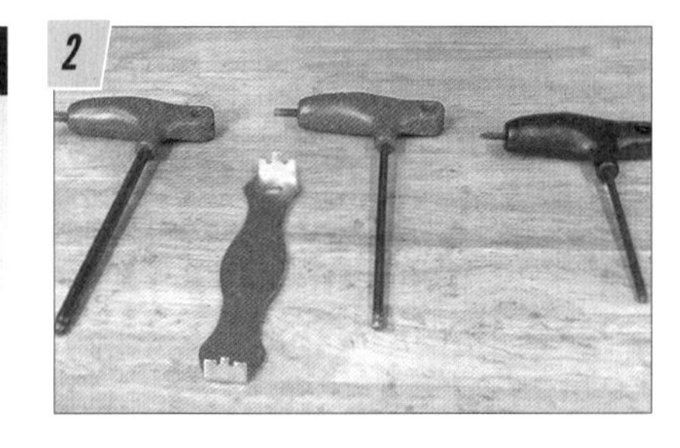

Depending on the type of chainring bolts you have fitted, you'll either need a 5mm Allen key and a chainring peg spanner, 5 and 6mm Allen keys, or a pair of Torx keys to remove them.

TOP TIP

If using a peg spanner to loosen chainring bolts, insert the three-pronged end in the female side of your bolt (on the inside of the chainring), while you wind out the male side with a 5mm Allen key. To fit a chainring bolt, use the two-pronged end of the peg spanner while you nip it up with your Allen key, then the three-pronged end and your torque wrench to tighten it.

Remove the bolts that connect your chainring to the spider and take the opportunity to give the bolts a good clean. While we've removed the crank arm from the bike in the photos here, it doesn't need to come off when changing your chainrings.

Before removing your chainrings, it's vital to note which are the inner and outer faces before you remove them. This will help you ensure the new ones you're fitting are orientated correctly. Taking some photos of your current set-up while it's still intact is a wise idea.

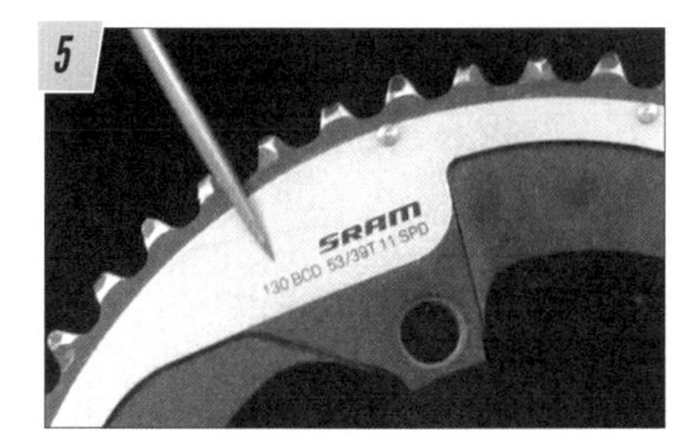

When fitting new chainrings, it is very common for any writing (manufacturer, size, etc) on the outer chainring to be facing outwards so it can be read from the drive side of the bike. While on inner chainrings, the writing usually faces inwards so it can be read from the non-drive side.

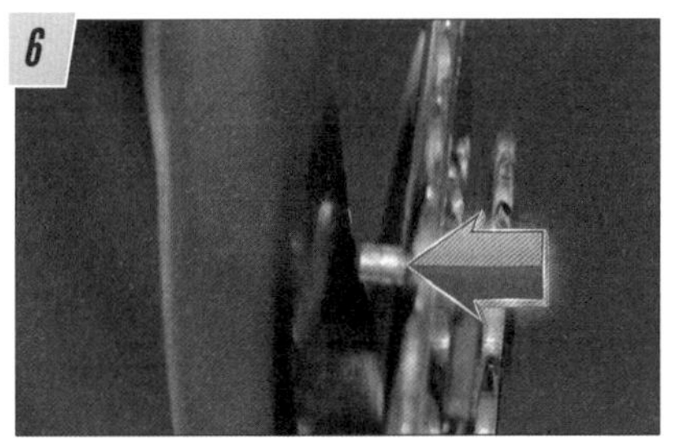

As well as getting the faces of the chainrings correctly positioned, you'll also need to orientate the bigger chainring so that the metal tab on the outer face lines up with the crank arm. This tab is designed to stop your chain getting wedged between chainring and crank should it fall off.

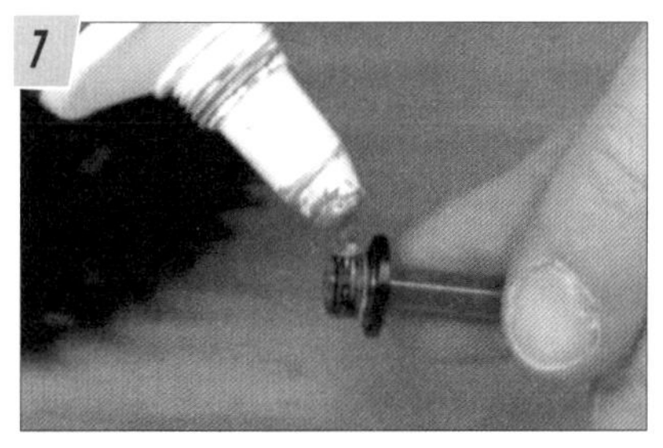

To fit your new chainrings, line them up on the spider, take your chainring nuts and bolts, and give each bolt a coating of grease before finger-tightening up. Next, grab your torque wrench and tighten every other bolt up in sequence, then go around again and tighten the remaining bolts.

Want Advice On New Chainrings?
See page 86 for changing gear ratios

ESSENTIAL REPAIRS

HOW TO CHANGE YOUR JOCKEY WHEELS

If the jockey wheels on your rear derailleur are damaged or not running smoothly, here's how to replace them

DIFFICULTY 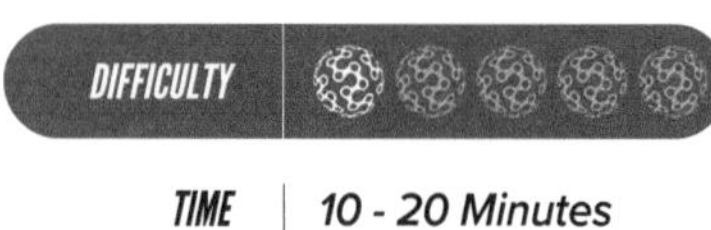

TIME	10 - 20 Minutes
TOOLS	• Allen keys • Grease or thread-lock • Torque wrench
WHEN	• Your jockey wheels are worn or damaged

Remove your rear wheel and have a look at your jockey (aka pulley) wheels. If they look misshapen or the teeth are pointed like a shark's tooth, then they need replacing.

Check to see if the jockey wheels spin freely by hand. If they feel really rough or you encounter any resistance, and they have sealed bearings, then it's best to replace them.

Some jockey wheels have bushings rather than bearings though. The bushings can be removed, cleaned and re-greased to get them running smoothly again.

Not all jockey wheels come with the same number of teeth, so it's vital you get like-for-like when choosing new ones. You can upgrade to fancier versions, such as ones with ceramic bearings, but ensure they are compatible with your derailleur.

Before removing your original jockey wheels, check that the first of the new ones you're fitting is the correct one for that position. Each one should be marked as upper and lower, guide and tension, or G and T.

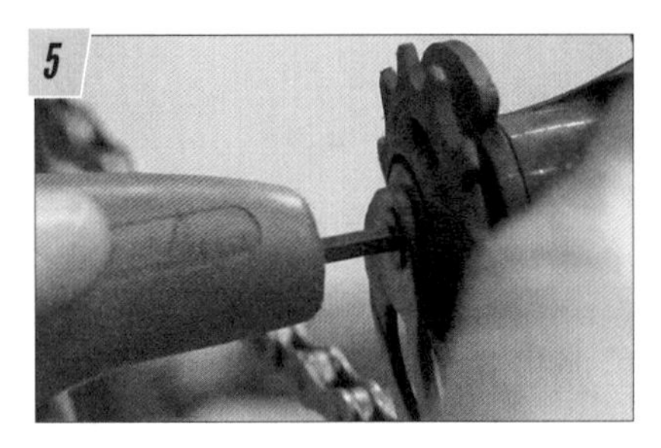

Start by removing your upper (or guide) jockey wheel. Hold the the rear derailleur cage then undo the bolt. In most cases, you'll need a 3mm Allen key. Once removed, put the tiny bolt somewhere safe as it's easy to lose it.

When replacing the jockey wheels, the easiest method is to do then one at a time so you don't fit the upper one in the lower position or vice-versa, so grab your new one and slot it in place.

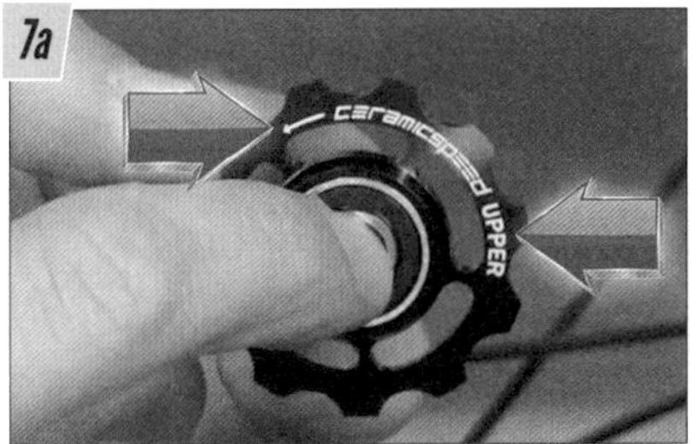

Before reinstalling the bolt, check that you've orientated the jockey wheel correctly as they are directional. The writing on the face is usually visible on the drive side and there may be an arrow to show you the direction of movement.

Working out which direction your jockey wheel will turn while pedalling forward can be confusing as the chain wraps around each jockey wheel, particularly if you've removed your chain.

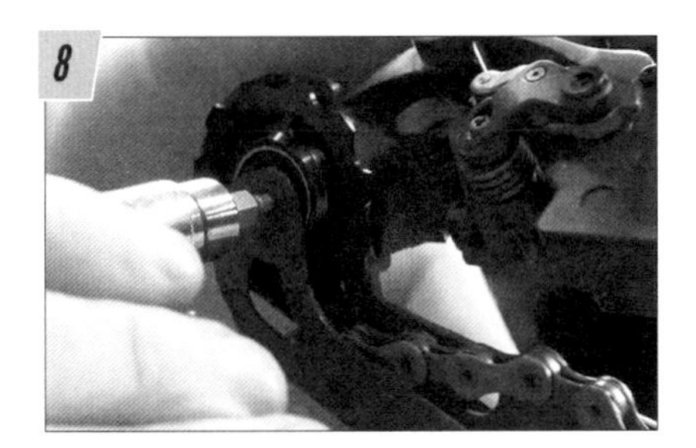

Using either a spot of grease or thread-lock (whichever is recommended by your derailleur manufacturer) on the bolt before installing, tighten it up to the recommended torque setting.

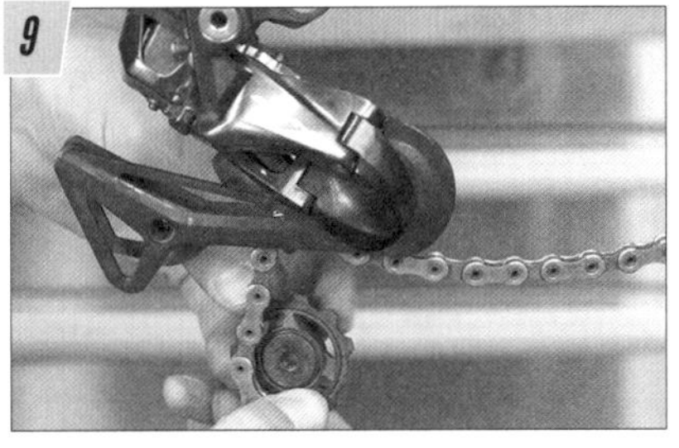

Remove the lower jockey wheel, but before you fit its replacement, take this opportunity to give the derailleur cage a thorough clean and degrease.

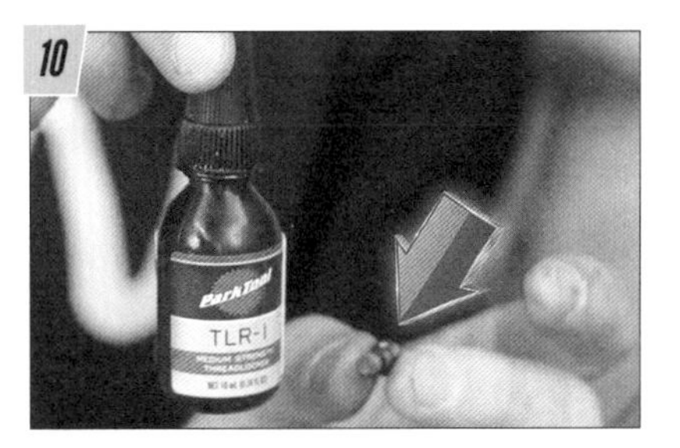

Finally, slot the second new jockey wheel in place, grease or thread-lock the bolt and tighten to the recommended level of torque.

Need To Replace Your Rear Mech?
Then head over to page 80

ESSENTIAL REPAIRS

HOW TO SERVICE YOUR SHIFTERS

If your shifters have lost their positive sounding click or shifting has become stiff, this servicing technique should get them back into shape

DIFFICULTY 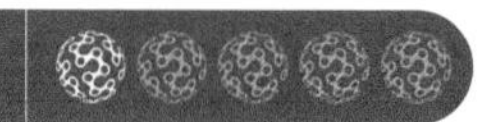

TIME	0 - 10 Minutes
TOOLS	• Spray degreaser • Spray lube
WHEN	• You've fitted new cables but shifting is still stiff

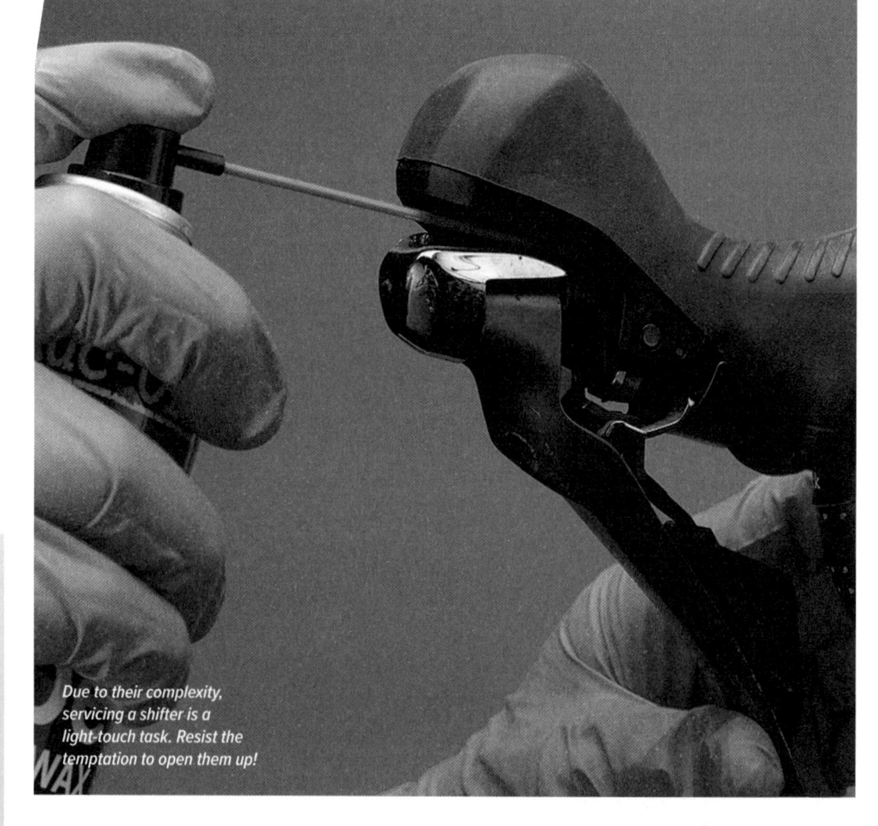

Due to their complexity, servicing a shifter is a light-touch task. Resist the temptation to open them up!

WATCH THE VIDEO

Free show-how and know-how

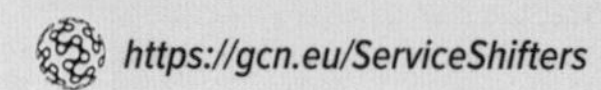

BEFORE YOU START

You only really need to service your shifters in the way described here if your gear mechanism feels particularly stiff and you're confident that sticky cables or a seized derailleur are not the cause.

Unnecessarily stripping out the factory applied grease from your shifters and replacing it with a much lighter spray grease means you'll have to service them more often as the grease you will be applying won't last as long.

One sign of a gunged-up shifter is that it no longer clicks through the gears in the usual way, but to be sure that your shifters are really the root of your problem, disconnect your gear cables at the derailleurs and see how the levers shift then. If the movement is lighter and sounds better, then you should first look at your sorting your cables and derailleurs before getting involved with your shifters.

To Get Super-Slick Shifting
Turn back to page 62

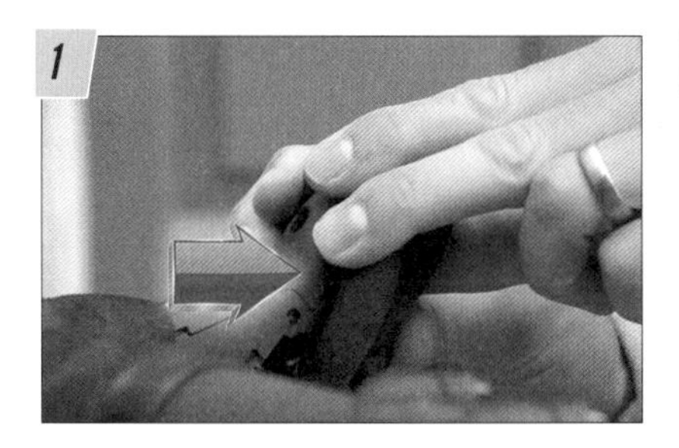

To access your shifter's internals, you need to first remove the lever hood. Do this by rolling it forward and down over the brake lever.

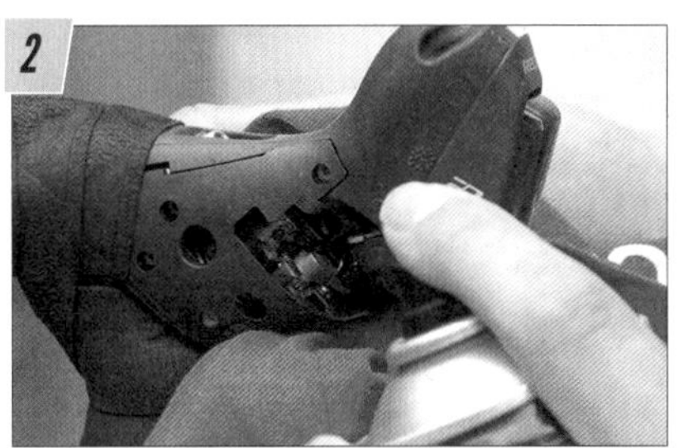

Next, grab your can of degreaser and liberally spray it into the internals of your shifter to help remove any build up of grease and gunk.

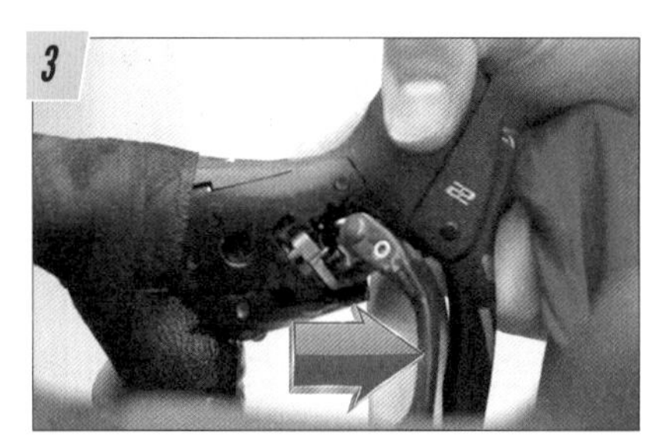

Move the shifter as you spray to help dislodge anything that might have worked its way inside. Hold an old rag below too soak up any excess and prevent it contaminating other parts of your bike.

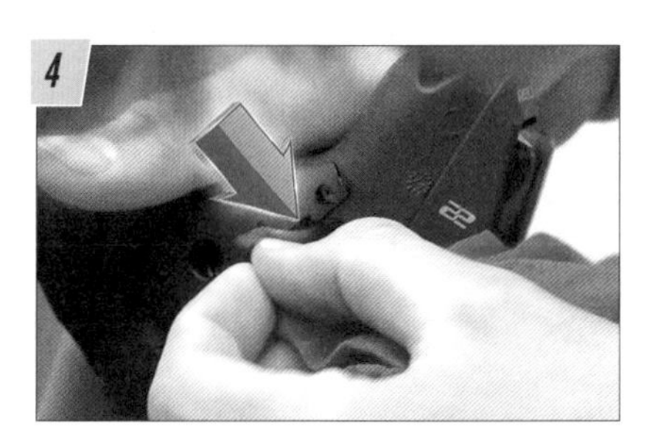

Wipe the shifter off with a clean cloth and really get inside the internals so as not to leave any pockets of degreaser in there.

COFFEE BREAK

Now is a good time to grab a brew to give your shifters time to let any degreaser you couldn't get to work its way out – or evaporate if it's a warm day. Once you've had your tea or coffee, use your cloth to give a second dry off of any areas where you can still see degreaser.

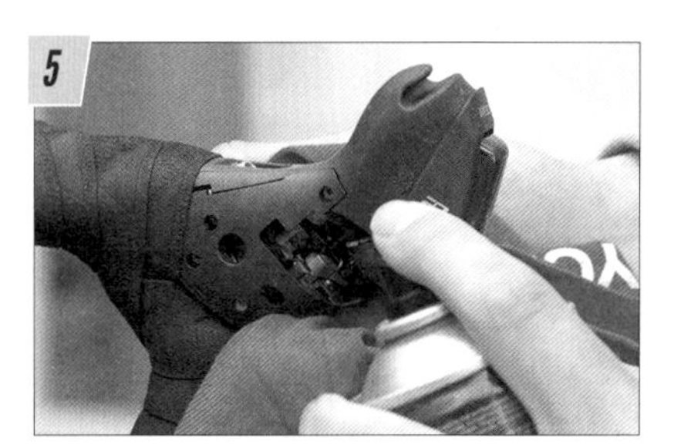

Now, grab your spray can of lube. Choose as thin a lube as you find so it will penetrate deep inside – and ideally use one that contains PTFE. Spray all the shifter internals, going through the gears as you do. Mop up any excess with a cloth, but don't completely dry any of the internal parts off.

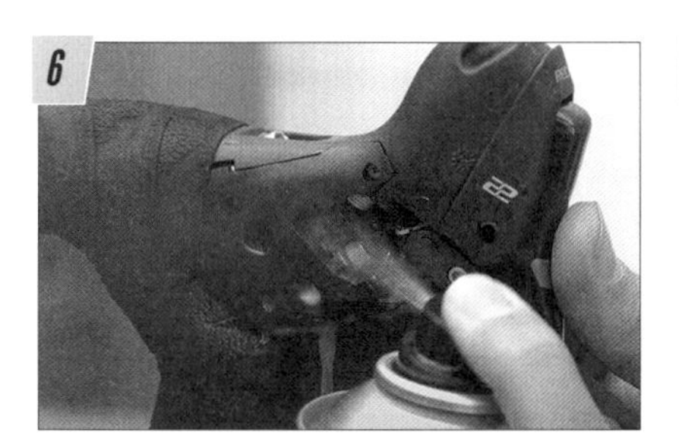

Before you put the lever hood back on, it's a good idea to put a little dab of grease on any moving parts you can reach to give the gear mechanism a little bit more weather-proofing.

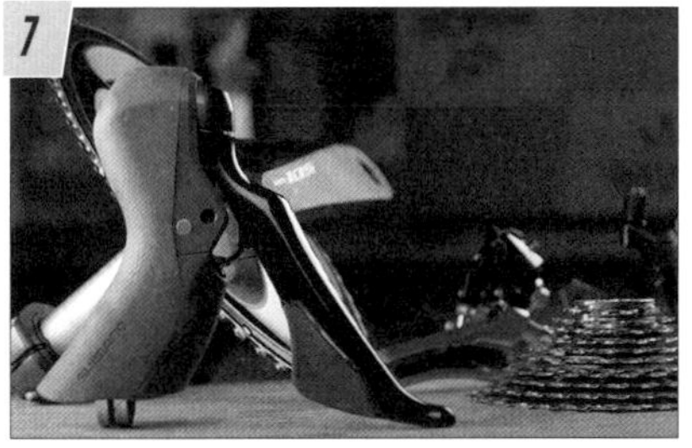

If your shifter still isn't working, you have two courses of action. The easiest and most expensive option is to go out and buy a replacement shifter/brake lever, while the second is to try and take the shifter apart to find out what is going on.

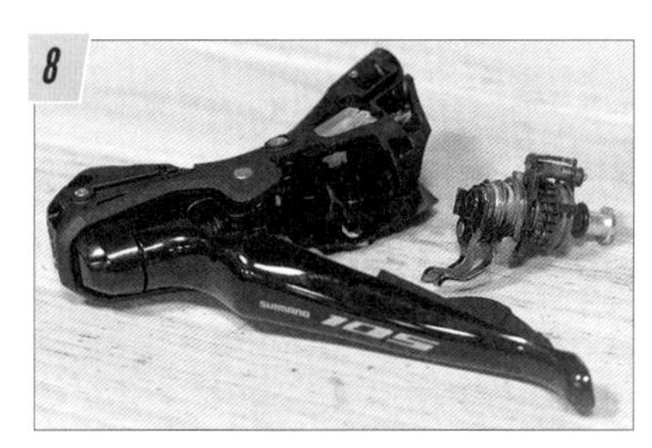

Should you go for option two, be warned that shifter internals have many small, complex parts and are notoriously difficult to piece back together. If you're riding a relatively new bike, it's also worth checking to see if your shifter is still under warranty.

ESSENTIAL REPAIRS

HOW TO CHANGE YOUR REAR DERAILLEUR

Your rear mech sits in a vulnerable position and can be easily damaged. Here's how to remove it and fit a replacement

DIFFICULTY 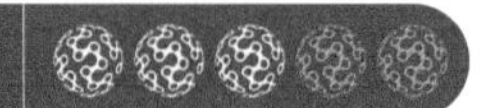

TIME 10 - 20 Minutes

TOOLS
- *Allen keys*
- *Chain-tool or long-nosed pliers*
- *Phillips screwdriver*
- *Cable cutters*
- *Torque wrench*

WHEN
- *Your derailleur is beyond repair or you want to upgrade*

WATCH THE VIDEO

Free show-how and know-how

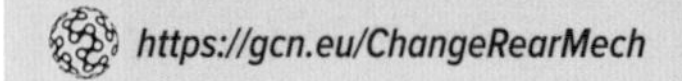

REMOVE THE DERAILLEUR

Begin by removing the chain, using your chain-tool to break the chain. If you have a master (aka quick) link, you can use a pair of pliers to remove it. See page 68 for more on removing and re-fitting chains.

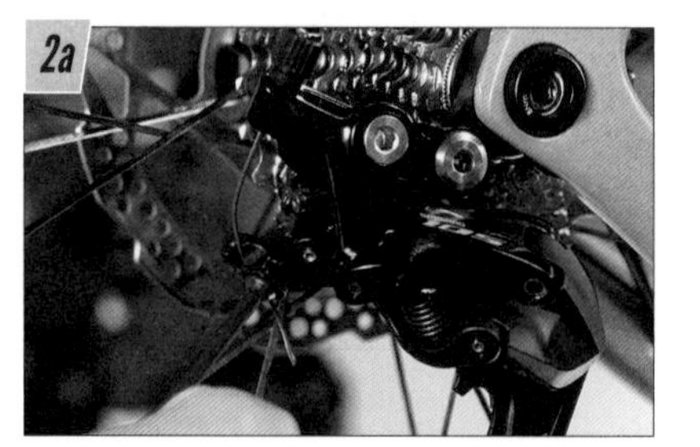

If you have a mechanical derailleur you'll need to remove the cable. Do this by pulling the crimp end off with the pliers, then undo the cable clamp bolt with an Allen key.

If you have Shimano Di2, then you'll need to unclip the cable, ideally using the Shimano TL-EW02 tool.

Once the cable is out of the way, you can remove the derailleur. Take a 5mm Allen key and undo the main mounting bolt, applying firm but even pressure to remove the derailleur from the hanger.

TOP TIP

With your rear derailleur removed, it's a good time to check for any damage to the derailleur (or mech) hanger. If it's damaged or looks bent it will need replacing. Simply unbolt it using an Allen key, and replace it like-for-like (you may need to track down the right one with help from you local bike shop).

FIT THE DERAILLEUR

Mount the derailleur with the 5mm Allen bolt, adding a little grease to the thread. Position the derailleur below the stop on the hanger. Unless otherwise stated, torque the bolt to 8-10Nm for SRAM and Shimano, or 15Nm for Campagnolo.

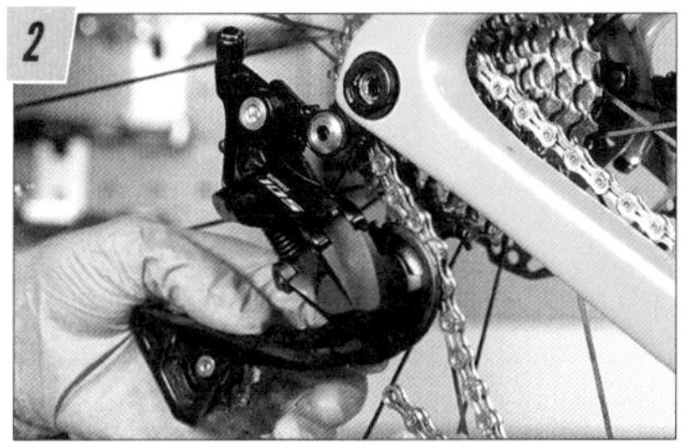

Thread the chain back through the cage and jockey wheels, reattaching with a master link. Then insert the gear cable back through the derailleur adjuster and under the cable clamp bolt. Pull the cable tight and tighten down the clamp bolt.

TOP TIP

Some mechanics prefer to set the H (high) and L (low) limit and B-tension screws on the derailleur before installing the chain – rather than after the chain is installed.

SET UP THE DERAILLEUR

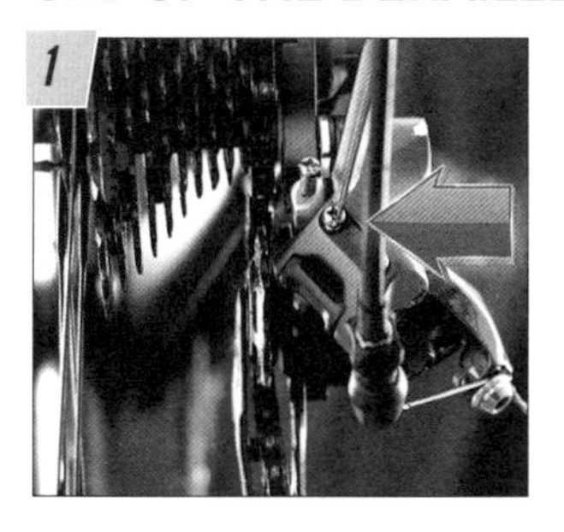

To adjust the derailleur, you need to set the H (high) and L (low) limit screws first. Turn the H screw until the top jockey wheel lines up with the smallest sprocket on the cassette.

Now shift the derailleur to the largest sprocket. Adjust the L screw until the top jockey wheel is in line with the largest sprocket on the cassette. As the cable tension is not set, move the derailleur by hand.

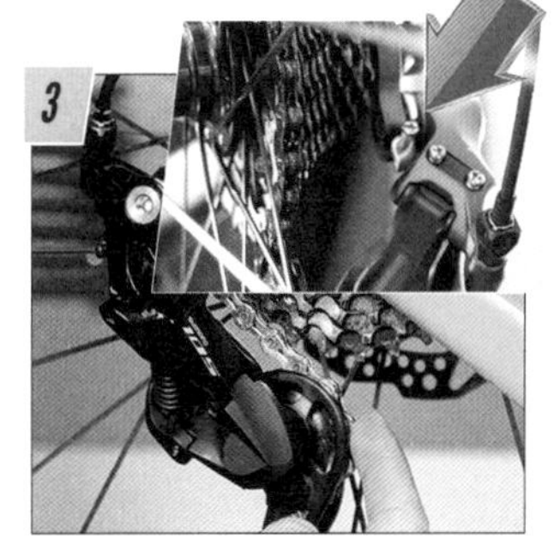

Staying in the biggest sprocket, adjust the long B-tension screw until the outside edge of the top jockey wheel sits around 10mm below the outside edge of the cassette teeth.

To set the cable tension, move to the smallest cog then shift one gear up. If the chain chatters but doesn't move, turn the barrel adjuster counter-clockwise until it does. For full details on setting this correctly, see page 67.

Want To Install A New Transmission?
Turn to page 90 for all the details

ESSENTIAL REPAIRS

HOW TO CHANGE YOUR FRONT DERAILLEUR

Fitting a new front mech is fairly straightforward, but getting it to shift smoothly is a little trickier. Here's how to get everything perfectly installed

DIFFICULTY 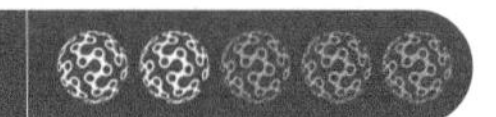

TIME	15 - 30 Minutes
TOOLS	• Chain-tool or long nose pliers • Allen keys • Small Phillips screwdriver • Cable cutters • Torque wrench
WHEN	• Your current derailleur is worn out or it's time to upgrade

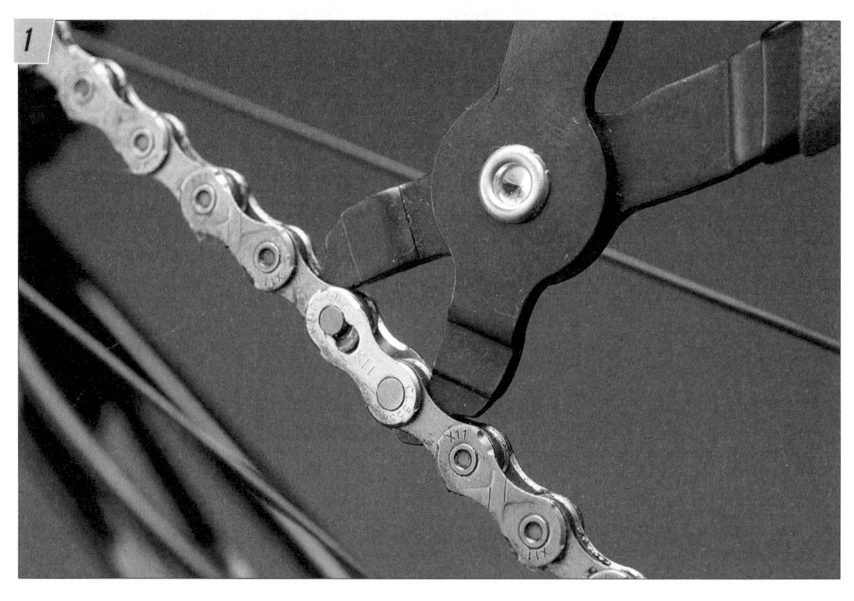
1

Begin by removing the chain, using your chain-tool to break the chain – see page 68 for how to do this. If you have a master (aka quick) link, you can use your pliers to squeeze the link together and remove it.

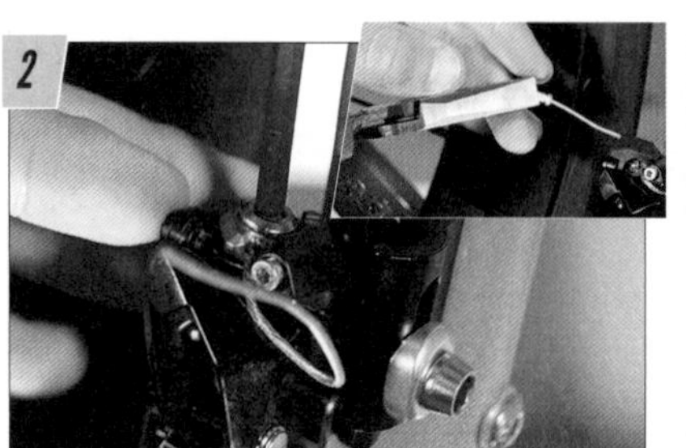
2

If you have a mechanical derailleur you'll need to remove the cable. Pull the crimped end off with the pliers, then undo the cable clamp bolt with a 4mm Allen key. If you're running Shimano Di2 electronic shifting, then you'll need to unclip the cable, ideally using the Shimano TL-EW02 tool (see page 98).

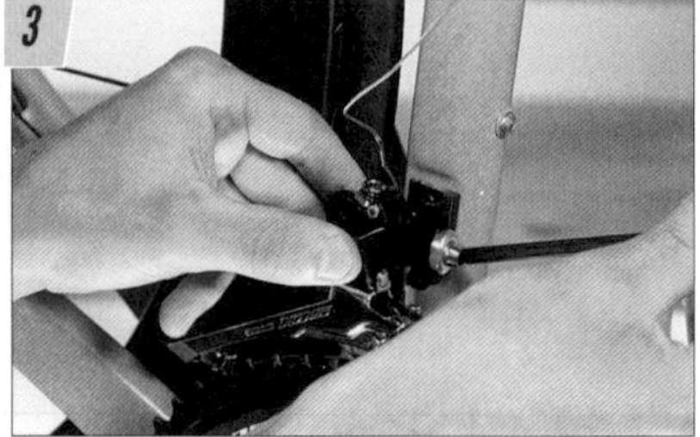
3

Once the cable is free you can then remove the derailleur from the frame. You'll either have a braze-on derailleur or a clamp mounted version. It'll likely be a 5mm Allen key to undo the bolt and free the derailleur. Make sure to remember or note the original position of any parts that come off.

WATCH THE VIDEO

Free show-how and know-how

https://gcn.eu/ChangeFrontMech

Need To Replace Your Cables?
Turn to page 70 to get them sorted

To refit the derailleur, mount with the 5mm Allen bolt, reconnect the cable to the derailleur, then thread the chain back through the cage and join it back together. Some new derailleurs come with a 'support bolt', which needs to be un-threaded most of the way before fitting the derailleur.

Position the outer cage of the derailleur so that it sits between 1-3mm off the tallest teeth of the outer chainring. Also, check that it's totally parallel to the outer chainring.

Once in place, the support bolt (if you have one) should be threaded back in to touch the bracket, and tightened until the rear of the outer plate is also in line with the outer chainring. Insert the cable behind the cable clamp bolt using the grove it should follow. Pull tight and clamp the bolt down.

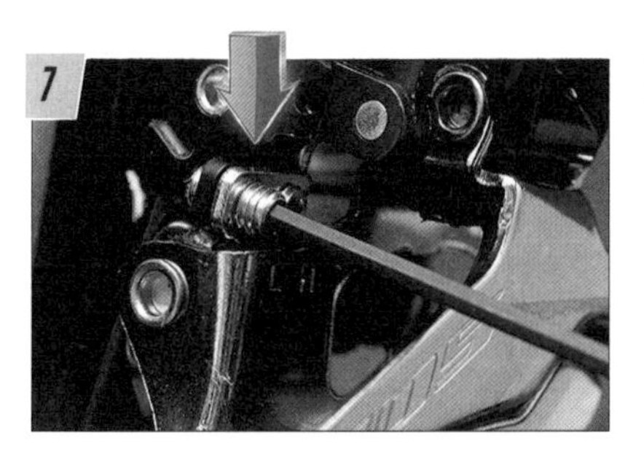

To adjust the derailleur, first make sure any barrel adjusters are screwed all the way in. Put the chain on the small chainring and the largest sprocket of the cassette. Adjust the L limit screw while pedalling in the stand until you can hear the chain rubbing on the plate, then back off a quarter turn.

Put the chain in the middle of the cassette and try using your shifter to move the chain to the large chainring. If it fails to shift, there's either too little cable tension or the H limit screw is too tight.

To check which it is, push the derailleur up by hand to test the shifting while pedalling. If the chain shifts properly, then you don't have enough cable tension. If the derailleur stops short then the H limit screw is too tight.

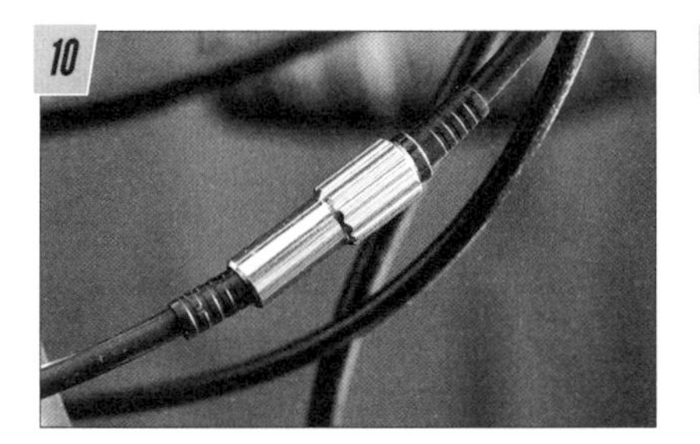

If it's cable tension, use the barrel adjuster to tighten the cable, testing the shift every so often. If it was the H limit screw, undo this a quarter turn at a time until the shift works properly.

Now the shifting is set up, you need to properly adjust the H limit screw. Put the chain in the big ring and the smallest cassette sprocket. Now turn the H limit screw in until you can hear the chain rubbing on the plate of the derailleur, then back off until there's about 1mm of space.

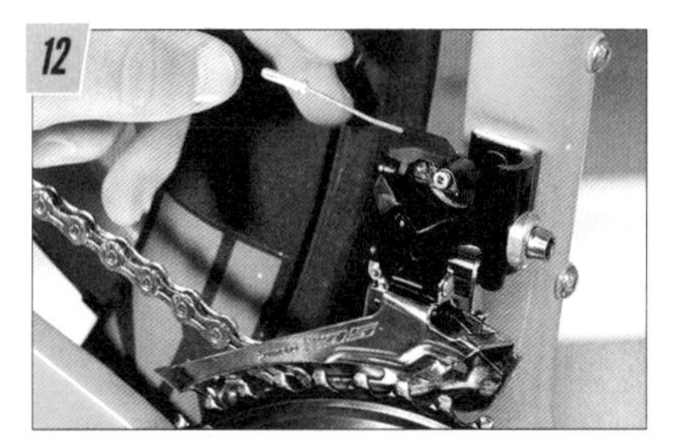

Finally, if you replaced the gear cable, use your cable cutters to cut it to length and apply a new crimp end.

ESSENTIAL REPAIRS

HOW TO REMOVE & INSTALL CRANKS

There are many different cranks out there, but here we'll look at two of the most common types from Shimano and SRAM

DIFFICULTY

TIME 5 - 15 Minutes

TOOLS

For Shimano:
- *Shimano pre-load tool*
- *5mm Allen key*
- *Small flat head screwdriver*
- *Nylon hammer*
- *Torque wrench*

For SRAM:
- *8mm Allen key*
- *10mm Allen key/pin spanner*
- *Nylon hammer*
- *Torque wrench*

WHEN
- *Servicing your bottom bracket or upgrading your crankset*

WATCH THE VIDEO

Free show-how and know-how

https://gcn.eu/FittingCranks

SCAN CODE TO WATCH THE VIDEO

SHIMANO CRANKS

Shimano cranks generally have a two-part system. This means that one crank arm is attached to the spindle or axle and the other arm is separate.

Start by undoing the non-drive side crank arm, loosening the bolts a little bit at a time. Once they're loose, you can use the pre-load tool to remove the plastic cap. Now you should be able to slide the crank arm from the spindle.

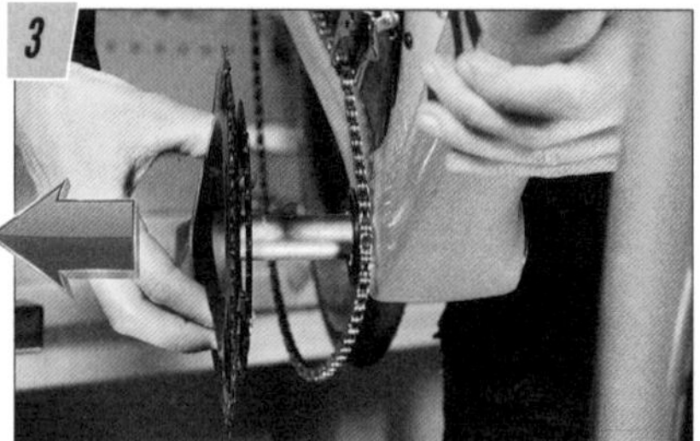

Use a small screwdriver to lift the retention spring away from the axle. Slide the spindle and chainset out of the bottom bracket. It will be pretty snug, but try not to wiggle it from side to side. If you're struggling, you can use a nylon hammer to persuade it through.

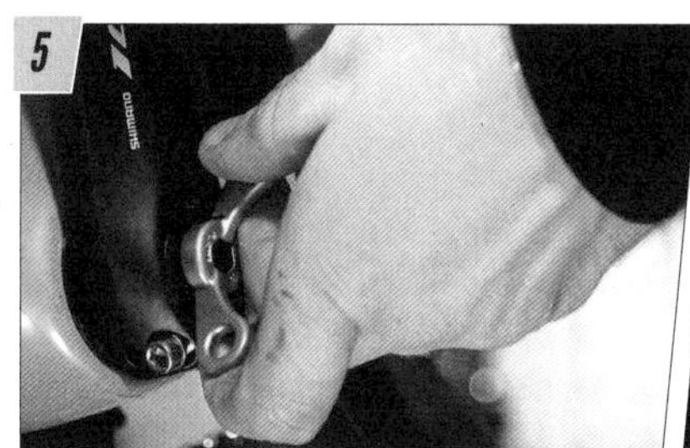

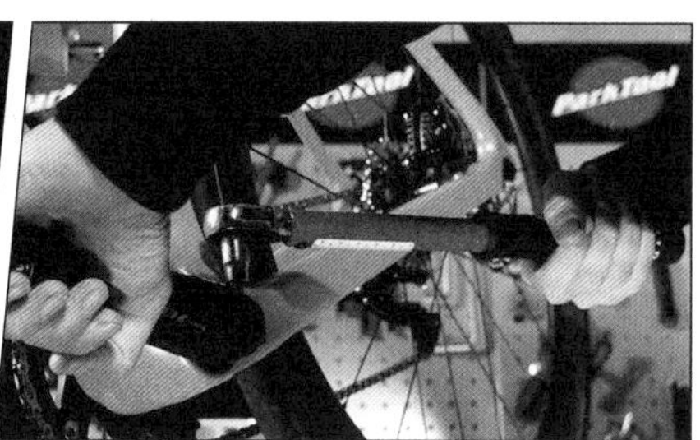

For reassembly, apply some grease to the drive side of the spindle, near the chainset, then rest your chain on the bottom bracket shell out of the way. Insert the spindle back through the bottom bracket – it might need a few gentle taps with your nylon hammer to go through.

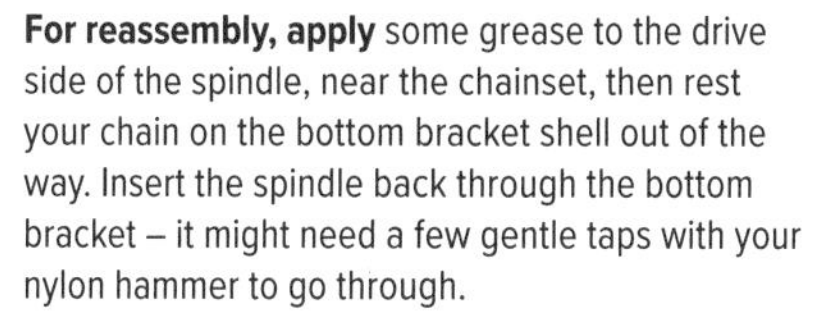

Put some grease on the splined part of the spindle then attach the non-drive side crank arm. Use the pre-load tool to tighten up the plastic cap, doing it up as tight as you can just with your fingers. Re-insert the retention spring using a small screwdriver and tighten up the 5mm bolts to the correct torque.

SRAM CRANKS

SRAM cranks are also a two-part system, but they use a self-extracting crank bolt. This system doesn't have the clamp with two bolts like Shimano, as it instead uses an internal bolt that holds the non-drive side crank arm onto the spindle and an outer retaining ring. Both are Allen key fittings.

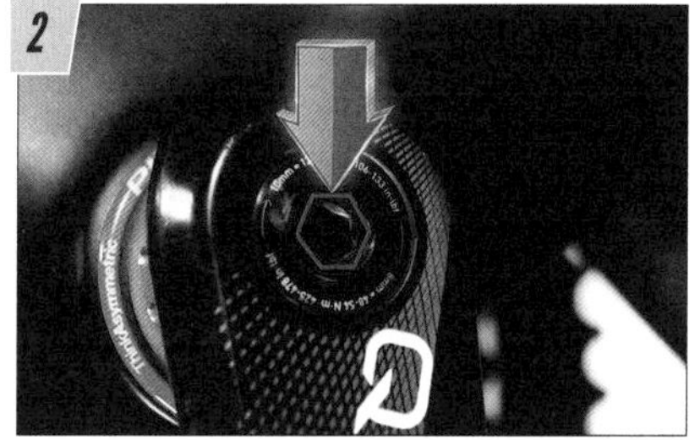

Start by ensuring that the outer retaining ring is firmly attached by tightening it with a 10mm Allen key. This ensures that when you start turning, the self-extracting bolt it has a solid connection with the ring.

Insert the 8mm Allen key through the centre of the retaining ring and undo it until the cranks come off. You'll feel an initial resistance as the bolt slackens off, then a period of no resistance, followed by firm resistance as you extract the crank against the retaining ring.

Take note of the position and order of any washers or spacers that might be behind the crank arm, before removing the drive-side chainset and spindle. Rest the chain on the bottom bracket shell out of the way and gently tap the spindle through with your nylon hammer.

To reassemble, grease the spindle and bolt threads. Insert the spindle through the bottom bracket, ensuring to correctly refit any spacers or washers. Replace the non-drive side arm and begin tightening the 8mm bolt into the spindle. Take care that it's on true, then tighten up with the Allen key.

Check the cranks or look online for the correct torque rating and then finish things off with the torque wrench. Finally, ensure the outer retaining ring is secure, then fit the chain back in place.

Want To Remove Your Bottom Bracket?
BB servicing starts on page 186

SET-UP SECRETS

HOW TO CHANGE YOUR GEAR RATIOS

Having the right gear set-up on your bike will make a huge difference to your riding experience. Here's what to consider if you want to alter them

DIFFICULTY
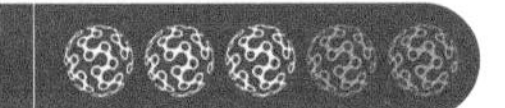

TIME 15 - 60 Minutes

TOOLS
- *Tape measure*
- *Chainrings*
- *Cassette*
- *Chainring bolts*
- *Derailleur*
- *Chain*

WHEN
- *You want to change your range of gears*

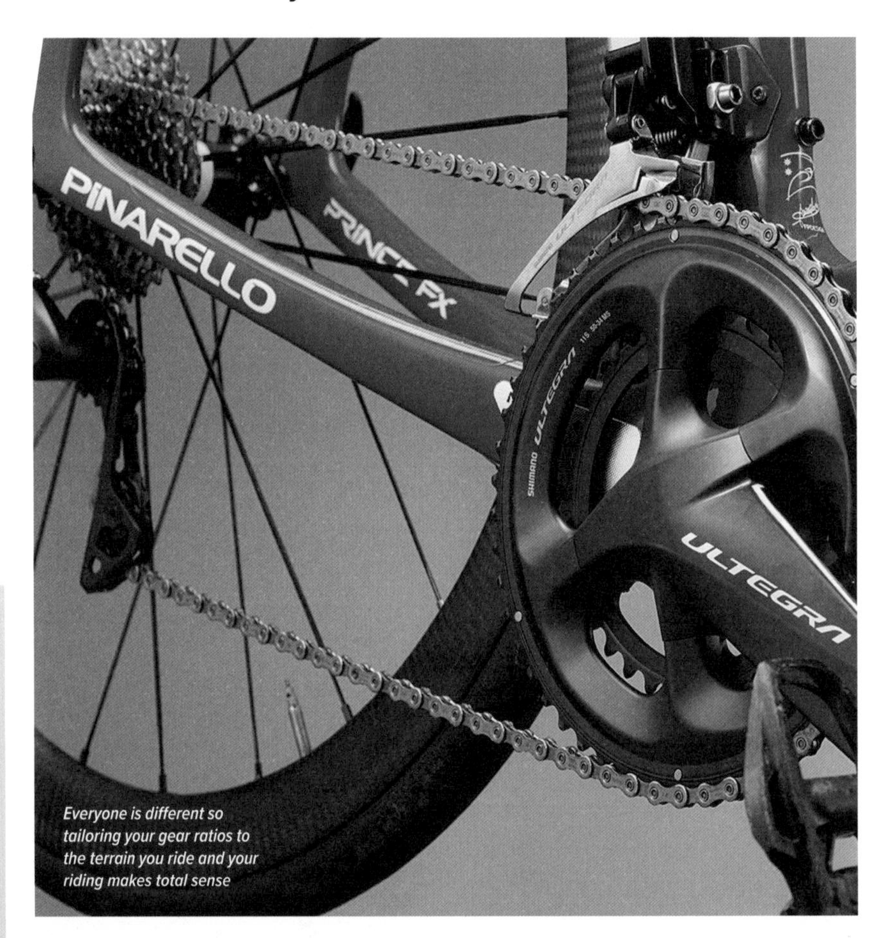

Everyone is different so tailoring your gear ratios to the terrain you ride and your riding makes total sense

WATCH THE VIDEO

Free show-how and know-how

GEAR RATIOS

https://gcn.eu/ChangeGearRatios

SCAN CODE TO WATCH THE VIDEO

Changing the ratio of the gears on your bike will have a profound effect on the amount of power you can put down and whether you muscle or spin up every climb, and whether you're able to power down the descents or are forced to coast down them as you've run out of gears.

Rather than walking you through how to physically change your cassette and chainset (we've got plenty of information on how to perform those procedures elsewhere in this section), we're going to discuss the different gearing options that are out there. We'll also look at how to work out which ones would be best suited to you and, crucially, how to ensure the changes you make to your gears will be compatible with your existing system.

1x delivers bigger jumps between gears but it has a similar gear range and is lighter than a double

WHICH GEAR RATIOS TO CHOOSE?

The simplest way to decide which gear ratios will suit you best is to think about the kind of riding you do and the terrain you mostly ride. If you like to race or enjoy short, sharp group rides on flatter roads, then a standard chainset and quite a close-ratio cassette will likely be a good fit for you. On the other hand, if you live in an area with a lot of steep climbs or you're not quite as fit as perhaps you'd like to be, a compact chainset with quite a wide-ratio cassette is likely to be a good fit for you.

There are many different chainring and cassette combinations that you will find on modern road bikes, three of the more typical set-ups though are: standard chainsets with 53/39t chainrings and an 11-23t cassette, mid-compact chainsets with 52/36t chainrings and an 11-28t cassette, and compact chainsets with 50/34 chainrings and an 11-32t cassette.

Standard chainsets are best suited to less hilly terrain or if you don't want to spin out when descending, while compact versions lend themselves well to allowing you to spin rather than grind up big hills. The wide-ranging gears of the mid-compact gives you the best of both worlds, but the drawback is bigger gaps between your gears.

SINGLE RING SET-UPS

If you ride a gravel bike and you're running a double chainset, you might want to consider switching to a 1x system. Removing a chainring and your front derailleur will make your bike a touch lighter, less complex and give you better clearance over obstacles. You should be able to get a similar range of gears with a wide-range cassette, though the gaps between gears will be bigger than you'll find on a double chainring system.

SWITCH YOUR CASSETTE

The simplest solution of all is just to change the range of your cassette. If going for a bigger one though, you will probably need a longer cage derailleur too – as your bike is likely to be running the biggest cassette your derailleur can handle.

HOW TO CHANGE YOUR GEAR RATIOS

TECH EXPLAINED

How Gear Ratios Effect Your Travel

The smaller the cogs on your cassette or the bigger the chainring on the front, the further you'll travel per complete revolution. For example, with a 50t chainring and an 11t cassette you'll travel 9.6m per revolution on regular sized road wheels, while conversely, using a combination of a 34t chainring and a 25t cassette, you'll travel 2.9m per revolution.

CHANGING YOUR CASSETTE

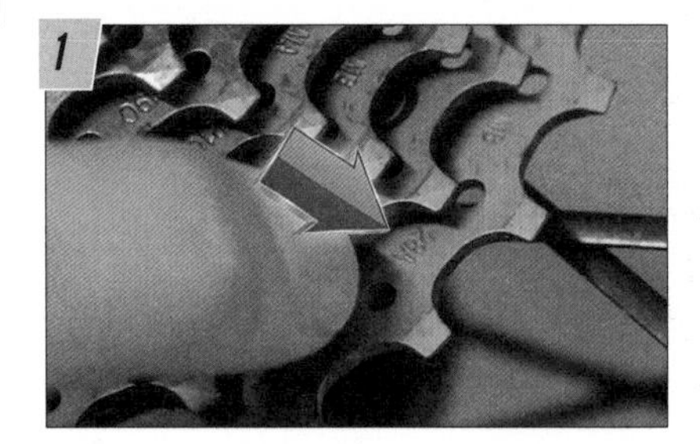

The easiest way to change your gear ratios is to swap your cassette for one with a different range. To see what you're currently running, check your biggest sprocket as the number of teeth it has will be marked there. Alternatively, count them yourself.

If your bike is already running a 23 or 25-tooth cassette, so you should be able to swap it over to 28 without any issues (see page 70 for how to change your cassette).

Once you've changed your cassette, you'll need to adjust the B-tension screw on your derailleur. The B-tension screw controls the distance between the top jockey wheel and the sprockets. Turning it clockwise will lower the jockey wheel and so clear the derailleur of the new larger cassette.

If you're already running a 28, then you could switch to a 32t cassette, but now it starts to get more complex as you'll need to check whether you've got a short or a medium length derailleur. When you increase the size of the cassette, you may also need to get a longer cage derailleur.

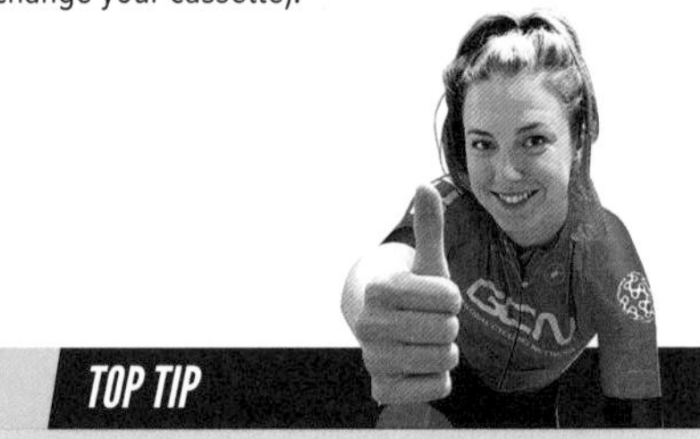

TOP TIP

It may seem obvious, but when buying a new cassette don't forget to ensure it is the same speed (has the same number of sprockets) as the one you're replacing. For example, if you're running 10-speed gears, your new cassette (and new derailleur if you need one) will also need to be 10-speed.

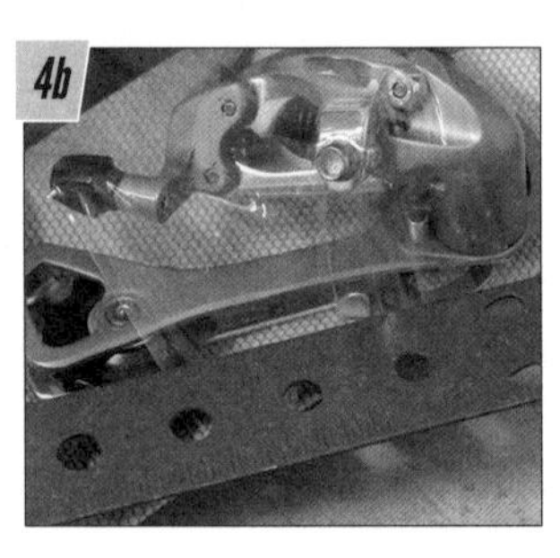

It's easy to check whether you have a short or medium rear derailleur as short cage versions have only 2cm between the jockey wheels whereas on medium cage derailleurs the gap is more like 6 or 7cm.

If you need a longer derailleur, the maximum size of the cassette it can work with is usually marked on the back of the box, so ensure to check before you buy.

If you want an even wider range or gears, you could fit an off-road cassette (such as found on a mountain or gravel bike), but as well as the cassette, you'll also need to run an off-road rear derailleur.

Switching to an off-road derailleur and cassette is only possible if you're running 9 or 10-speed though, as 11-speed road gears have a different cable pull ratio to what is used on 11-speed mountain or gravel bikes.

To Remove & Install Cranks
Flip back to page 84

CHANGING YOUR CHAINRINGS

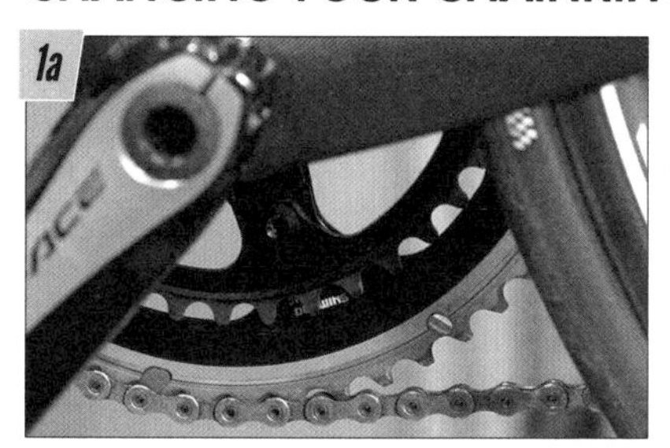

To swap out a chainring for a different size, you'll need to ensure you get one that has the same BCD (bolt circle diameter) as your old one. If going for a bigger chainring, check you have enough frame clearance to run it.

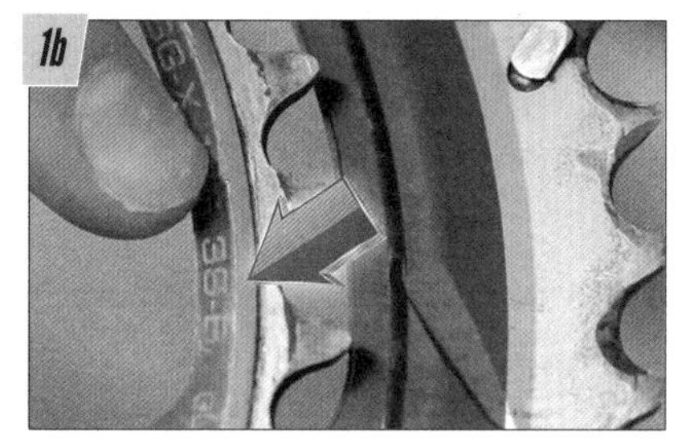

While you can measure the BCD for yourself, you'll usually find it marked on most chainrings. On a standard 53/39t chainset, the BCD is 130mm (or 135mm if you're using Campagnolo), while on a compact or mid-compact chainset it's 110mm.

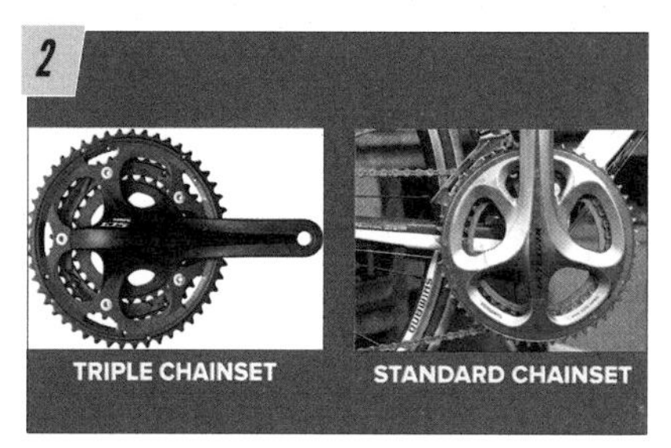

If you want really low gears with a huge range, you could fit a triple-ring chainset which has three rings as opposed to two. You'll also need to fit a new front derailleur and shifter, as well as a long cage rear derailleur though.

FITTING A 1X DRIVETRAIN

Another option is to fit a 1x system. This means running a single chainring and a wide-range cassette. You can convert a double chainset into a single, but you'll need to check your BCD as double gravel chainsets can come with a BCD of 130 or 110mm, depending on the size of the chainrings.

Without a front derailleur, it's easier for the chain to fall off the chainring, so ensure your replacement chainring is a narrow/wide version. Narrow/wide chainrings are designed specifically with 1x systems in mind and have teeth that hold the chain more securely so it's less likely to get dropped.

It's also a good idea to fit a clutch-equipped derailleur. The clutch mechanism will keep the chain taught and help avoid it getting dropped.

A more expensive, but arguably simpler and slicker option is to buy a complete 1x drivetrain. There are a range of 1x combinations particularly at 11 and 12-speed. 1x drivetrains can have a front ring that usually vary from 34 to 40t and wide-ranging cassettes of up to 42t. See page 94 for more on 1x.

When changing your drivetrain components it's a good idea to fit a new chain too. If you decide to stick with your original chain though, always check that it's still long enough after you've made your changes to your cassette and/or chainring. To do this, run the chain in the biggest gears at the front and back and then also in the smallest chainring and sprocket too – just to make sure that it is still functioning correctly.

SET-UP SECRETS

HOW TO INSTALL A CABLED TRANSMISSION

Installing a groupset can seem like quite a daunting task, but once you understand the basics of how gears work it's actually quite straightforward

DIFFICULTY 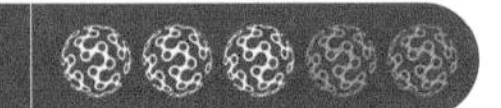

TIME 90 - 120 Minutes

TOOLS
- *Allen keys*
- *Hollowtech crank bolt tool*
- *Chain tool*
- *Cable cutters*
- *Cassette tool*
- *Chain installation tool*
- *Grease*

WHEN
- *You want to replace or upgrade your transmission*

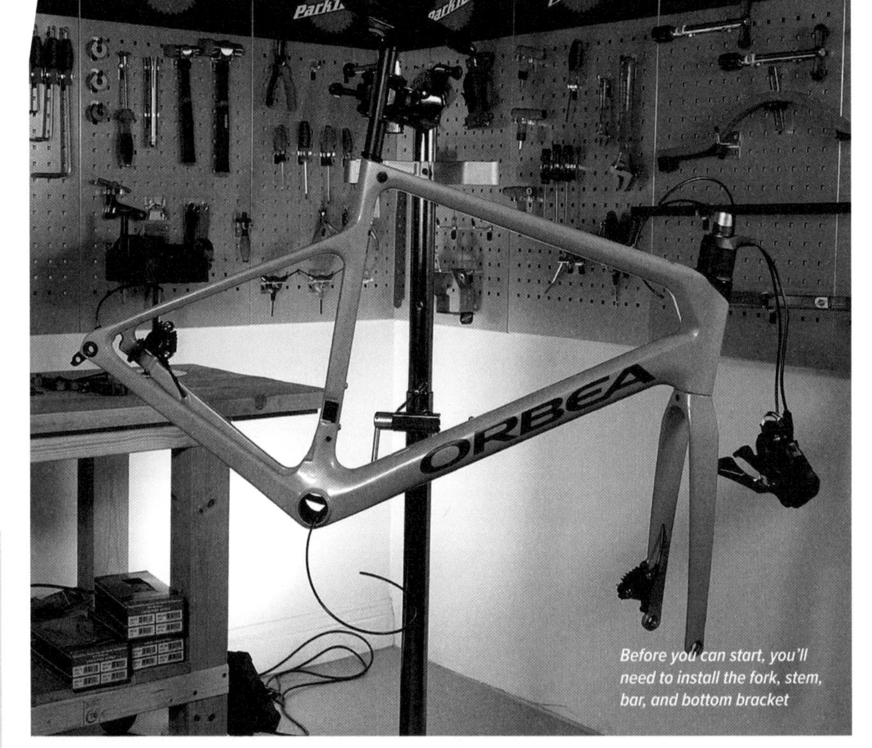

Before you can start, you'll need to install the fork, stem, bar, and bottom bracket

WATCH THE VIDEO

Free show-how and know-how

GCN TECH

HOW TO INSTALL A MECHANICAL TRANSMISSION

https://gcn.eu/FitMechanicalGears

SCAN CODE TO WATCH THE VIDEO

Taking a heap of different parts and cables, adding a bit of grease and building a seamlessly shifting, wheel spinning transmission out of it is the nearest you'll get to being the Doctor Frankenstein of bikes. You don't need a lightning storm to make it happen either, you just need the instructions here and a patient, methodical approach to the sections where you need to do a bit of back and forth tweaking. This is one of the longer jobs in the book too so have some snacks, a supply of drinks ready and be ready to take a break if you find yourself getting frustrated or too task-focussed at any time. Often looking at a problem with fresh eyes can be a big help.

BEFORE YOU START

If you're building a bike up from scratch, before beginning this process you'll need to fit the bottom bracket, seatpost, bar and stem. If you need any help fitting any of these parts, their installation is all covered in the relevent pages of this book so check them out and then come back to crack on.

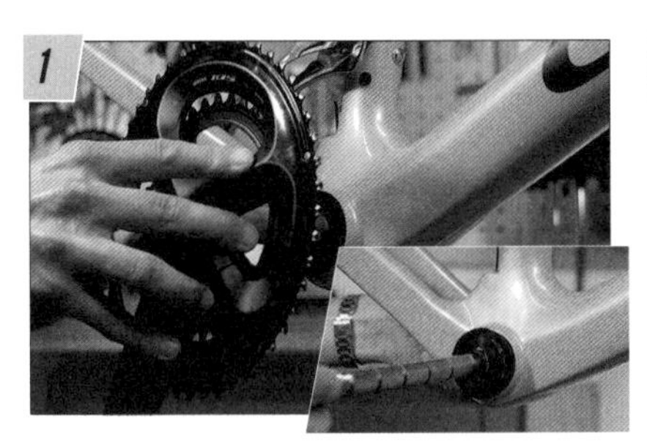

First install the chainset. If it has a fixed spindle then just slide it through the bottom bracket and then fit the arm on the far side. Use the built-in bolt to tighten it firmly into place. Shimano cranks use a plastic tightener and then secure with the two pinch bolts on the bottom of the arm.

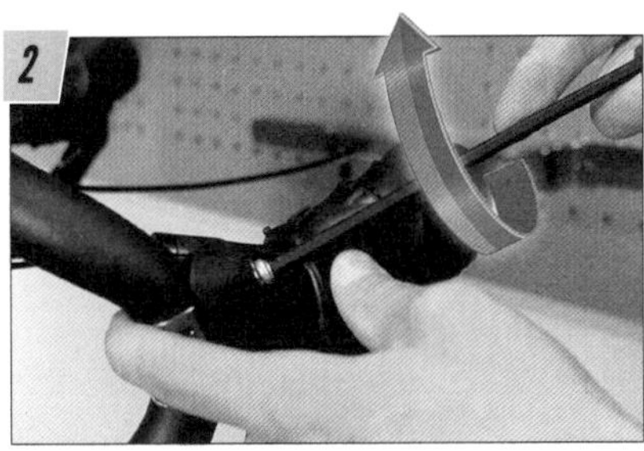

Now install the shifters. Simply peel back the rubber shifter hood so you can access the clamping bolt, and loosen this just enough that you can slide the shifters onto the drops of the bar. Work them round until they're in the correct location, and tighten the bolt back up to between 4 and 6Nm.

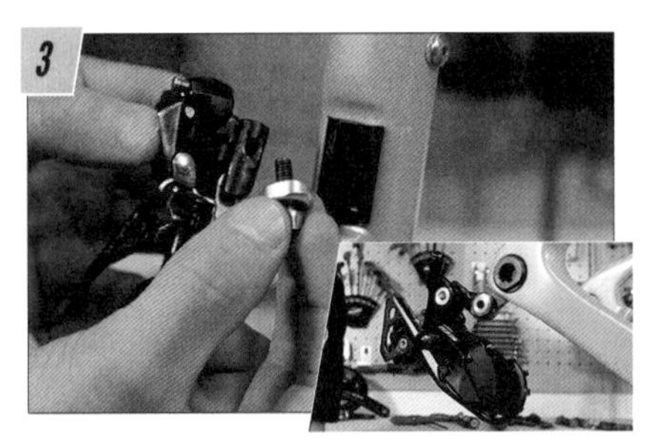

Fit the rear derailleur to the hanger and tighten to about 5Nm. Loosely fit the front derailleur to the derailleur mount – though if you're using a band-on front mech, wrap this around the seat tube. Tighten the bolt enough so it won't move on it's own but you can still adjust its position.

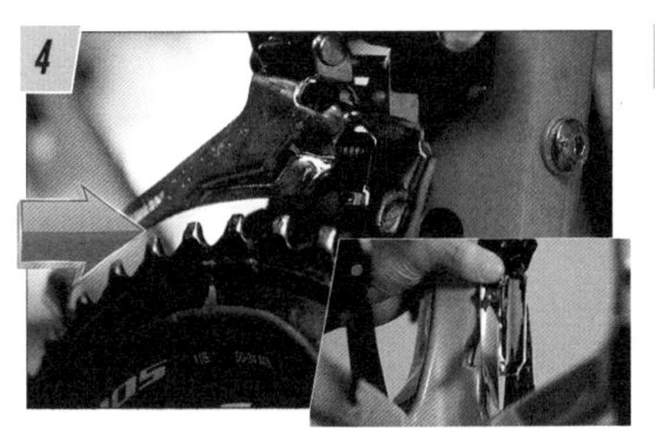

Line the front derailleur up so the outer part of the cage is sitting 2 to 3mm above the large chainring. You'll also need to make sure the cage is parallel with the chainring when looking at the derailleur from the front. When you're happy it's in the correct position, torque the bolt up to 5Nm.

Fitting the cassette is really straightforward. Smear a small amount of grease or anti-seize on the freehub body. Line up the cassette splines with the splines on the freehub, put a dab of grease on the lockring, and tighten the lockring down using the cassette tool. See page 70 for more.

Find the ideal chain length by wrapping the chain around the largest chainring and the largest sprocket on the cassette (don't thread it through the derailleur). Add two full links and you'll have your correct length. You could install the chain now or after the cables are installed if you prefer.

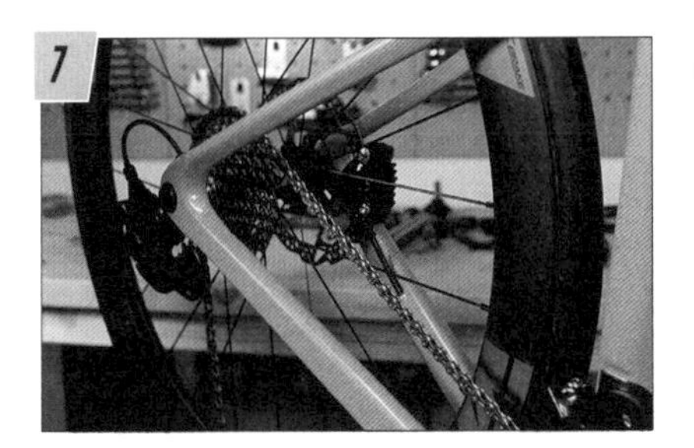

Remove the excess links then thread the chain around the inner chainring, smallest sprocket and through the derailleurs. Ensure to thread the chain clockwise around the upper pulley wheel on the rear derailleur so it doesn't rub on the tab and then anti-clockwise around the lower pulley wheel.

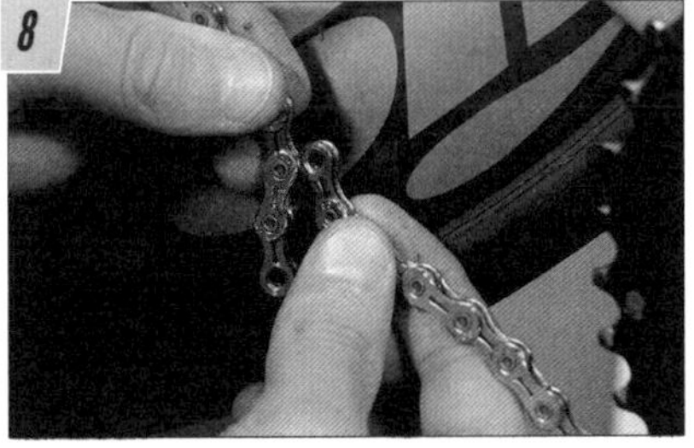

Pull the two loose chain ends together and hold them in place with an installation tool or an old spoke. Quick-links make fitting the chain easy as you just fit a plate to each end of the chain, join them together and pull on both sides to lock in place. If you have a joining pin, see page 69.

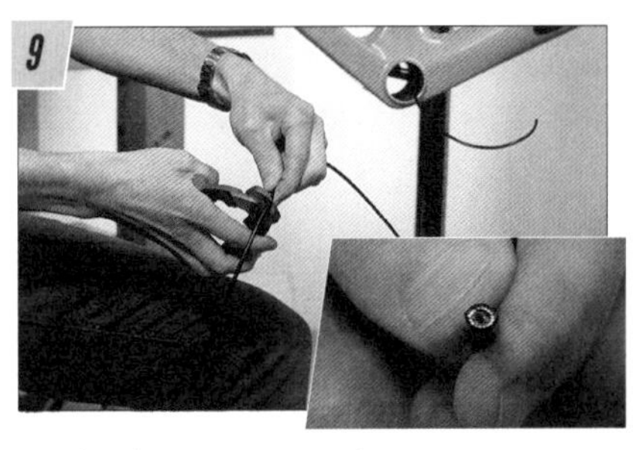

Now it's time to measure and cut your outer cables. To correctly measure your outers, hold the outer between the brake or mech, and the shifter or cable port on the frame. You want to make sure you have a nice smooth curve to the cable without any tight angles as this will impact your shifting.

HOW TO INSTALL A CABLED TRANSMISSION

TOP TIP

Make sure you have a nice, sharp pair of dedicated cable cutters – and NOT side cutters or pliers. Side cutters will compress the end of your outer and make it really tricky to thread the inner cables, as well as add a bit of resistance and make it harder to get smooth shifting and braking.

For the outer cables that leave the shifters, make sure you measure the outers with the bars turned in such a way that the cable is in its most extreme position. This will ensure that the cables won't be yanked out of place when the bars turn.

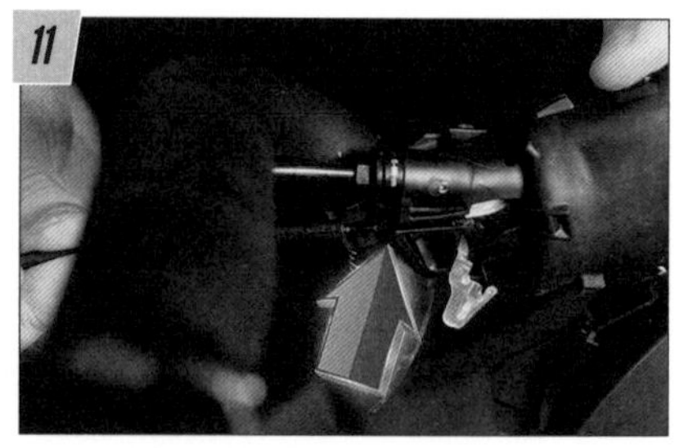

Peel back the shifter hoods, insert the outer cable for the rear derailleur into the correct port. Thread the other end of the cable through the frame or the cable guides. Do the same for the front derailleur. Fit the brake hoses/cables at the same time using the instructions on pages 87 and 99.

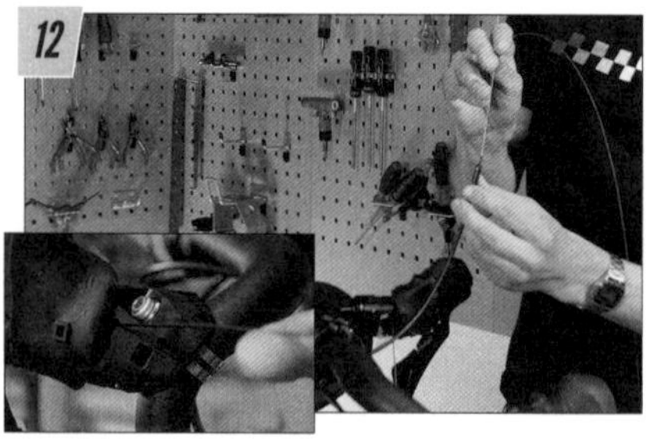

Now the outers are in place, you can install the inner cables. At the shifters, thread the cable into the cable holder, pulling it all the way through until the barrel is seated correctly inside the shifter. You can then thread the other end of the cable through the outers to the derailleurs or brake callipers.

Now you need to connect the rear derailleur. But before you do that, you'll need to adjust the limit screws. These screws determine how far inboard and outboard the derailleur can move and stop the chain going over the largest sprocket into your spokes, or off the smallest sprocket into your frame.

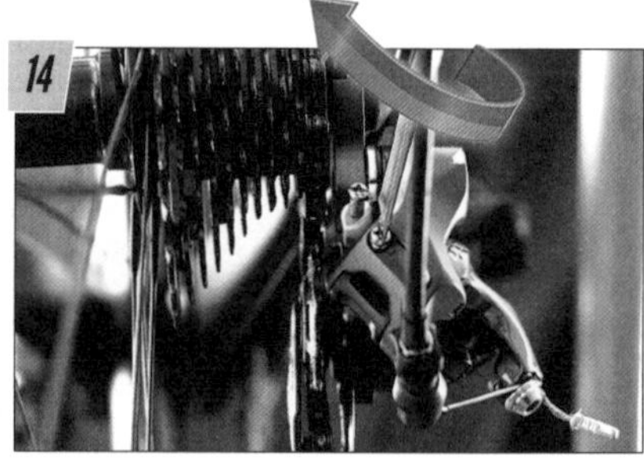

Start with the H (high limit) screw. Loosen it and the derailleur will move outboard, making sure you get all the gears. Tightening moves the derailleur inboard making sure it doesn't fall off the end of the cassette. Adjust it until the upper pulley wheel and smallest sprocket are parallel with one another.

The L (low limit) screw stops your chain going over the lowest gear and into the spokes. Push the derailleur into the biggest gear position while turning the cranks. If the chain won't go that far, loosen the L screw. If it wants to carry on past the largest gear into the wheel, tighten the L screw.

Now click the rear shifter into the smallest cog. Check all the outer cable is properly snug in the guides, the shifter and the derailleur. Check that any barrel adjusters on the cables are wound fully in. Thread the inner gear cable around any guides on the derailleur, pull it tight and clamp into place.

Not all front and rear derailleurs have cable guide segments but when they do they are crucial for making the mech run through it's full range of movement at the correct leverage. If you're unsure where the cable goes, check the relevant online installation guides for the mech model you have.

If you pedal through the gears you'll probably find they're a bit jumpy and you won't be able to access them all. You now need to micro-adjust each gear using the barrel adjuster at the point the outer cable enters the rear mech. Starting in the smallest sprocket, click the shifter up one gear.

If the chain doesn't move to the next sprocket straight away, turn the barrel adjuster a quarter turn anti-clockwise at a time until it does. Repeat this process for each gear. If you find the chain jumps all the way over a gear to the next sprocket, turn the barrel adjuster clockwise until it doesn't over-shift.

Moving on to the front derailleur. Double check that the outer part of the cage sits 2-3mm above the large chainring and it's parallel from the front. Install the inner cable through the outer between the shifter and frame, thread this down to the front mech, pull it tight, and clamp it into place.

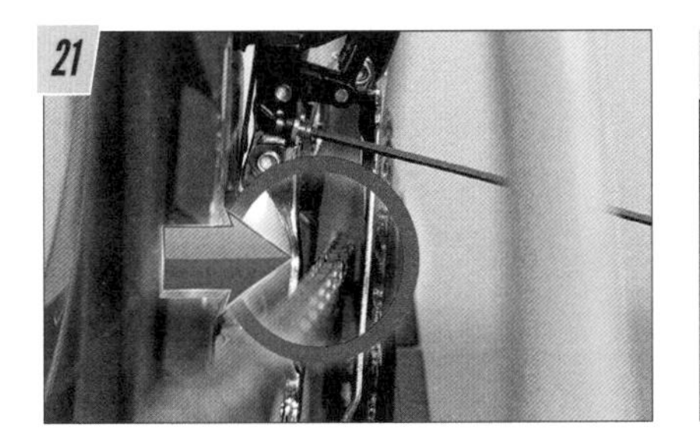

With the chain on the inner chainring, adjust the L limit screw until there is as small a gap as possible between the inner derailleur plate and the chain without it rubbing when pedalling. Turning the L limit screw clockwise will move the derailleur outboard, and anti-clockwise will move it inboard.

When working on the front derailleur, turn the L limit screw clockwise as you pedal until you hear chain rub, then slowly back the screw off until the rubbing noise stops.

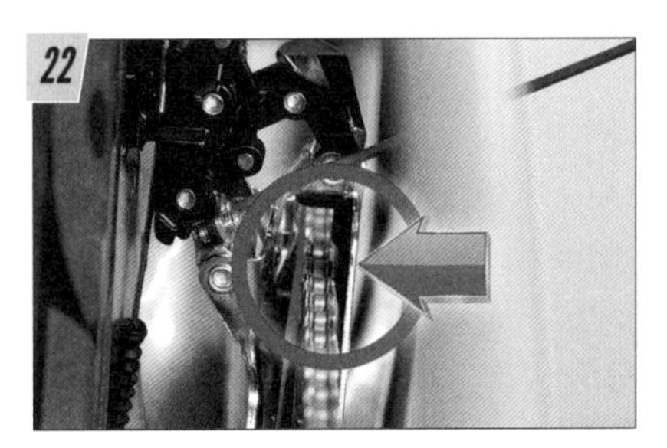

Shift into the big ring and repeat the process for the H limit screw. Again, aim for as small a gap as possible between the outer plate of the mech and the chain, so repeat the adjustment process in the large chainring.

Now shift through all the gears at the back in each chainring. If you hear any rubbing, take a look at the front mech and see where this is occurring. If the inner plate is rubbing on the chain, move the mech inboard. If the chain is rubbing on the outer plate, move the mech outboard.

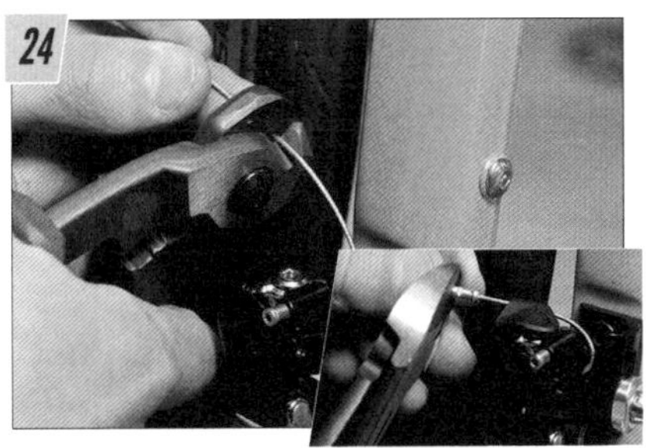

When you're happy with this, shift between the chainrings as you're pedalling to make sure everything is working correctly. Adjust if needed and then you can trim the excess gear cables and fit cable ends to stop them fraying.

TOP TIP

After a few rides your gears might start to creep out of adjustment and shifting will get noisy or slow. This is down to the outer cables settling into place and compressing a little. As soon as you notice this, re-tighten the cable by turning the barrel adjusters slightly, just like you did when you set the gears up.

Need To Set Up Your Cable Brakes?
See page 124 and page 138 for how

SET-UP SECRETS

HOW TO INSTALL A 1X TRANSMISSION

Single-ring drivetrains are simpler, look neat and work well on gravel, cyclo-cross and TT bikes. Here's how to set up SRAM or Shimano-based 1x system

DIFFICULTY 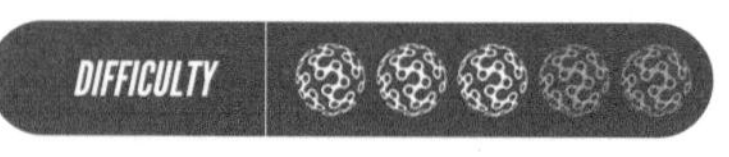

TIME 30 - 60 Minutes

TOOLS
- *Allen keys/Torx keys*
- *T25 Torx key*
- *A torque wrench*
- *Cable cutters*
- *Chain tool*
- *Master link*
- *SRAM chain gap guide*

WHEN
- *You want to run a less complex gear system*

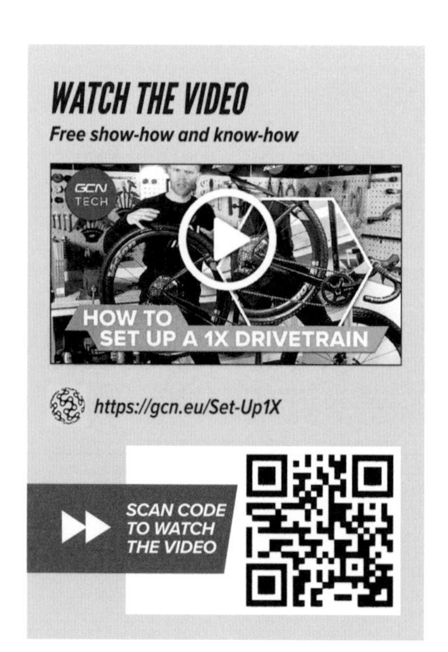

They started on mountain bikes, then moved into specialist set-ups like cyclo-cross and time trial, but now more and more 'all rounder/gravel/adventure' bikes are using single ring '1x' transmissions. So what do you need to know to set them up correctly?

For most of a 1x set-up you can follow our instructions for setting up a regular groupset. For example, fitting shifters, a bottom bracket and a chainset is essentially the same, but there are some key differences which we'll run through here.

We'll also talk through Shimano, SRAM and Campagnolo set-ups separately where they differ.

SINGLE MINDED

The main difference with a 1x groupset over a 2x, is of course the lack of multiple front chainrings and a front derailleur which makes setting up a lot easier.

With no front derailleur to guide the chain you need to make sure it doesn't fall off the chainring – particularly on rough gravel or in cyclo-cross situations. That's

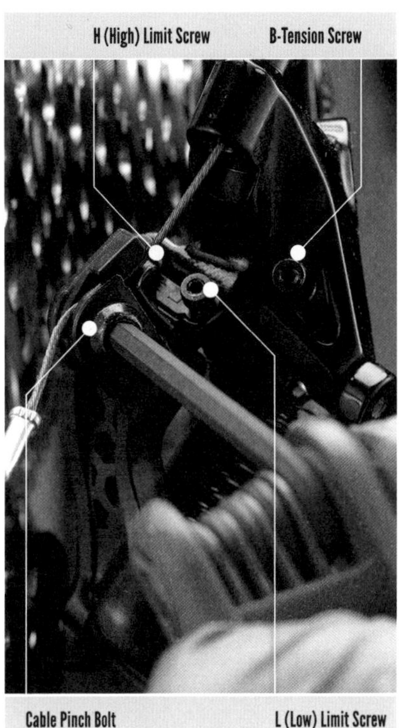

why 1x groupsets have specific chainrings. The next significant difference is the rear derailleur itself. This usually has a larger jockey wheel cage and modified linkage path to accommodate a wider spread of gears and a longer chain. It will also have a stabiliser spring/clutch to help keep the chain under tension and stop it thrashing around.

1X GROUPS AREN'T ALWAYS LIGHTER

It sounds crazy considering they don't have a front mech or a second chainring or a left hand brake with a shifting mechanism in it, but single chainring set ups aren't much different in weight to double ring groups. That's because to get the same gear ratio spread you need to use a cassette with much bigger cogs on the low end and rear mechs with longer cages. Also, those shifting guts and the front mech don't weigh much at all, so don't be surprised if there's literally just a few grams difference between 2x and 1x groups of the same type.

SINGLE SPECIFIC CHAINRINGS

While exact designs vary, all 1x chainrings use a tooth profile designed to hold the chain in place better. Most are a variation on the alternating thick tooth, thin tooth design pioneered by SRAM.

STABILISED REAR MECH

To stop the chain whipping around too much and flying off the chainring, 1x specific rear derailleurs have 'stabilisers'. These increase the force needed to pull the jockey wheel cage forward and create chain slack. SRAM used to call them a 'clutch', but now call them 'orbital dampers'. They also use a 'Cage Lock' button to hold the mech open for removing/fitting your wheel more easily. Shimano use both 'clutch' or 'chain stabiliser' to describe their system which you're able to switch on or off. Campagnolo Ekar has a clutch with a catch hook like SRAM.

HACKS & BODGES

You can create your own 1x set-up by just using the small chainring you already have and your existing gearing. You'll only have a narrow gear spread though and your chain is likely to fall off as soon as the bike starts rattling around. In other words it's OK for a hack/commuter/pub bike, but we wouldn't recommend it for your regular ride.

BEFORE YOU START

Single ring chainsets fit in the same way as doubles or triples, so we'll assume you already have the chainset installed. We'll also assume you have the shifter in place on the bars and the rear derailleur outer cable already threaded through the bike.

HOW TO INSTALL A 1X TRANSMISSION

TOP TIP

Something to note is the floating bracket that holds the Shimano GRX derailleur in the correct position. It needs to extend backwards and the little tabs on the reverse of the plate should not foul on the gear hanger, so bear this in mind when you're bolting it in place.

First you need to install the rear derailleur. This mounts in the same way as a standard rear derailleur but ensure you lock out or turn off the clutch. On Shimano, move the little lever to the 'off' position, while SRAM and Campagnolo push in the button marked with the 'lock' symbol.

Make sure the shifter is in the top (smallest gear). Check the outer cable is tight against all the cable stops from the shifter to rear derailleur. Thread your derailleur cable through the outer cable, through the barrel adjuster and through the guides to the clamp area. Pull it tight and then clamp securely.

When it comes to adjusting the angle of a Shimano GRX 1x rear derailleur, there's not too much that's dissimilar to a regular version. You'll want to pay more attention to the B-limit screw though, as that'll affect shifting way more than on a regular road derailleur.

As you shift up, and this is unique to 1x, you need to make sure the top jockey wheel has enough clearance to move up to the next largest sprocket, without fouling on it. And that's where the B-limit screw comes in. Turn counter-clockwise to decrease the gap, clockwise to enlarge it.

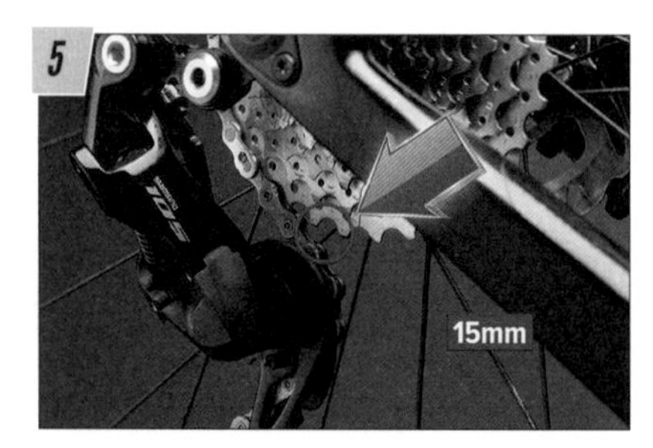

SRAM make setting the gap easier by providing a plastic template for correctly positioning the upper jockey wheel in relation to the cassette. If you haven't got this template, then aim for a gap of 15mm between the two sets of teeth.

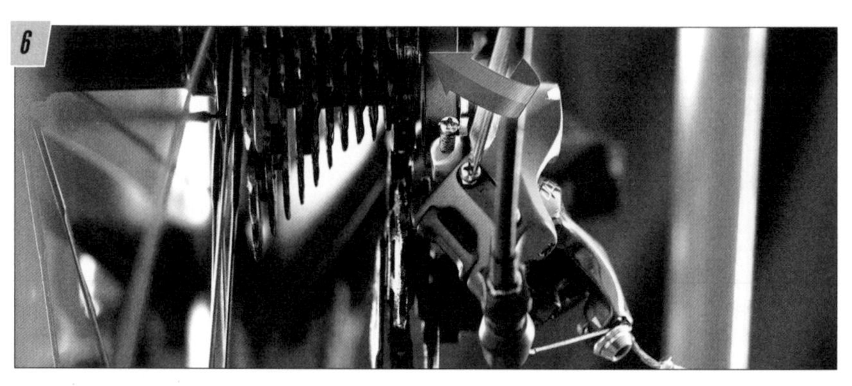

To stop the chain falling off the inside or outside of the cassette, getting jammed and potentially damaging the frame or wheel, you need to set the high and low limit screws. First turn the H-screw until the top jockey wheel is in line with the smallest sprocket on the cassette.

Need To Fit Your Cassette?
See page 70 for how to install it

Now shift all the way up to the largest sprocket. On Shimano and Campagnolo the top jockey wheel should be in line with the largest sprocket on the cassette. Turn the L (low) limit screw so that you can't push the rear mech any further towards the spokes (to stop the chain running off the cassette).

TOP TIP

With SRAM 1x, the best place to set the low limit is *just* past the largest sprocket. What this does is allow a dummy shift, essentially keeping you in that gear rather than dumping the chain back down a gear. Careful not to set it too wide though otherwise the derailleur will make contact with the spokes.

Now to fit the chain – using a sizing method that differs from the norm. Wrap the chain around the chainring and the largest sprocket on the cassette without running it through the derailleur. Hold the ends of the chain together and then add four links to its length – including the joining link.

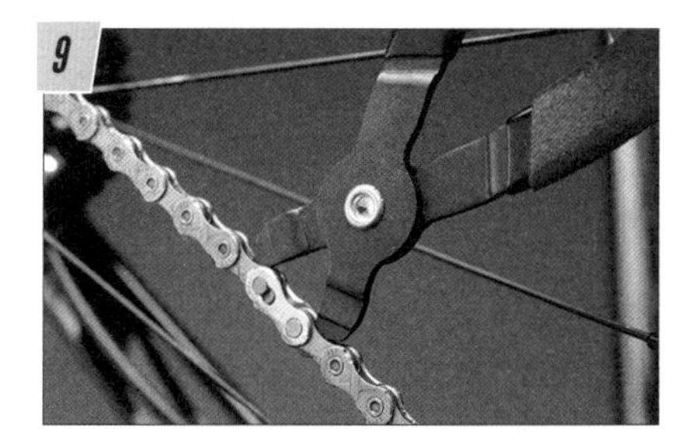

Pull the chain through the cage around the jockey wheels and chainring, making sure the broader links sit on the broader teeth. Now link the chain with the joining link and pull it tight. Check that it runs smoothly, flexing it gently sideways if there's any stiffness. See page 66 for more on chains.

Once you've broken the chain down to the correct length, disengage the rear derailleur's clutch. On Shimano you pull the little lever to the 'off' position, while SRAM and Campagnolo have a push button lock out.

Now try the shifting. If your cable tension is too high, then the chain will rub on the next largest sprocket. If it does, loosen off the barrel adjuster slightly. If it doesn't change up when you shift then increase the tension. Keep adjusting tension until you find the sweet spot.

If when you shift down from that largest low gear it still seems a little sluggish, you can turn the B-limit screw anti-clockwise to bring the jockey wheel in a little closer, which should speed things up.

Once everything is working well. Check the cables are all clamped securely, then trim the spare length off and fit a cable cap to stop it fraying.

SET-UP SECRETS

HOW TO SET UP SHIMANO Di2

Shimano's Di2 electronic shifting system is a fully wired system which needs setting up with care for quiet and accurate operation

DIFFICULTY 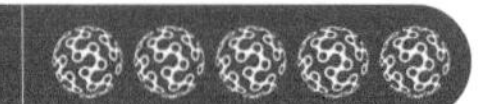

TIME 90 - 120 Minutes

TOOLS
- 2mm and 5mm Allen keys
- Shimano TLEW02 Di2 tool
- Tools to remove and refit your chainset, bottom bracket, chain and derailleurs

WHEN
- You want to upgrade to Shimano electronic shifting

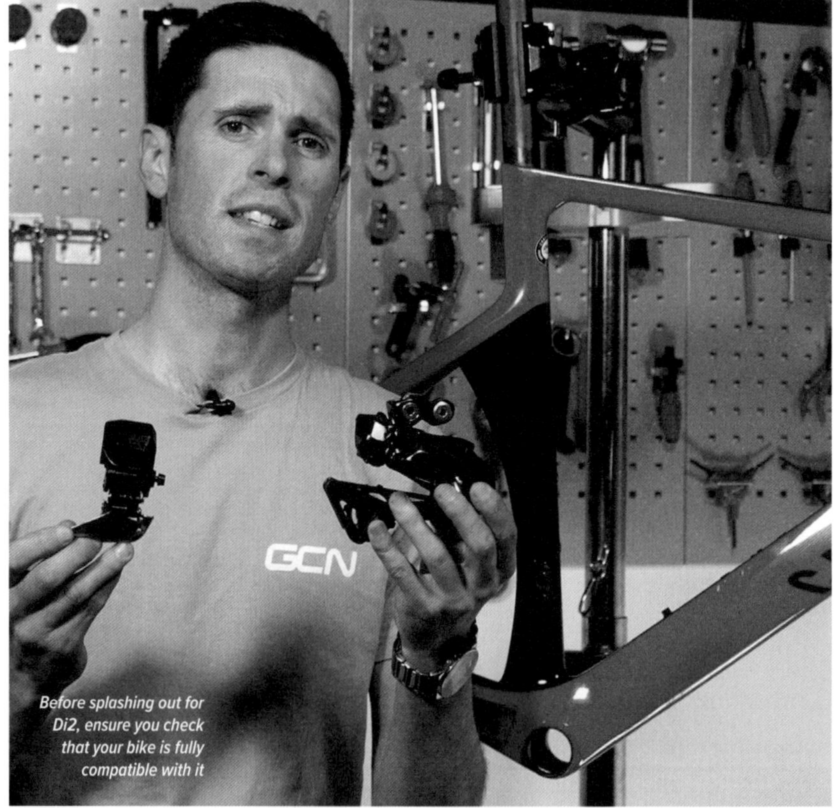

Before splashing out for Di2, ensure you check that your bike is fully compatible with it

With a nest of wires connecting shifters, derailleurs and battery, Shimano Di2 is a lot more time consuming to install than SRAM's wireless eTap system. For a clean installation you need a bike that's compatible with the necessary wiring and battery too. You also need the specific kit for your bike as there are lots of different ways batteries or junction boxes can be mounted. Add potentially awkward diagnostics using a hardwired connection rather than Bluetooth and this is a job that can cause some serious headaches. Once completely set up though, you can be justifiably proud of your achievement.

"Shimano Di2 is a lot more time consuming to install than SRAM's wireless eTap system"

Remove your bottom bracket, stem and other components before you begin Di2 installation

WILL YOUR BIKE WORK WITH DI2?

In theory, you can make any bike compatible with Di2 if you don't mind using the existing gear cable infrastructure backed up with zip-ties and gaffer tape to secure the battery, junction box and wiring where necessary. Some bikes don't have a big enough space to fit a battery inside the frame though (especially steel or alloy bikes), so you may have to use an external battery mount if your frame doesn't have that capacity.

You'll obviously get a lot neater result if your frame is specifically ported where the cables need to come out and has a proper battery and junction box mounting plan. That's fairly common on mid to high-end bikes from the previous decade, but be warned that some brand new bikes are now purely rigged for wireless or cable. Smaller bike sizes or shorter/more unusual stem designs can also create mounting issues so be prepared to get creative to get an acceptable result.

Don't Hack Your Frame

Don't be tempted to get a drill out to do a bit of Di2 surgery either as frames aren't designed to have extra holes in them and the warranty will certainly reflect that.

Osymetric Off Limits

While Di2 works OK with Rotor's slightly eccentric chainring design, you're likely to get significant chain drop issues with the most extreme shaped Osymetric rings. While Chris Froome seems to make it work, that's only by using a massive carbon fibre chain guide moulded onto his frames to keep the chain in place.

BEFORE YOU START

We're making the assumption that you're building from scratch, rather than replacing your current groupset, but the steps remain the same if you are. You might need to do some more preparation and removal of existing components. That includes removing the bottom bracket and chainset as well as fork and stem/washers if you've got an integrated 'hidden cable' front end.

A new Di2 kit should come with everything you need for installation, but you need to make sure you have exactly the right kit for your bike. That includes the correct battery, junction boxes and any hardware to mount the battery and junction boxes in the frame/seatpost/stem depending on their design. If in any doubt, ask for some professional advice from your local shop or contact your bike's manufacturer.

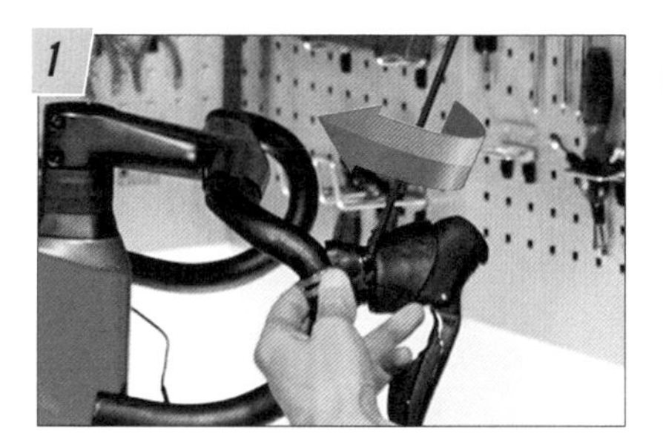

Mount the brake/shift levers onto the handlebars. Simply slide them over the drops, ensuring they're on the correct sides, then clamp in place with the 5mm allen key. If you need advice on positioning head over to page 110.

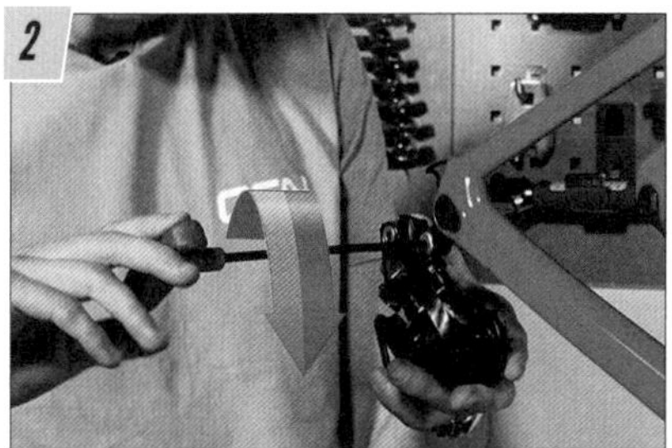

Attach the rear derailleur, using the 5mm Allen bolt. Apply a little grease to the thread and tighten on to the derailleur hanger. Then set the high and low stops on the derailleur, which is the same process as a mechanical version. If you're unsure on this step, flip to page 64.

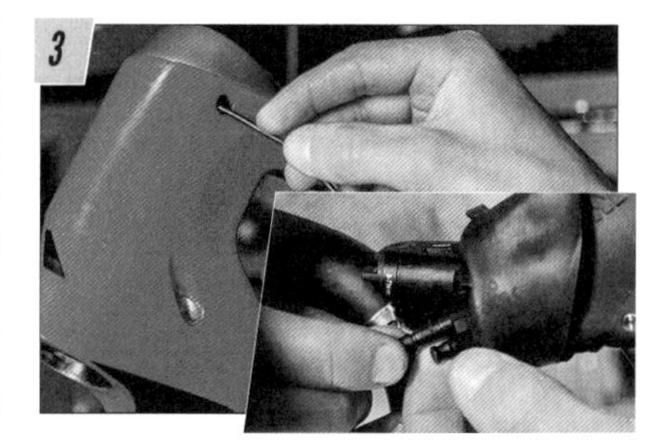

Next, you need to fit the cables. Starting at the shifter, attach a cable to the top of the three (or two) holes on each shifter using the special Shimano tool, ensuring there's enough slack to reach the first junction box.

HOW TO SET UP SHIMANO DI2

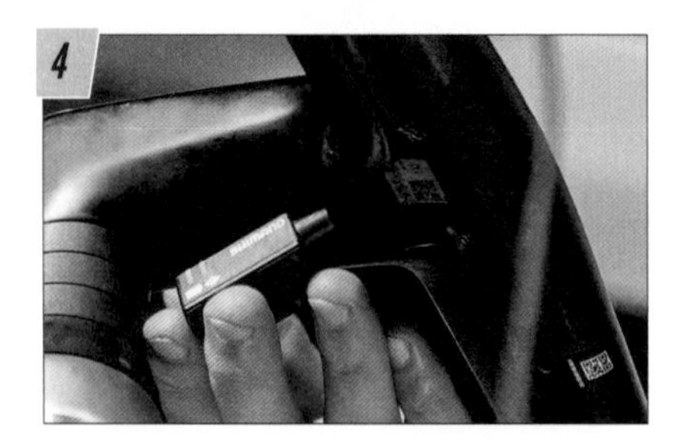

4

If you are running an external junction box, use the rubber strap to mount it onto the underside of the stem. If the junction box is in the bar end, then insert it loosely as you'll need to pull it out slightly to tape the bars in a few steps time.

TOP TIP

When plugging in the cables you'll get an initial loose fit, but don't mistake this for pushing the cable fully home. Use the dedicated forked Shimano tool to press firmly until you feel a definite click as it engages. This ensures a fully secure and watertight connection.

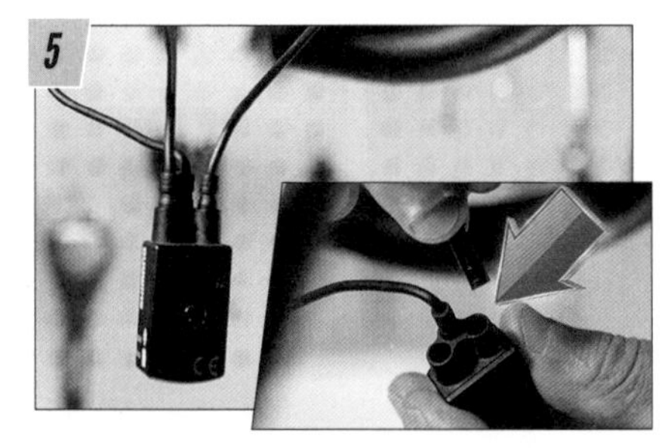

5

If you have internal cable routing on your bars, thread the cable through it and pop the ends into either side of the junction box using the Shimano tool. Otherwise tape the cable on the outside of the bars alongside the brake cable/hose. Now wrap the handlebar tape over the top as normal.

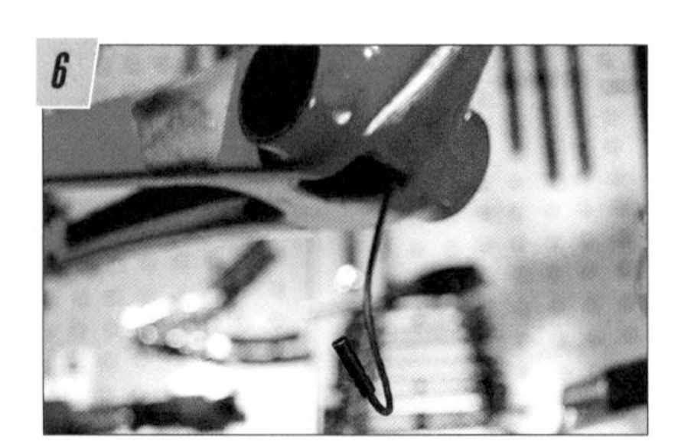

6

Take a longer cable and connect it to the junction box. On internally routed frames, thread the cable through the downtube and out of the BB. Then thread a shorter cable through the hole near the front derailleur until it also emerges at the BB.

TOP TIP

Make sure you use the little sprigs or tiny zip-ties supplied with your cable at regular intervals. These press the cable against the tube walls and stop it slapping and rattling around which is way louder and more irritating than you might expect.

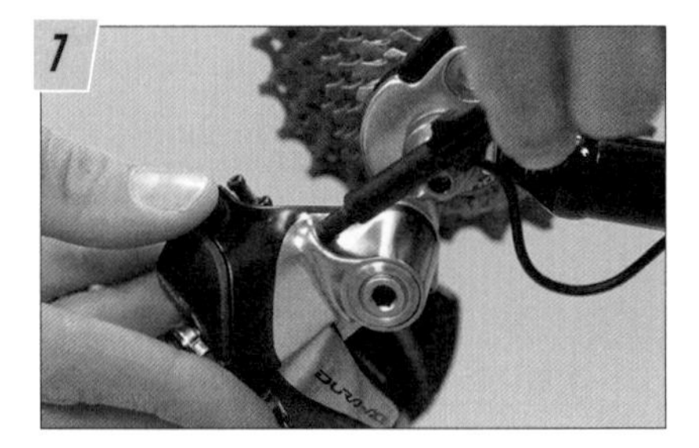

7

Finally, take another long cable and thread it through the little hole near the rear derailleur, along the chainstay and out near the bottom bracket. Fit the rear derailleur and use the dedicated Shimano tool to insert the cable into it.

8

You then need to add the battery into the mix. Some batteries mount inside the mainframe and some sit inside the seat tube. Wherever it is, you need to thread another cable from the battery down/along to the bottom bracket.

TOP TIP

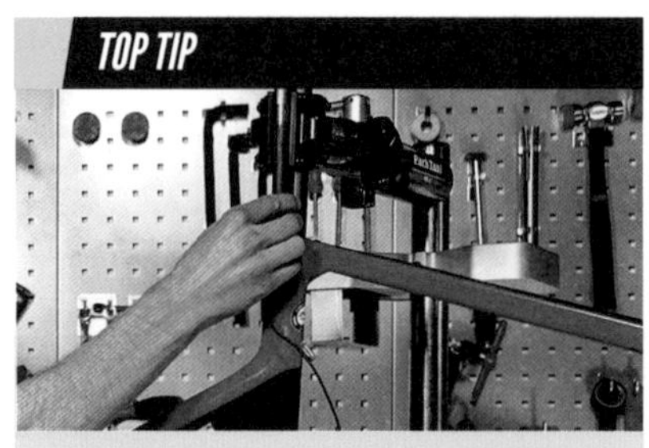

If the battery is in the seatpost, be very careful when you insert the seatpost into the frame. It's really easy to snag the cable and damage it as you're pushing the seatpost in.

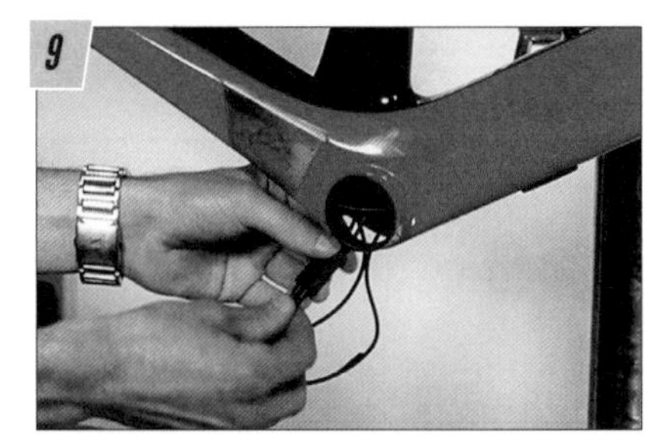

9

Now you have four cables coming out from the bottom bracket, take the secondary junction box and attach all the cables here. It doesn't matter which hole you use for each cable, but you may as well put the front cables in one end, and the rear cables in the other.

New To Installing A Chainset?
See page 84 for how to do it

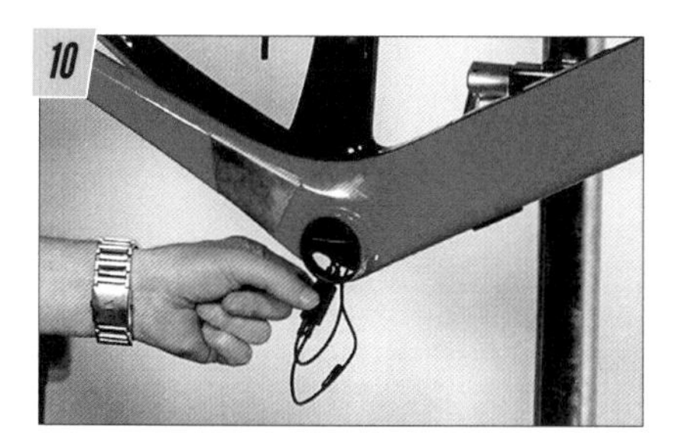

You can now hide away the junction box and cables inside the frame, either up inside the seat tube or in the downtube. You can now go ahead and reattach your bottom bracket (see page 186 and page 188) and chainset (see page 83).

TOP TIP

Wrap the lower junction box in a generous amount of bubble wrap or foam to stop it making any annoying rattles or shifting around once you've reassembled the frame.

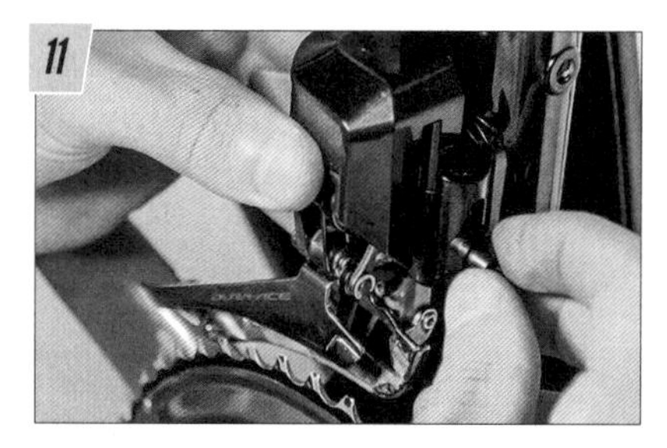

Mount the front derailleur, whether it's a band-on or braze on-mount. Clamp it in place, ensuring the outer cage is 2-3mm from the top of the outer chainring teeth. Once in place, use a 2mm Allen key to set the frame stop screw, aligning the cage of the derailleur with the outer chainring.

Attach the cable to the front derailleur. Then set the high and low limit screws on the derailleur – which is the same process as a mechanical version. You can now refit the chain to the bike and move on to the final adjustments.

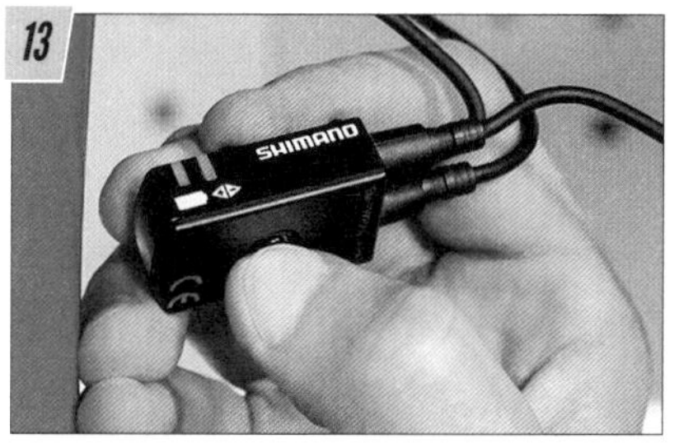

Press the button on the main junction box (at the stem/bar end) until a solid red light appears. You're in adjustment mode now and will be for a minute, or until you press the button again.

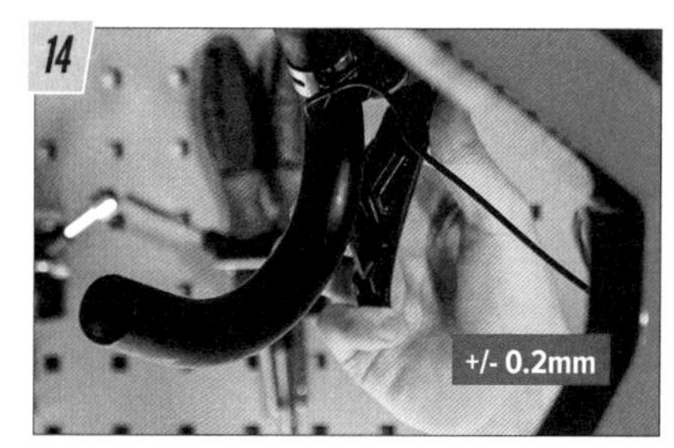

Use the up and down shifters to move the derailleurs into the correct position in the same way as you would by turning the barrel adjuster on a conventional cable set-up. Every press of the shifter buttons will move the derailleurs by 0.2mm in your desired direction.

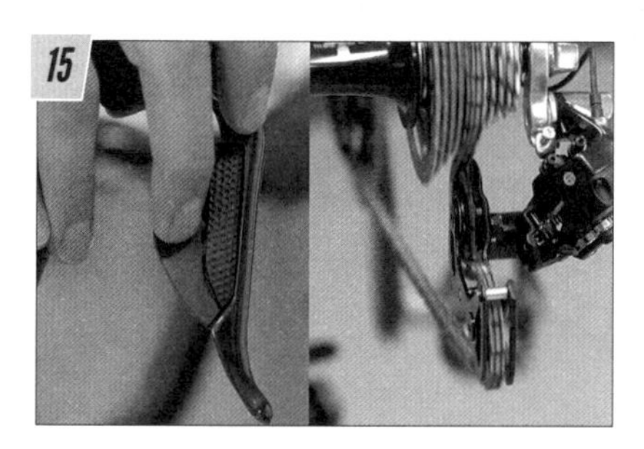

Continue to adjust until you're happy with the shifting across the cassette and between the front chainrings. When it's all working well, press the button on the junction box again to exit adjustment mode. Run the gears all the way through to double-check they're OK and then you're good to go.

TECH EXPLAINED

Setting Up Shimano E-TUBE

To get the most out of your Di2 system you need to sync it to Shimano's E-TUBE app. This will let you choose between three shifting modes: Conventional, Synchronized (linked front and rear from one shifter) and Semi-synchronised (rear shifts to sequential gear if you shift the front). You can also check the battery health of the system and upload the latest firmware updates when available. The syncing process can be a little clunky and slow though, so be prepared to be patient and keep your phone or tablet as close to the bike as possible in order to get the best connection.

SET-UP SECRETS

HOW TO SET UP SRAM ETAP

SRAM's wireless eTap shifting system is super-easy to set up but a bit of extra knowledge always helps

DIFFICULTY 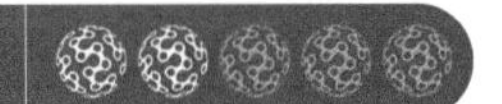

TIME	30 - 60 Minutes
TOOLS	• Torx keys • Smart phone with AXS app
WHEN	• You're adding to your current system or installing for the first time

WATCH THE VIDEO

Free show-how and know-how

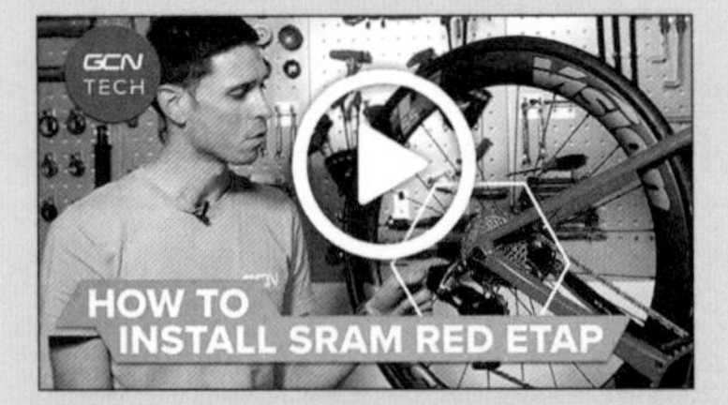

Go To:
https://gcn.eu/Set-UpEtap

SRAM's eTap system has been around for a while now but the AXS range is constantly expanding eTap Force. You can run eTap 1x or 2x, depending on the system you've purchased and the bike you have. Either way, the process is the same, though obviously you don't have to set up the front mech if you don't have one.

Bonus Add Ons

As we've said in the intro, because the AXS system components all use the same connection protocol there are all sorts of extra bits you can add on to the default drivetrain options. The simplest and most useful are the extra 'Blip' or 'Multiclic' buttons. These plug into the shifters or an additional Blipbox controller and let you put shift buttons wherever you want on your bars. There's even a set for sticking in the end of Tri bar extensions.

You can control any AXS component with any shifter too. That means you can add an AXS Eagle XX1 or X01 rear mech with a 10-52 cassette for ultra-wide gravel gearing or switch between Wide Range and conventional Force rear mechs and cassettes. The only thing you need to double-check is that the rear mech you use has the right capacity in terms of how

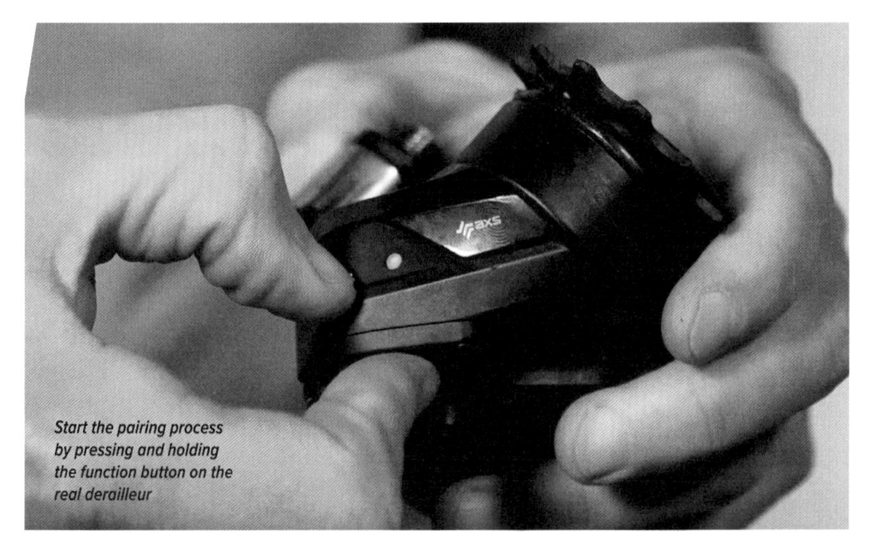

Start the pairing process by pressing and holding the function button on the real derailleur

"Because there are no wires involved you can share components like the Reverb or even rear mechs and cassettes between bikes, as long as the frame dimensions are compatible"

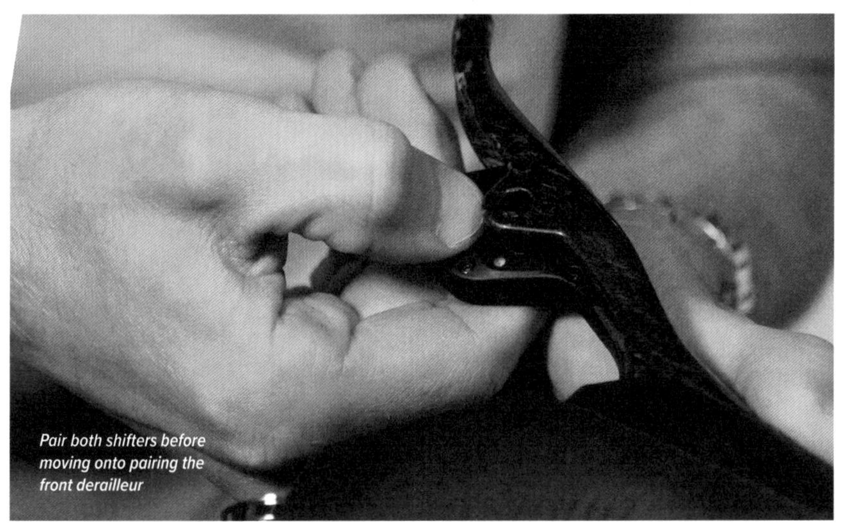

Pair both shifters before moving onto pairing the front derailleur

big a cassette or difference in ratios it can cope with. If you really want to push drop bar bike performance off-road, you can also add a remote controlled AXS Reverb dropper seatpost for full bodyweight mobility and extra control on descents. Because there are no wires involved, you can share components like the Reverb or even rear mechs and cassettes between bikes, as long as the frame dimensions are compatible.

AXS Software

As well as the mechanical advantages of SRAM AXS there's a rapidly developing software side that can give you a huge amount of useful data about your riding and how you use your transmission. The basics of this are accessible through the AXS Mobile smartphone app, but the AXS Web online site can be linked to a Garmin head unit (Wahoo compatibility is currently in beta testing) and gives a whole extra level of ride recording feedback – including gear usage data. There's more servicing and other features in the pipeline too and as it's all free, it's definitely worth signing up for.

Make sure you keep up to date with firmware updates for your AXS components too as SRAM are continually refining the shift management processes.

BEFORE YOU START

The first step is to pair the shifters with the derailleurs so that they, and only they, can communicate with one another.

Each component has a small button called the 'function button' and it's this that you use to pair them up.

The rear derailleur is the master in this system, so first press and hold the function button until the little LED next to it blinks quickly. This opens the pairing process and enables the system to be ready for setting up.

Next, press and hold the function button on each shifter until they blink quickly – and then finally the front mech. You only have about 20-30 seconds until the pairing process times out and all the parts need to be paired in the same session.

Although you can do this when the parts are bolted onto your bike, it makes it slightly harder to complete the pairing process. It also means you miss out on the fun of having them creeping across your workbench.

HOW TO SET UP SRAM ETAP

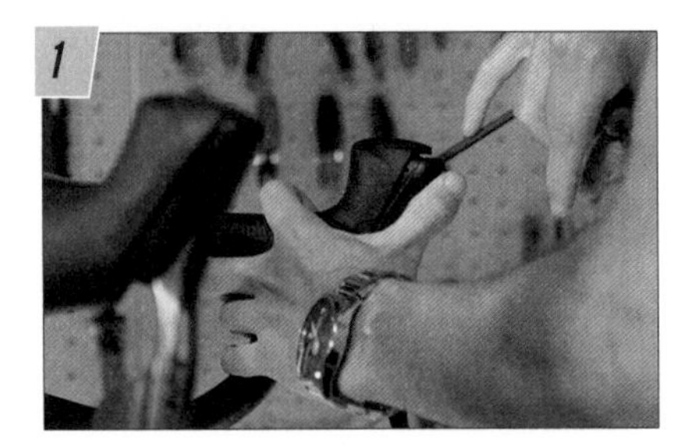

Once the components are paired, you can bolt them onto the bike. Shifters fit as usual, so peel back the hood to find the head of the clamping bolt, loosen the clamping band slightly and then slide them on your bars. If you're fitting Blip/Multiclic buttons, plug them in now before taping your bars.

TOP TIP

If you're fitting extra shifters under bar tape on the tops or in the drops for shifting, then use the new Multiclic buttons. These have small flanges either side of the button to hold them in place while they poke through the tape.

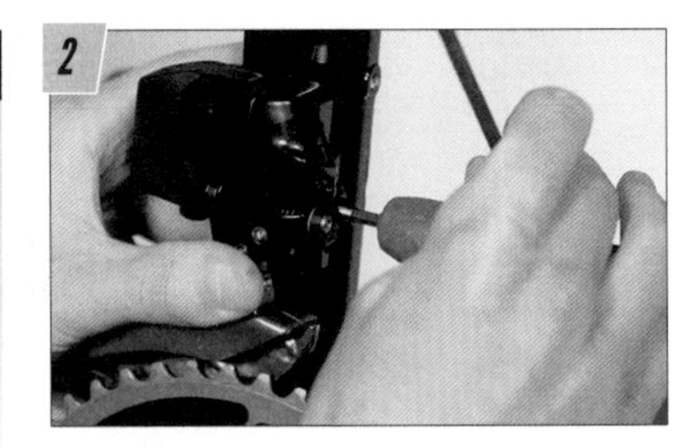

Now fit the front mech. The function button changes the position of the derailleur – you want it in the outboard position as if you're in the big ring. Bolt on the mech with a 4mm Allen key, then line up the adjustment mark (on the inner cage) with the top of the teeth on the outer chainring.

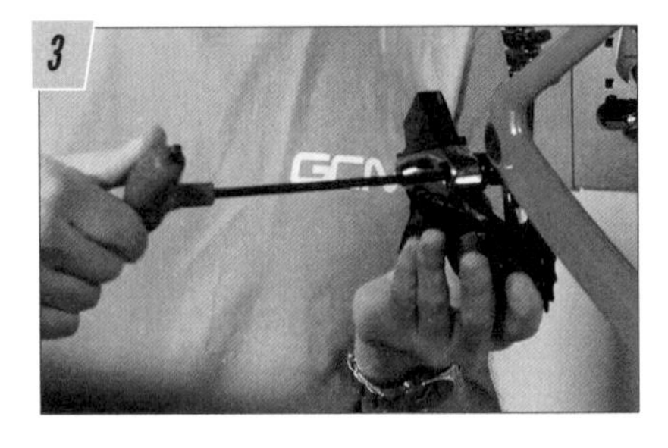

Next, looking down on the derailleur, line up the white marks on the front and back of the derailleur, again with the teeth on the outer chainring. Getting this angle right means that you won't get any rub on the front mech when in any gear combination. You can then tighten the clamp bolt down to 7Nm.

Move to the rear derailleur. Unlike mechanical systems you need it to be inboard for setting up, so press the function button or the shifters to shift the mech underneath the largest cog. Bolt the mech on making sure the B-limit screw is in the correct position against the stop on the gear hanger.

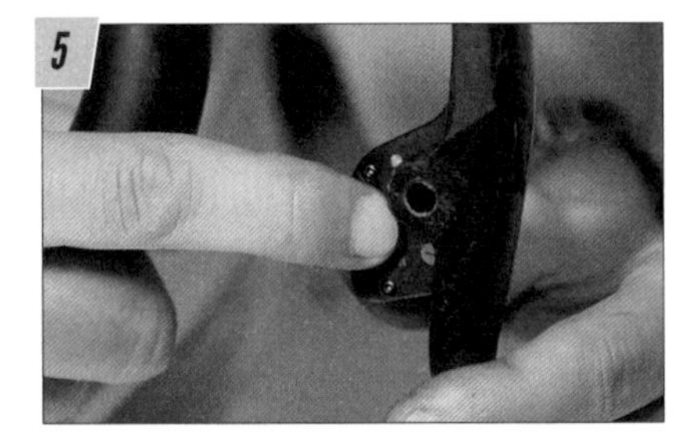

Move to the back of the bike and see whether the jockey wheels are lined up underneath the cog. If not, press the function button on a shifter and shifting simultaneously to micro-adjust. The right shifter moves the derailleur outboard, the left shifter inboard. Each movement is 0.2mm at a time.

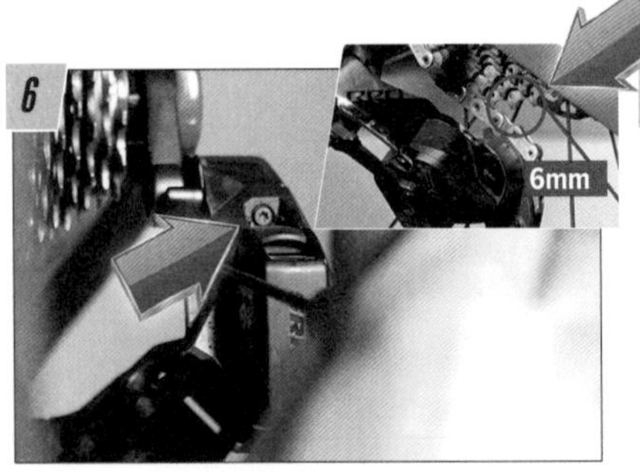

Still on the rear mech, you need to adjust the B-tension screw. This is familiar to mechanical systems as it sets the height of the pulley wheels under the cassette. With the chain in the largest cog look for a gap of about 6mm between top of chain and the closest part of the large cog.

Also familiar are the high and low limit screws that stop the derailleur overshifting at either end of the cassette. With the chain in the largest cog, adjust the lower limit (L) screw until it lightly touches the mech, then shift into the smallest cog and repeat the process with the higher limit (H) screw.

If you haven't already, now it's time to fit the batteries into the holders on the back of the mechs and put the chain on. If you're starting from scratch make sure you get the length of the chain right. Head over to page 68 for full instructions.

Need To Fit A New Cassette?
See page 70 for how to install it

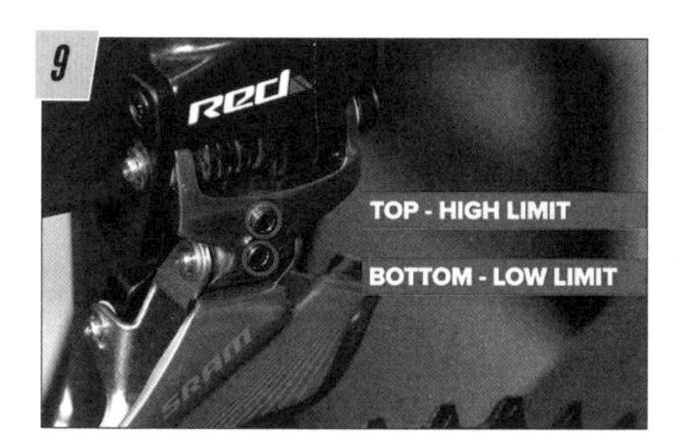

With the chain on you can now set the high and low limit adjusters on the front derailleur. Shift into the big ring and the smallest cog at the back. Adjust the H screw either in or out so that you get a gap of 0.5mm between the outer cage and the chain.

TOP TIP

The limit screws of mechanical and electrical mechs all work in the same way. That means you need to turn the screw anti-clockwise to move the mech inboard (towards the centreline of the bike) and clockwise to move it outwards.

Next, shift into the small ring and the largest cog at the back to set the lower limit screw. Using the same process, you want about 0.5mm between the chain and the inner plate of the cage so use the limit screw to adjust that. Turn anti-clockwise to move inboard, clockwise outboard.

To make sure the shifting is as crisp as it can be, eTap comes with little bracing wedges that fit between the mech and the frame. Choose the one which fits best and then slide into place. Check it's not pushing the mech outwards too much or that there's not enough room left for a bigger spacer.

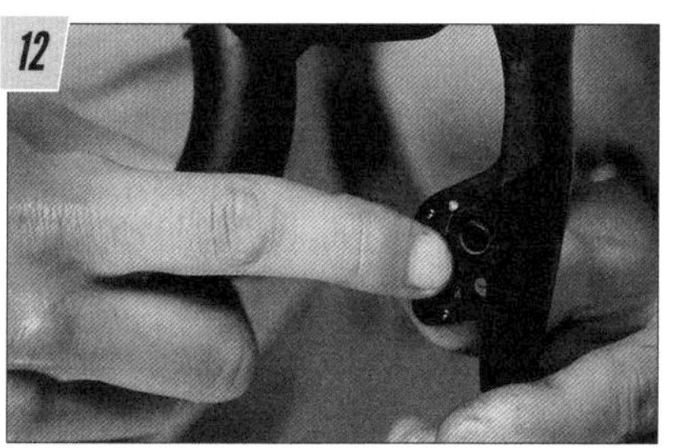

The only thing left is to run through the gears to double-check they work. Remember that you can do those little micro-adjustments (from Step 5) to the rear derailleur if it's not indexing quite right, or if it's making any grinding noises rather than running smooth and quiet.

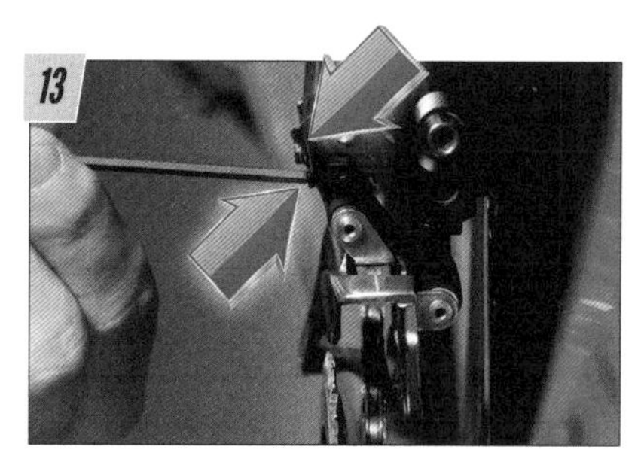

If the front shifting isn't quite right and you don't have that facility, just recheck the alignment, height and then H and L screws. Those are the only points of adjustment so you'll just have to juggle them until it all falls into place smoothly.

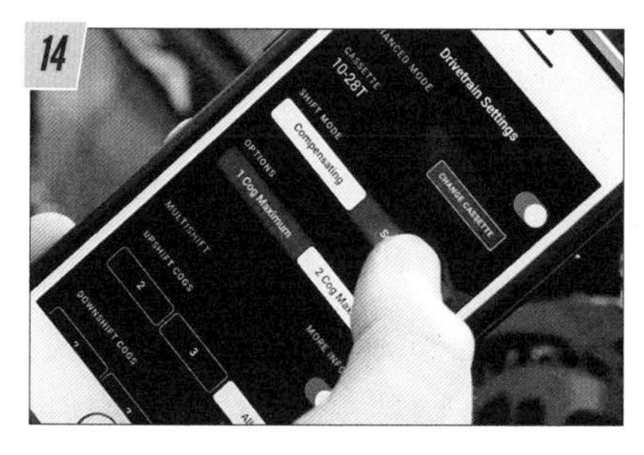

The final step is to sync the system to your SRAM AXS mobile app so you can program the shifters to your preferred normal, sequential or compensating modes. Once that's done, pair the system to your GPS (if you're compatible) and you're good to go.

TECH EXPLAINED

Battery Life

The amount of battery power you have remaining is a worry with any electrical component and the individual mech batteries on SRAM AXS are smaller than the single master battery on Shimano Di2. They'll still last for at least 60 hours of riding though and they can be swapped from front to rear if one mech (likely the rear) runs out faster. As well as a flashing warning light on the mechs when the battery is low, you can also set up an alert notification for your GPS screen via the AXS Mobile app. The shifters run on CR2032 coin cell batteries which should last at least two years of normal use, but we know some riders who keep a spare taped to the shifter body under the hood just in case.

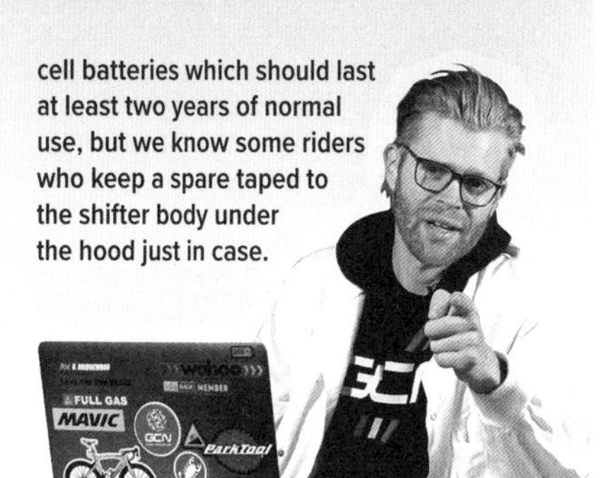

SET-UP SECRETS

HOW TO CONVERT TO SINGLE SPEED

Single speed bikes are lighter, simpler and look super-clean. Here's how to convert your bike to run just one gear

DIFFICULTY 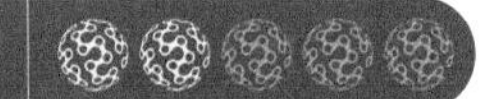

TIME 45 - 90 Minutes

TOOLS
- Cable cutters
- 4 or 5mm Allen key
- T25 Torx wrench
- Chain tool
- Master link
- Chainring bolt spacers
- Single speed conversion kit
- Chain tensioner

WHEN
- You want to ditch all but one of your gears

WATCH THE VIDEO

Free show-how and know-how

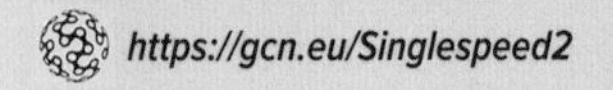

1

The first step is to remove your existing gears. Break the chain using your chain-tool or the split-link – if there is one. Undo the gear cables, snip off the end caps and pull them out of the outer cable and shifters. Unwrap the tape from the tops of your bars and remove the outer cables.

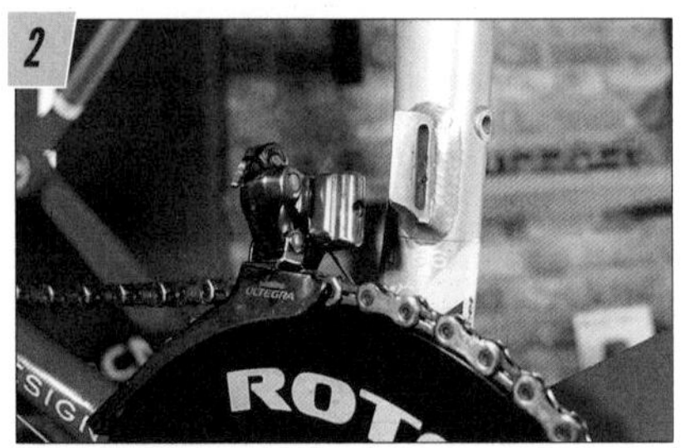

2

Unbolt the front and rear mechs and keep them safe with your cables in case your knees decide they want them back later. Now remove your chainrings using 4 and 5mm Allen keys or a T25 Torx key to loosen the chainring bolts.

TOP TIP

If you're really keen you can remove the shift levers or even the whole gear changing mechanism from your shifters. They can be a fight to re-install though, so wait until you're certain you like single speed before starting this surgery.

3

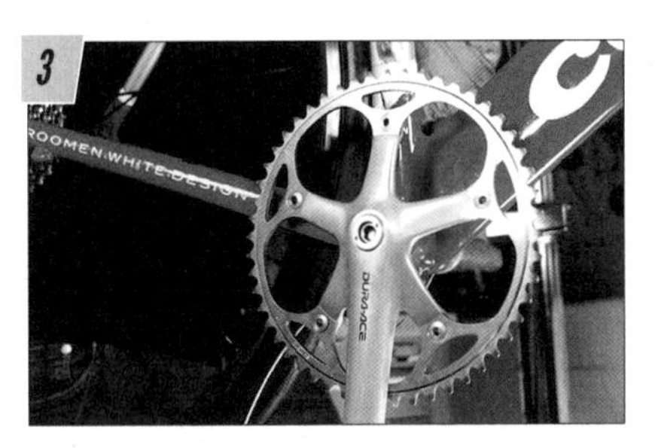

Swapping to a specific single ring will support and secure the chain better. Using a 44 or 46 tooth chainring will work well with a 16 tooth rear sprocket for general riding. You can just use one of your existing chainrings but you might find you are straining or spinning more than you want.

4

Whichever ring you use, mount it onto the inner position on your chainset to give the best chain line. Add the chainring bolt spacers to the chainring bolts where the outer chainring should be and tighten them up hard. See page 74 for more on fitting a new chainring.

5

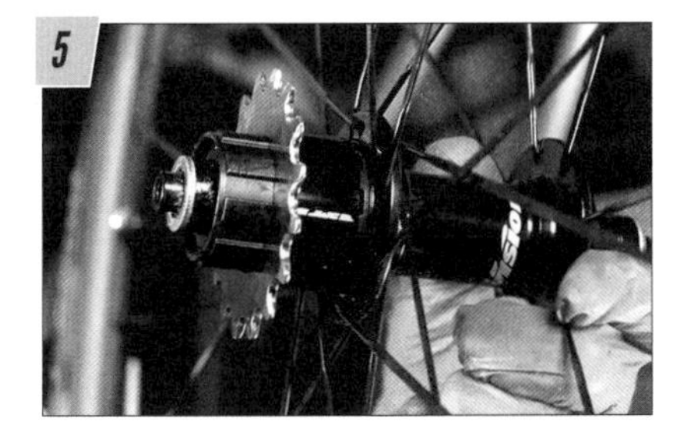

Remove the rear cassette. Follow the instructions on the single speed conversion kit to fit it onto the freehub. Don't tighten the lockring until you've adjusted the spacers either side of the sprocket to get the best chainline. Re-fit the rear wheel, then fit the chain tensioner into the rear mech mount.

TOP TIP

If you're converting an older bike with slotted rear dropouts you might be able to move the rear wheel back or forward enough to take up the chain slack without a separate tensioner. You'll need to tighten the quick-release very firmly though or switch to a bolted skewer.

6

Take your chain and wrap it around the chainring and sprocket to check the chain line is as straight as possible when looking from above. If it isn't, shift the sprocket by swapping the spacers from one side of the freehub to the other until it is. Now tighten the lockring fully and refit the wheel.

7

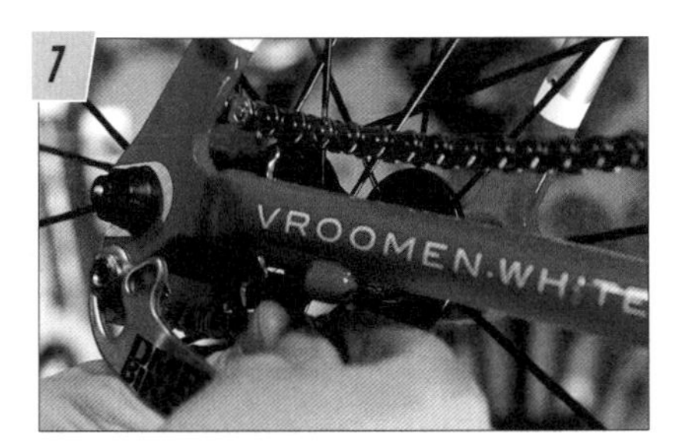

Wrap the chain around the chainring and sprocket, then remove links to make the shortest possible length that still runs smoothly. Rejoin with the chain tool and fresh chain pin or a quick link. Now hook the jockey wheel of the chain tensioning tool inside the chain so that it takes up the slack.

8

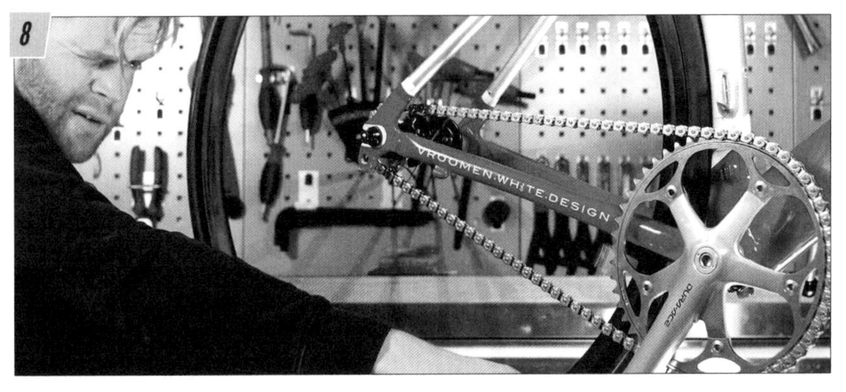

Check everything works smoothly by spinning the chain gently backwards and then forwards to turn the wheel. If it's all OK, stand back and admire how clean and simple your bike looks now.

Tune Up Your Rim Brakes
See page 118 to sort your stoppers

PIRELLI

SECTION 3

BRAKING

Whether you're running rim or disc brakes, here you'll find how to get the most out of your existing set-up, fix any problem and replace braking components

SET-UP SECRETS

HOW TO SET UP & ADJUST BRAKE LEVERS

Here's how to fit a new set of brake levers or adjust the position of your existing lever set-up

DIFFICULTY 

TIME	10 - 20 Minutes
TOOLS	• 5mm Allen key
WHEN	• You want to tweak your brake lever set-up

WATCH THE VIDEO

Free show-how and know-how

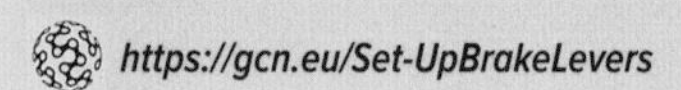

https://gcn.eu/Set-UpBrakeLevers

LOCATE THE MOUNTING BOLT

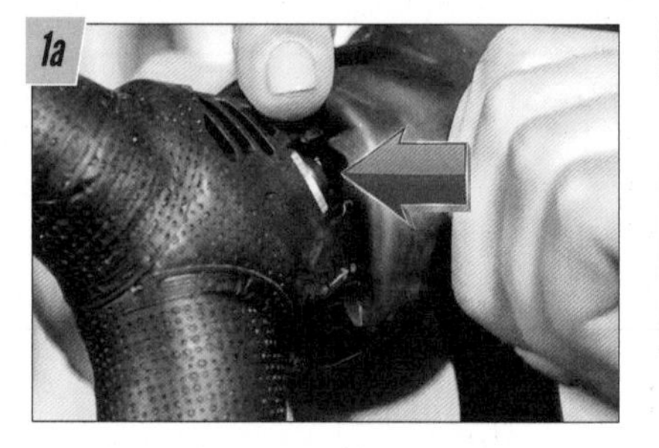

Before you can adjust anything you'll need to locate the mounting bolt that tightens the clamp holding the levers to your bars. Peel back your brake hood to expose the 5mm bolt.

If you can't find it, some models of brake levers have an access channel from the front of the hood, marked by a little slot or groove. You can insert your Allen key through there to access the bolt.

SETTING UP NEW BARS

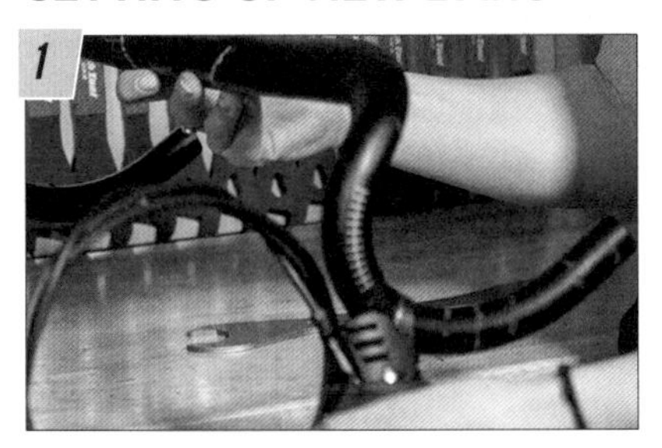

If you're building a new bike from scratch or you've got unwrapped bars with no cables attached, it's much easier to set your levers up.

Loosen off the 5mm clamp and slide the brakes onto the drops, getting them roughly in the position that you want them. Using a straight edge of some kind, place it under the flat drop section of the bars and line up the bottom of your levers with it.

You can position the levers higher on the bars for easier access when riding on the hoods or lower to make it easier in the drops. Of course, raising them will make it harder to reach when in the drops and lowering them will make it harder on the hoods.

If your levers allow you to adjust their reach, use this adjustment to make it easy to get your fingers around the levers on the hoods as well as when in the drops. The reach is normally adjusted via a bolt on the top of the hood using an Allen key. Turning the bolt will adjust the lever reach to/from the bar.

Once you're happy with the position, gently tighten up the lever and match the same position on the opposite side. Using a straight edge or a piece of string stretching from one lever to the other will help ensure they're even, and don't forget to check from above as well.

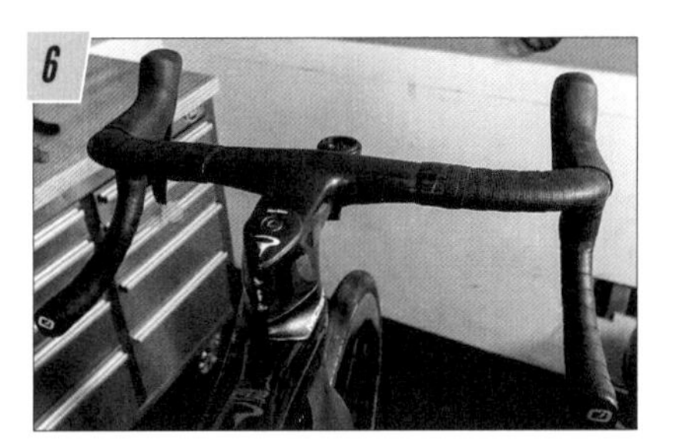

As a general rule you want the brake levers facing straight forwards. Though, if you have flared bars this might need extra adjustment to take account of the flare.

ADJUSTING AN EXISTING SET-UP

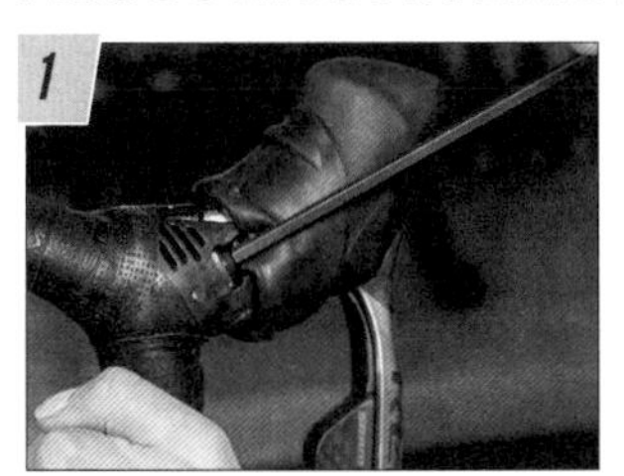

If you've got your bars wrapped and cabled already, it's a little trickier to adjust your levers. For tiny adjustments you can get away with pulling back the hoods, loosening the bolt and wriggling the levers around.

Be aware however, that your brake and gear cables might not like being pulled around while secured under the bar tape and could become unseated in the lever.

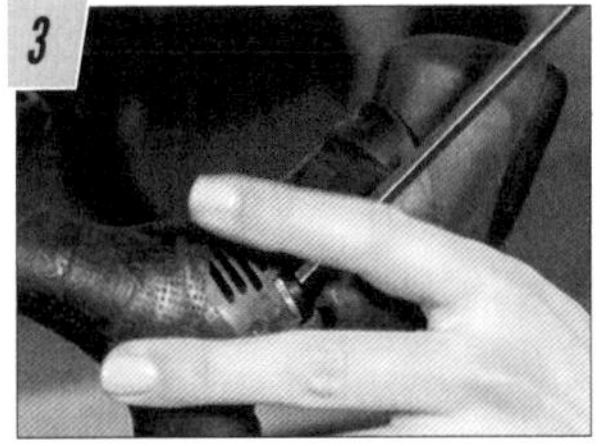

You might need to unwrap your bars to give the free movement required for proper adjustment of the lever – depending on how closely the tape has been wrapped.

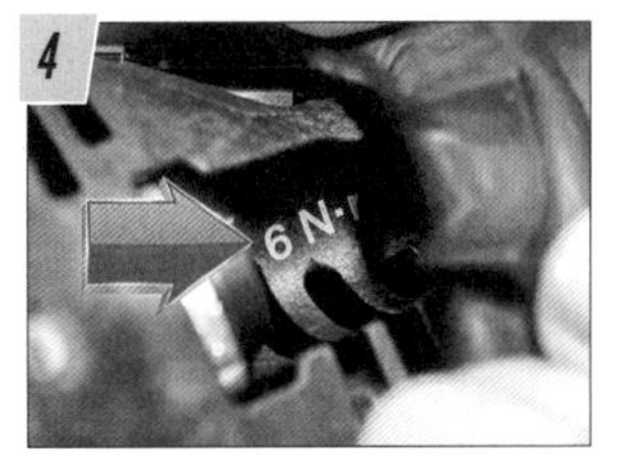

Re-tighten the bolts to the manufacturer's specified torque rating. If you haven't got a torque meter, the levers need to be clamped so they don't move easily. Too tight and you may well damage the bar.

Need To Replace A Brake Cable?
We show you how over on page 114

ESSENTIAL REPAIRS

HOW TO CHANGE YOUR RIM BRAKE PADS

Daily commuting, wet weather and big descents can soon eat through your brake pads. Here's how to change them and set them up properly

DIFFICULTY 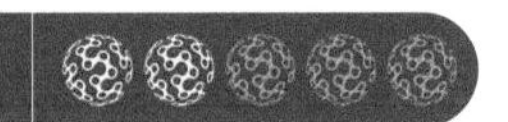

TIME 10 - 20 Minutes

TOOLS
- *Allen key*

WHEN
- *Your pads are near their wear limits*

Properly fitted pads will give much better braking performance than a badly set-up pair

WATCH THE VIDEO

Free show-how and know-how

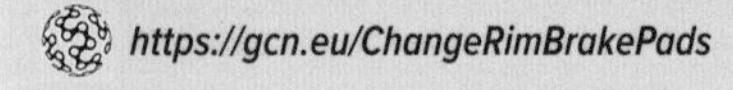
https://gcn.eu/ChangeRimBrakePads

TECH EXPLAINED

Brake Blocks Vs Brake Pads

Your rim brakes will either have brake blocks, where the pad is integrated into the mounting system, or a cartridge brake pad in which the pad can be removed from the mount. The cartridge pad system has the advantage of a mount that stays in place on the brake calliper. This saves you from the faff of repositioning them when you change pads.

> "The cartridge pad system has the advantage of a mount that stays in place on the brake calliper"

Toe-ing in your pads or blocks will massively reduce brake noise

First, remove the wheel by loosening the quick-release skewer or through-axle, then push up the release mechanism on your brake to open the calliper and drop your wheel out.

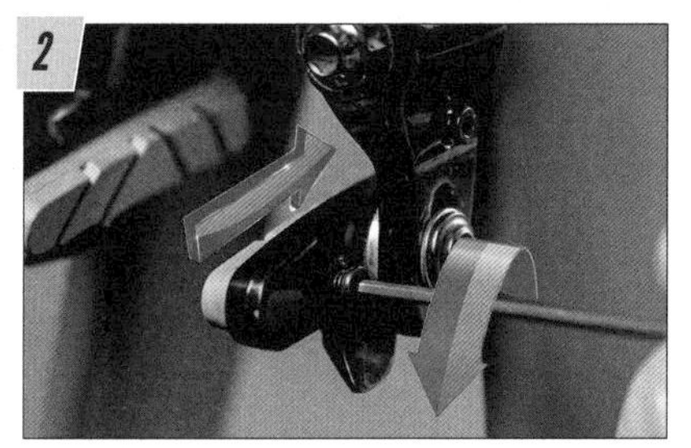

To remove brake blocks, you'll need an Allen key, or a spanner if you're working on an old bike. Simply undo this bolt and the pads will loosen and come off. If you have brake pads, there's usually a little grub screw that holds the pad in place. Loosen it off and slide the pad out of the mount.

Loosely refit your new pads or blocks into the brake calliper, then refit your wheel. Position the pads so that the entire pad makes contact with the rim's braking surface. Too high and the pad could rub on the tyre, too low and it won't make full contact with the rim.

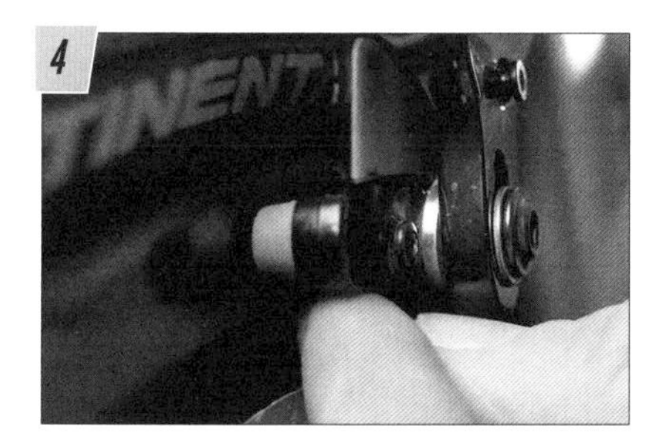

You also want to position the pad so the forward-most three quarters of it touches the rim a fraction before the rear – which is about 0.5mm difference. This is called toeing-in the brakes and it helps eliminate braking noise and judder.

With your new pads fitted, you'll likely need to adjust your brake cable tension, so wind in the barrel adjuster and release the clamp holding the brake cable. Then hold the brake pads against the braking surface with one hand and retighten the cable clamp with the other.

Want More On Setting Up Rim Brakes?
Then head over to page 118

ESSENTIAL REPAIRS

HOW TO CHANGE BRAKE CABLES

If your brakes are feeling rough, fit some fresh new brake cables to regain your bike's super-smooth stopping

DIFFICULTY 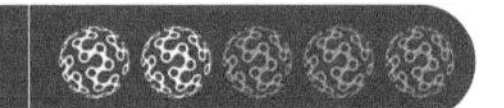

TIME 10 - 20 Minutes

TOOLS
- 5mm Allen key
- Cable cutters
- File
- Small pick

WHEN
- Your shifting is sluggish

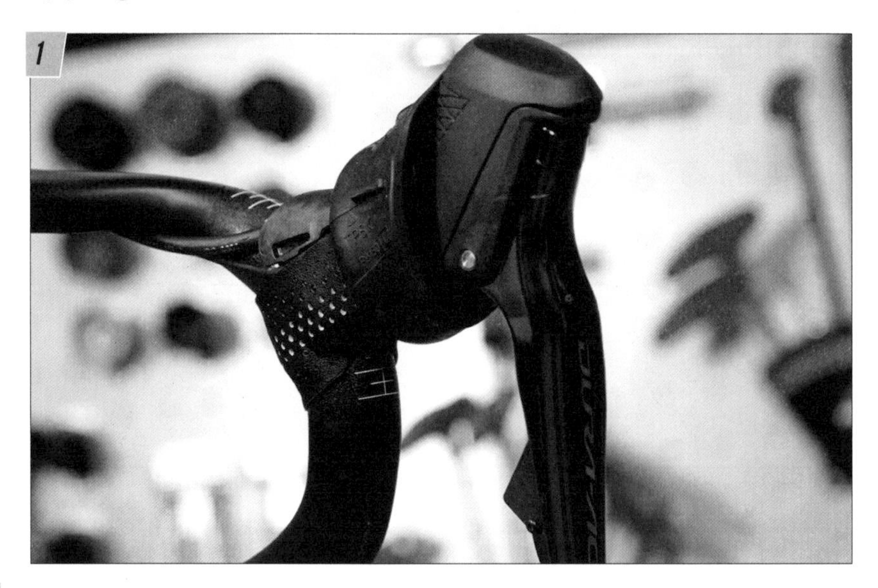

1

If you're replacing an outer cable, start by removing the top part of the handlebar tape. Once you've unwound this back to the shifter area, peel back the shifter hood to gain access to where the outer cable enters the shifter. Undo any electrical type tape that might be holding the cable in place on the bars.

WATCH THE VIDEO

Free show-how and know-how

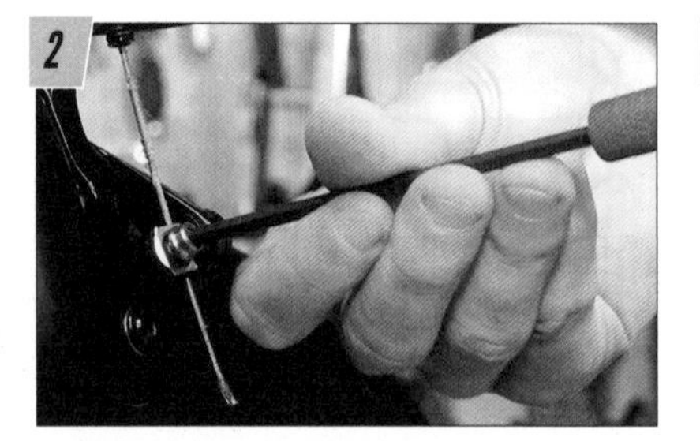

2

On the brake calliper, release the cable clamp bolt using the Allen key. Cut off the ferrule and any fraying strands so the inner can pass through the outer when you pull it out.

3a

If you have an internally routed frame and you're working on the rear brake, do not remove the inner or outer cable just yet – as you're likely to need to use one of them as a guide for your new cable. Read Internal Cable Routing Hacks on page 174, before going any further here.

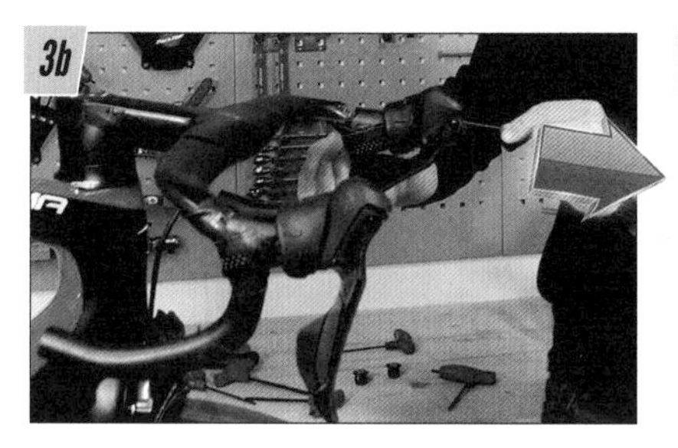

Move up to the lever and pull the lever inwards to expose the end of the cable. With a bit of jiggling, grab the cable end and pull out the old inner cable completely. Take note of where the cable leaves the lever as you'll need to insert the new cable into the same place.

Remove the outer cable from the lever and the calliper of the front brake, or the various sections of outer if you're working on the rear brake.

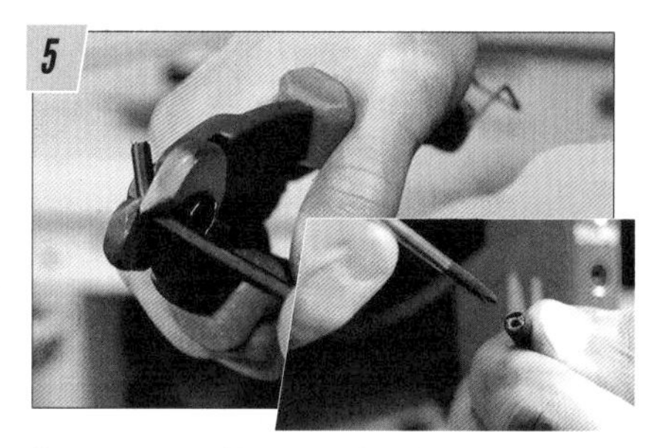

Cut your new cable outer to length – using the original outer section(s) you've just removed as a guide. Once cut, use the pick to gently open the inner part of the outer housing. You can also use the file to gently take off any rough edges.

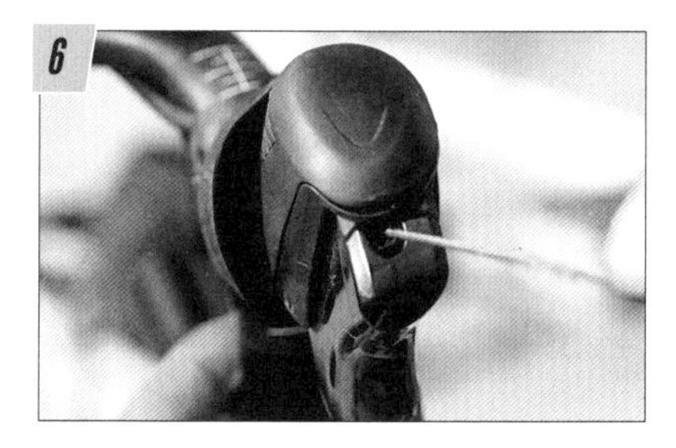

Thread your new inner cable through the lever, then add the first (or only) section of cable outer onto the inner and push the outer fully home into the base of the lever. If working on the rear brake, thread the inner cable through the frame and/or any other required sections of outer cable.

Thread the inner through the brake calliper barrel adjuster, making sure the barrel adjuster is turned all the way in.

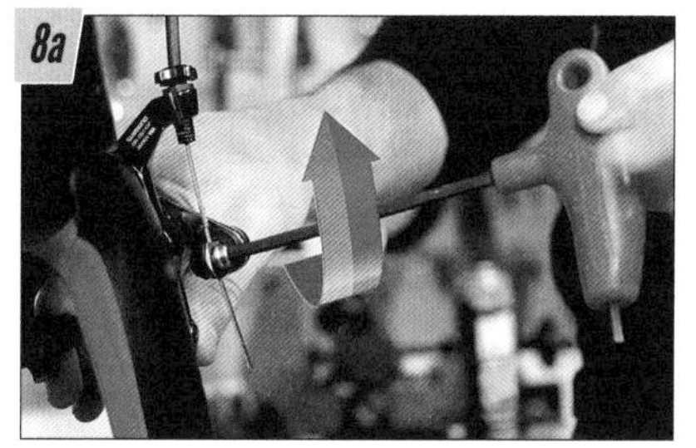

Pull the cable through the brake calliper clamp while simultaneously holding the brakes closed on the rim with the other hand. Hold the brakes in place while securing the 5mm bolt with your Allen key.

When you release the hand holding the brakes in place, they should settle into a good position. Trim the excess inner cable leaving 3 or 4cm past the clamp, then crimp an end ferrule on the end of the cable.

Now that's all in place, you can go ahead and tape the cable outer back against the handlebar and re-wrap the bar tape – there's more on fitting bar tape over on page 200. That's it, now you should have a lovely new responsive brake.

For The Perfect Rim Brake Set-Up
Turn over to page 116

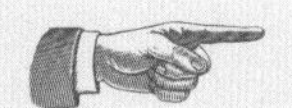

SET-UP SECRETS

HOW TO SWAP FRONT & REAR BRAKES

If your brakes are 'the wrong way round', it's simple enough to switch them back. Here's how to do it

DIFFICULTY 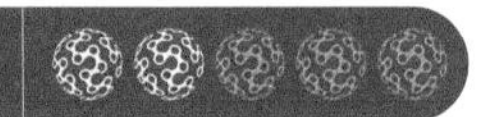

TIME 20 - 40 Minutes

TOOLS
- *Allen keys*
- *Cable cutters*
- *Cable outers*
- *Stanley knife*
- *Electrical tape*

WHEN
- *You want switch your brakes around*

TECH EXPLAINED

Brake Orientation

While in the UK, Ireland and Australia, bikes are sold with the rear brake on the left-hand side of the handlebars, in the vast majority of the world, it is the other way around.

If you buy a bike from another country or region, e.g. one coming from Germany into the UK, it may come with the brakes on the opposite side to what you're used to. Alternatively, you might have moved to a country which uses the a different standard to the one you usually ride with.

Either way, it's a very good idea to switch your brakes over to match what is ingrained in your head rather than retrain your braking habits. While you will likely be fine most of the time you ride, in a braking emergency you may well instinctively go for the brake orientation you're used to – which could result in serious consequences.

"If you buy a bike from another country or region, e.g. one coming from Germany into the UK, it may come with the brakes on the opposite side to what you're used to"

WATCH THE VIDEO

Free show-how and know-how

https://gcn.eu/SwitchFrontAndRearBrakes

To Adjust Your Brake Levers
Head over to page 110

1

First you need to remove both inner cables, so loosen the clamp bolt on your brake callipers which secures the inner cables and snip off the cable end caps with your cable cutters.

2

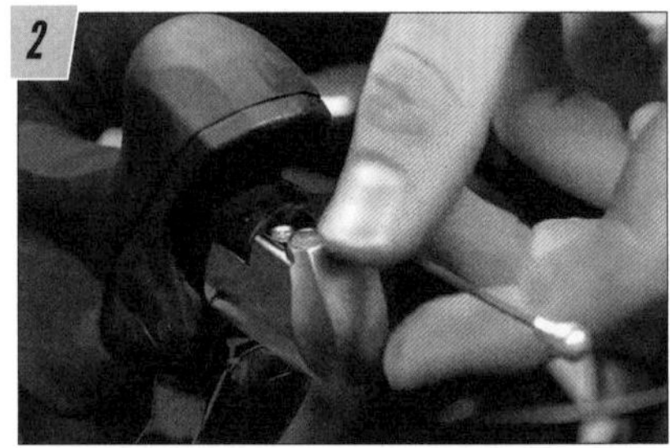

To remove the cable end from the brake levers, squeeze the lever to expose the end cable end, then pull the inner cable all the way out. Do this on both of the brakes.

Unfortunately, you're going to have to remove the bar tape to expose the outer cables secured beneath it, as they are unlikely to be the right length to work with the opposite brake.

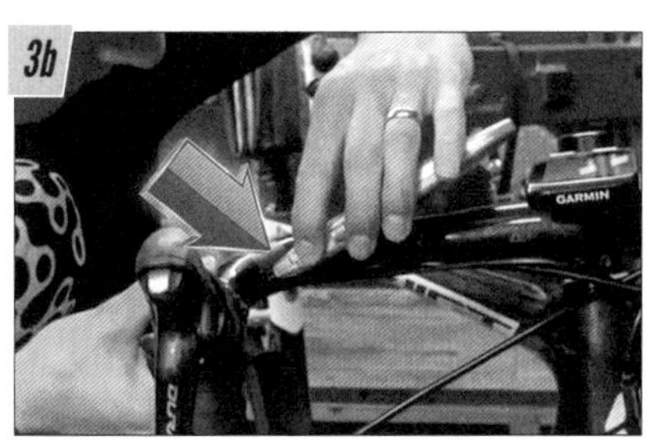

Use your Stanley knife to remove any tape that's helping to secure your bar tape, then unwind the tape to expose your outer brake cables.

Rethread your inner cables into the opposite brake to which they came from. You should be able to reuse the ones you've just removed unless they have frayed ends, in which case you'll need to replace them.

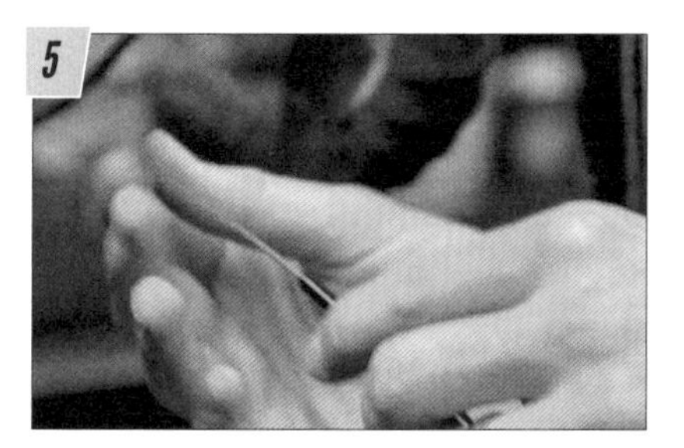

Thread your outer cables onto the inner cables, also ensuring you switch sides and the ferrules which attach onto each end of the outer are in place and orientated correctly (the pointed ferrule is the one that enters your frame).

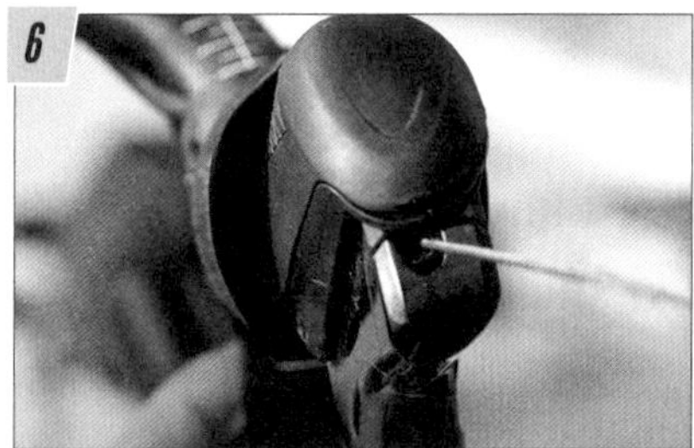

Thread the inner cables through your braking system and back to the brake callipers.

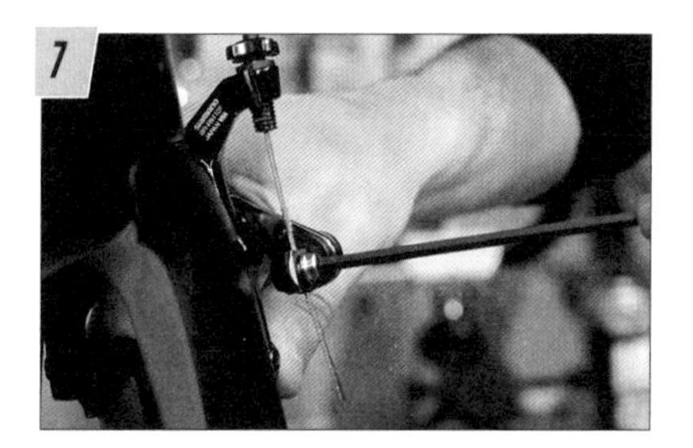

Slide your inner cables back through the retaining clamp and correctly tension the cables before tightening the clamp bolt back up. Ensure to screw your barrel adjusters on your brakes back down before setting the cable tension.

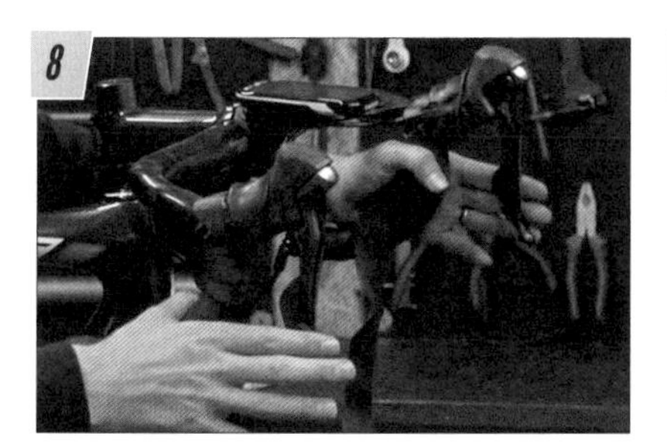

Before reattaching your bar tape, test your brakes just to make sure that everything is working 100 per cent.

Secure your outer cables onto the handlebar with some electrical tape, then carefully wind your bar tape back on and secure the free ends with electrical tape. See page 200 for details on how to wrap bar tape.

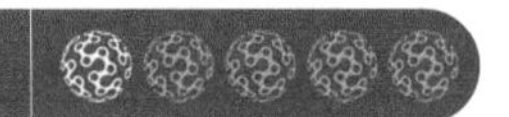

TOP TIPS

HOW TO CARE FOR YOUR RIM BRAKES

Follow these brake care tips to ensure your stoppers are always in top condition and performing at their best

DIFFICULTY

TIME: *15 - 30 Minutes*

TOOLS:
- *Allen keys*
- *Teflon-based oil*
- *File or sandpaper*

WHEN:
- *After every few rides*

CHECK YOUR BRAKE PADS

Brake pads can wear out at an alarmingly fast rate, particularly in bad weather. This means it's a very good idea to keep an eye on the amount of brake compound left on your pads – so you don't end up with massively reduced braking power in the midst of a ride.

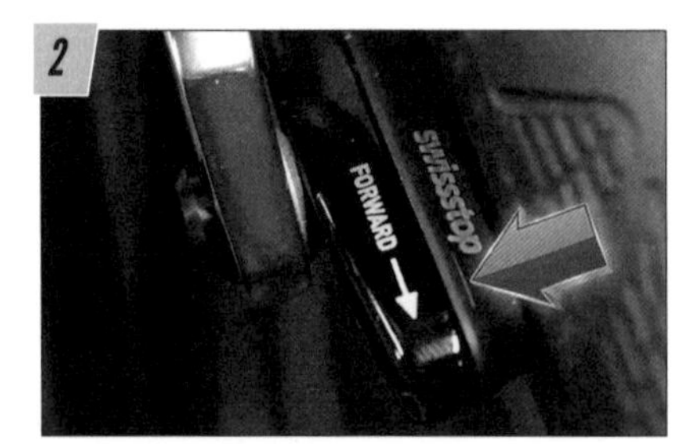

Some brake pads have wear indicators that tell you when to replace them, however, other brands don't. A basic rule of thumb is that anything less than 1.5mm of brake compound remaining and it's time to for some new pads.

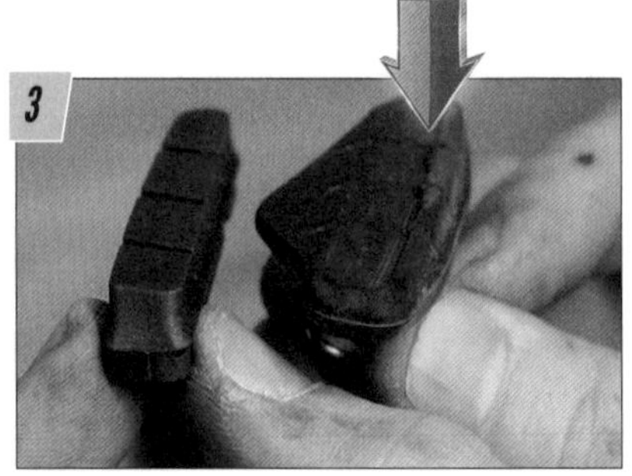

Check your brake pads are wearing evenly across the whole surface of the pad. If your pads have a ridge at the bottom, they are not properly positioned on the rim and you may be using the tyre wall to brake. If you find a ridge, remove the pad and file it flat, then properly reposition it.

WATCH THE VIDEO

Free show-how and know-how

https://gcn.eu/CareForRimBrakes

Need To Replace Your Pads?
Head over to page 112

When aligning your brake pads you want the front of the pad to touch the rim 0.5mm before the rear (called toeing-in, see page 121). If you're struggling to get that set correctly, then just make sure that the whole pad connects at the same time – but avoid the rear of the pad touches first.

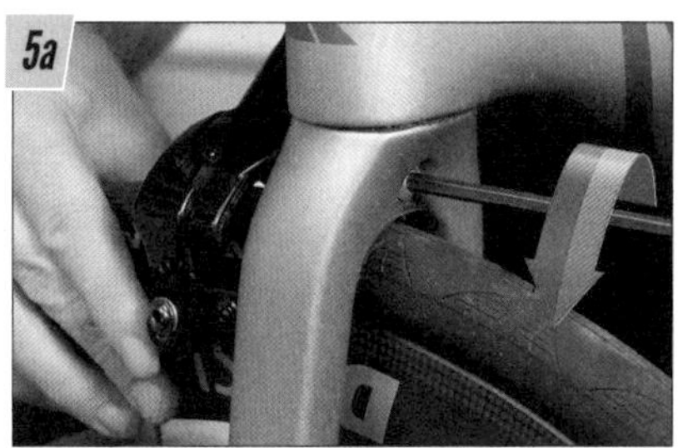

Also, check to see if both pads on each brake are wearing out at the same rate. If not, you'll need to make sure that that brake is aligned centrally. You may need to release the actual mounting bolt to line the brake up.

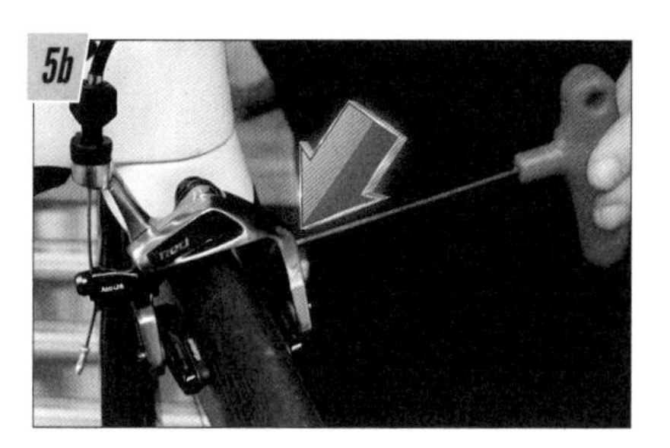

Alternatively, you could adjust the centring screw, just to make sure that both sides are touching the rim at the same time.

Closely inspect the brake pads. If you've got any grooves or channels in them, check closely for any embedded debris and pick it out. The same goes for any tiny shards of metal that are embedded in the pad. Any of these can reduce braking performance and prematurely wear the rim.

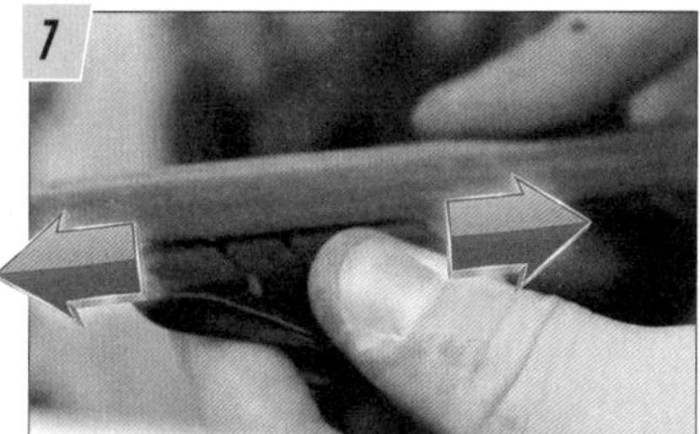

Sometimes your brake pads can become shiny which will reduce their effectiveness. So either use a file or some sandpaper and just take off a thin layer off the surface. This will help the pads stick better onto the rim and slow you down faster.

CHECK YOUR BRAKE CABLES

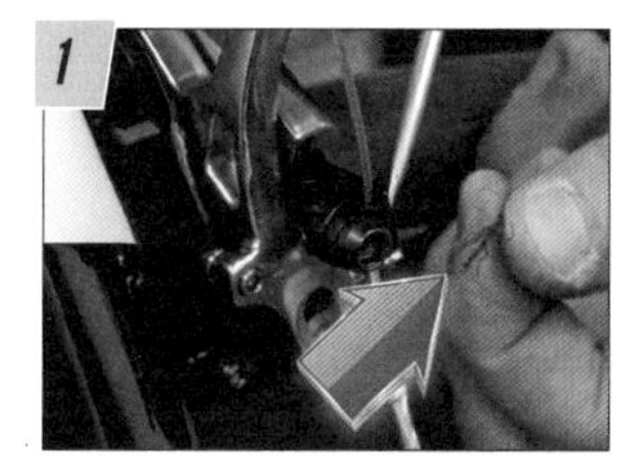

First, check your inner cables for any fraying where they clamp onto the calliper.

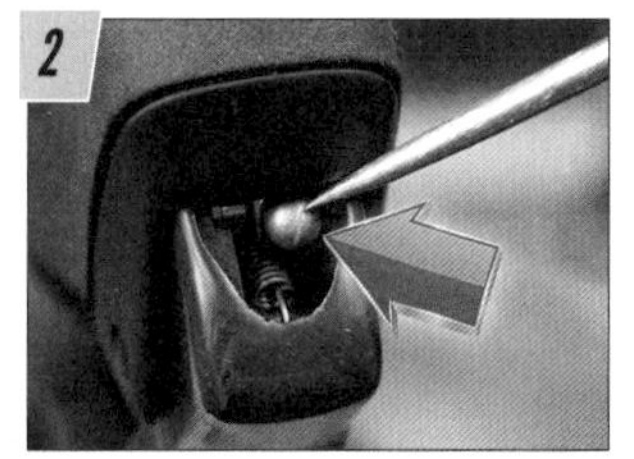

Pull the brake lever and check for fraying where the cable end sits in the lever. If you find any broken strands at either end of the cable, replace that inner cable before riding your bike as it could fail completely.

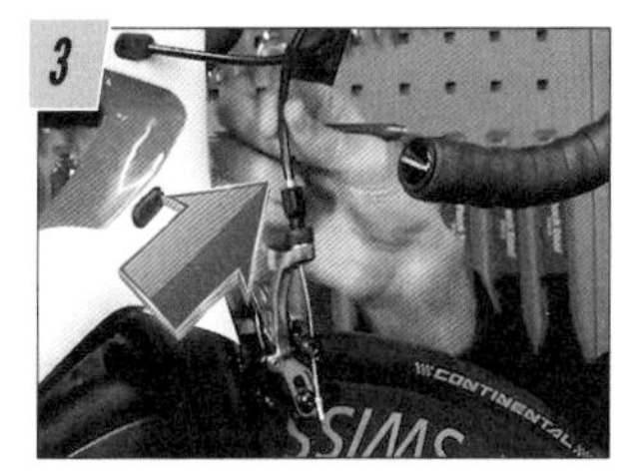

Check your outer cables for any splits, corrosion or other damage. Should you find any issues, that outer will need replacing – see page 114 for how to change it.

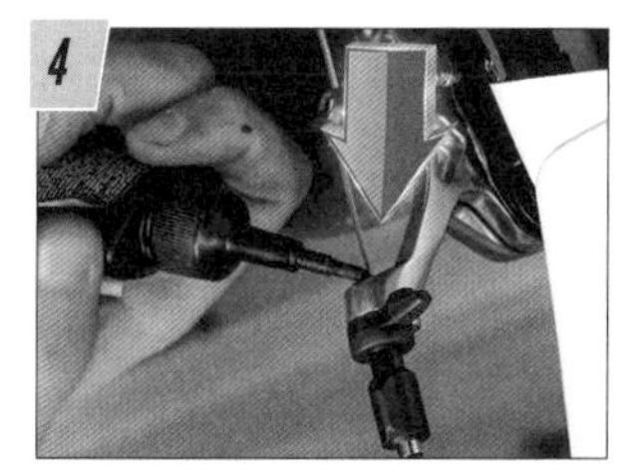

If your brakes are feeling a little bit gritty, a temporary solution is to turn your bike upside down and run a few drops of Teflon-based oil down the inners. Gravity will then help it coat the rest of the cable.

ESSENTIAL REPAIRS

5-MINUTE RIM BRAKE TUNE UP

If your brakes aren't running quite right but you're short of time to give them a proper service, follow our quick tips on putting them right

DIFFICULTY

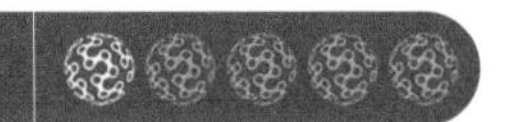

TIME	5 Minutes
TOOLS	• *Allen keys*
WHEN	• *Your brakes need a tune up, but you're in a rush*

WATCH THE VIDEO

Free show-how and know-how

BRAKE TUNE UP

GCN TECH 5 MINUTE...

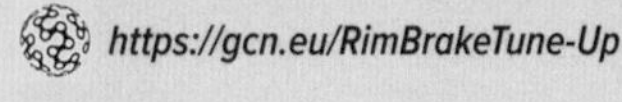
https://gcn.eu/RimBrakeTune-Up

CHECK YOUR CABLE TENSION

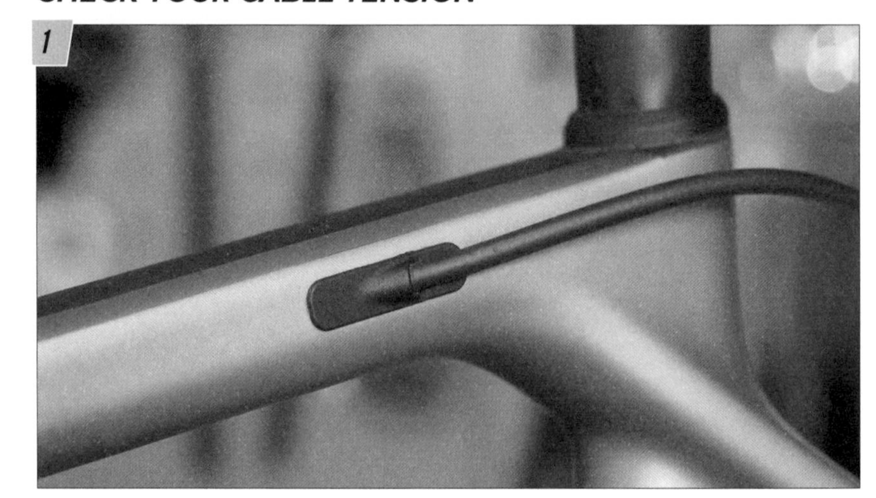

Check to make sure that your inner cable doesn't have any slack in it. This is especially important with the rear cable because there are often a couple of different cable stops where it could become stuck, e.g., where it enters or exits the frame. Make sure the cable is nice and tight throughout its length, otherwise you could find yourself grabbing a brake and very little happens.

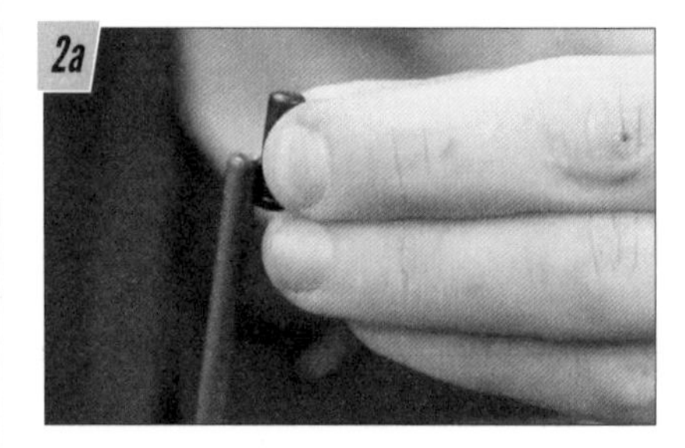

If you have ferrules on the ends of your outer cable, make sure that the outer cable is pushed all the way inside of them. If they aren't fully home, the outer cable may move instead of the inner cable when pulling the lever and result in poor braking.

If you don't have ferrules on the end of your cables, check that the outer cable is cut dead-straight, then push it all the way home into the housing of either the brake calliper or the brake lever for perfect braking.

SET YOUR CABLE TENSION

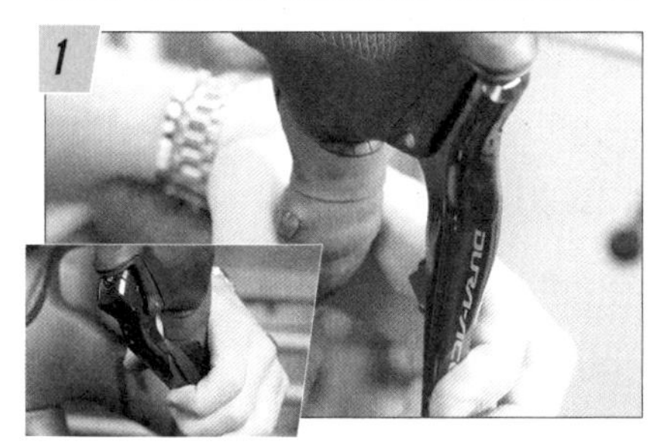

The distance of your brake pads from the rim is mostly personal preference. Some riders like them super-close for ultra-responsive braking, whereas others like to almost touch the bar before the brakes fully engage.

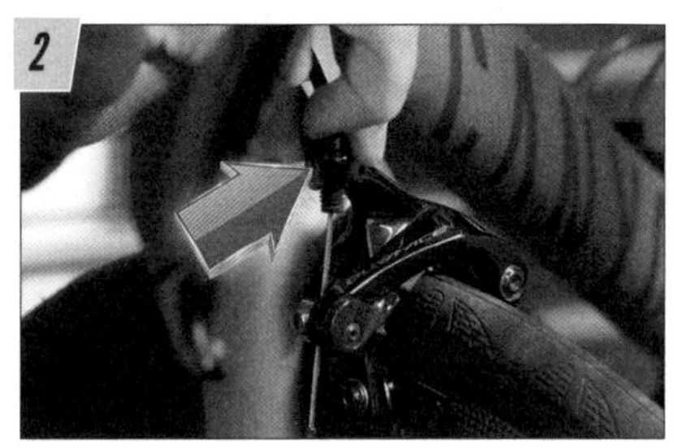

A good place to start is to hold the pads against the rim, then pull the cable through the clamp on the calliper and tighten it up, then use the barrel adjuster to fine-tune your brake lever pull to how you want it.

CENTRE YOUR BRAKES

To ensure your brake callipers are aligned centrally, release the brake mounting bolt either behind the forks or behind the seat stay bridge, then get the callipers as central as possible and retighten the bolt.

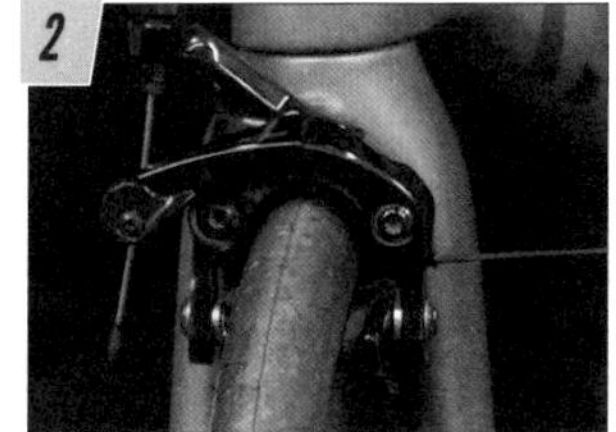

Most brakes have a screw or Allen key head on the brake calliper that allows you to fine-tune their pull. Adjust it so that both brake pads touch the rim at the same time when you pull on the lever.

ALIGN YOUR BRAKE PADS

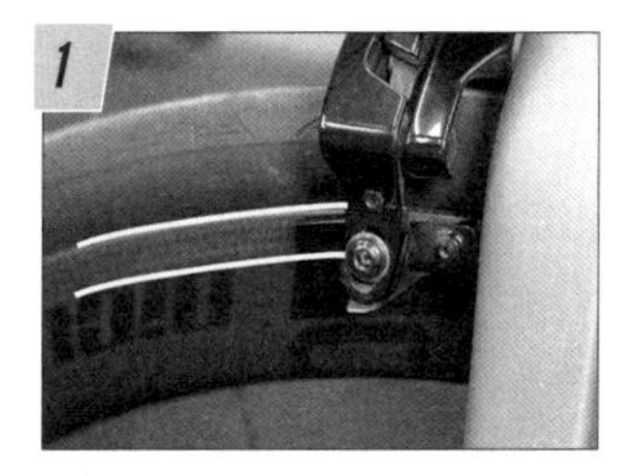

Check that your brake pads are in the centre of the braking surface. Too low and your braking will be poor. Too high and you're going to run the risk of your brake pads going through the sidewall of your tyre.

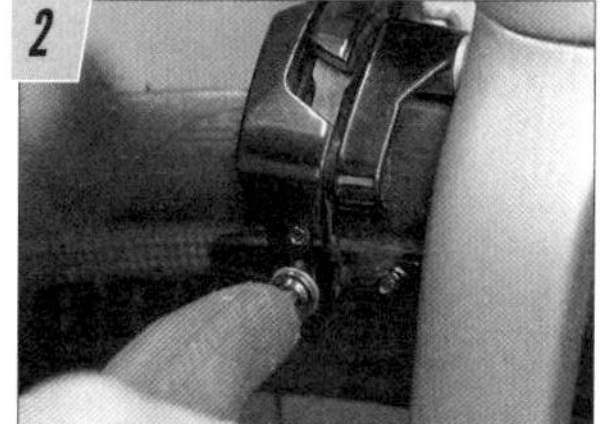

If you need to adjust them, use an Allen key to loosen the pad, then line it up and retighten it. Before you do it right up though, hold the pad firmly in your hands to make sure it doesn't move, then fully tighten it up.

TOE-IN YOUR BRAKE PADS

Check the angle of your brake pads as they touch the rim. You want the front part of both brake pads to touch the braking surface before the back third. This will give better braking and reduce noise.

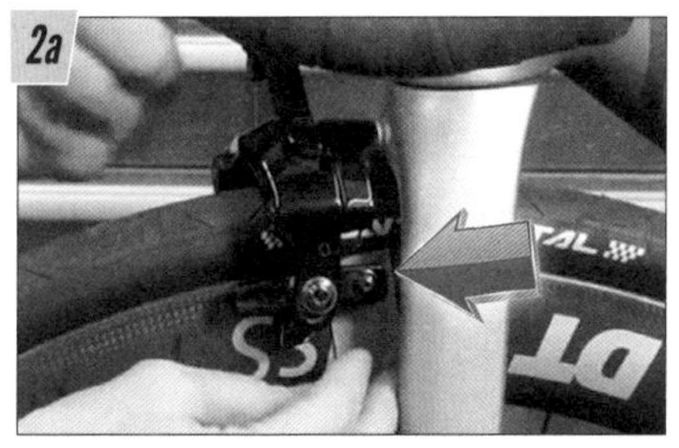

If they do not look toed-in properly, grab an old business card, or a bit of card from a cereal packet, and place it in-between the brake pad and the rim covering the rear third of the pad.

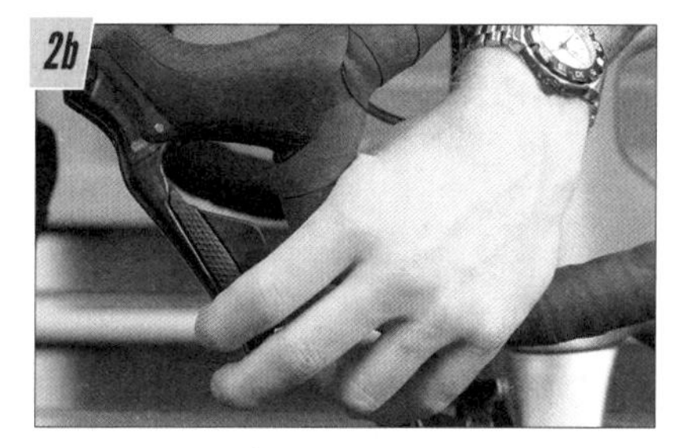

Now pull on your brake level and while keeping it firmly on, loosen then retighten the brake pad's mounting bolt. Repeat this process on the opposite side and you will have a perfectly toed-in brake.

To Recondition Your Callipers
Head over to page 126

SET-UP SECRETS

HOW TO FIT & SET UP CABLE RIM BRAKES

Upgrading your brakes can massively improve your control as well as stopping power. Here's how to install a new set

DIFFICULTY 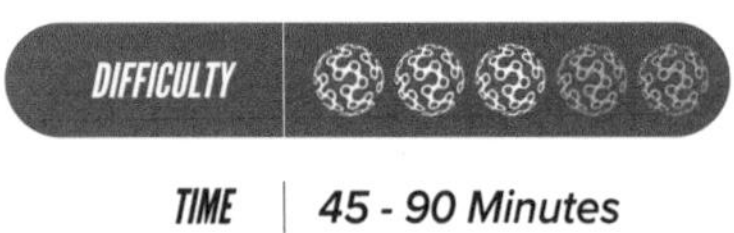

TIME 45 - 90 Minutes

TOOLS
- Allen keys or Torx keys
- Pliers
- Fresh inner cable
- Cable cutters
- Cable nipples
- Small piece of folded card
- Torque wrench

WHEN
- Your old brakes are beyond repair or you want to upgrade

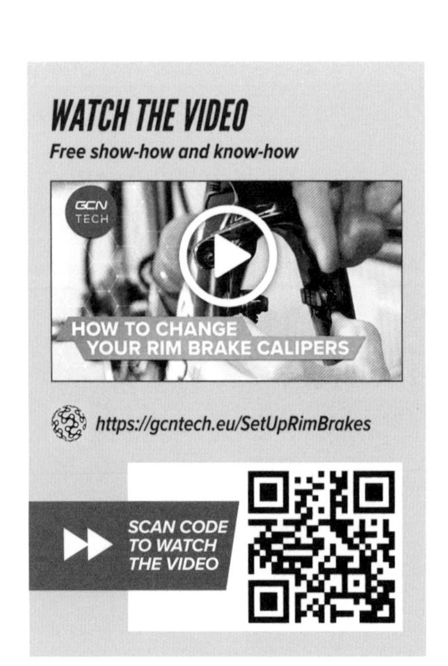

WATCH THE VIDEO

Free show-how and know-how

https://gcntech.eu/SetUpRimBrakes

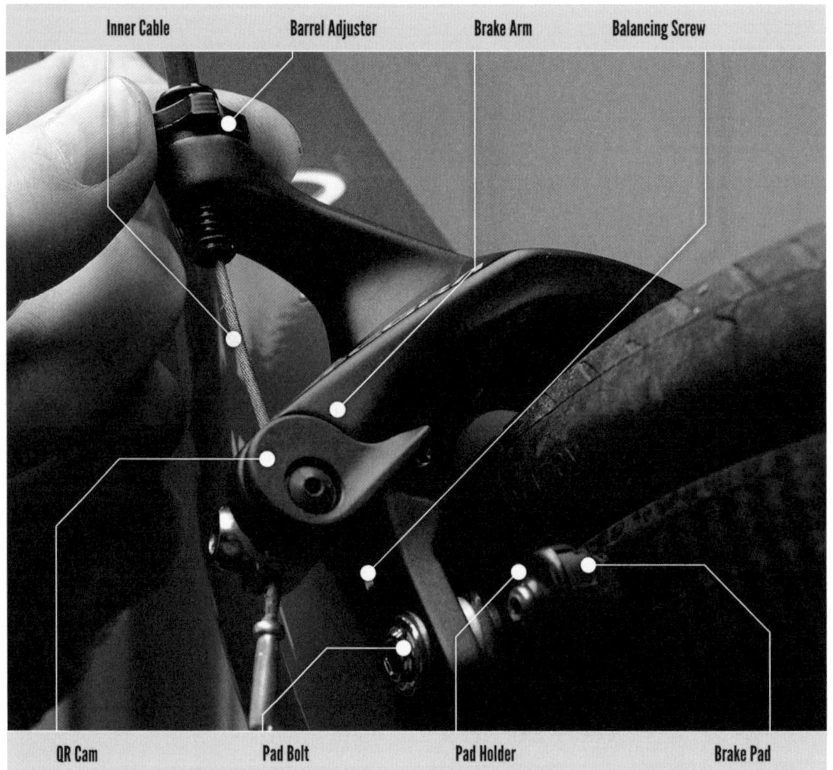

While many bikes are switching to disc brakes, including much of the WorldTour peloton, it's worth noting that the 2020 Tour de France was won by Tadej Pogačar (UAE Emirates) on a Colnago, the Giro d'Italia won by Tao Geoghegan Hart (INEOS Grenadiers) on a Pinarello and the Vuelta a España won by Primož Roglič (Jumbo-Visma) on a Bianchi – all of them with rim brakes. With over a century of development behind rim brake callipers they're now seriously powerful and sensitive – and still the lightest type of bike anchor too. So how do you fit and set them up so they perform at their best?

DIFFERENT BRAKE TYPES

There are two main types of rim brake – centre-bolt brakes and direct-mount brakes. Each requires a different frame/fork design so make sure you get the right ones for the chassis you're using.

Centre-mount brakes are the classic design, using a central bolt through the calliper arms. That same bolt extends

Direct-mount brakes are fixed to the frame by two bolts rather than just one

straight through the fork crown at the front and the brake bridge on the frame at the rear. This makes centralising the brake very easy as you can simply pivot it on the bolt from left to right to equalise rim clearance. The design means more flex in the brake arms though, as there's a longer lever between the mount point and brake pad. They generally have less room for tyres inside the arms too, with many topping out at 25mm officially.

Direct-mount brakes extend the two pivot-bolts of dual-pivot brakes into receivers on the fork/frame rather than a separate central bolt. That puts the mount point much closer to the brake pad for much better stiffness and fine control. They also have a wider stance so can take 28-30mm tyres and are compatible with chainstay mounts on aero bikes. Centralising them is harder though as you have to balance the springs not just rotate the brake on a central mount.

Centre-mount brakes are connected with just one bolt

BEFORE YOU START

Remove Old Callipers

Begin by unbolting the old callipers from your bike. First remove the cable crimp ends with your pliers and then loosen the cable clamp bolt with the appropriate Allen key. Pull the inner cable out of the brake but check whether it moves freely in the outer by holding the bare end and pulling the lever. If it still feels smooth with no resistance, then you can save time by re-using the current cable outer with a fresh inner. That's particularly useful if you're using an internal cable set-up which can be a nightmare to rethread a fresh outer through. It'll also save you re-taping your handlebars.

Once you've assessed the cables, undo the brake mounting bolts. These are located on the back of the brake bridge and fork on centre-bolt brakes or on the front of direct-mount brakes. Then remove the brakes.

> "There's over a century of development behind rim brake callipers and they're now seriously powerful stoppers"

INTEGRATED/INTERNAL CABLE SET-UPS

Routing cables through the frame has some aero benefits and looks tidy too. Trying to feed new outer cables through a frame to the right exit hole can be a real pain though. Which becomes even worse – unimaginably horrible in some instances – if your bike has internal routing through stem spacers/stem and bars of a semi or fully integrated cockpit. Unless you've got a proper vintage set-up with the cables coming out of the lever top, even external cable routing will require you to rewrap the bar tape over the top.

If that's all sounding like a proper battle then you'll realise why we suggest re-using outer cable runs wherever possible. If you're working on a new bike or the cables are corroded or 'gritty' in feel though you'll have to fit fresh outers. At that point it's up to you to assess your patience and competence levels against the cost of just dropping your bike off at your local shop and saving yourself the DIY hassle.

RECOMMENDED COMPONENTS

Quality Cables

If they're not supplied with the brakes, use the best quality cables you can. Reduced friction means more control at your fingertips and can be the difference between making a corner and hitting the deck. They'll also shrug off foul weather to give longer periods between servicing, so they're always worth the investment. To minimise cable friction, spray a little lubricant down the brake housing, so the cable runs extra smoothly.

Brake Pads

New brakes should always come with new pads installed, but if you're using carbon wheels you'll need to swap them to the correct pads. It's crucial that you use the pads designed to create the right amount of friction/heat to work with the specific braking surface lay-up of your wheels. If in doubt, check with the manufacturer for compatible pads or you risk damaging your rims, or just not stopping; either is a really bad outcome.

HOW TO FIT AND SET UP CABLE RIM BRAKES

Fitting fresh brakes is a simple reverse process, but make sure the mounting bolts either have thread lock on them (a light grey or blue 'paint' band on fresh bolts), or a dab of grease to stop them seizing into place.

TOP TIP

You need to make sure you're fitting the front calliper to the fork and the rear calliper to the brake bridge. This is easy to figure out on centre-bolt brakes as the rear brake has a far shorter mounting bolt than the front.

On centre-bolt brakes simply slide the mounting bolt through the brake bridge or fork, then affix the retaining nut to the bolt. Centralise the calliper by eye and then tighten until the calliper is difficult to move from side to side. It needn't be any tighter.

Direct-mount brakes fix onto the frame with two bolts – one each side. Hopefully they should come pre-balanced so that the pads are the same distance from the rim on each side. Be prepared to use the adjuster screw to shift the arm alignment one way or the other if they're not though.

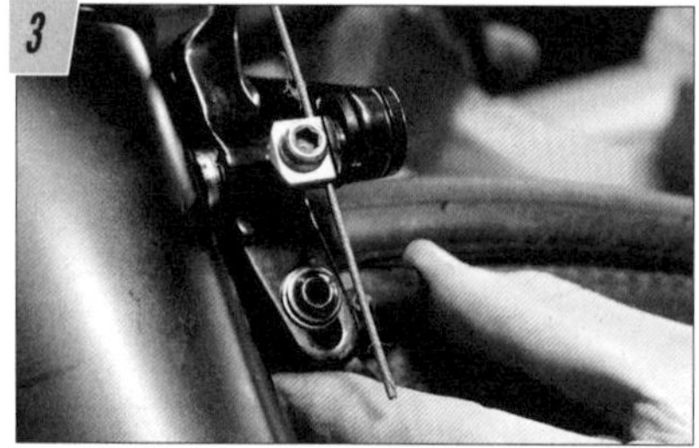

Next you need to make sure the brake pads are properly aligned to the rim. Use a 4mm Allen key to loosen the retaining bolts on the pads and wiggle them until they're aligned with the braking surface of the rim. The 'safe zone' can differ on carbon rims so always check before setting the height.

TOP TIP

To help prevent brake squeal with fresh pads on longer arm, centre-bolt rims, place a small bit of folded card under the back of the pad to 'toe them in' when setting up – see page 114 for more. You won't need to do this with stiffer direct-mount brakes though.

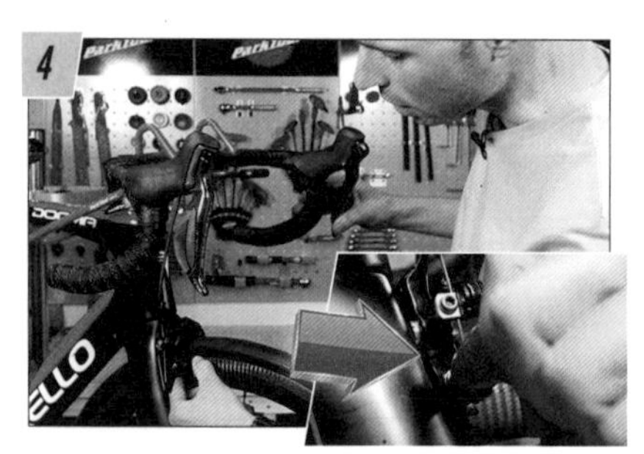

Hold the calliper closed against the rim with one hand, while tightening up the brake pad retaining bolt with your Allen key. Be careful that the pad doesn't rotate or move while tightening though. Repeat the process for each pad on each brake.

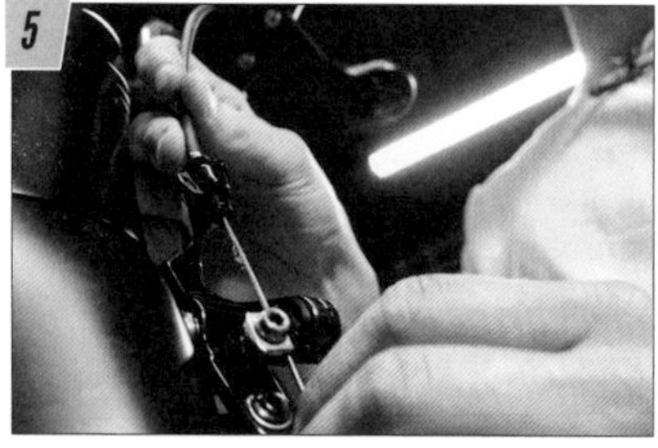

Now you can re-attach the cable. Wind down the barrel adjuster on the brake so that it's only slightly out and check that the quick-release on the calliper is in the closed position (usually pointing downwards). On Campagnolo brakes check that the lever is in the operating rather than open position.

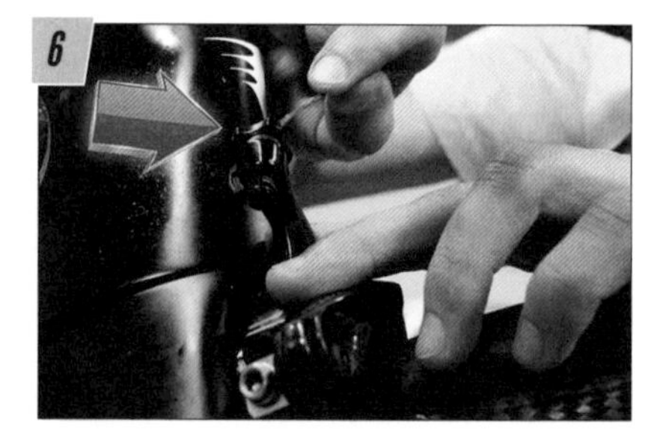

Insert the inner cable through the top of the barrel adjuster and make sure the outer cable end cap is firmly slotted home. Thread the inner cable through the groove under the clamp bolt. Check that the outer cable is securely fixed into the lever and brake ends as well as any cable stops.

TOP TIP

Always use a fresh inner cable even if the outer is fine. The fixed tip will stop it fraying and will make it much easier to install. It will slide a lot more freely for longer once installed too. Again, always use the best quality you can afford.

7

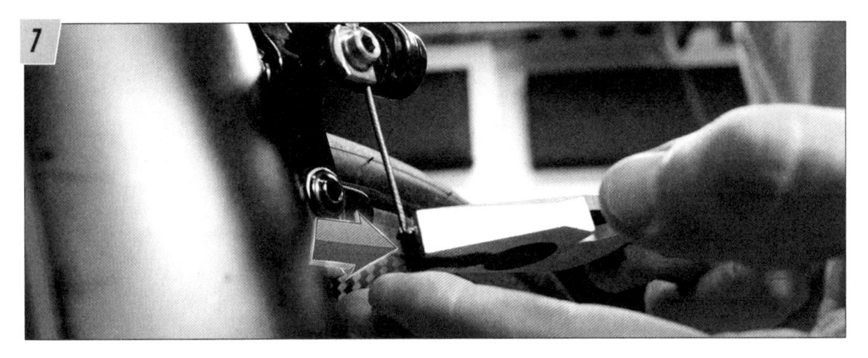

Pull the inner cable through firmly while holding the calliper firmly closed and then tighten the cable clamp to hold it in place. Release the brake calliper and spin the wheel. If the brake pads rub slightly then use the barrel adjuster to feed some slack into the cable so it spins freely. Trim the inner cable and crimp an end cap onto it to stop it slipping.

8

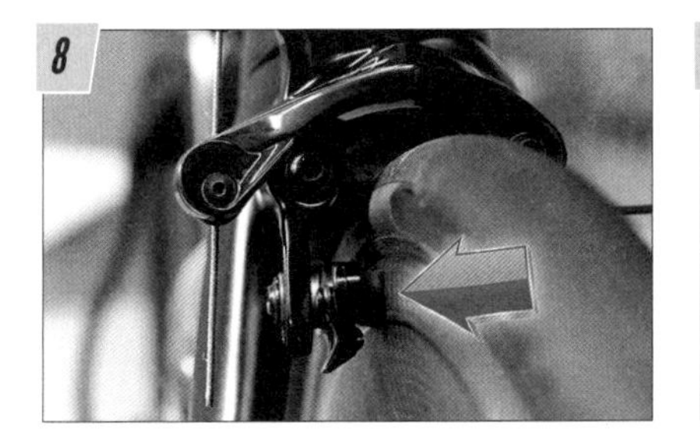

Check that the brake pads both hit the rim at the same time from the same distance apart. Centre-bolt brakes can be aligned by twisting the calliper slightly on the bolt. Direct-mount brakes will need balancing using the spring adjuster bolt on the top of the calliper though.

9

Once everything is adjusted and rebalanced, spin the wheels again to check for brake pad alignment. Pull the brake levers a few times to check everything returns to the right position. Check the wheel rims for damage or dirt. If they need it, give them a wipe with bike cleaner and then rinse.

10

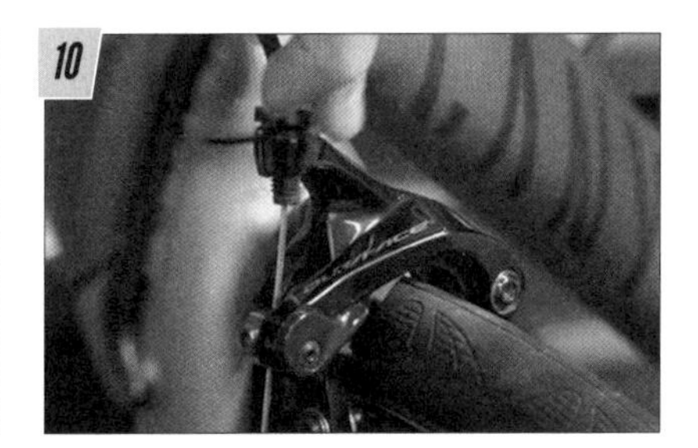

Before putting everything away take the bike out for a quick test ride. Pull progressively harder on the brakes while stopping to make sure the pads or the cables don't slip and that the lever position is where you want it. If not, adjust the barrel adjuster to adjust the rim contact in the lever pull.

TECH EXPLAINED

Pad Wear & Adjustment

As the pads wear down, the gap between pad and wheel rim will increase, resulting in you having to pull the levers further to get the same stopping power. Offset this by winding out the barrel adjuster to tighten the cable as the pads wear down. Keep checking the wear indicators (normally a groove or line on the pad) to be sure that there's still adequate life in the pads though.

"As the pads wear down, the gap between the pad and wheel rim will increase"

Need To Replace Your Pads?
See page 130 for how to change them

HOW TO RECONDITION CALLIPER BRAKES

If you've got a calliper brake that just won't pull evenly or is difficult to pull at all, this reconditioning procedure should get it back to full working order

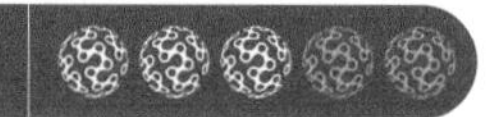

TIME 20 - 30 Minutes

TOOLS

- *Allen keys*
- *Ring spanners*
- *Spray degreaser*
- *Thick grease*
- *Cleaning rags*

WHEN

- *You have a calliper brake that's not working properly*

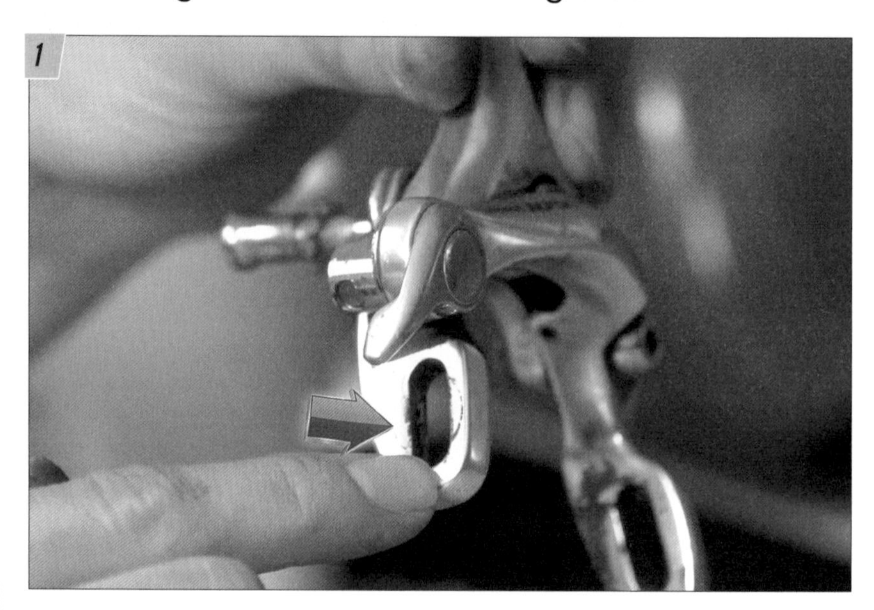

Remove the brake calliper from your bike and ensure to also take off the brake pads so as not to contaminate them during the cleaning and re-greasing process you'll be doing later on.

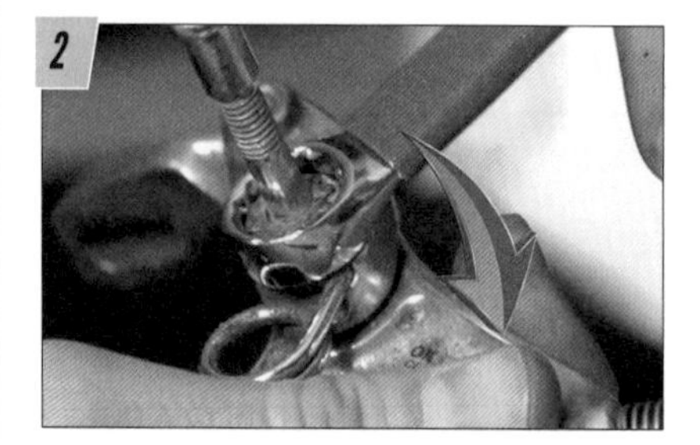

Next, you need to disassemble the central pivot which will allow you to remove the calliper spring and make the whole process easier. Loosen the central nut with a ring spanner, then you should be able to remove it by hand.

When removing each part in turn, it's essential to remember the order in which they will be re-assembled, so ensure to keep each one in a safe place and in the correct order.

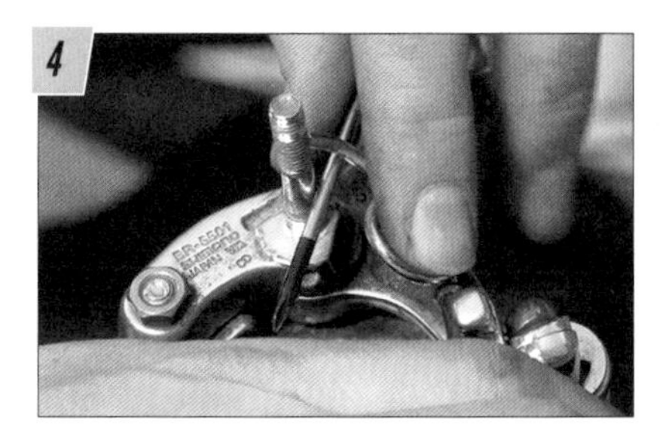

Without the central nut in place, you should be able to remove the spring. Gently lever it out with a small screwdriver or something similar.

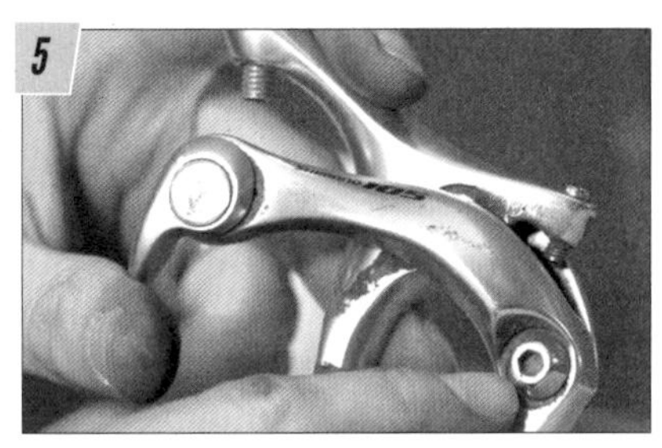

With the spring removed, you'll now be able to feel how your brake pivots are moving. If they are not moving freely, the pivot bearings are likely to be the cause of your problems.

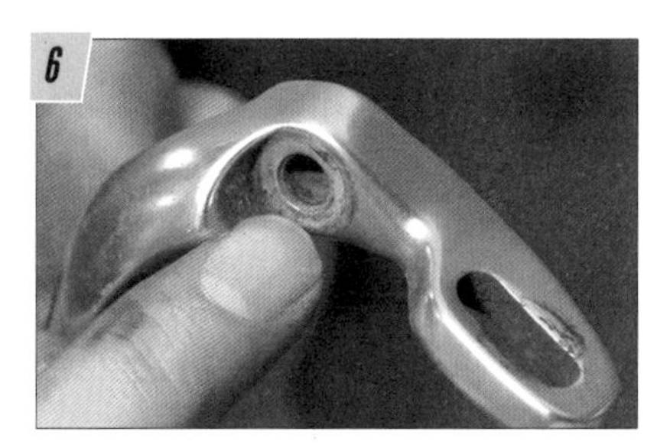

Next, disassemble the pivots themselves. Use an Allen key and a spanner to remove the first pivot bolt and its locknut, keeping an eye out for any bushings the pivot bolt may run through.

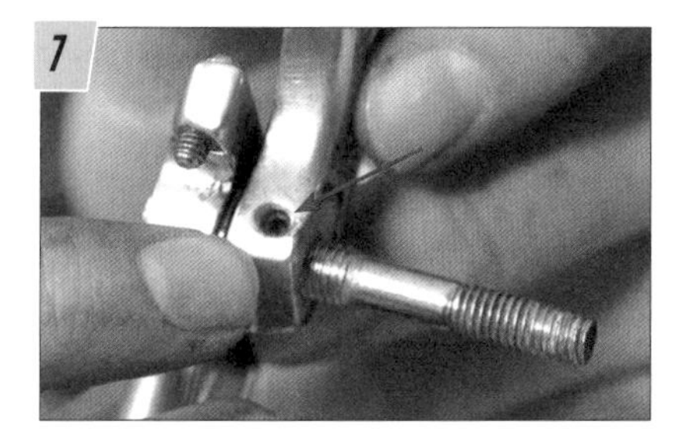

Check to see if there is a retaining grub screw that will need loosening (like the one on the Shimano 105 brake in the picture here) before you can remove the second pivot bolt.

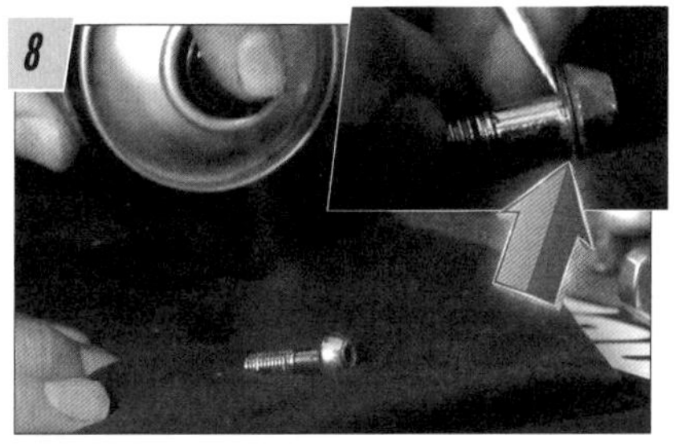

Grab your degreaser and liberally spray all the parts, then use the rags to thoroughly clean every part. If anything looks split, pitted or worn away, you may need to replace it, likely through cannibalising another brake of the same type.

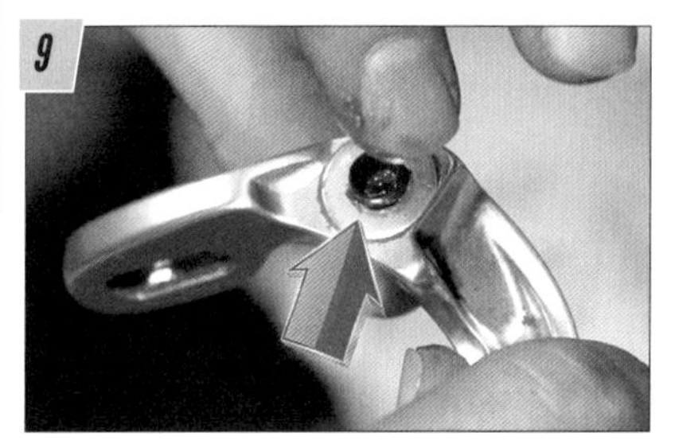

Now to reassemble the pivots, but before you do, ensure to apply some thick weatherproof grease to the inside of the pivots as this will help them keep moving freely as long as possible.

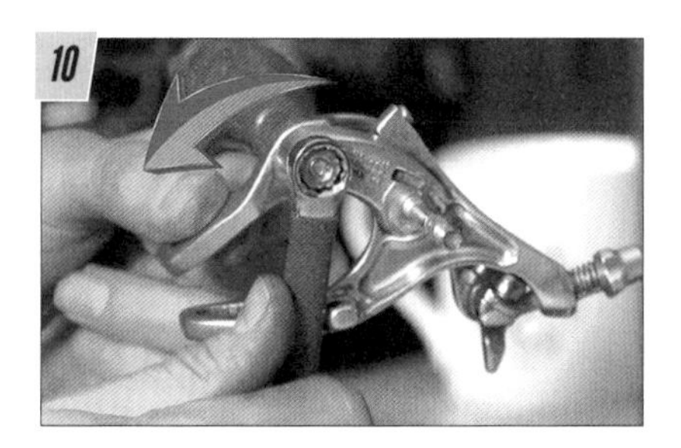

When reinstalling the second pivot, ensure not to over-tighten it as you'll stop the pivot from working. Once the bolt is tight enough to remove any unwanted play, replace the locknut at the rear and tighten that right up while holding the pivot bolt in place with your Allen key.

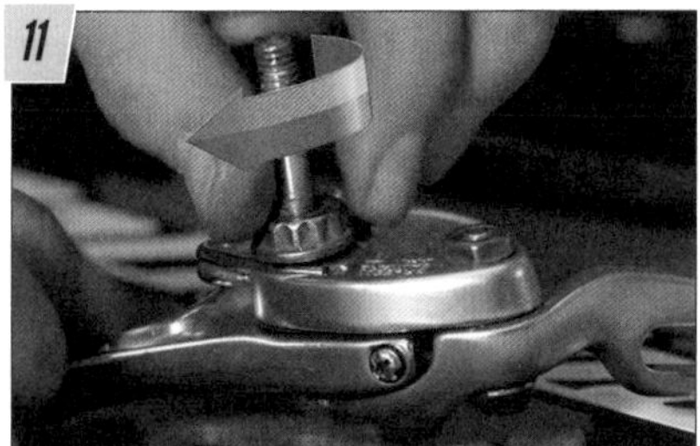

Attach the end of the spring that sits behind the central nut in place, then reinstall the nut. Tighten using a ring spanner.

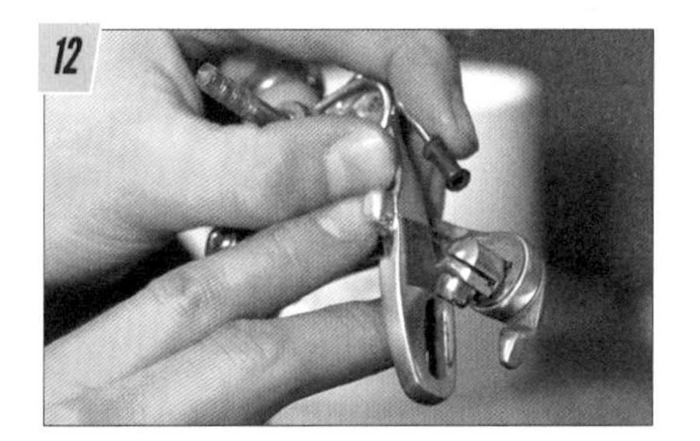

When seating the opposite end of the spring to tension the brake, it's a good idea to use something like an old rag to protect your fingers just in case the spring slips free and pinches them. Once done, you're ready to reattach the brake blocks and install the brake back on your bike.

Fed up with punctures?
See page 156 for how to go tubeless

SET-UP SECRETS

HOW TO FINE-TUNE CANTILEVER BRAKES

Cantilever brakes may not be the most powerful, but here's how to wring every last bit of braking force out of them

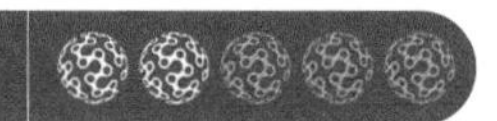

TIME 30 - 60 Minutes

TOOLS
- Allen keys
- Degreaser
- Grease

WHEN
- You want to improve your braking performance

INCREASE THE MECHANICAL ADVANTAGE

To get maximum braking power from your cantilevers you need to set the straddle cable as low as possible. There is a trade-off for increased power though as you'll reduce your mud clearance slightly both here at the forks and also at the brake blocks themselves.

Loosen the retaining bolt on the yoke, lower its position, then retighten the bolt. You'll also need to take up the slack in the straddle cable. Squeeze your levers to gauge how efficient your system is. The squishier the better, while a wooden feel means they're not as powerful as they could be.

> "To get maximum braking power from your cantilevers you need to set the straddle cable as low as possible"

WATCH THE VIDEO

Free show-how and know-how

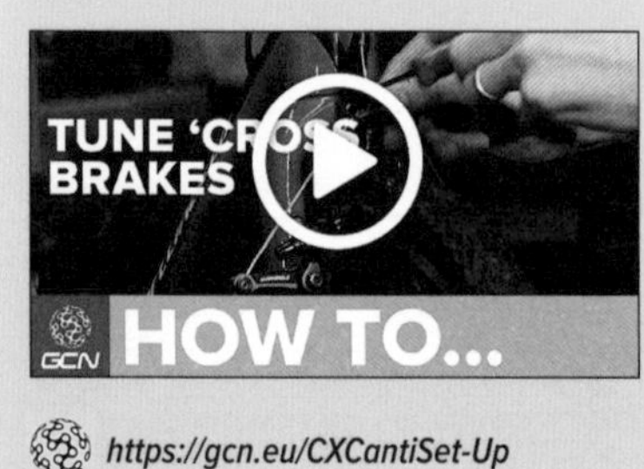

REDUCE FRICTION IN THE SYSTEM

So you lose as little braking force as possible through friction in the system, you need the cables to be running as smooth as possible. If they feel sticky or gritty, then you need to replace them.

Keeping the cable lengths to a minimum will help and if you've got the money, compression housing cables make a huge difference. See page 114 for more on setting up your cables.

SPRING TENSION

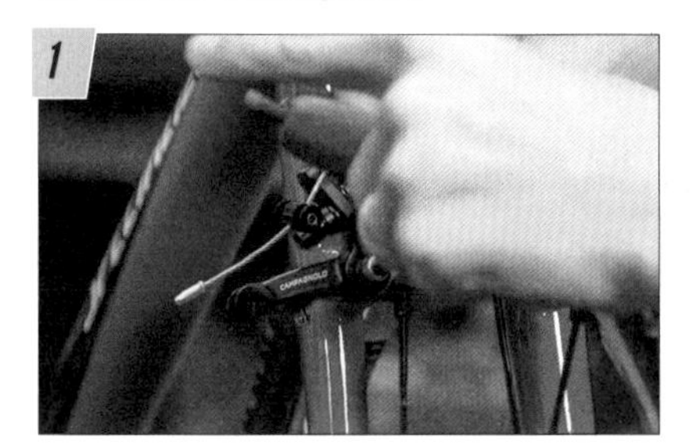

With the brakes unhooked from the cables, manually pivot them on the bosses to check for any excessive friction. If not, the chances are that the issue is coming from the bosses themselves. So unbolt the brakes and clean the bosses so they feel super-smooth and are free from any dirt or grit.

If there's any visible corrosion on the bosses themselves, gently them down with some fine emery paper. Once done, lightly re-grease them then replace the cantilever brake. Then tighten the brake mount bolts back up using an Allen key.

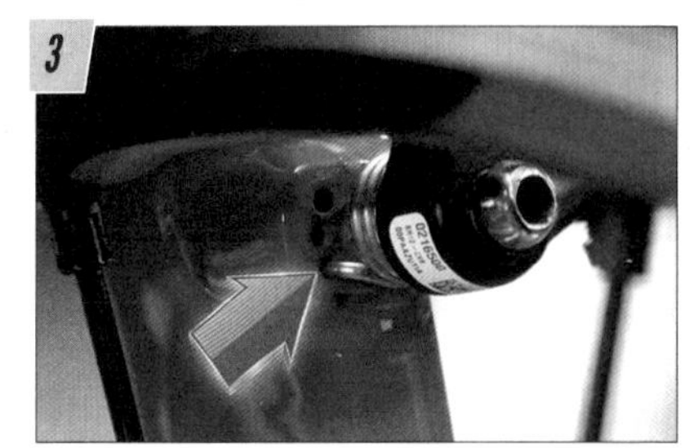

When you're putting the brake back on, fitting the spring in the middle hole is supposed to give the best balance for spring tension. If you want to experiment, the lower hole gives less spring tension while the upper hole increases it.

TOP TIP

Some cantilever brakes have their own bearings on in which case you need to look at those rather than the boss itself. If your brakes are the bearing type, then just clean and re-grease the bearings instead.

CHECK YOUR BRAKE BLOCKS

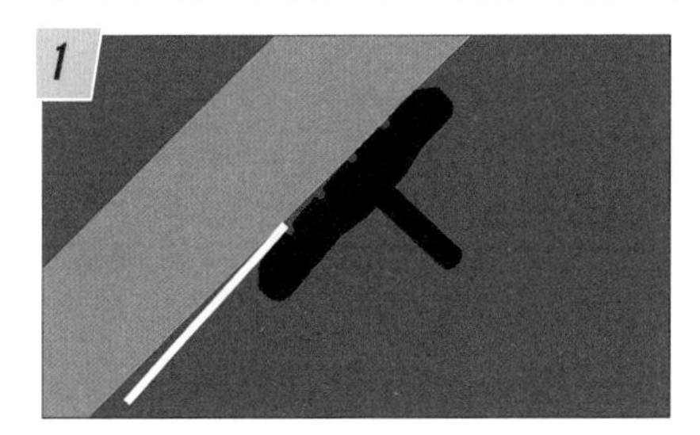

To help prevent brake squeal, you want the leading edge of the blocks to touch the rim slightly before the rear. To help position them correctly, place a thin piece of card at the rear of the pad as you tighten them up.

Check your brake blocks for excessive wear and to see if they have any small stones or anything else embedded in them. Remove anything you find jammed in there and replace your blocks if they are well worn.

BRAKE JUDDER

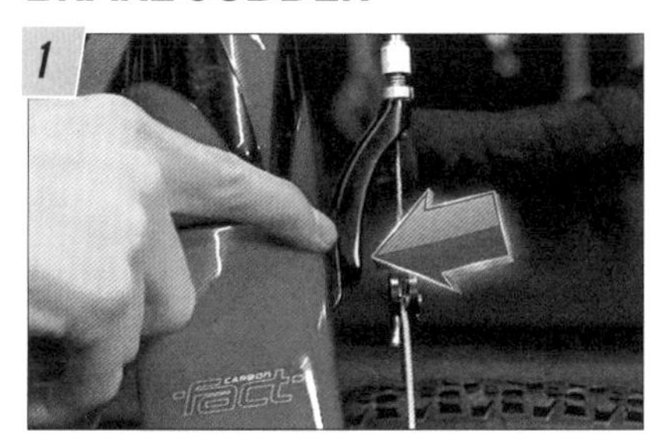

Juddering brakes are something that a lot of cyclo-cross bikes suffer from. If you have this issue, look at the position of your brake hanger. If it's up under the stem, move it down onto your fork if possible.

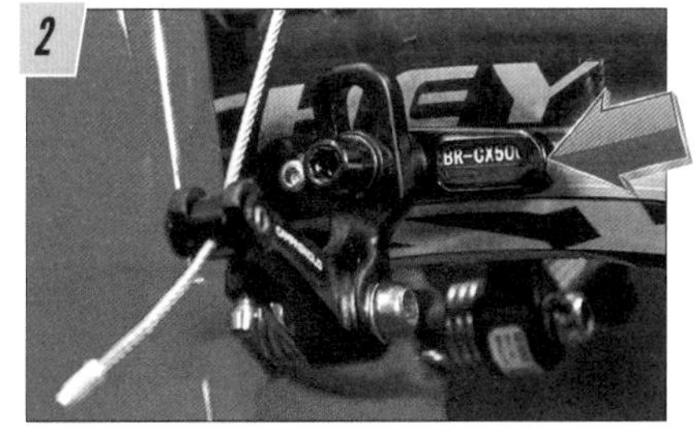

Another option is to increase the angle of toe-in on your brake blocks and see if that has an effect. Ultimately it could come down to there being a lot of flex in your forks, which is a costly upgrade.

To Adjust Cup & Cone Bearings
Head over to page 168

ESSENTIAL REPAIRS

HOW TO CHANGE DISC BRAKE PADS

Your disc brake pads will wear out over time, but fortunately it's a pretty simple job to replace them. Here's now to do it

DIFFICULTY 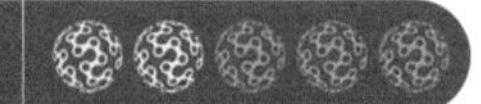

TIME	*10 - 20 Minutes*
TOOLS	• *Allen keys* • *Tyre levers or brake piston tool* • *Nitrile gloves*
WHEN	• *You have less than 1mm of braking compound left*

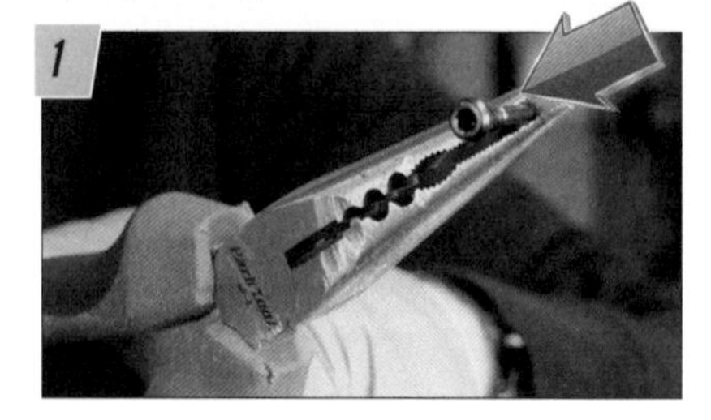

Remove the wheel to help access the brake calliper. Then remove the retaining pin or bolt and circlip. If you have less than 1mm of braking compound on your pads, it's time to fit new ones.

Remove the pads. This can vary from model to model, but they can usually be pulled out from the back of the calliper. Some pads have a metal clip to help the pads move back after braking.

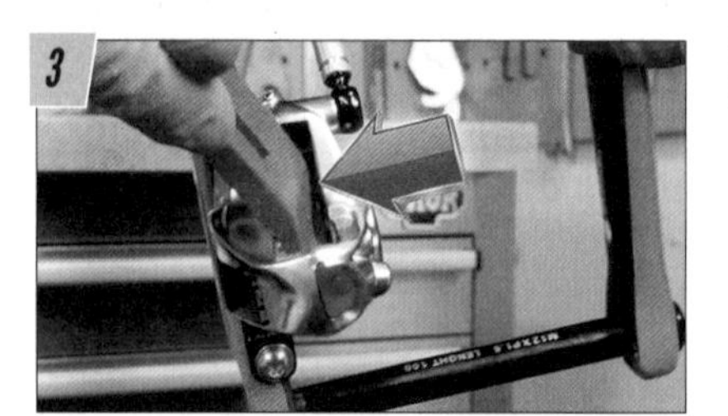

Before fitting your new pads, push the pistons back inside of the calliper with a tyre lever or brake piston tool, as the callipers would have been positioned to fit your old worn out pads.

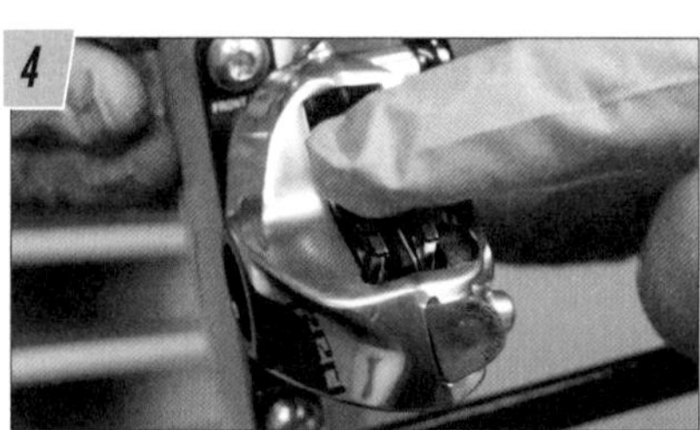

Carefully fit the new pads and metal clip, then refit the retaining bolt to the torque setting – if marked. If not, the bolt head needs be snug against the calliper. Then fit the circlip to other end of the bolt.

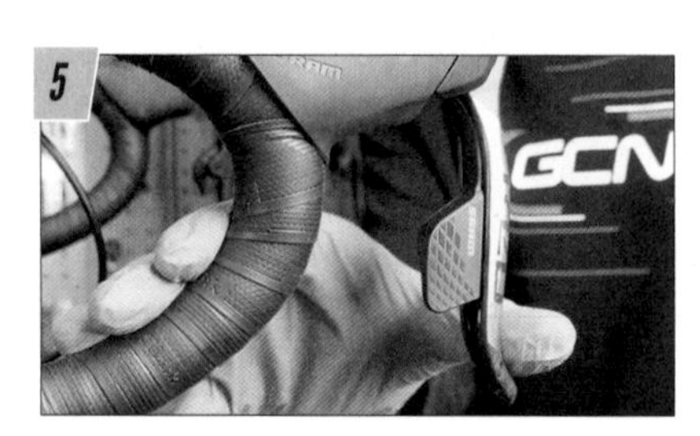

Give the lever a few pumps and the pads should find themselves back in a good position. But before going out for a ride, bed in the pads with repeated firm braking at medium and fairly fast speeds.

WATCH THE VIDEO

Free show-how and know-how

https://gcn.eu/ChangeDiscBrakePads

TECH EXPLAINED

Different Pad Types

Organic pads work well when cold, are quiet, but wear out quickly and are less effective when hot, while metallic pads work less well when cold, can be noisy, wear well and are effective when they heat up. Semi-metallic pads combine elements from both organic and metallic.

ESSENTIAL REPAIRS

HOW TO TRUE A DISC BRAKE ROTOR

If you've repositioned your brake calliper, but you're still getting disc brake rub, your rotor may well need truing

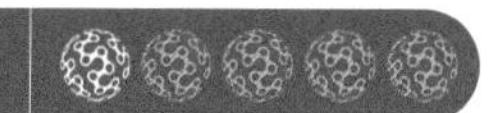

TIME 10 - 20 Minutes

TOOLS
- *Workstand*
- *A4 sized piece of paper*
- *Rotor truing tool or large adjustable wrench*

WHEN
- *Your rotor is bent and rubbing on your pads*

Usually disc brake rub can be cured by repositioning your callipers (see page 138 for how to do exactly that), but it's also possible that it's caused by a bent rotor.

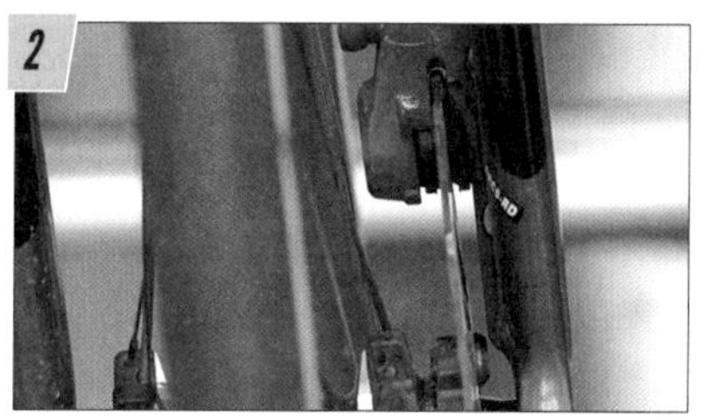

With your bike in a workstand, place your piece of paper on the floor below the rotor and spin the wheel. Look through the calliper to see where the rotor is bent and in which direction.

Take your rotor truing tool, fit the split end over the offending bit of rotor and bend it back into shape. There will be a bit of spring in your rotor, so carefully give it a bit of force.

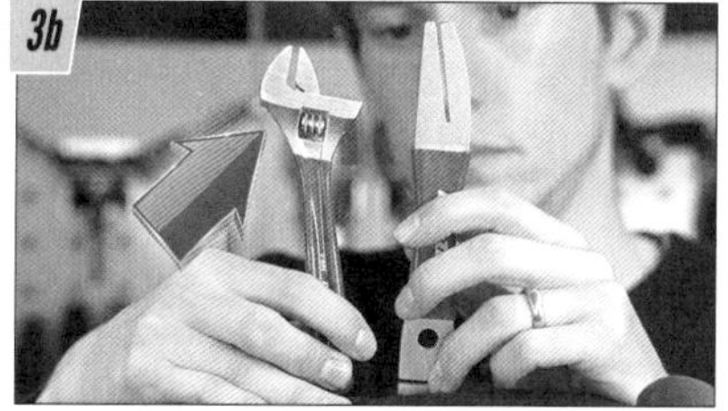

If you don't have a specialist tool, an adjustable wrench can do the job. However, given the spanner isn't as deep as the truing tool, take care that you're not just bending the outside of the rotor.

Getting rid of your rotors kinks can take a little time, but stick with it. You're unlikely to get it totally true once again, but the object is to get it true enough so as not to rub on your brake pads.

Avoid sticking your fingers through the rotor and then spinning your wheel – it hurts a lot. Also, try not to touch the rotors with your bare hands, their natural oils can contaminate the metal surface.

WATCH THE VIDEO

Free show-how and know-how

https://gcn.eu/TrueDiscRotor

SCAN CODE TO WATCH THE VIDEO

Need To True A Wheel?
Head over to page 164

TOP TIPS

HOW TO LOOK AFTER YOUR DISC BRAKES

If you're new to disc brakes these maintenance tips will help you look after them and ensure they're performing at their best

DIFFICULTY 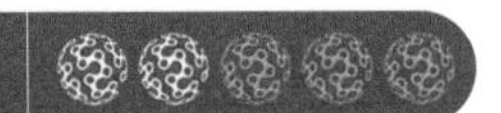

TIME	20 - 40 Minutes
TOOLS	• Tyre levers • Disc brake cleaner • Emery cloth • Allen keys
WHEN	• You want to get the most from your disc brakes

WATCH THE VIDEO

Free show-how and know-how

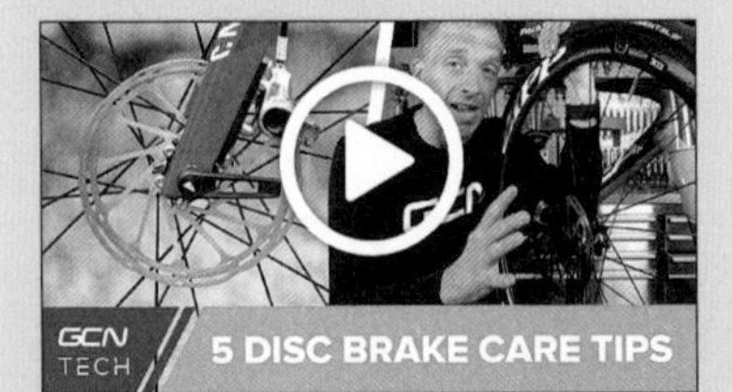

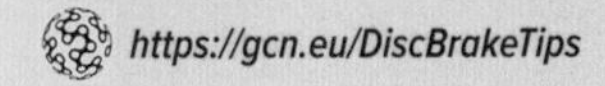
https://gcn.eu/DiscBrakeTips

BRAKE PADS ARE TOO TIGHT

1

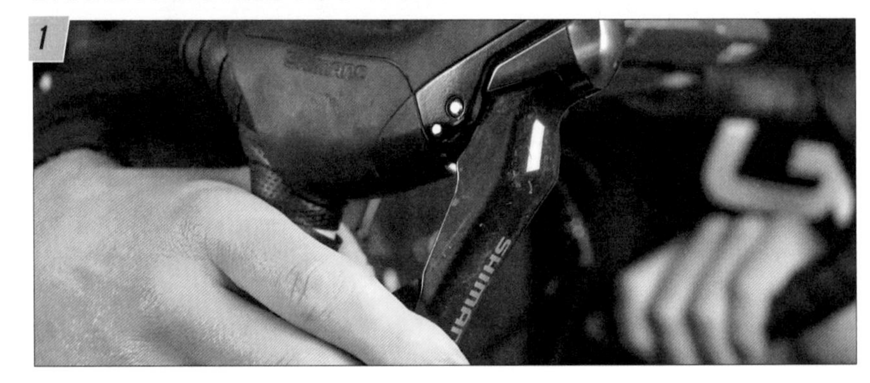

If you've accidentally pulled a brake lever with your wheel out, your self-centring brake pads will likely now be so close together that you can't get the wheel back in, or the pads may have even fallen out.

> **"If travelling with the wheels off, jam something between the brake pads to stop any accidental activation"**

2

To push the pads and the brake pistons back in, grab a tyre lever or something similar and work around the pads to push them back in. If you can't get enough leverage this way, try taking the pads out and pushing the pistons until they are flush with the body of the brake.

3

If you're transporting your bike with the wheels off, jam something between the brake pads to stop any accidental activation. Your bike may well have come with special blocks which are made just for this purpose.

LOST BRAKING PERFORMANCE

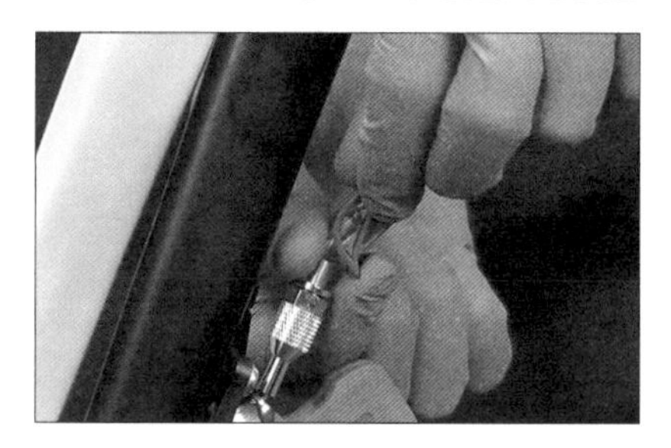

If your hydraulic brakes are starting to feel squishy and aren't performing as well as they once did, you're going to have to bleed them to remove any trapped air that's got into the system. For lots more on bleeding your brakes, head over to page 140.

CONTAMINATED ROTORS

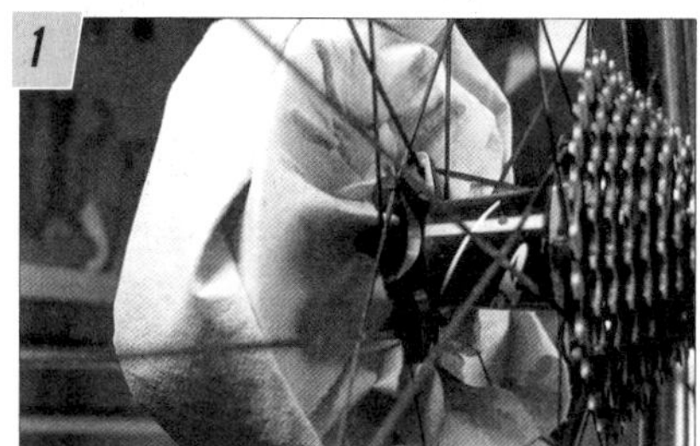

When spraying lubricant, degreaser or anything else on your bike, it's important to keep your brake rotors covered by something clean to prevent contamination. Loud screeches or poor performance are signs of contamination.

Disc brake cleaner will help restore your brakes. Just spray it on your rotors and your pads and let it dry. If that doesn't work, try rubbing some isopropyl alcohol onto the rotors, or lightly rubbing them with some emery cloth as a last resort.

TOP TIP

When handling your brake rotors or pads, always wear some disposable gloves as even when totally clean, the natural oils in your skin can be enough to contaminate the braking surfaces and cause the dreaded and deafening brake squeal.

RUBBING ROTORS

The tolerances between brake rotor and pad are much finer than you'll find on rim brakes. This means that the slightest bend or knock in the rotor will cause it to rub on the pads, so take great care or them especially with the wheels out.

If you have got a rotor that's not quite as flat as it once was, it is possible to get special tools designed to get them back in shape (see page 131). Failing that, the only alternative is to replace the rotor with a new one.

Your brake rotor could be rubbing because the calliper is just slightly out of line. To correct this, loosen off the calliper mounting bolts and squeeze the lever while re-tightening the calliper bolts.

BEDDING IN BRAKE PADS

Just like new rim brakes, disc brake pads don't work to their full effect when they're brand new as they have a very slight glaze on them which needs to be scrubbed off.

The best way to bed them in is to ride along between 10 and 15mph then pull the brake enough to bring you to a sharp stop. Repeat this 15 times, then do the same again at around 20mph.

Got SRAM or Shimano Disc Brakes?
Learn how to bleed them from page 144

TOP TIPS

ROAD BIKE DISC BRAKE HACKS

Here are three quick techniques to help improve the power and alignment of your disc brakes

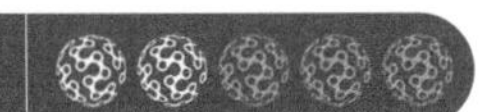

DIFFICULTY

TIME 20 - 40 Minutes

TOOLS
- *Allen keys*
- *Piece of card*
- *Isopropyl alcohol*
- *Clean cloth*
- *Bleed bucket*
- *Hydraulic fluid*

WHEN
- *You want to improve the stopping power of your disc brakes*

ALIGNING THE CALLIPERS

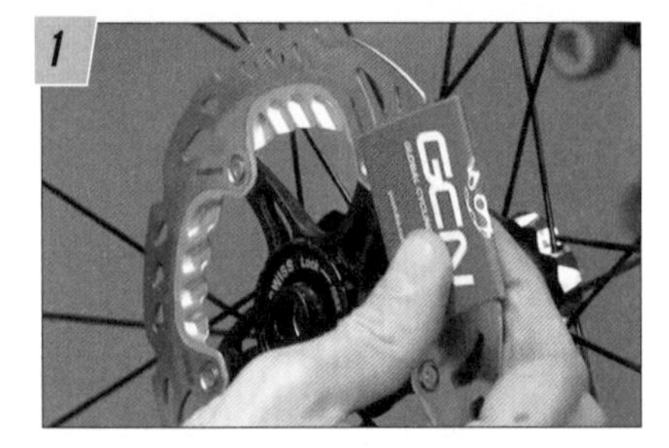

We've already discussed how to realign your brake callipers on the previous page, but if you have flat-mounted callipers (rather than post-mounted), you might need to try this additional hack. Remove your wheel, then take a thin piece of card and bend it over both sides of the rotor.

Reinsert your wheel so that the card covered section of your rotor sits in the calliper. Loosen off the calliper bolts, pull the brake lever, then retighten the bolts. The extra distance provided by the card should now have stopped any brake rub.

"If you ride a lot in bad weather, you may end up with brake pistons that are slow to retract or don't do so fully"

FIXING STICKY PISTONS

If you ride a lot in bad weather, you may well end up with brake pistons that are slow to retract or don't do so fully. If this is the case, cleaning will get them working properly again.

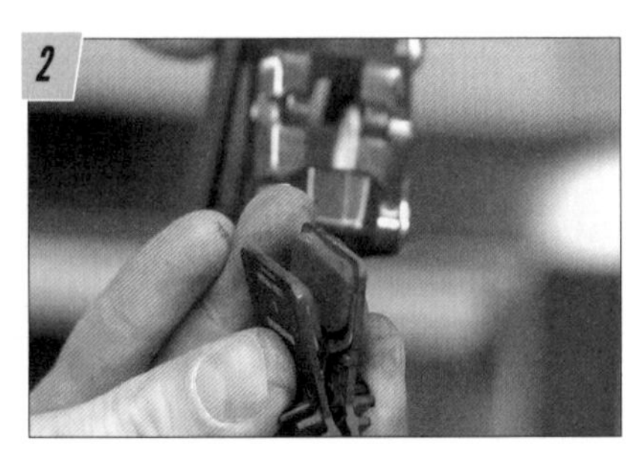

To get at the pistons, remove your wheel and brake pads – ensuring to to put the pad retaining pin and clip somewhere safe.

WATCH THE VIDEO

Free show-how and know-how

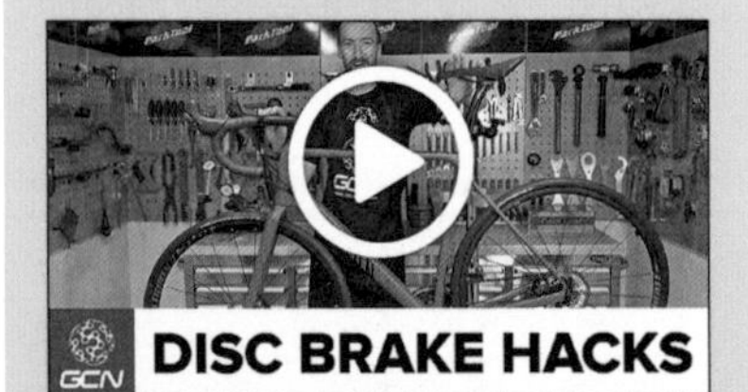

https://gcn.eu/DiscBrakeHacks

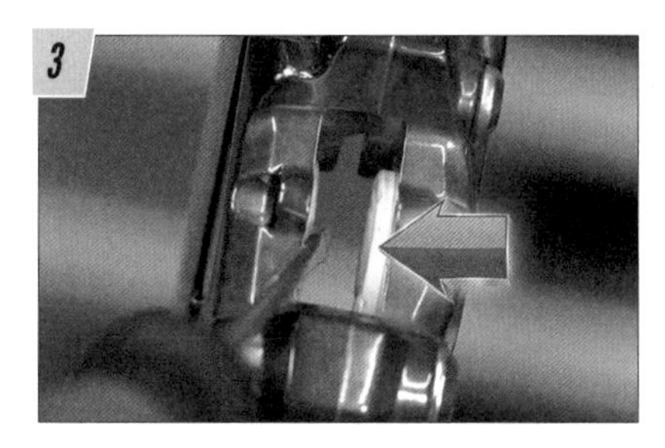

Once the pads are out, gently squeeze on the lever a few times to push the pistons out by 3 or 4mm. Take care not to overdo it, as you can push the pistons completely out of the calliper and you'll then need to do a full brake bleed to fix them.

Next, take your isopropyl alcohol and carefully spray or wipe some on the exposed sides of the pistons, then clean them up with your cloth.

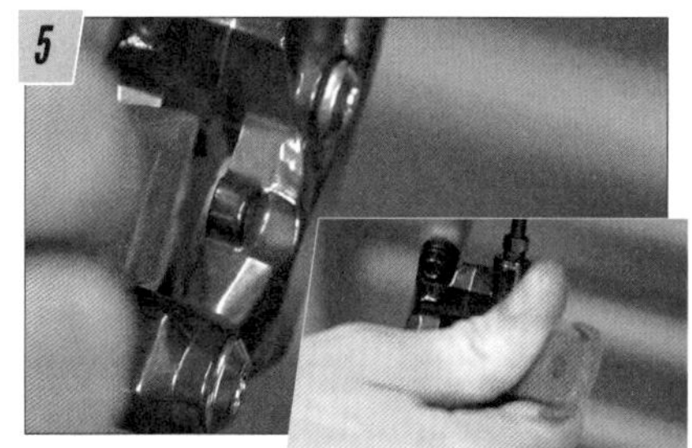

Should you have a piston that's stickier than its counterpart and refuses to fully comply when pulling on the levers. Clean the one that has come out, then by pushing the cleaned one back in with a tyre lever, the change in fluid pressure should force the stubborn to emerge.

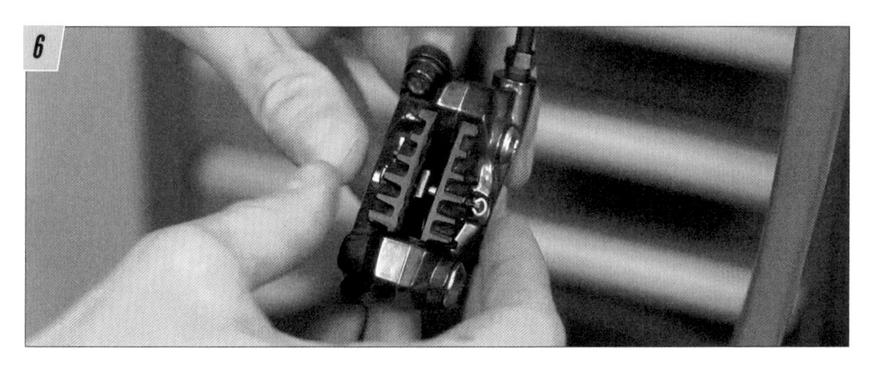

Once both pistons are clean and dry, push them back into the calliper with your tyre lever and give the brake a few pumps to check they are both now moving smoothly and evenly. Push them back in again, refit your brake pads and finally your wheel.

BLEEDING HACK

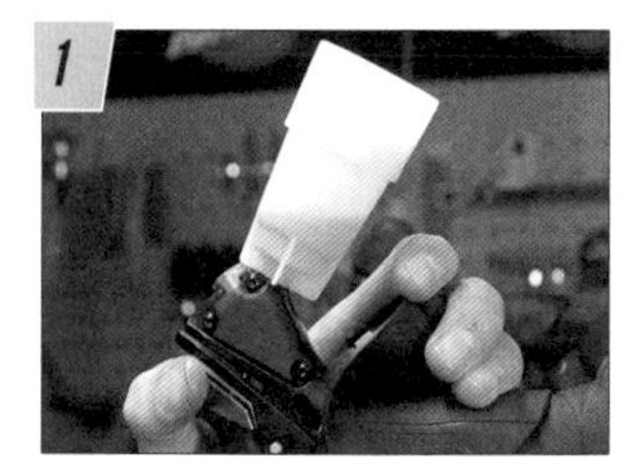

If your brakes are feeling spongy, you'll likely need a full rebleed. But, if the fluid in your system is fairly new, you might get away with this hack. Fill a third of a bleed bucket with brake fluid and fit it to your brake.

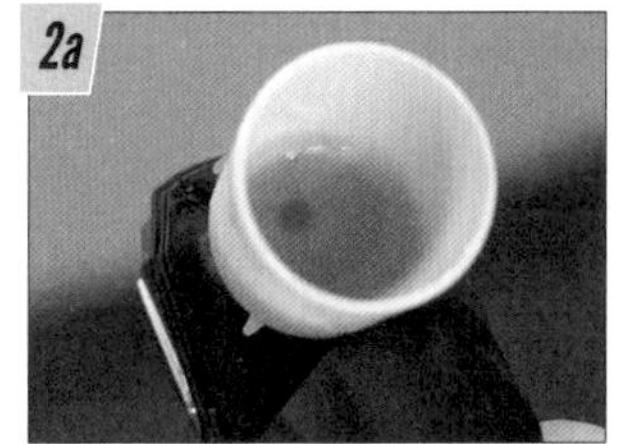

Remove the bucket top and plunger. Squeeze the lever a few times and you should see some bubbles in the fluid. Replace the lid and squeeze the lever while tapping the wheel on the floor to release any trapped bubbles.

If you're working on the rear brake, use gravity to assist you by lifting the bike onto its rear wheel while squeezing the lever and tapping the wheel on the floor.

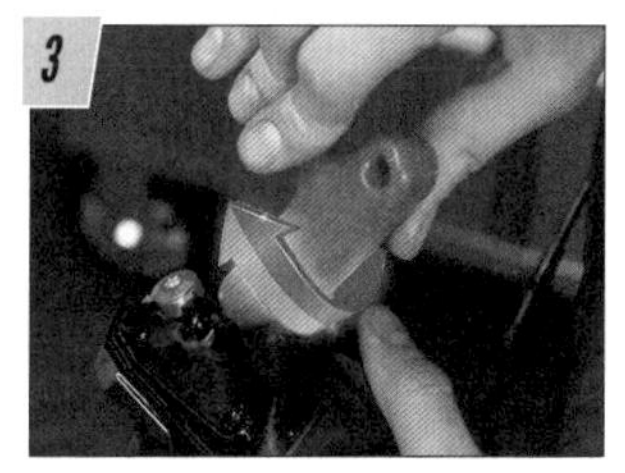

Remove the lid from the bucket, then replace both plunger and lid, remove the bucket and replace the bleed screw. Wipe up any excess fluid and your brakes should now feel a lot more solid.

Want More Helpful Hacks?
Turn to page 224 for loads more

SET-UP SECRETS

HOW TO SET UP CABLE DISC BRAKES

Cable operated disc brakes offer a more affordable alternative to hydraulic brake callipers and are easy to maintain. Here's how to get the most from them

DIFFICULTY 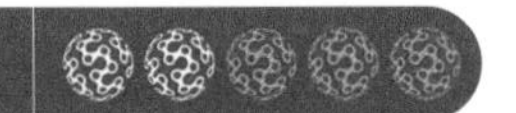

TIME 30 - 60 Minutes

TOOLS
- 3mm, 4mm or 5mm Allen keys or Torx keys (depending on your brakes)
- T25 Torx wrench (depending on your brakes)
- A torque wrench and bits is useful

WHEN
- Your brakes are not as efficient as they were

Cable disc brakes are common on more affordable road and commuter bikes

WATCH THE VIDEO
Free show-how and know-how

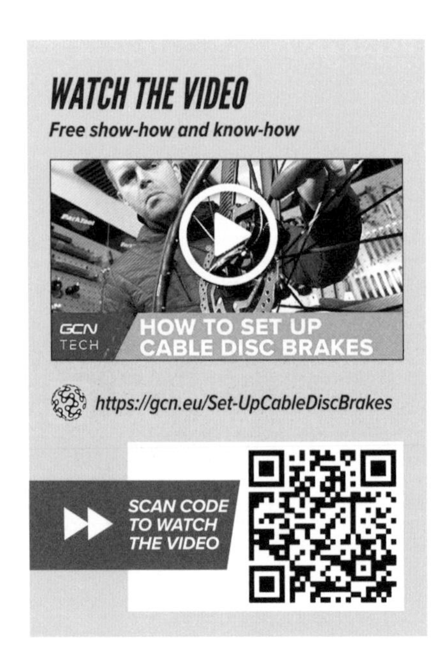

https://gcn.eu/Set-UpCableDiscBrakes

Disc brakes are a common feature on bikes now as they offer increased braking performance in all conditions. There are two main types of disc brakes found on bicycles – hydraulic discs and cable discs. Cable discs use a cable to actuate the calliper and close the brake pads, whereas hydraulic brakes use a line filled with hydraulic fluid. A lot of bikes come supplied with mechanical disc brakes as they're a more affordable alternative to their hydraulic counterparts and they are simpler to work on too.

Types Of Cable Disc Brakes

Now there are slightly different variations of mechanical disc brake callipers. Some just move the pad from one side (single lever arm/ piston, sometimes also known as 'one-pot'), while others move the pads onto the rotor from both sides (dual lever arm/piston or 'two-pot'). Two-pot designs deliver the best performance and allow pad adjustment for both the inner and outer sides, while single piston brakes may have both inner and outer pad adjusters or just inner pad adjustment depending on the model.

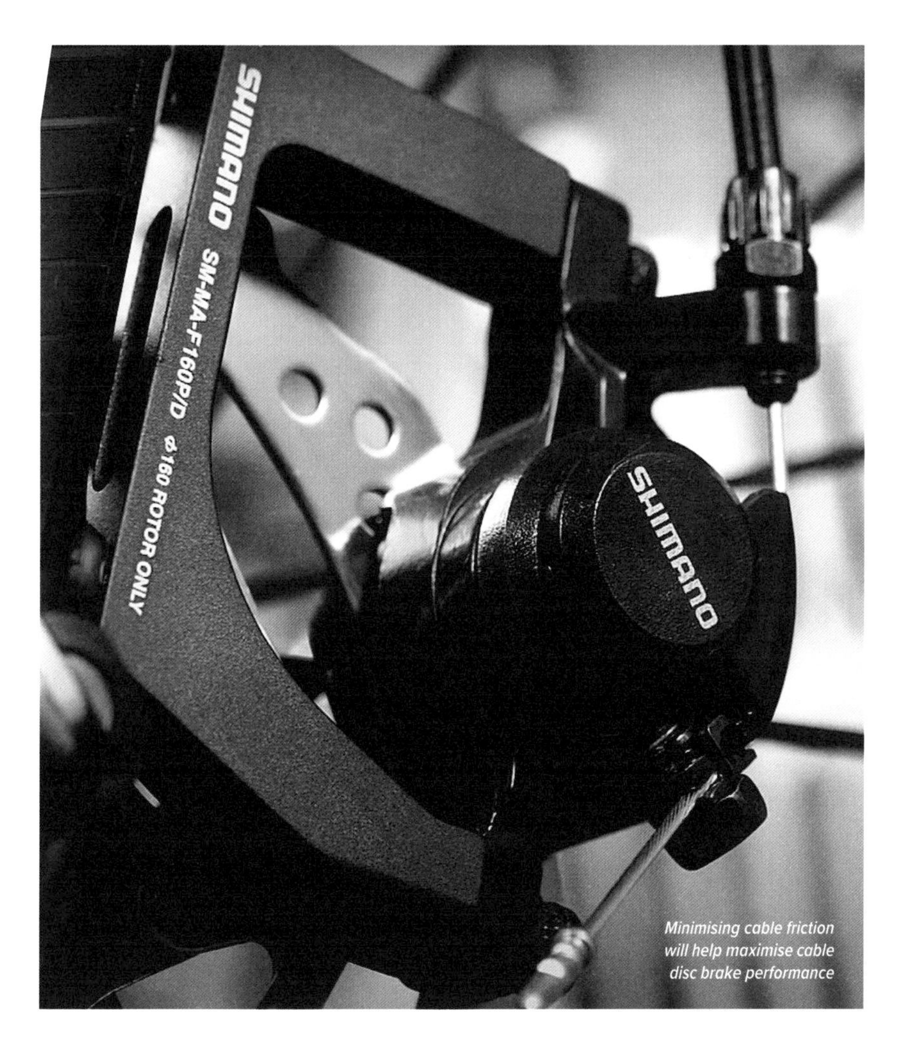

Minimising cable friction will help maximise cable disc brake performance

RECOMMENDED COMPONENTS

To get the best from your mechanical disc brakes there are some components that we recommend:

Cable Housing

First and foremost, you will get performance benefits from using compressionless brake cable housing. This eliminates any in-line compression of the outer cable, meaning when you brake more force is transmitted to the cable and calliper – rather than on the cable outer compressing. Several brands produce these so check your local bike shop to see what they've got.

Inner Cables

Next, we'd suggest using Teflon-coated cables. They run more smoothly with less friction through the cable housing to provide a lighter lever feel than standard stainless steel cables.

Brake Pads

Over time your brake pads will need replacing. Different brands and designs use different shaped pads, so ensure to replace yours with the correct type. You can choose from two different brake pad compounds – organic (resin) or metallic (sintered). Organic pads are quieter and manage heat better, but they wear down more quickly. Metallic pads last longer, make more noise, but can lose power when they get hot.

BEFORE YOU START

Make sure everything else on the bike is in order. The wheels should be properly seated in the dropouts and check the rotors are not loose.

Check the rotors are true and aren't warped (you can do this by lifting the bike, spinning the wheel and looking through the calliper, you'll be able to see if the rotor has any lateral, side-to-side movement).

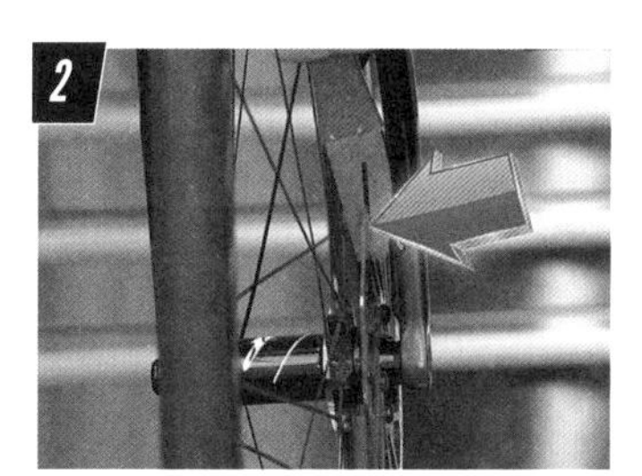

If the rotors need truing, use a rotor truing tool to get them running straight again. Turn to p131 for our walkthrough showing you how to do this.

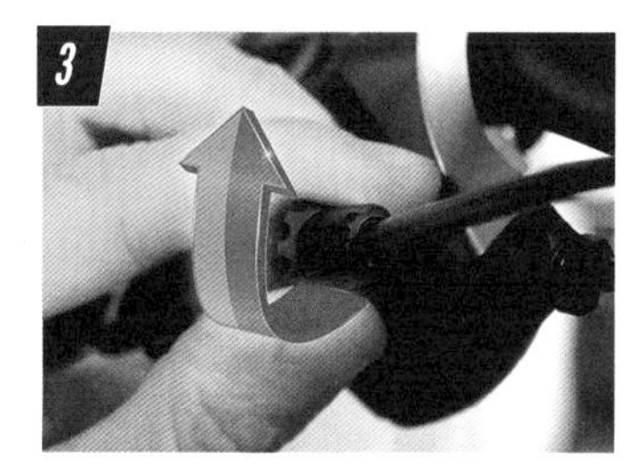

Next, make sure the barrel adjusters on the levers (and sometimes also on the calipers) are turned fully clockwise, leaving plenty of room for adjustment later on.

HOW TO SET UP CABLE DISC BRAKES

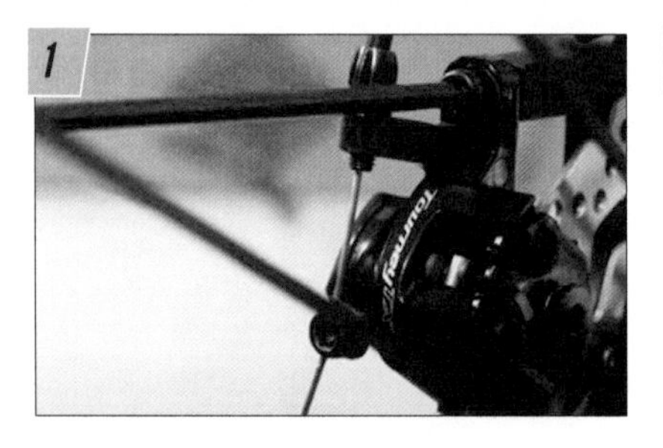

Begin by using the right size of Allen key for your brake (usually a 5mm) to loosen the caliper mounting bolts. This allows the calliper to float freely (move from side to side) on the mount.

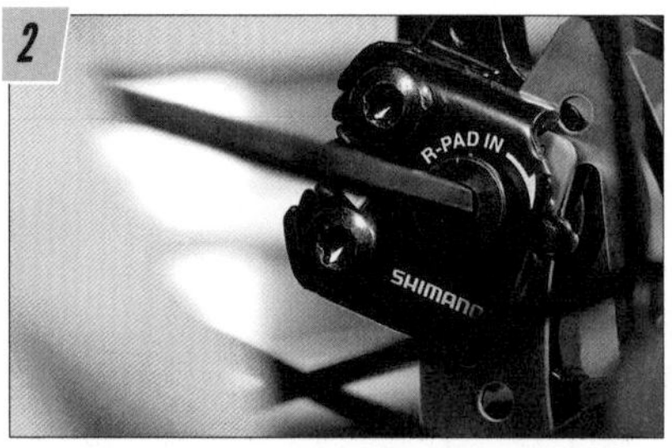

Using the correct Torx or Allen key (usually a T25 Torx, or a 3 or 4mm Allen key), turn both the inner and outer pad adjusters on either side of the calliper body all the way in (clockwise), then back off about a quarter of a turn. This leaves room for fine-tuning and future adjustment.

Pull and hold the brake lever tight (with the calliper bolts loosened off), this naturally centres the calliper body on the rotor.

Still keeping the brake lever down tight, tighten the calliper mounting bolts, then release the brake lever.

TOP TIP

You can also fine-tune lever feel by turning the barrel adjusters on the brake levers. Turn them anti-clockwise little-by-little to tighten the cable and reduce the lever throw (how far the levers move until the brake pads engage the disc rotor). To loosen the cable tension, turn the barrel adjusters clockwise and this will increase the lever throw.

Back off the pad adjuster another quarter turn anti-clockwise.

For both flat bar or drop bar brake levers, you want to make sure the levers have the correct amount of travel in them – meaning they engage the brakes at about half way through their entire possible movement when you pull them. If they engage too soon, you won't be able to apply enough pressure through the lever. If they engage too late, the lever might bottom out on the handlebar before the brakes fully engage.

If they require some fine adjustment, you can dial in or out the pad adjuster(s) until the lever is in the correct position.

Now, check the rotor is rotating freely when you spin the wheel and isn't rubbing on the disc brake pads. You'll either be able to hear this, see this or feel the wheel dragging. If there's no rubbing, you can skip to Step 8.

If you do detect some rub, check the alignment of the rotor in the calliper. The rotor may be slightly warped, or the calliper is misaligned.

TOP TIP

When using a two-ended Allen key with a ball end and a square end, use the square end when you need to use force to tighten/untighten a bolt so you don't round the bolt out. The ball end is just for light adjustment.

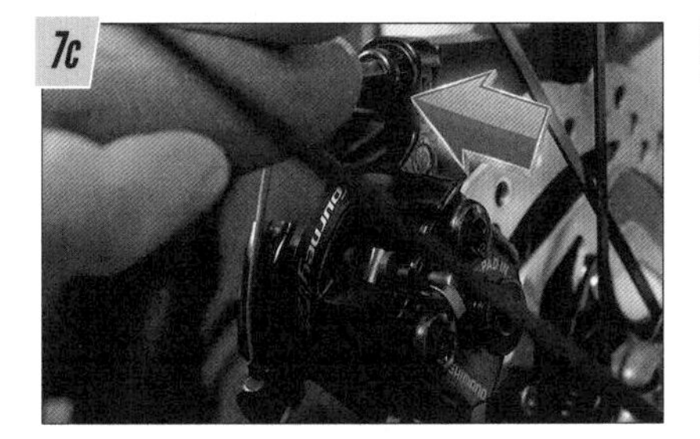

If the calliper is misaligned, repeat steps 3 and 4. If your brake only has inner pad adjustment, you'll need to loosen one mounting bolt at a time to make fine adjustments to the calliper alignment (by moving it a little towards the side that's rubbing), then snug it up to test again. Repeat as necessary.

If the calliper's aligned but brake pads are still rubbing, fine-tune the inner and outer pad adjusters (or both, as needed) on either side of the calliper body by turning them in or out a little by little to move them towards or away from the disc rotor until the rubbing stops.

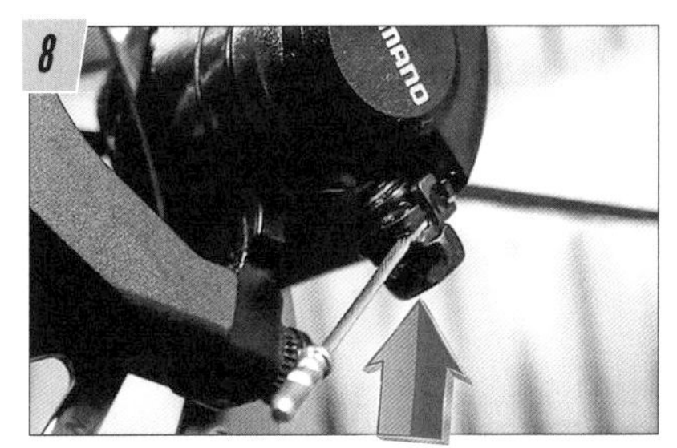

With everything set up and aligned perfectly, ensure the cable pinch bolt and the calliper mounting bolts are snug and tight. If you've a torque wrench, they should be around 6Nm for the mounting bolts and 4Nm for the pinch bolt.

With everything cinched up, it's time to check it's all working as it should on a test ride. Repeat any steps above until it's all working sweetly.

TECH EXPLAINED

Pad Wear & Adjustment

One key point to remember is that cable disc brakes will require adjustment as the pads wear, unlike hydraulic brakes that self-adjust. Sort your brakes when the levers start to feel spongy or the lever throw (the amount the lever pulls back to the bar) starts to increase. This can become dangerous when the bite point of the brake lever is too close to the bar to properly engage.

> "If the calliper's aligned but brake pads are still rubbing, fine-tune the inner and outer pad adjusters"

Need To Replace Your Pads?
See page 130 for how to change them

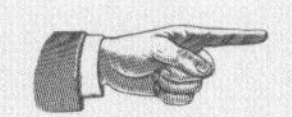

SET-UP SECRETS

HOW TO FIT & SET UP HYDRAULIC DISC BRAKES

Hydraulic discs offer brilliant all-weather braking control but fitting them can be a daunting prospect. Here's how to get it right first time

DIFFICULTY

TIME 60 - 120 Minutes

TOOLS

- *Allen keys or Torx keys*
- *Mineral oil or DOT brake fluid*
- *Bleeding kit for your brakes*
- *A torque wrench with crow foot adaptor*
- *A lockring tool for centrelock brake rotors*
- *7 and 8mm open-ended spanners*
- *Nitrile gloves*
- *Hose cutting tool*
- *Small Phillips screwdriver*
- *Electrical tape*
- *Handlebar tape*

WHEN

- *You want to upgrade or fit a new hydraulic brake system*

WATCH THE VIDEO

Free show-how and know-how

GCN TECH
HOW TO FIT AND SET UP HYDRAULIC DISC BRAKES

https://gcn.eu/FitHydraulicsDiscBrakes

SCAN CODE TO WATCH THE VIDEO

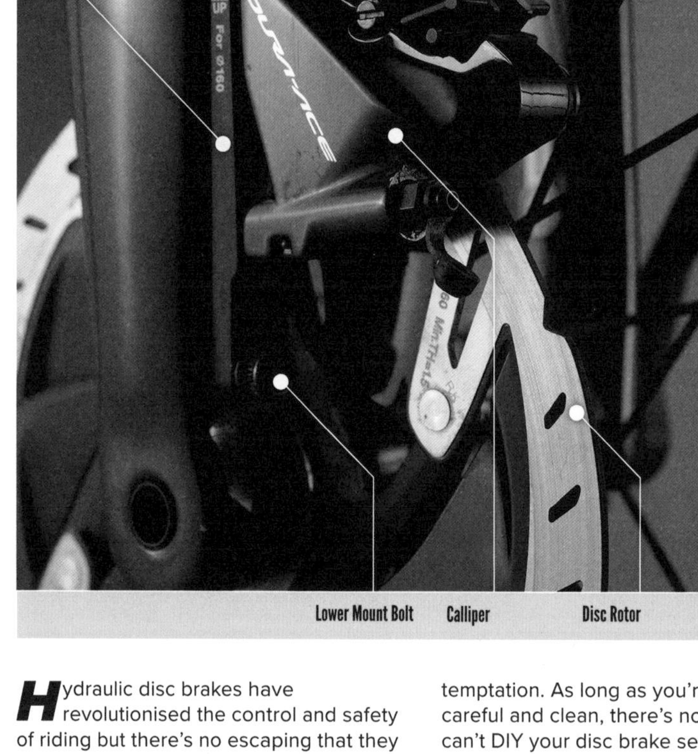

Hydraulic disc brakes have revolutionised the control and safety of riding but there's no escaping that they are a lot more complicated to install than a set of cable rim brakes. The process also involves several specific tools that you might only need very rarely afterwards. While we've tried to include all the tips and hacks we know, there's a big difference to reading them in a book compared to making them work in real life. That all makes just taking your bike into your local shop and asking them to do it a definite temptation. As long as you're patient, careful and clean, there's no reason you can't DIY your disc brake set-up and feel very proud about the results.

BEFORE YOU START

The first step is to make sure that your frame is ready and prepared to install the brakes. If you're buying a brand new frame then you won't have the headset or the bottom bracket installed. That makes

Fit and prepare your brake hoses before fitting the brakes themselves

it much easier to reach into the frame to help pull or push the hoses through the routing, so don't fit them until you've threaded the hoses through.

If you're installing new brakes to an existing frame or bike then you might find it easier to remove them, but we'd suggest you try fitting the hoses first to save yourself some extra work.

New frames usually come with guide tubes pre-installed through the hose routing path in the frame. Bars with integrated routing should hopefully have guidelines as well and as you'll see in the install section this makes life a lot easier.

FITTING YOUR HOSES

As we've said the difficulty of this job depends a huge amount on the frame, bar and stem you are using and how simple the routing around or through them is. Some brakes come with the hoses, levers and callipers separately in the box, while others come ready connected. This is great if you have external cable routing as you can just clip them straight into place. If you need to thread the hose through the cockpit and/or stem, then remove the pads from the calliper and carefully undo the hose at the calliper end. You'll probably have to cut off the very end that has the barb installed and the olive crushed round it. That will let you slide the fixing nut/collar and any rubber cover off the hose.

"There's no reason you can't DIY your disc brake set-up and feel very proud of the results"

To minimise brake fluid leak out of the hose put a small cap of cling film over the end or push half a cocktail stick into it. This works very well if you then stick the other end of the stick into the guide tube that's already threaded through the cockpit and/or frame. By the way, we say half a cocktail stick not a whole one as the half is easier to get round tight corners. A short piece of coat hanger wire or cut spoke can work well too though and it has the added advantage of being magnetic so you can use a strong magnet to guide it through from outside the frame.

If you're using an existing bike then use the old hoses as the guide for pulling the new ones through. However, while it might be tempting to use the existing hoses with fresh brakes and callipers and save yourself some installation hassle, we wouldn't recommend it. The hoses will be contaminated by old fluid and any other gunk that's got in there. Also once you've removed the old hardware the hoses might be too short or damaged. If you're switching between brakes that use mineral oil (Shimano, Campagnolo, FSA) and brakes that use DOT fluid (SRAM, Hope) it's a definite no. That's because even a tiny amount of the wrong fluid will make the seals swell and totally destroy your brakes and levers.

Brake Fluid Precautions

Always keep brake fluid away from paint work as it can damage it. Keep it away from rotors and brake pads too, as if it gets on them you won't be able to get them clean and stopping properly again. Remove your wheels and brake pads before starting the fitting process and keep them clear until the whole system is installed securely and you've cleaned the bike and brakes of any spills.

HOW TO FIT & SET UP HYDRAULIC DISC BRAKES

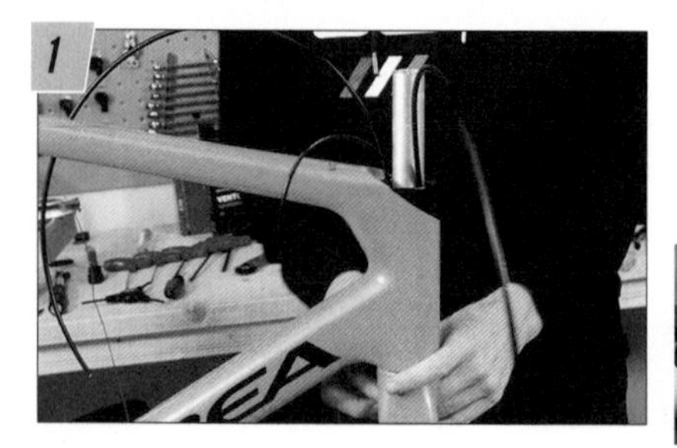

Once the hoses are in place and the frame and fork are together it's time to install the brake callipers. If you're using flat mount brakes the callipers themselves are identical, so it doesn't matter if you use either one for front or rear. What is different are the mounting plates.

The front mounting plate has two bolting options. Install it one way round for 160mm rotors or bolt it onto the calliper the other way for 140mm rotors. On the rear calliper, if you mount it without the plate it's set up for 140mm rotors. Mount it with the wedge plate added for 160mm rotors.

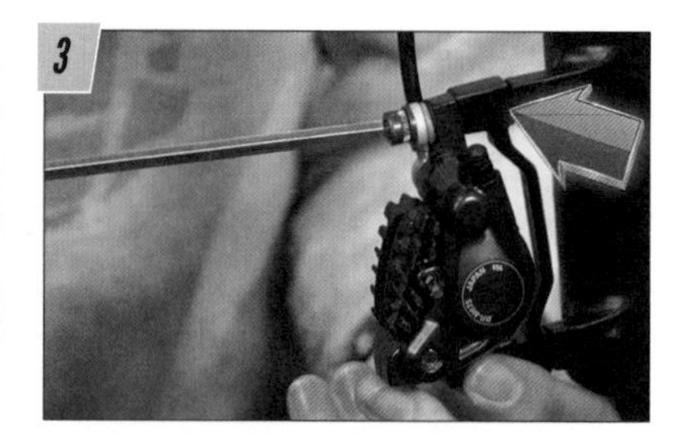

If you're using older post mount or even older IS mount brakes then you'll need the appropriate spacers or bracket to work with the rotors you want to use. If in any doubt check the bits go together correctly with a 'dry install' first to save you suddenly running into trouble half way through.

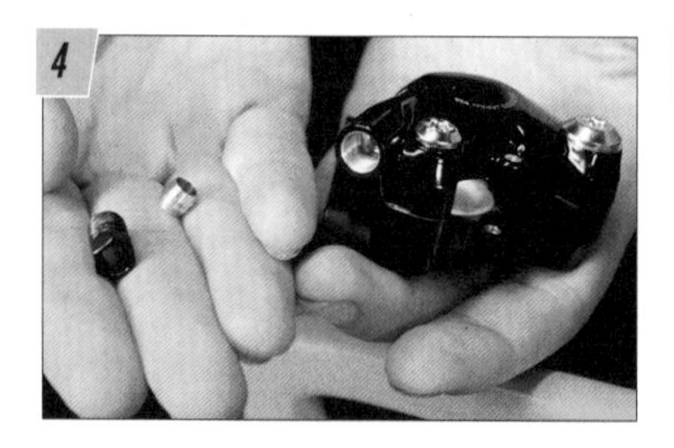

Before mounting the callipers, you'll need to fit the hoses. Different brakes attach in different ways, but take the hose collars and/or rubber grommets and any hose clamping nuts/collars off the brake and slide them onto the hose in the correct order (the reverse of how they 'meet' the calliper).

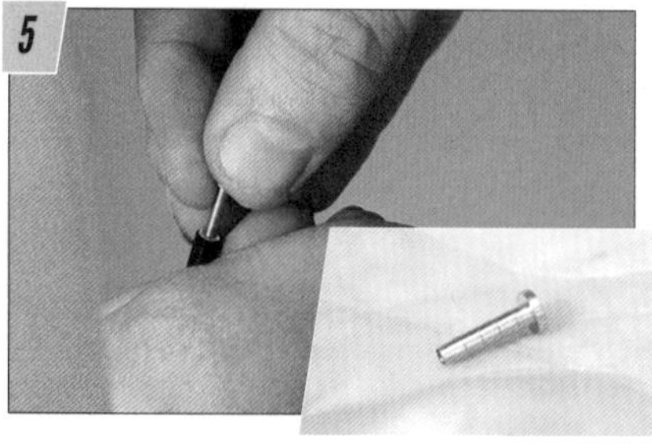

Now slide the olive (the barrel type sleeve that creates the tight hose fit) onto the hose and fit the barb. If you don't have a barb tool use the small Phillips screwdriver or ball-ended Allen key. Push and twist this carefully into the end of the hose to open it slightly so the barb slides in more easily.

TOP TIP

Make sure that you have the correct size barbs for your brakes. They can differ slightly between different brake set-ups and brands.

PRO HACK

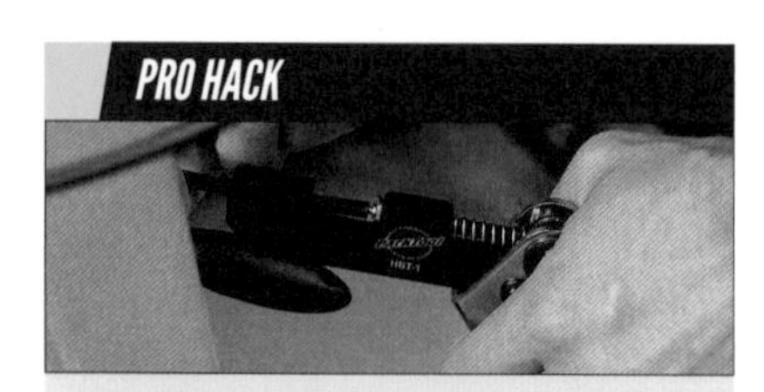

If you've got a barb tool, use the tapered push pin to open up the hose. Then push the hose all the way through until the end is protruding from the clamp. Tighten the clamp firmly, then press the barb in by hand. Now use the barb driving tool to press the barb fully into the hose. Unclamp, slide the hose back out and you're good to go.

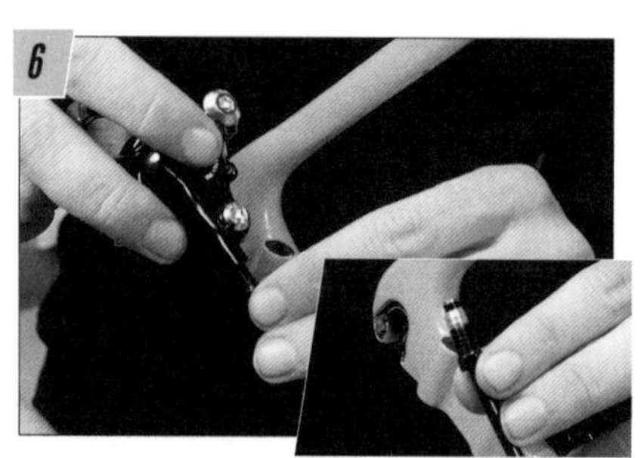

Push the hose into the receiver on the brake calliper and then slide the fixing nut/collar down the hose. This will push the olive down towards the end of the hose where it will stop on the flared end created by the barb.

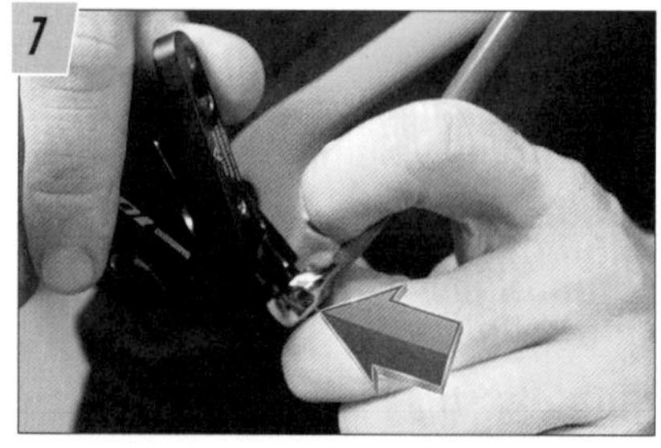

Carefully thread the hose clamping collar/nut into the calliper and then use an 8mm or 7mm spanner to tighten it. This will crush the olive to create the hydraulic seal, so tighten it firmly. Don't overdo it though as the fixtures are often alloy to save weight, but this also makes them easy to damage.

TOP TIP

Never use an adjustable spanner, pliers or similar to tighten the locking nut/collar. The fit won't be tight or consistent enough to keep it secure and you seriously risk damaging your spanner and your brake fastenings. That means you might not be able to tighten or remove the nut/collar which is a real problem.

8

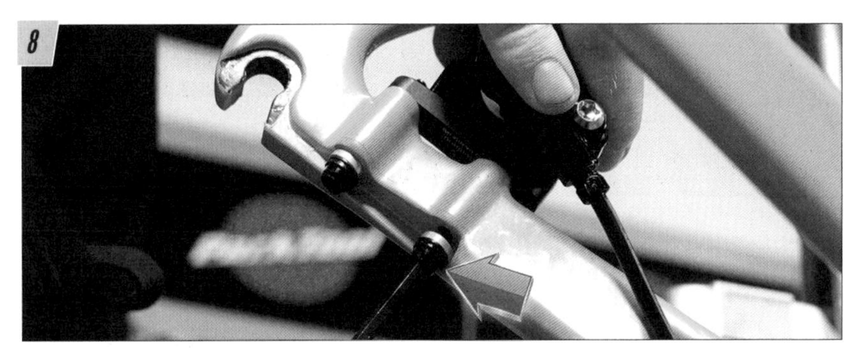

Now to bolt the callipers to the frame. There is a standard length bolt that comes with callipers. Some frames have a slightly different design, and if so, are usually supplied with the correct length bolts. Don't fully tighten the bolts just yet, as you'll need to align the callipers on the rotors later.

9

Put the brake levers briefly onto the bar. This is to position them so you can make sure the hose lengths are correct and cut them down if needed. They don't have to be exactly right as you can push excess hose into the frame, but make sure you don't cut them too short.

10

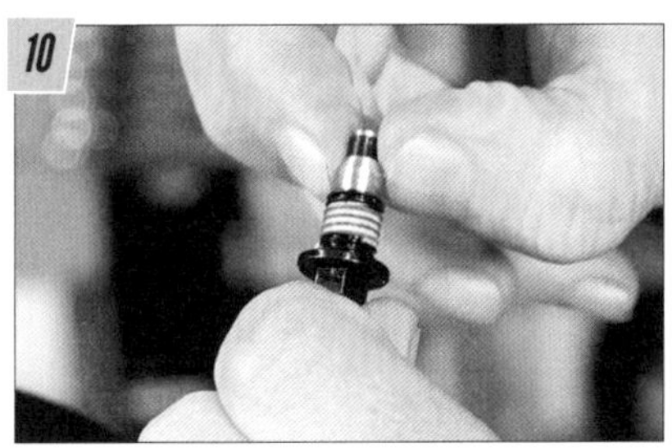

Take them off again as it's much easier to work on the brake levers and hoses with them hanging free. Prepare the hoses as you did at the brake end – by sliding the retaining nut and olive down the hose and then the olive. Now, push the barb into the end.

11

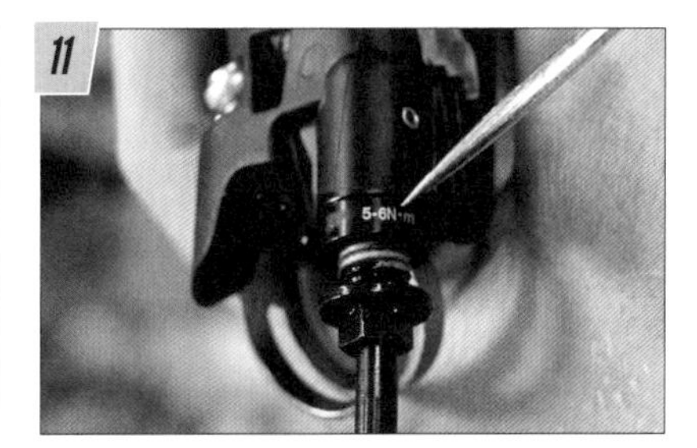

You are now ready to fit the hose into the brake lever. Plug the hose into the port, slide the olive up as far as it can go and then tighten the locking nut into place. Be very careful not to overtighten it though as it's quite easy to damage the shifter and they are very expensive to replace.

12

You can carefully use a standard open-ended spanner, but if you have one, use a crow foot adapter and a torque wrench to tighten to 5 to 6Nm. Once the hose is in place, slide the brake lever back onto the bars, positioning them as per the advice on page 110.

13

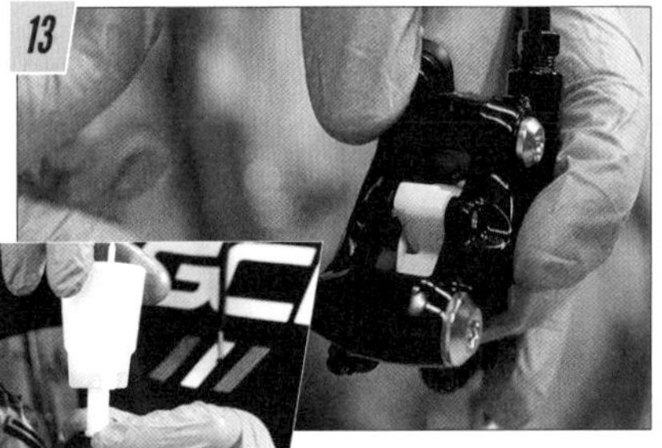

Once the brake levers are fitted you'll need to bleed both brakes to fill them with hydraulic fluid. Even if you've split and re-used a sealed set-up, you'll need to bleed it to get rid of air bubbles that have crept in while the hoses were unplugged. You can find bleed instructions starting on page 144.

TOP TIP

If you've pulled apart and re-joined a sealed system it's always worth checking your brakes in case you've been lucky enough to put together a leak free install. Sometimes just pulling your brake levers, strapping them to the bar at full pull and leaving them for a few hours will 'auto bleed' the system too.

Now You'll Need To Tape Your Bars
Turn to page 200 for full instructions

ESSENTIAL REPAIRS

HOW TO BLEED SRAM DISC BRAKES

Bleeding your hydraulic discs may sound like a technical job, but with the right equipment and our guide it's far more straightforward than you might think

DIFFICULTY 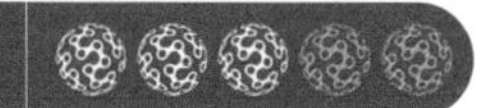

TIME	20 - 30 Minutes
TOOLS	• Bleed kit • Clean cloths • Hydraulic fluid • Long-nose pliers • Nitrile gloves • Isopropanol alcohol • Toe strap • 2.5mm Torx key • Allen keys • Bleed block
WHEN	• Your brakes have lost their sharpness or the levers pull too near the bars

WATCH THE VIDEO

Free show-how and know-how

GCN TECH HOW TO... BLEED SRAM BRAKES

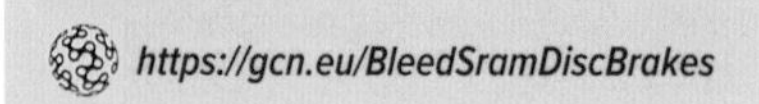

https://gcn.eu/BleedSramDiscBrakes

Remove the front wheel from the bike. Remove the brake pads by pulling off the retaining clip on top of the pads, then unbolt the pin and pull out the pads. To stop the brake pistons from moving, insert the bleed block into the space where the pads were.

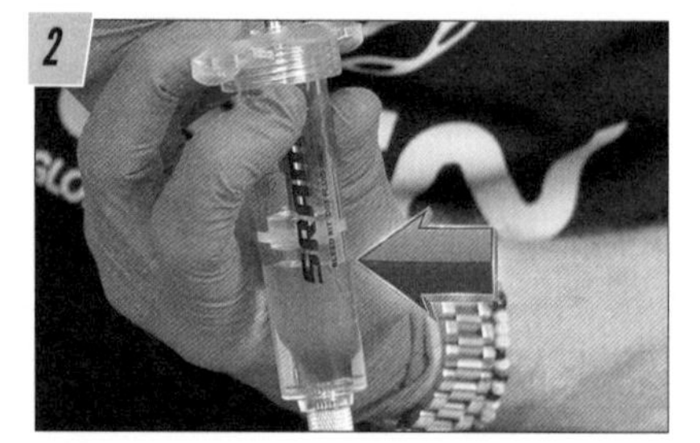

With your gloves on, assemble your syringes. Fill the first syringe half-full with brake fluid, then with the end of the syringe pointing upward, push down on the plunger to remove the air trapped in the syringe and catch any spills with your cloth.

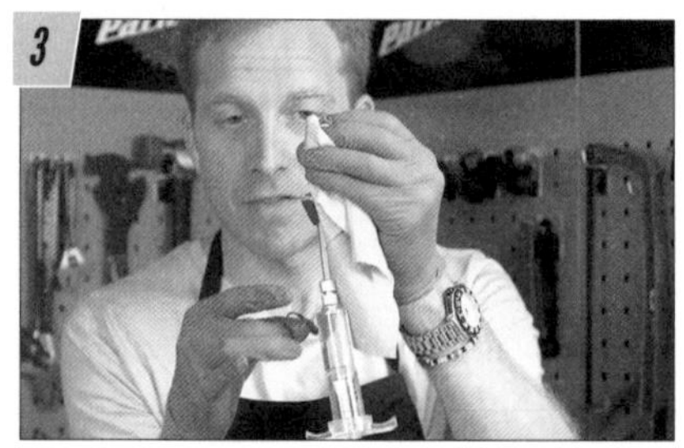

Close the red hose clamp, then repeatedly pull down on the plunger and flick the syringe with your finger to remove the last of the air from the fluid. Now, repeat the whole process on the second syringe, but only fill it a quarter-full of fluid.

Before starting the bleed, you need to ensure that the brake lever is 90mm or less away from an imaginary line that runs from the lever hood. If it is, you'll need to adjust your lever reach with your Allen key to bring it nearer the bar.

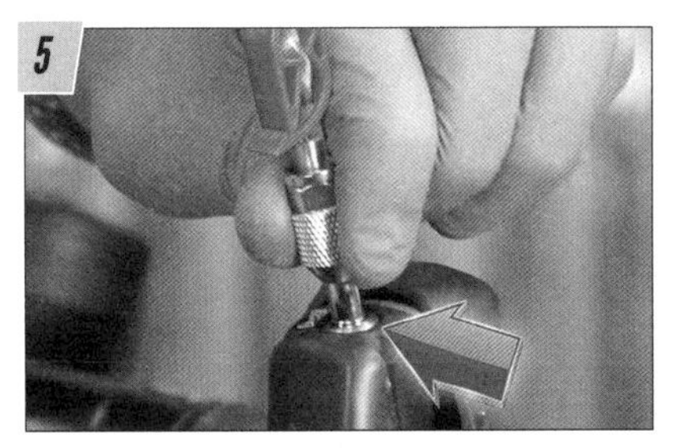

Pull back the brake lever hood and remove the bleed port screw with your 2.5mm Torx key, ensuring to put it somewhere safe. Then thread the quarter-full syringe into the hole where the bleed screw was.

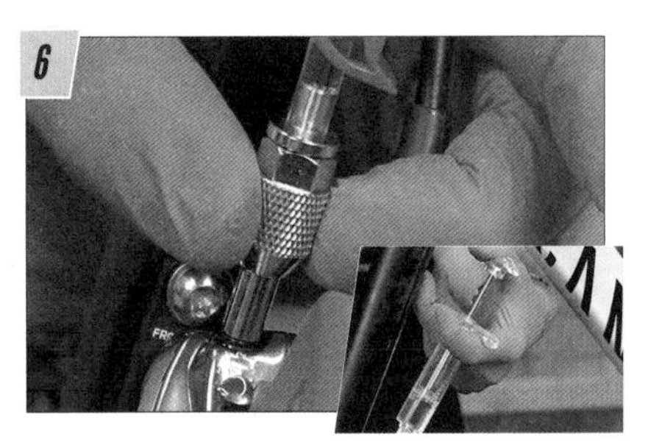

Remove the bleed port screw from the calliper and attach the half-full syringe in there. Release both hose clamps. Push gently on the calliper syringe until the syringe on the lever is around half-full, then lock down the hose clamp on that syringe.

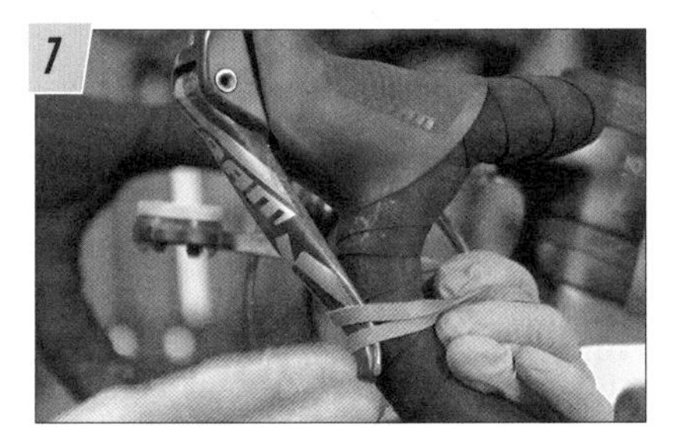

Pull in the brake lever and using your rubber band (or an old toe strap), secure the lever in place on the handlebar.

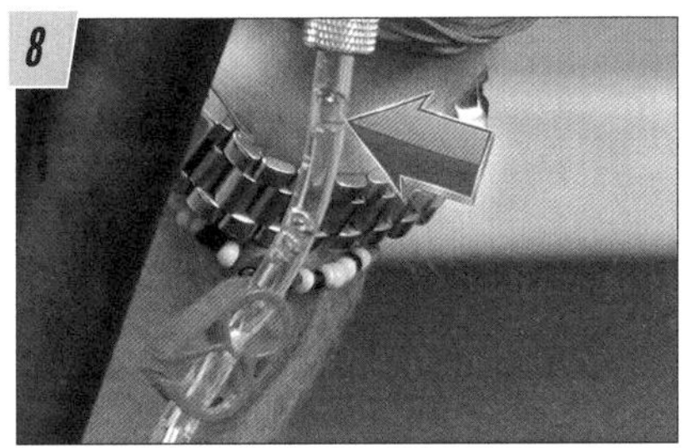

On the calliper syringe, hold the body in one hand and start to pull on the plunger with the other to remove any trapped air bubbles from this side of the system. When the bubbles stop rising, push the lever in and repeat the process a few times.

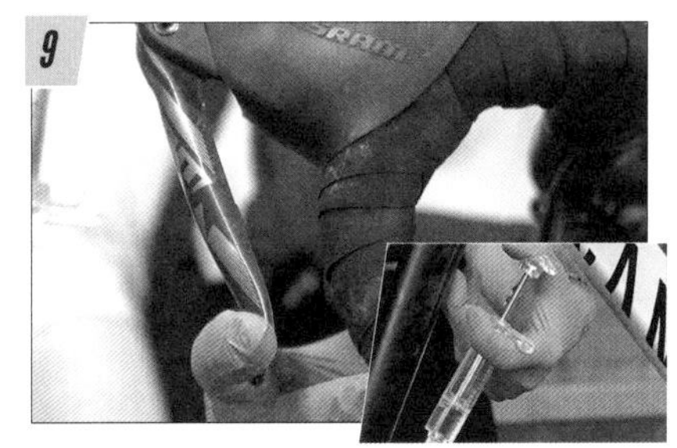

Remove the rubber band from the lever, but keep it in place with your hand. Then start to push on the syringe plunger at the calliper and allow the fluid pressure to push the lever back into position, but apply some light resistance with your lever hand as it does so.

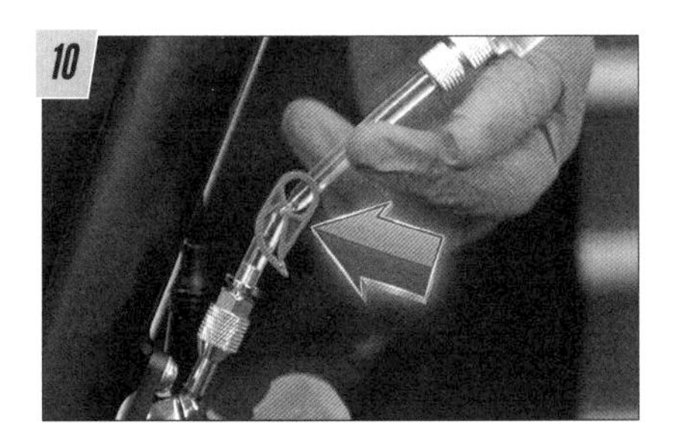

Once the lever is fully released, clamp both syringe hoses and gently unscrew the syringe from the bleed port on the calliper and reinsert the bleed screw, tightening to 1.5Nm. Ensure to wipe up any excess brake fluid.

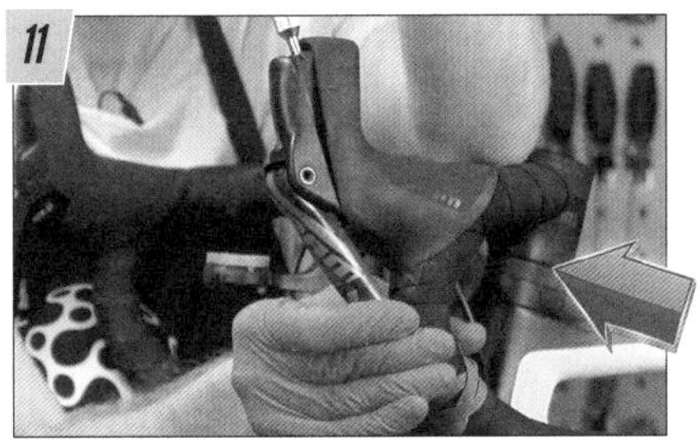

Release the clamp on the lever syringe and then pull on the plunger to extract the trapped air from the lever reservoir. Push down on the plunger and repeat this a few times. Fully squeeze and release the brake lever 10 times, then return to pulling and pushing the plunger to extract the last few bubbles.

Finally, push down on the plunger to gently push some fluid back into the system, clamp the hose, remove the syringe and re-install the bleed screw. Wipe up any excess brake fluid and clean the lever and calliper with your alcohol. Re-install the brake pads and wheel and you're ready to test ride.

Want To Bleed Shimano Disc Brakes?
Then just turn over the page

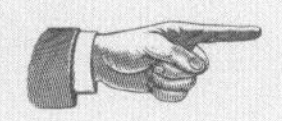

ESSENTIAL REPAIRS

HOW TO BLEED SHIMANO DISC BRAKES

If your hydraulic disc brakes have started to feel mushy or erratic then you need to bleed them. Here's how to sort Shimano brakes

DIFFICULTY 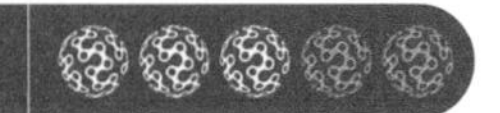

TIME 30 - 60 Minutes

TOOLS
- *Drip rag/kitchen towel*
- *Shimano hydraulic mineral oil*
- *Shimano disc brake bleed kit*
- *Bleed block*
- *Bleed port adaptor*
- *7mm spanner*
- *2mm Allen key or Torx key*
- *Small flat-head screwdriver*
- *Pad spacer tool or a large flat-head screwdriver*

WHEN
- *Your brakes are feeling spongy or your levers have excess travel*

WATCH THE VIDEO

Free show-how and know-how

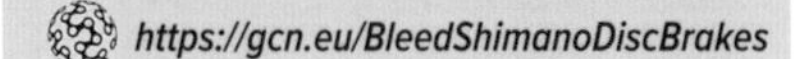
https://gcn.eu/BleedShimanoDiscBrakes

1

If you're bleeding the front brake, put the bike in a workstand angled slightly down to stop the forks from moving around. When you're working on the rear brake, angle the bike upwards to help with bubble flow and use a strap or similar to secure the bars. We'll just concentrate on the front wheel for now though.

2

Remove your front wheel. Reset the pistons by pushing them gently back into the calliper with the piston tool or a big flat screwdriver. You don't want to go in too hard and gouge the brake pads as you can easily damage them.

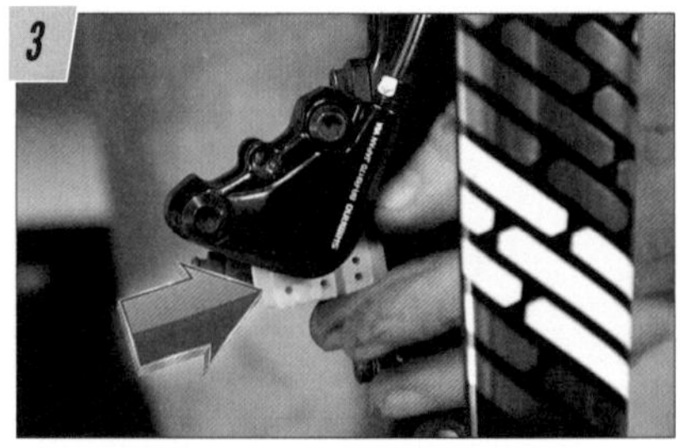

3

With the pistons reset, remove the brake pads to stop them getting ruined by any spilt fluid. First remove the little clip on the right-hand side and then undo the little retaining rod with the flathead screwdriver. Insert your bleed block into the calliper to hold the pistons in place.

TOP TIP

With your pads out it's a good opportunity to inspect them for wear and see if you need new ones. Fresh pads always make the system easier to set up anyway, so if in doubt, install a new set later.

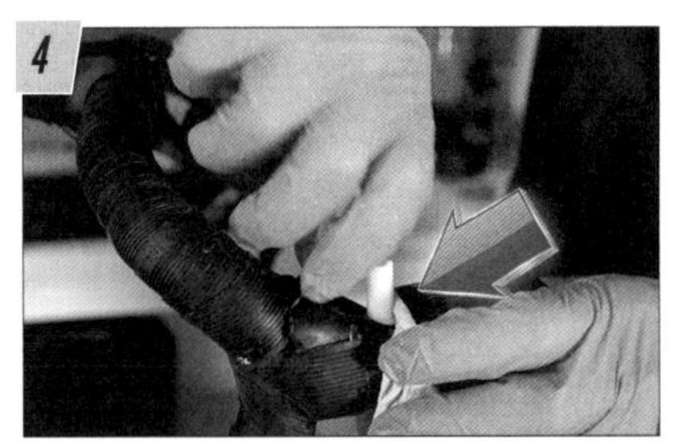

4

Peel back the shifter hood and undo the bleed port screw on the top of the shifter body. It's quite easy to round these out, so ensure to use a good quality, undamaged Allen key. If you've got more recent Shimano brakes you'll need to use the bleed port adapter which screws into the top of the bleed port.

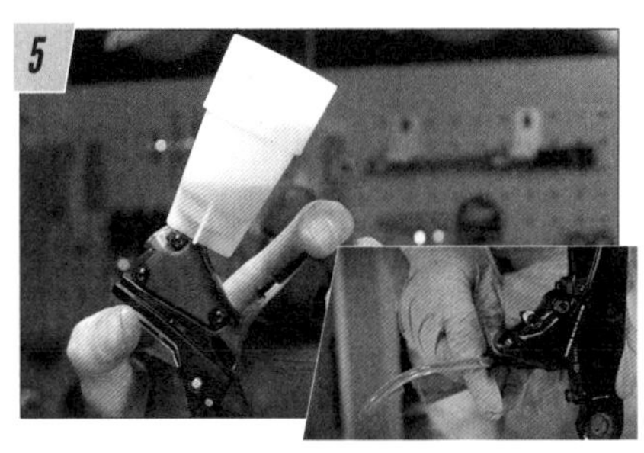

5

Take the fluid reservoir and screw that into the top of the adapter or bleed port. Grab a syringe and fill it halfway with the hydraulic mineral fluid. Move to the brake itself and take off the little rubber dust cover on the calliper bleed port nozzle and push the syringe hose onto it.

6

Use your 7mm spanner and undo the bleed port quarter of a turn. While still holding the syringe in place, carefully go back up to the bar and remove the plug pin out of the reservoir 'bucket'. This opens up the system so the oil can flow up into the reservoir taking any bubbles with it.

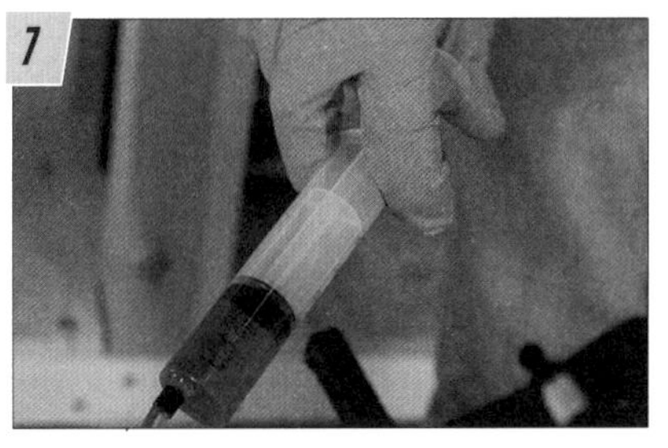

7

Depress the syringe carefully to push the fluid through the system. Don't push too hard as this can cause it to leak. You should see air bubbles coming out of the system and into the reservoir. Continue to push fresh fluid through until the bubbles stop or you only have 10ml or so left in the syringe.

TOP TIP

Tapping the brake hose from the brake end up to the lever end can help detach air bubbles stuck to the sides of the brake or hose and 'burp' them up to the top.

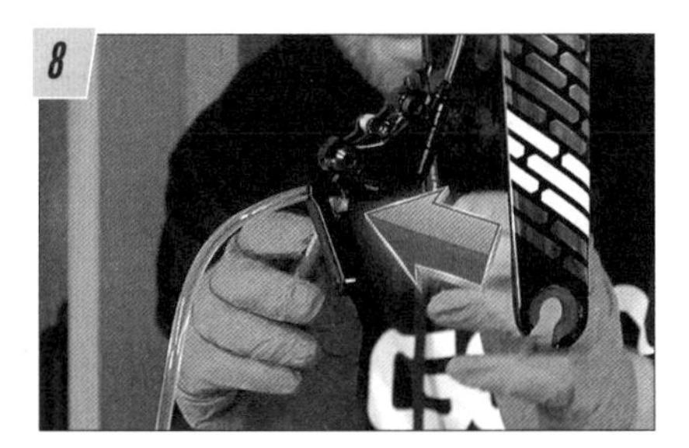

8

Tighten the calliper bleed port with the 7mm spanner. Then pull back slightly on the syringe plunger while removing it to reduce spillage. Clean up any oil with a rag or paper towel.

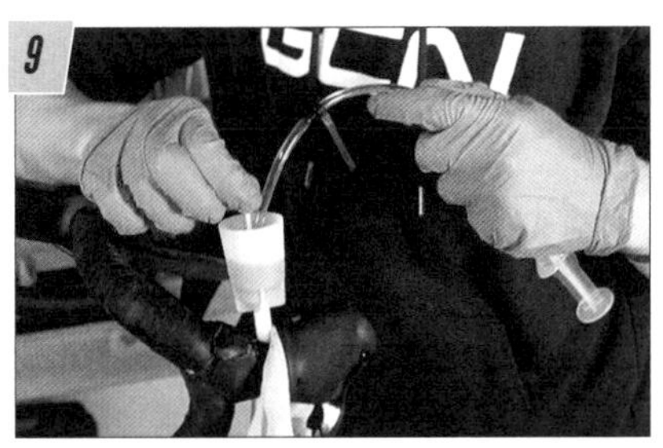

9

Now stick the syringe hose carefully into the reservoir bucket at the lever end and see if you can suck any stubborn bubbles out of the system from the top end. Replace the plug pin and remove the reservoir – cleaning up any spilt fluid.

10

Remove the piston spacer, refit the pads and replace the front wheel. Pull the brakes several times to settle them in and then spin the wheel to check for alignment or drag. Now you're good to ride, but remember that fresh pads will take a while to bed in and get to full power.

Want Our Favourite Workshop Hacks?
See page 226 for 12 top tips and tricks

SET-UP SECRETS

HOW TO SWAP QUICK CONNECT HOSES

Here's how to use Shimano Quick Connect hydraulic brake hoses to swap which lever operates which brake

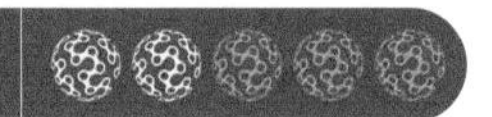

DIFFICULTY	
TIME	15 - 30 Minutes
TOOLS	• Workstand • 2 x 8mm spanners • 6mm Allen key • Brake pad spacer or folded up cardboard • Alcohol-based cleaner • Cleaning rag
WHEN	• You want to switch your brake hoses over!

TECH EXPLAINED

Quick Connect Hoses

First check if your bike has got quick-release connectors on the hoses between the bar and the frame or fork. Shimano, SRAM and others make them for their brakes, but unfortunately not many manufacturers fit them. Without them, swapping hoses becomes a complex and time consuming job you might want to leave to your local bike shop.

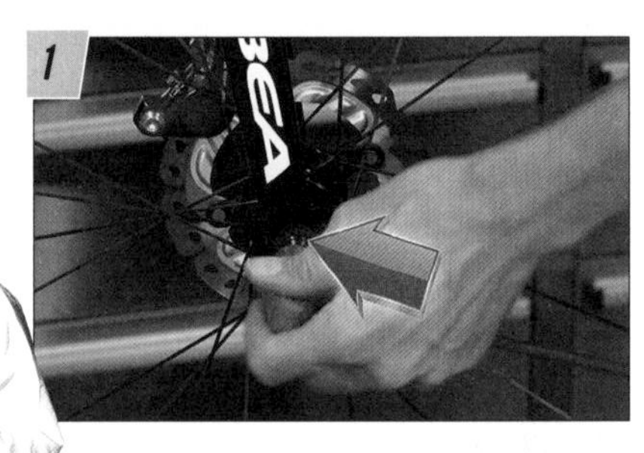

Put the bike into your workstand and before touching the brakes, remove the front wheel so there's no danger of brake oil getting onto the disc. Unscrew the axle with the 6mm Allen key and put the wheel safely to one side.

"You can sometimes hack a temporary bleed by pulling your levers to your bars and securing them with a zip-tie"

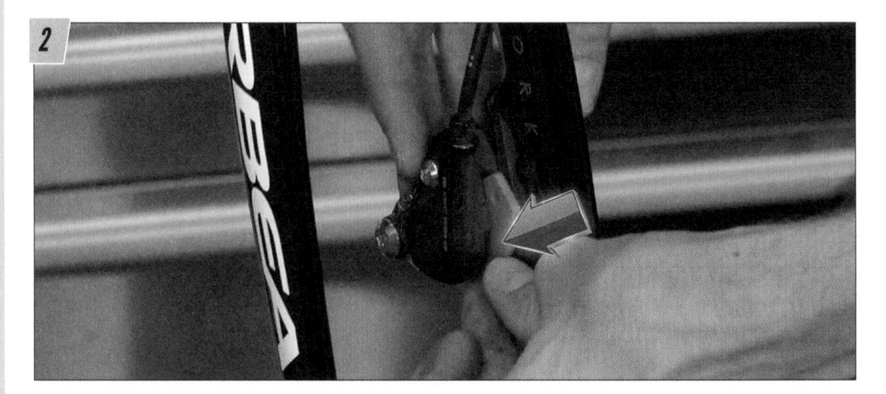

Put your travel spacer or folded cardboard between the brake pads when the wheel is out – just in case you knock or pull the brake levers. Cover the calliper with a clean rag to stop oil drip contamination too.

WATCH THE VIDEO

Free show-how and know-how

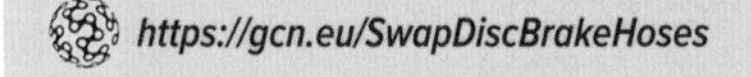

Need To Set Up Disc Brakes?
See page 140 for how to get it right

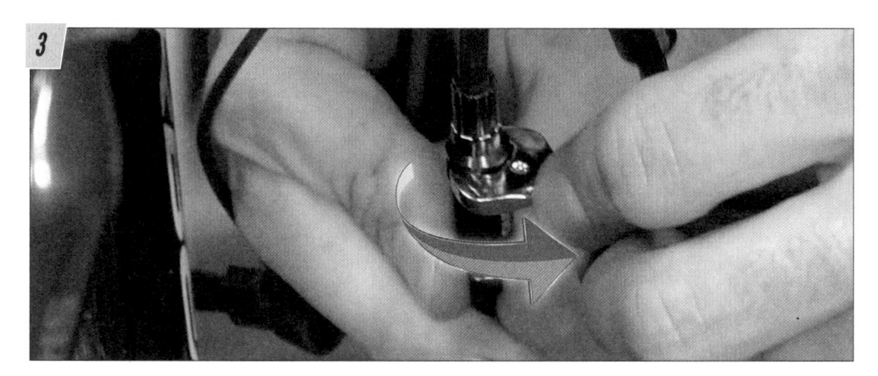

Pull off the rubber covers on the junction sections to expose the fixings underneath. Then get your two spanners (most bikes use 8mm but check beforehand) and fit top and bottom onto the junction piece. Undo each hose on each brake very slightly – about quarter of a turn – until you feel a slight jolt.

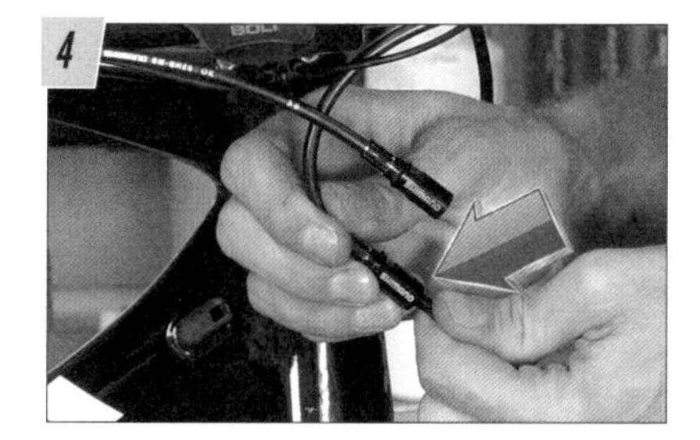

Undo both hoses completely. Try not to knock them as that can spill fluid and definitely don't touch the levers. Switch the hoses over, push them back into the junction piece and carefully tighten by hand to avoid cross-threading. Use the spanners to fully tighten them into place.

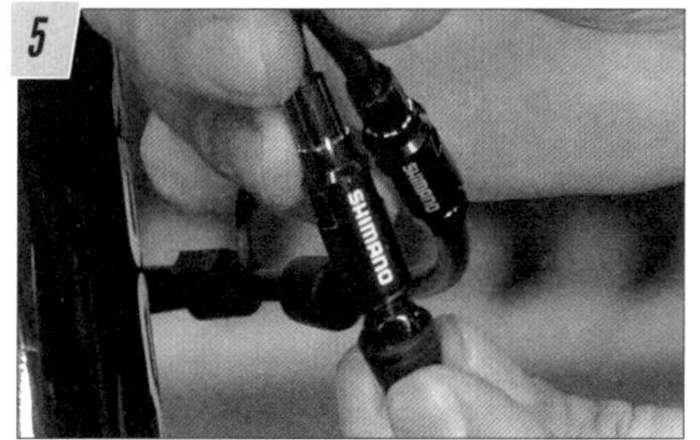

Spray the junction pieces with the cleaner and then wipe down to remove any leaked oil. Replace the rubber covers and if you've been careful and not spilt much fluid that might be job done.

Refit the front wheel and carefully pull each brake lever in turn. Don't give them a hard pull in case those junction pieces aren't together properly. If they feel OK, then increase the pressure and then pull the brakes repeatedly to check feel and pull distance are consistent on both sides.

If brake feel is still inconsistent, spongy or the levers pull straight to your bars then there's an air bubble somewhere in the system. That means you need to bleed your brakes. The technique for bleeding Shimano brakes is on page 146.

TOP TIP

You can sometimes hack a temporary bleed by pulling your levers to the bars and securing them with a zip-tie or similar and leaving them for a few hours. This lets trapped air move up into the oil reservoir where it doesn't affect function. Even if that works, do a proper bleed as soon as possible though.

SECTION 4

WHEELS & TYRES

From fixing your first puncture to truing your first wonky rim, you'll find all the wheel-related techniques you need to know in this section

BEGINNER BASICS

HOW TO CHANGE A TYRE

If it's time to replace a worn out clincher tyre or you're upgrading to a better quality one, here's the easiest way to do it

DIFFICULTY 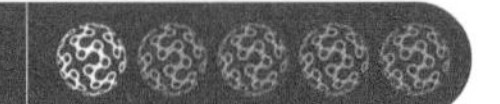

TIME 10 - 15 Minutes

TOOLS
- *Tyre levers*
- *Track pump*

WHEN
- *You've reached the wear indicators on your tyre or it looks excessively worn*

Remove the wheel with the tyre that needs replacing. You will probably need to release your brake calliper (by operating the small lever at the top) to get your tyre though the brake. Once out, remove the air from the tyre. With the most common valve type: Presta, that's by unscrewing the top of the valve and pushing it down. If you have a Schrader (car) type valve, depress the centre section.

WATCH THE VIDEO

Free show-how and know-how

Next, insert one of the tyre levers in between the bead of the tyre and the wheel rim and hook it underneath the bead. Once in place, pull it back towards the spokes and try and hook it behind one of them. It's a good idea to work away from the valve, so it doesn't get in the way.

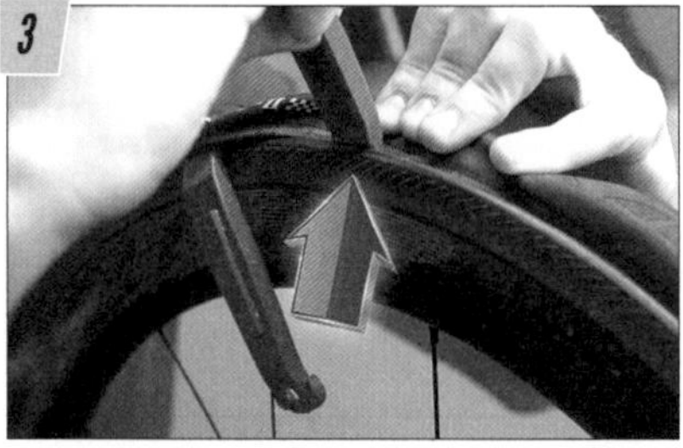

Take your second lever and insert it underneath the bead of the tyre, position it fairly close to the initial one. You should now be able to use it to pull some tyre bead over the rim, though sometimes you might need to pull down both levers together to get this process started.

Continue to work your way around pulling the bead over the rim with the lever until the enough of the tyre is loose to be able to do it by hand. Alternatively, you could carefully slide the lever around the rim, taking care not to damage the inner tube as you do though.

Now you've got half of the tyre off the rim, you need to remove the inner tube. Working opposite the valve, carefully pull the tube out until you get to the valve. Unscrew the retaining nut on the rim side and pull the valve from the wheel. Then the rest of the tyre should easily come away from the rim.

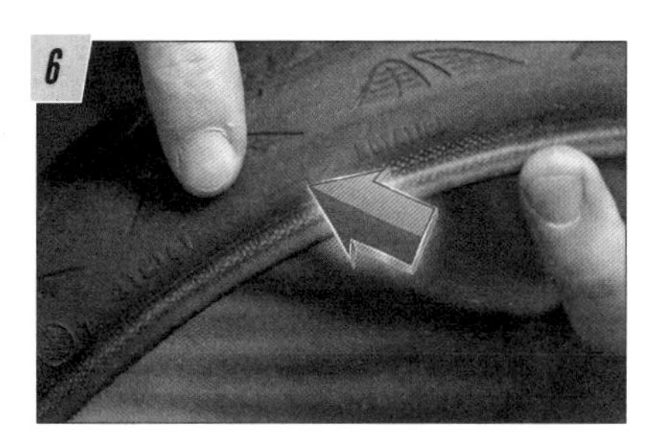

Grab your new tyre and get ready to start fitting it, but before you do, check the sidewall to see if there are any marks indicating the direction of rotation. Ensure you correctly orientate the tyre so the arrow is pointing in the direction of travel when the bike is moving forwards.

Insert one side of the tyre bead into the rim bed and start working your way around until the whole side has been fitted.

Next, pick up your inner tube and inflate it slightly just to give it a little shape. Push the valve through the hole in the rim and start fitting the inner tube inside the open side of the tyre.

Starting at the valve, work around the tyre tucking in the remaining side of the tyre bead over the rim. If the final section is tough, go around the tyre squeezing both walls together so they sit in the middle of the rim bed. This should create enough slack to easily push that final section over the rim.

TOP TIP

Should you encounter a particularly tight tyre that you just can't get over the rim using your hands, you can resort to using a tyre lever to pop that final section in place. Place it between the bead and the rim and gently lever it up over the rim, but take great care not to snag the inner tube as it could get pinched or torn.

Before starting to re-inflate the tyre, just check that the tyre bead isn't sitting on top of the inner tube at any point. If it is, then gently wiggle the tyre off it in that section.

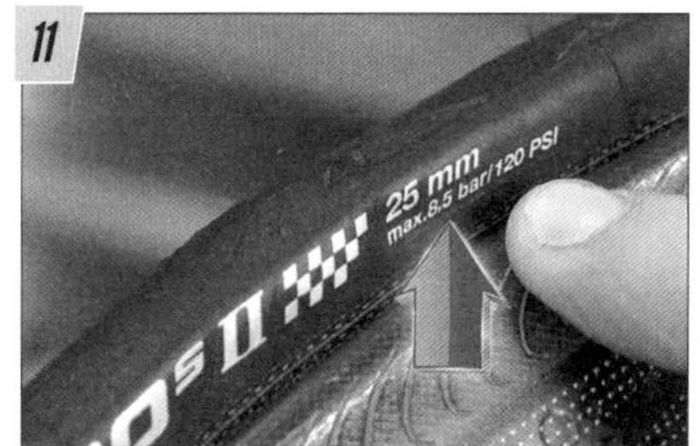

Start to add some air though the valve. Stop at around 15psi to check for any pinches and wiggle the tyre if necessary to remove them. Pump it up to the maximum pressure indicated on the tyre's sidewall to ensure that it's properly seated on the rim, then adjust to your usual riding pressure.

Want To Repair A Puncture?
Turn over to page 154

BEGINNER BASICS

HOW TO FIX A PUNCTURE

It's easy to repair punctured inner tubes rather than replacing them. It will also save you money and it's better for the environment. Here's how to do it

DIFFICULTY 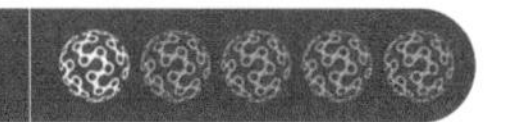

TIME 5 - 10 Minutes

TOOLS
- *Tyre levers*
- *Pen or crayon*
- *Puncture repair kit*
- *Pump*

WHEN
- *You get a flat tyre*

WATCH THE VIDEO

Free show-how and know-how

REMOVE THE INNER TUBE

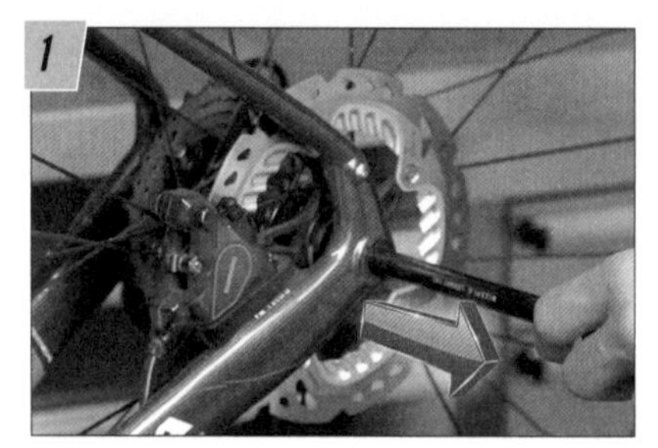

Remove the wheel from your bike by releasing the quick-release skewers or undoing your through-axle.

To get to the punctured inner tube, you need to remove one side of the tyre from the rim. To do that, take a tyre lever and slide the thinner end between the rim of the wheel and the bead or the tyre.

"Two holes side by side usually means you've suffered a 'snakebite' puncture caused by a pothole"

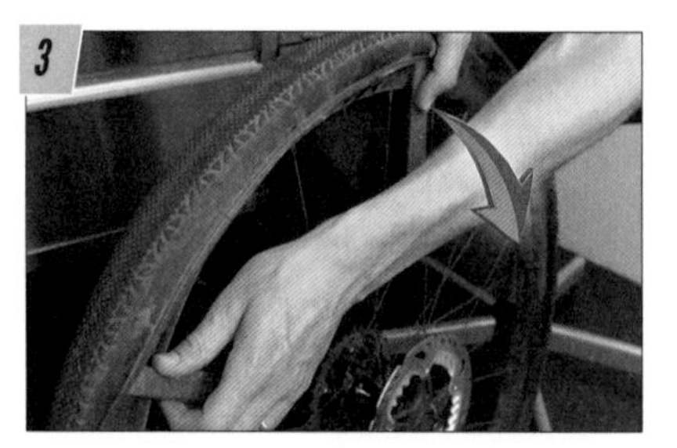

Once worked into position, push the tyre lever down and pull a section of tyre bead over the rim. Take the other tyre lever and work that between the rim and bead in the same way to pull a wider section of bead over the rim. Slide one of the levers around the rim to remove the remaining tyre bead.

With one side of the tyre off, you can now pull the inner tube free from inside the tyre and push the valve out through the hole in the rim. You may need to remove the valve locknut from the spoke side of the rim first though.

LOCATE THE PUNCTURE

1

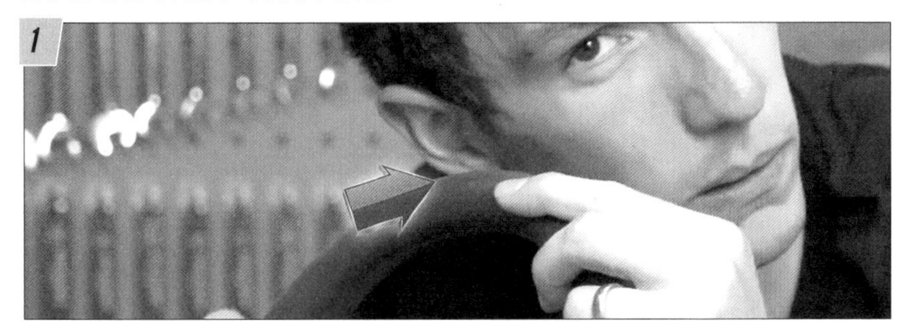

Partially inflate your inner tube so you can feel and hear where the air is escaping from. If you're by the side of a road or anywhere noisy, run the inner tube near the side of your face to help you better feel and hear the escaping air. Once you've found the hole, mark the spot with your pen.

2

Run your fingers over the inside of the rim to check that nothing is poking through to where the inner tube sits. The rim bed should be covered with rim tape and feel completely smooth.

TOP TIP

If you're repairing a puncture at home, get a bucket full of water and submerge the inner tube. Then slowly rotate it under the water and watch for a stream of air bubbles. If you have a slow puncture which only lets out a tiny bit of air, this may be the only way to locate it. Two holes side by side usually means you've suffered a 'snakebite' puncture caused by the inner tube being pinched on the rim when riding over a pothole or other sharp edge – this also may indicate that your tyre pressures are too low.

3

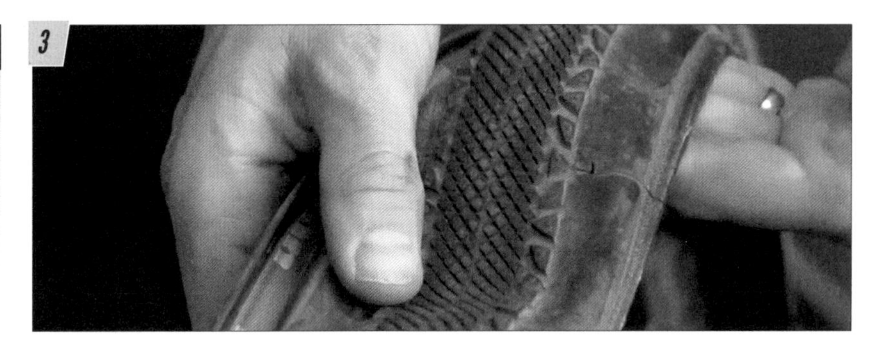

Open out the tyre and visually inspect the outer side for any visible cuts or objects such as thorns sticking out of it. At the same time, carefully run your fingers along the inside of the tyre to feel for objects that might not be visible from the outside, pulling out anything you find.

REPAIR THE PUNCTURE

1

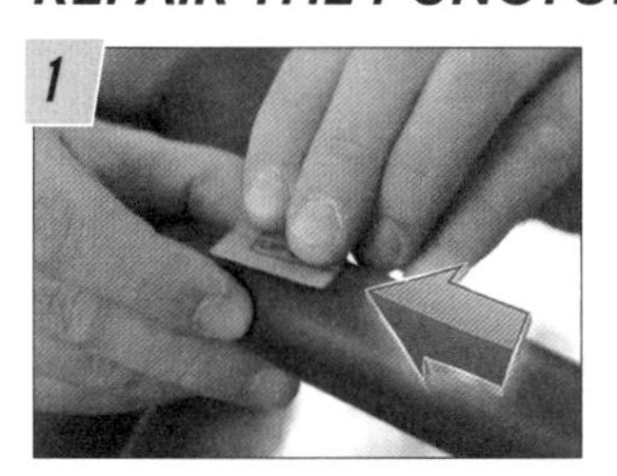

Remove the air from your tube and use the piece of sandpaper that usually comes in a puncture repair kit to lightly roughen the area around puncture. This will help form a better bond between the patch and tube.

2

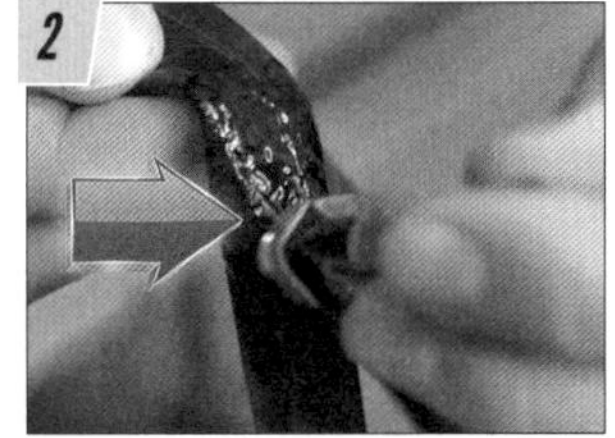

Choose an appropriate patch from your repair kit, then put a thin layer of glue over the site of the puncture that's slightly bigger than the patch. Wait a few minutes to let the glue dry before applying the patch.

COFFEE BREAK

Leave the patch in place for at least three or four minutes, ideally with something on top of it to weight it down. When you return to it, grate the piece of glass chalk usually found in puncture repair kits over the patched section. This will cover it with chalk dust and stop the repair from sticking to your tyre.

3

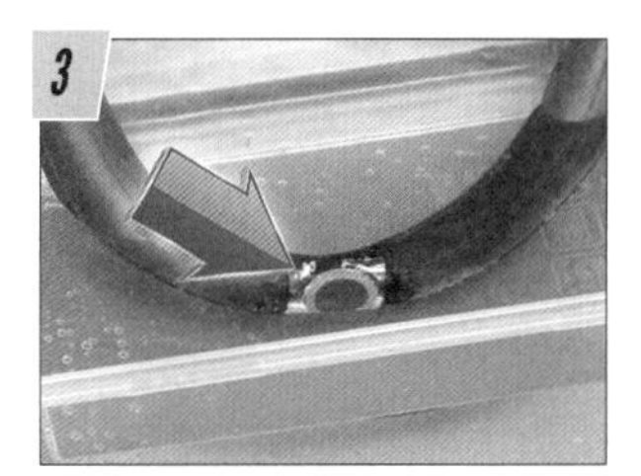

Partially inflate your inner tube and check the repair for leaks. If all's OK, insert it back into the tyre, refit the tyre on the rim and re-inflate it to your usual tyre pressure.

Banish Punctures Forever!
Turn the page to see how to go tubeless

SET-UP SECRETS

HOW TO INSTALL & SET UP TUBELESS TYRES

Make punctures a thing of the past by installing tubeless tyres. Here's how to set them up

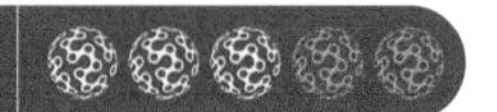

TIME 30 - 60 Minutes

TOOLS
- Track or tubeless inflation pump
- Sharp knife
- Valve core remover
- Bucket of soapy water
- Large brush
- Tubeless tyres
- Tubeless compatible wheels
- Tubeless valves
- Tubeless sealant
- Tubeless rim tape

WHEN
- You want to punctures to be a strange and distant memory

Going tubeless will help reduce the number of punctures you'll need to fix

Making the switch to tubeless tyres will protect your bike from all but the most serious of punctures and will also enable you to run lower tyre pressures. This will actually make your bike go faster on most surfaces as your tyres will soak up more road buzz. Many people are put off by the initial set-up, which can be a bit fiddly in some instances, but the extra installation hassle is well worth it for a puncture-proof bike. Here we show you the easiest method to frustration-free tubeless installation.

BEFORE YOU START

Be sure to check that you have tubeless compatible wheels and tyres (often called 'tubeless ready'). Tyres specifically designed to run tubeless have thicker beading to give a tighter fit on the rim, while tubeless wheels have a larger rim bed diameter to make installation easier.

While it is definitely possible to run standard tyres and wheels without an inner tube, setting them up will be more difficult or may not work at all. You also run the risk of the tyre bead unseating from the rim while you ride, which could well have serious consequences.

Fortunately many new bikes now come with tubeless compatible wheels and tyres even if they are running inner tubes – be sure to check the manufacturer's information if you're uncertain.

Check Your Pressures

While the benefits of going tubeless are many, tubeless tyres don't tend to hold air over long periods quite as well as their inner-tubed relatives. This makes it a good idea to check your tyre pressures before every ride and top them up as required.

If you use CO_2 cartridges, make sure your tyre sealant is CO_2 compatible

TECH EXPLAINED

Tyre Sealant

Most tubeless sealants are made from natural latex and small, suspended fibres. When you get a puncture, lower pressure inside the tyre forces the sealant through the hole which quickly gets plugged by the fibres and the coagulating latex which quickly forms a secure bond.

1

While some wheels come pre-taped or don't require tape at all, most wheels on the market will need tubeless tape to prevent air escaping via the spoke holes. Make sure the tape you buy is the right width for the internal diameter of your rims.

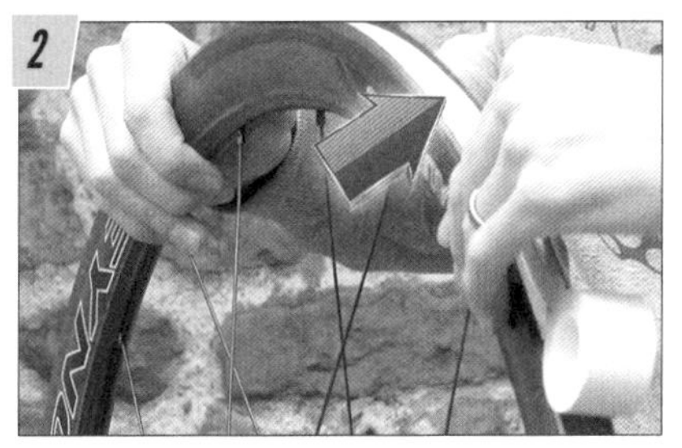

2

Ensuring your wheels are clean and dry, start applying the tubeless tape to the rim bed of your wheels. Keep the tape nice and tight as you run it around and ensure to overlap the point at which you started by at least 8cm or so.

3

Use your knife to carefully make a nice clean hole in the tape above the valve hole, then insert your valve and loosely do up the retaining collar.

TOP TIP

Tubeless valves with removable cores make adding sealant much easier. In addition to the initial set-up, you'll also need to top up your sealant every few months. Removable cores mean you can add it directly through the valve stem (with the core removed) instead of having to prise the bead away from the rim to pour the sealant in.

4

If your valves have removable cores, now is a good time to take them out either with a valve core remover or with a pair of pliers – taking great care not to damage them – particularly if using pliers.

5

Now it's time to seat the tyre. Start by seating one side of the tyre in the well of the rim as you would normally, then work around the bead until it's all inside the rim. See page 152 for more on this.

HOW TO INSTALL & SET UP TUBELESS TYRES

6

When fitting the other side of the tyre, it helps to have the wheel resting at your feet with the valve down at the bottom.

7a

Given the tighter bead on tubeless tyres, you might find it difficult to fit the final section inside the rim on the second side. To make it easier, you want to squeeze the bead on both sides of the tyre together so that it sits in the middle of the rim – which is the smallest diameter point on the wheel.

7b

If the bead is still refusing to sit in place, you can try forcing your thumbs around the bead to push any slack to the bottom of the wheel, which should then enable you to pop that final stubborn section over the rim.

7c

While some tyre manufacturers produce a tyre lubricant in order to help seat really difficult tyres, a DIY option is to use soapy water to lubricate the tyre and help it slip over the rim.

8a

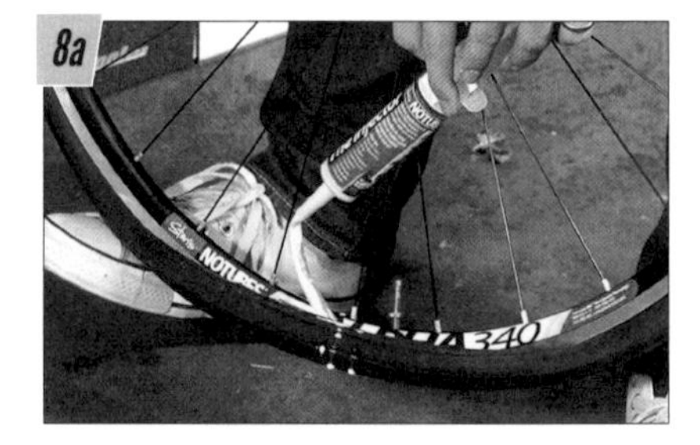

If you don't have a removable valve core, before you seat the tyre completely you'll need to add your sealant. Shake the bottle well, then pour around 55ml (2fl oz) into the open section of the tyre.

8b

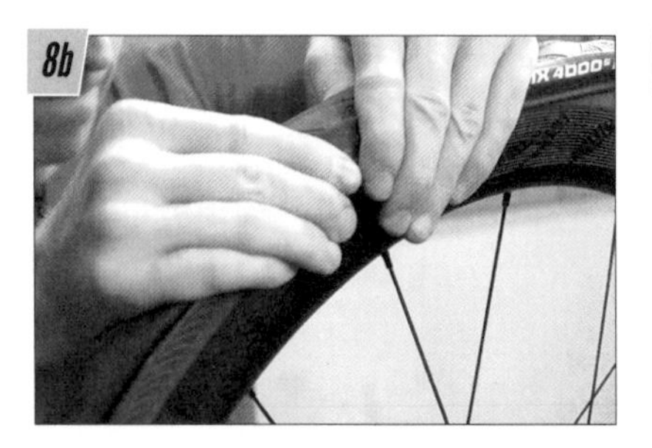

Carefully rotate the wheel around so that sealant sits in the sealed part of the tyre and push the open section of bead over the rim.

9

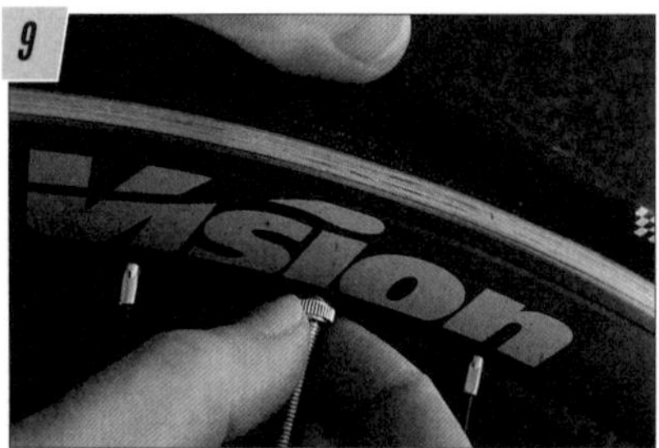

With the tyre now fitted, push the valve up to ensure that the bead of the tyre is definitely sitting either side of it, then push the valve back down and firmly do up its lockring.

10a

If your valves have removable cores, now is the time to add the sealant. Shake the sealant bottle to help distribute all the little micro-particles evenly throughout the solution.

Most sealant bottles come with a clear hose that fits over your valve stem which makes it easier to squeeze in the sealant. Use around 55ml (2fl oz) depending on the size of your tyre – bigger tyres need more sealant.

Now it's time to inflate the tyre and if your tyres had really tight beads and were tough to fit, this next process is likely to be much easier.

To make getting getting that initial seal easier, brush some soapy water between the rim and the bead of the tyre.

Next, roll the wheel along the ground to force sealant onto the bead of the tyre which will also help get the initial seal.

By vigorously pumping away with a standard track pump you should be able to get the tyre to inflate. If you're struggling, however, a track pump with a dedicated inflatable air canister specifically designed for setting up tubeless tyres will make the process a lot easier.

Once you've got that initial seal, inflate the tyre to about 50psi – which is when you should hear a load of little popping sounds as the tyre bead snaps into place on the rim.

Once the tyre is seated on the rim, hold the wheel up and spin it to check for any bulges or wobbles. If there are any, squeeze the tyre or bounce the wheel to remove them. If all looks good, reinstall the wheels, set your tyre pressures and take your bike for a test ride.

Want Tubeless Maintenance Tips?
All the info you need is on the next page

TOP TIPS

HOW TO MAINTAIN TUBELESS TYRES

While going tubeless will make punctures a distant memory, tubeless set-ups are not quite fit-and-forget, as they still need some maintenance

REGULAR INSPECTIONS

Periodically checking your tyres for signs of punctures is a good idea. Sometimes you'll get a tubeless puncture and you won't even notice because it will seal it so effectively and so quickly. Look carefully though and you should be able to see little holes or cuts in the tyre, or sometimes small traces of sealant. Also check for signs that sealant has sprayed out on your frame and fork. It can leave residue on the fork crown, on the rear brake or around the bottom bracket and seat tube area. It's difficult to judge how much sealant you've actually lost though, so your best bet is to top it up regardless.

TOPPING UP

To top up your sealant, there are two ways you can go about it. First, you can undo your valve core with a valve key and then inject sealant into the tyre system. The other way is to unseat the tyre, fully deflate it, unseat a section from the bead and then pour in the sealant. Undoing the valve core is a preferred method because it's usually less messy and less hassle than having to reseat the tyre on the rim.

CLEANING UP AND REPLACING SEALANT

Over time your sealant can dry out and if you've replaced your sealant a couple of times, there's probably a fair amount of congealed and dried up sealant accumulated in the tyre. It's a good idea to completely remove the tyre and clean the interior and the rim with a wet cloth every six months or so. This also gives you the opportunity to inspect the inside of the tyre for any big cuts or damage that you might need to pay attention to. If there's a hole in your rim tape or it's become worn, you might need to replace that as well. Just bear in mind that when you remove the tyre it can be quite messy as you can get sealant everywhere.

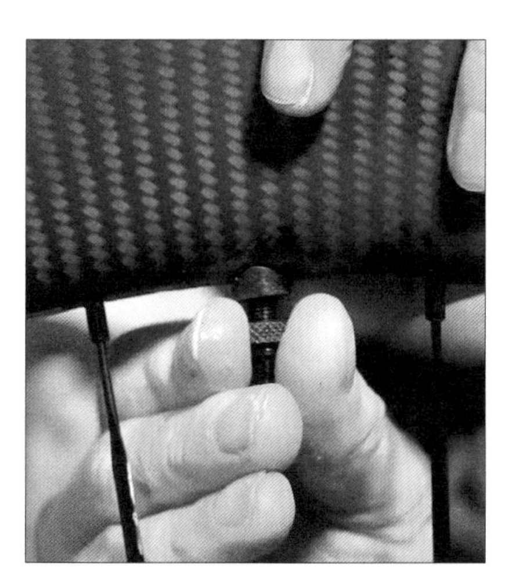

SERVICE YOUR VALVES

With the tyre off, it's a great opportunity to remove your tubeless valves and give them a service as well. Over time, sealant can build up inside the valves and then stop them from working effectively. Once removed, take the valve cores out and give them a good clean from both ends – a pipe cleaner is really helpful here.

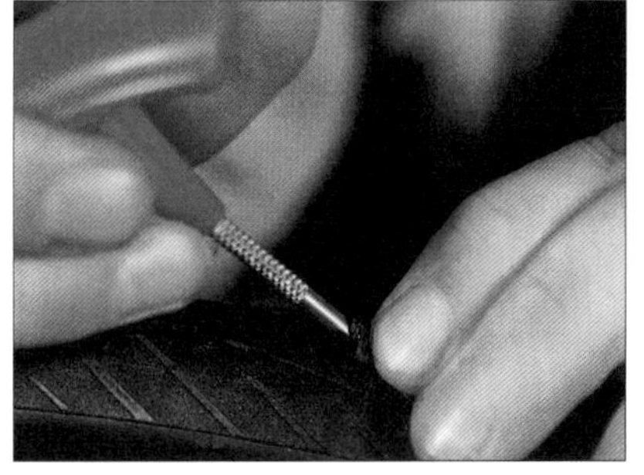

BIG CUTS

To repair a hole in your tubeless tyre that's too big for the sealant to fill, or one that seals at first but won't hold pressure, there are a few different options. You could try the DIY approach using an old piece of tyre as a patch by gluing it onto the inside, or you can buy dedicated products such as tyre boots and tyre plugs. There are a few different types of tubeless plugs, but basically you wind or push in the plug from the outside to fill the cut and enable the sealant to form a bond. There will be a protruding lump left on the outside, but this gets worn down as you ride.

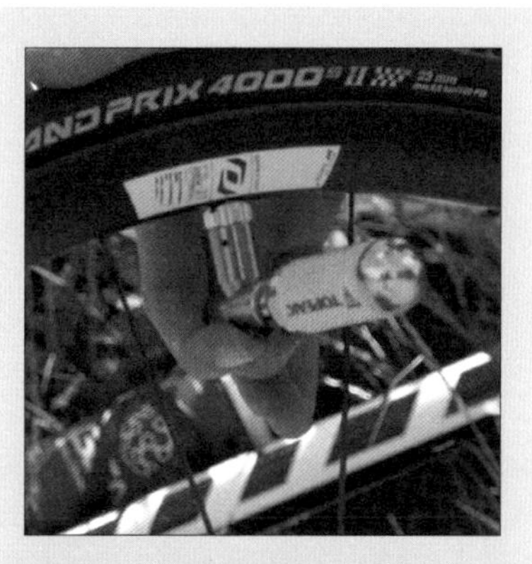

FROZEN SEALANT

One last tip, if you are re-inflating a tubeless tyre by the side of the road, take care when using CO_2 cartridges. The CO_2 is very cold when it comes out of the cartridge and as sealant is water-based, the cold gas in your tyre can cause it to freeze. Frozen sealant is unlikely to seal your puncture, so you may have to try a different approach.

ESSENTIAL REPAIRS

HOW TO REPLACE A BROKEN SPOKE

Broken spokes are a wheel nightmare, but – depending what wheelset you have and whether it's front or rear – they're relatively easy to replace at home

DIFFICULTY 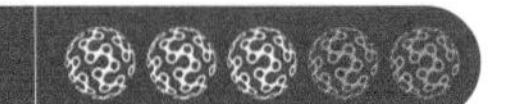

TIME 30 - 60 Minutes

TOOLS
- *The correct spoke for your wheel*
- *Spoke nipple*
- *Spoke key*
- *Flat head screwdriver*
- *Cassette removal tools (if the spoke is on the drive-side rear)*
- *Disc rotor removal tools (if on the brake side)*
- *Tyre removal tools*
- *Cable cutter*

WHEN
- *You have a broken spoke*

WATCH THE VIDEO

Free show-how and know-how

https://gcn.eu/ReplaceABrokenSpoke

First check your wheel to see how the spoke attaches. 'Straight pull' spokes thread through a block on the hub. 'J bend' spokes hook through a raised flange from the side. Some spokes thread into a nipple that sticks out of the base of the rim. Some deeper wheels use 'hidden' spokes inside the rim.

If you have 'hidden' spokes then you'll also have to remove the tyre and rim tape to get at the nipple from inside the rim, so grab the tools you need for that too. See page 152 for details.

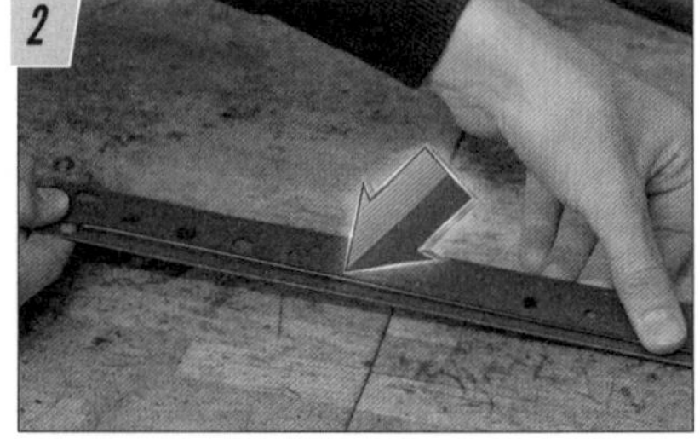

Measure the spoke length very accurately as just a few millimetres too long or too short won't work. Check the type of spoke it is – blade/aero (flat in the middle), butted (thinner in the middle than the ends), straight pull or J bend. If this is all sounding too complicated, ask your local shop to sort it out.

Carefully remove the broken spoke from the hub. If it's on the drive side rear you might have to remove the cassette. If it's on the rotor side of a disc brake wheel you may have to remove the rotors. See pages 70 and 140.

Even if you can wiggle a short stub of broken spoke out, don't forget that you'll need to get a full spoke back in. If removing obstructions is going to help this process you may as well do it now.

Rotate the wheel with the nipple positioned at the top so it doesn't fall into the rim and get lost. Unscrew the spoke from the nipple end using the spoke key to hold the nipple in place. Put the broken spoke to one side as it might come in useful later.

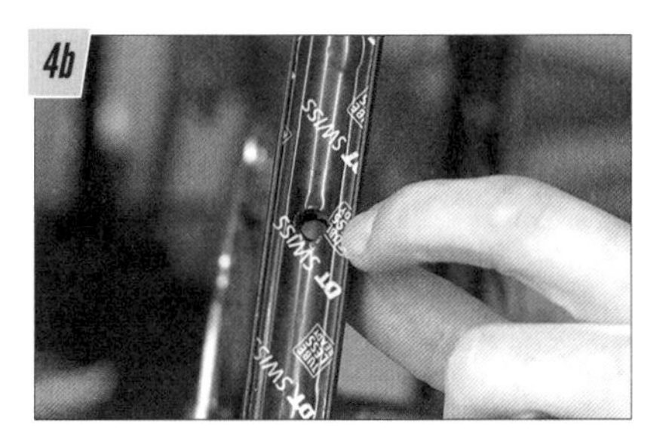

If the spoke and nipple are seized then remove the tyre and rim tape and pull the whole spoke and nipple out through the rim.

Fit the fresh spoke by checking how the other spokes on the same wheel and side are laced. Some wheels use radial spokes, while others cross three other spokes between the hub and the rim (shown). J bend spokes can insert from inside or outside too, so check and copy correctly.

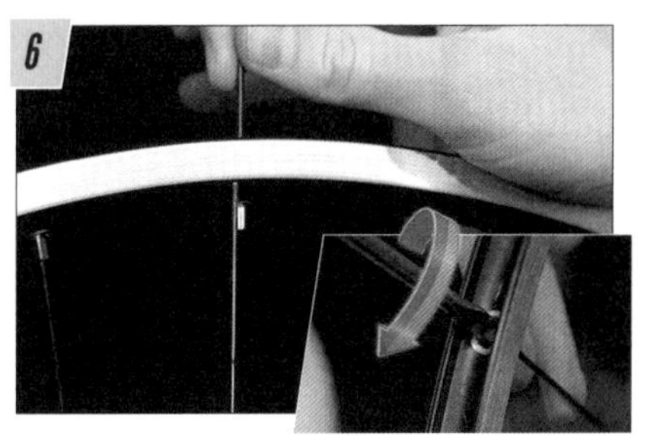

Place the new nipple through the rim. If it's awkward to hold then try threading the broken spoke you saved into the far end a couple of turns to create a useful handle (remove once in-situ). Then, using the screwdriver, start screwing the spoke carefully into the nipple.

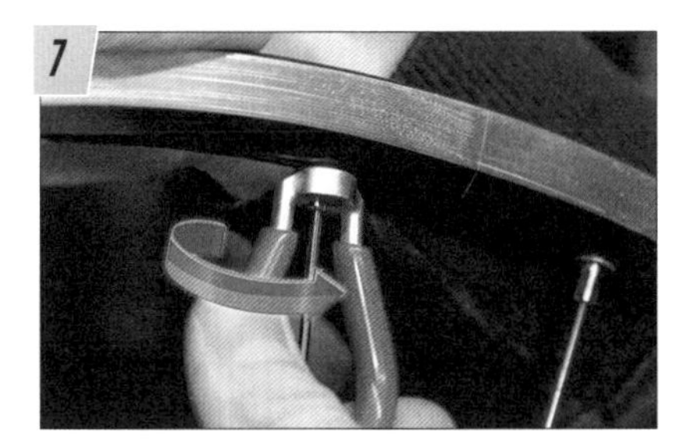

Using the spoke key, slowly tighten the spoke a quarter of a turn at a time until it's no longer slack. If you've removed the rim tape and can see the end of the spoke, check that it is not poking out of the nipple as it could push through the tape and cause punctures. Trim off any excess with a cable cutter.

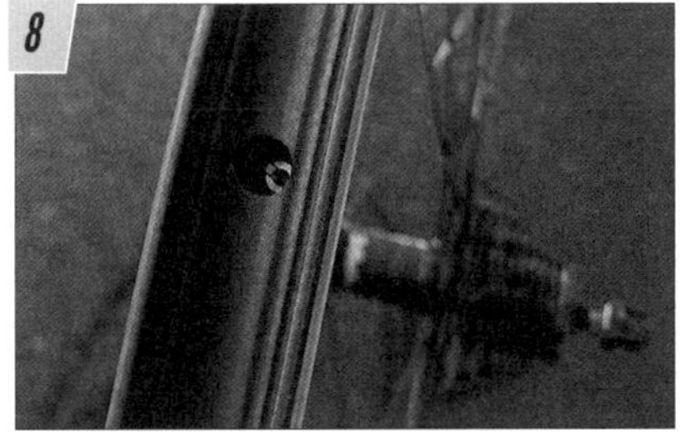

Once you've got the spoke back into place correctly and checked there's nothing pointy protruding then you're ready to re-straighten or 'true' your wheel. See page 164 for how to do that.

Need To True Your Wheel?
Turn to page 164 for how to get it right

ESSENTIAL REPAIRS

HOW TO TRUE A WHEEL

Straightening a wobbling wheel takes patience, but 'truing' is a really satisfying skill to master and the basics are really simple to learn

DIFFICULTY ●●●●○

TIME 15 - 30 Minutes

TOOLS
- *Exactly the right spoke key for the nipples*
- *Spoke clamp or pliers for aero spokes*
- *Pencil/chalk*
- *Elastic band*

WHEN
- *You have a wheel with a wonky rim*

1

If you don't have a professional truing jig, then make your fork or frame into one. Do this by fixing the pencil, chalk, or a pen onto the stay or fork leg level with the rim using the elastic band. Move it inwards while the wheel is spinning slowly until the biggest bit of the wobble touches the end.

WATCH THE VIDEO

Free show-how and know-how

GCN TECH HOW TO TRUE A WHEEL

https://gcn.eu/TrueAWheel

SCAN CODE TO WATCH THE VIDEO

TOP TIP

Once you've located the wobble, always check the condition of the rim at that point. If the wheel has been knocked out of shape by a big impact then the rim wall may be cracked or dented. You may see stress marks around the nipples too. If this is the case, give up on truing and replace the rim.

2

Work out how long the wobble is in relation to the spokes as that shows which spokes you need to adjust. Normally the spokes on the side away from the wobble will have slackened off so it's these you need to tighten up.

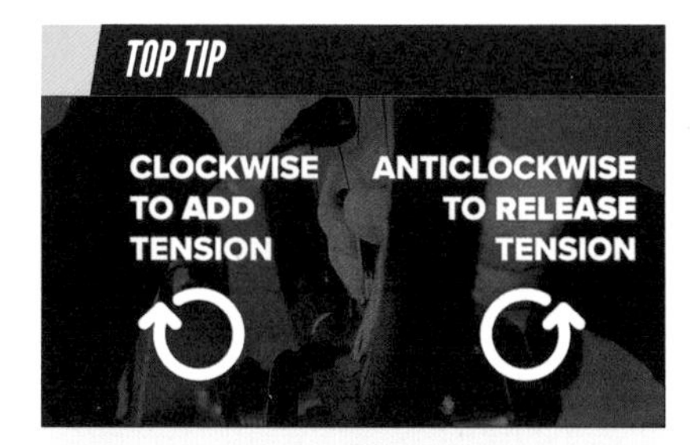

Looking from above, spokes tighten clockwise and loosen anti-clockwise. Always make sure you have exactly the right spoke key for your nipples too, as a rounded off nipple is a nightmare to remove and replace.

Never turn the nipple by more than a quarter of a turn at a time, and use your spoke clamp tool or pliers to hold aero spokes straight.

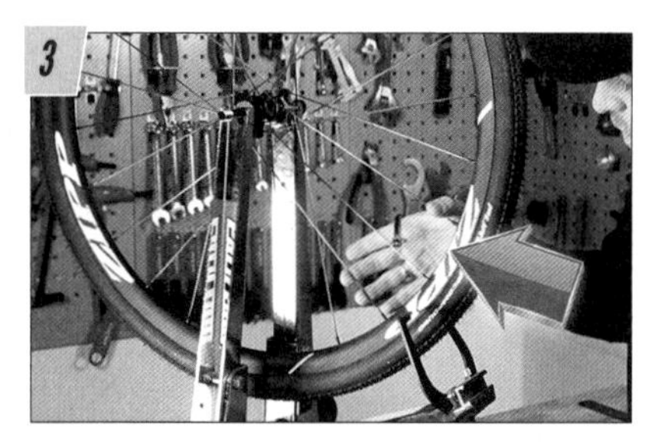

Start with the relevant side spoke nearest the biggest part of the wobble and increase tension by quarter of a turn. Spin the wheel to see what effect that has had. If the wobble has decreased then move the chalk/pencil in closer till it contacts again.

If not, tighten the spokes either side of the first spoke you tensioned too, then spin and check again. If necessary move the chalk/pencil and then continue until the wobble is mostly gone. Don't go mad chasing absolute perfect straightness though as you risk over-stressing the wheel.

Now 'ping' the spokes in the rest of the wheel with your fingers to check your adjusted section is at a similar tension to everything else. Lightly tighten any obviously slack spokes before they start to let the wheel wobble.

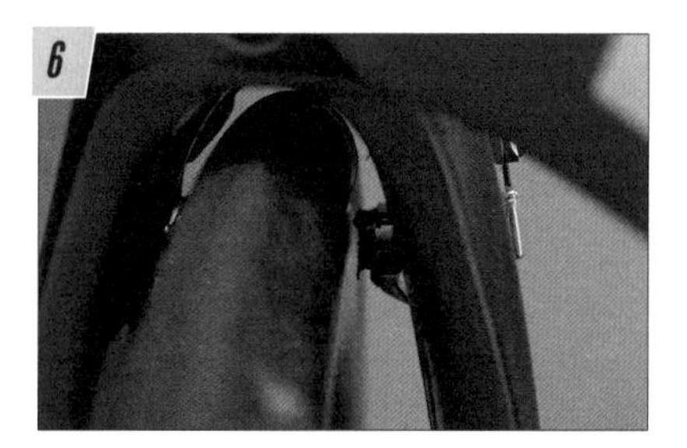

Once you're done tweaking, check that the centre of the wheel is still on the centreline of the bike by sighting it against the seat tube or head tube. Check there is no obvious 'hop' or any flat spots in the wheel at the same time too. If it's all good you're ready to ride.

If you can't get the wheel straight or you've ended up with obviously different or excessive spoke tensions, a shift to one side or a vertical hop in the wheel. Don't make things worse by chasing the mistake, take the wheel to your local bike shop or wheel builder instead.

You may get some creak or 'ping' from the spokes when you start riding but that's normal. Check rim wobble and new spoke tension regularly for the next few rides though and take your spoke key with you in case it does needs adjusting.

For The Lowdown On Bottom Brackets
Head over to page 180

ESSENTIAL REPAIRS

HOW TO SERVICE CARTRIDGE BEARINGS

Are your wheels' sealed cartridge bearings noisy or wobbly? Here's how to get them riding fast and super-smooth once again

DIFFICULTY 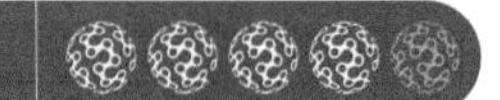

TIME 20 - 45 Minutes

TOOLS
- *Degreaser*
- *Cleaning rag*
- *Good quality grease*
- *Correct size replacement bearings*
- *Bearing removal punch*
- *Bearing press*

WHEN
- *Your wheels aren't running as smoothly as they used to*

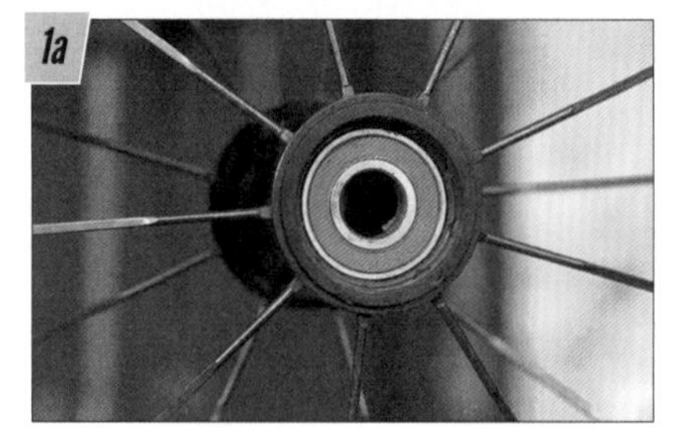

1a

First check the bearing system on your wheels. Most cartridge bearing wheels are non-adjustable and you just need to refresh the grease or replace the cartridges when they wear out. That's what we're dealing with in this walkthrough.

1b

Some wheels use a similar adjustable preload collar/locknut system to cup and cone bearings though. If that's the case then follow our walkthrough on page 168 for regular servicing but come back here once they need refreshing or replacing.

WATCH THE VIDEO

Free show-how and know-how

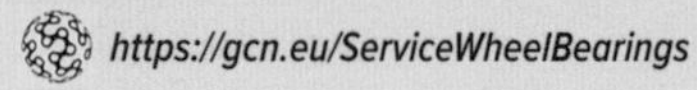

https://gcn.eu/ServiceWheelBearings

> *"If your bearings feel dry and squeaky, but aren't wobbling, fresh grease might be enough to revive them"*

2

If your bearings feel dry and squeaky, but aren't wobbling, fresh grease might be enough to revive them. Remove the protective end caps. These will either pull off or unthread depending on the wheel design, so check for spanner flats or a fitting for an Allen key as a clue that they unscrew.

3

Once you've removed the protective caps you'll see the rubber seal rings on the bearings. Use the knife or screwdriver to very carefully lift the seal away from the bearing. Any cut, nick or split here means a new bearing though, so be REALLY careful. Once off, clean it and put it somewhere safe.

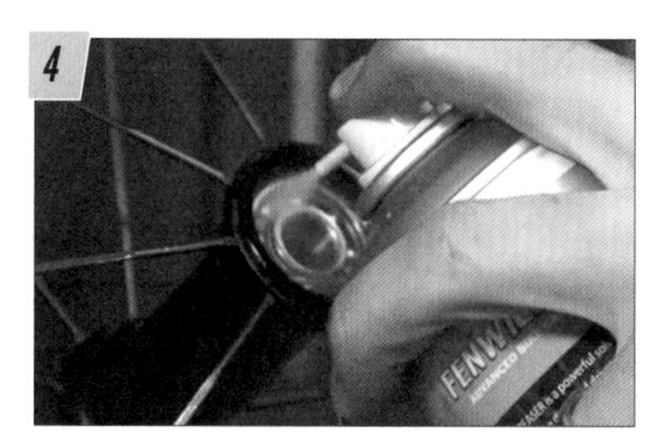

Use a degreaser spray to clean any old dirty grease and grit out of the bearings. Give the bearings a wipe without knocking them out of place and then let the degreaser evaporate. Pipe in fresh grease and then carefully replace the seals making sure they don't get kinked or trapped.

Now repeat for the other bearings and see if that's done the trick. If it hasn't or the bearing has gone wobbly, then you need to completely remove and replace it. For most riders, asking a shop to do this is the simplest option and saves buying specialist tools for a job you won't do that often.

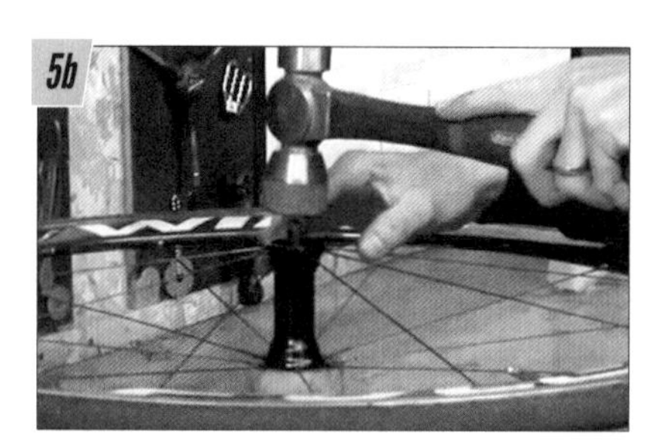

If you decide to continue, first you need to remove the axle. Most axles press-fit into place so just need tapping out carefully with a soft-faced hammer. Be aware that the axle can also take the freehub body and other internals with it when you remove it too, so do it somewhere clean and uncluttered.

TOP TIP

Never use a metal hammer on your axle as it can easily flare the ends which means it won't go through the bearings or the end caps anymore and will need replacing. If you have no other option, use a piece of wood or thick plastic between the hammer and axle to protect the ends.

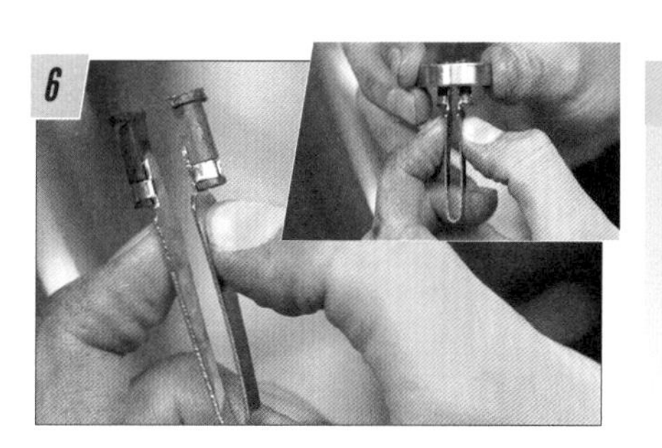

Once the axle is removed, use the bearing removal punch or puller to tap out the bearings from the other side of the hub. Again, go gently as the punch and bearings can fly out the far end at speed if you're not careful. Once the bearings are out, check for corrosion inside the hub and clean if needed.

TOP TIP

Don't be tempted to drift the bearing out with a chisel/screwdriver or similar. We know it doesn't matter if you damage the old bearings but you could easily damage the hub shell in the process and that could mean a whole new wheel.

Use your bearing press to carefully push each new bearing into place. Never try and fit both sides at once as they rarely line up right. Always use the correct adaptor that presses on the outer edge of the bearing – not the inner one too, otherwise you can distort and completely ruin the bearing.

TOP TIP

You might spot a theme here, but again, don't be tempted to knock the bearings in with a hammer or piece of wood. You'll almost certainly damage and/or misalign the bearings so they'll never spin properly. You could also damage the hubs too.

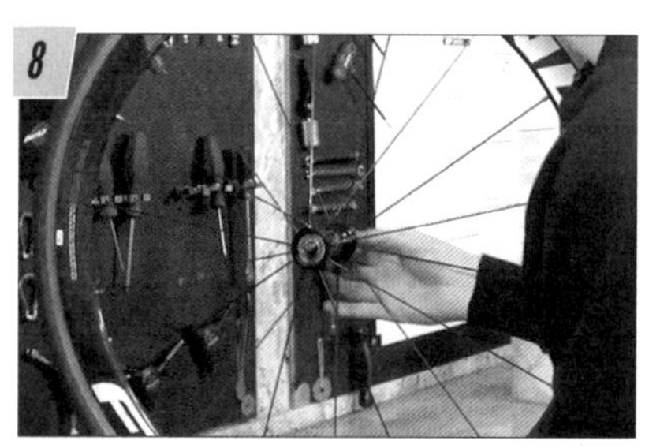

Once the fresh bearings are all installed, lightly grease the axle and push or tap that back into place gently. Refit the end caps, check everything spins sweetly and then you're good to go.

Is Your Wheel Wobbling At The Hub?
See page 168 for how to adjust it

ESSENTIAL REPAIRS

HOW TO ADJUST CUP & CONE BEARINGS

Cup and cone bearings are a brilliant way to make a bike wheel spin smoothly, but they do need looking after and adjusting correctly

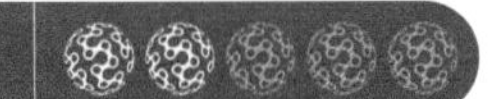

TIME 15 - 45 Minutes

TOOLS
- Cone spanners
- Bench vice
- Bearing grease
- Cleaning rag

WHEN
- Your bearings aren't running smoothly

1

Cup and cone bearings are faster rolling through corners due to less resistance. However, friction builds up on each individual ball bearing as they are in angular contact with one another. As a result, they need to be serviced more regularly than cartridge bearings.

WATCH THE VIDEO

Free show-how and know-how

https://gcn.eu/AdjustCupAndConeBearings

TOP TIP

Some of the cartridge bearing systems out there work on a very similar preload system as cup and cone bearings. Follow the bearing tensioning and locknut clamping process shown here to properly adjust them and get them running perfectly.

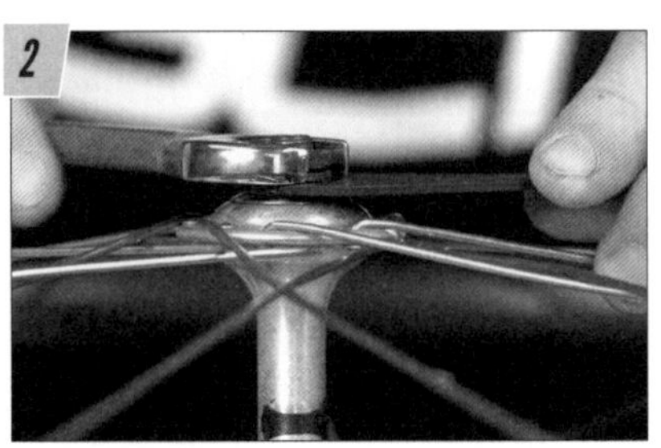

2

Hold the flat faces on the inner cone with your cone spanner and then loosen the outer locknut slightly. Now, hold the locknut on the other side and loosen the cone on the first side very slightly so you can see into the bearings, but not so much that they fall out.

If everything looks clean and smooth, dab in some fresh grease for good measure and lightly tighten the cone back into place.

If the grease is dirty or the bearings look rough, it's worth completely removing the bearings, cones and axles and giving everything a good clean. Repeat for the other bearings too.

TOP TIP

If the bearings are looking worn but the cup and cone races are still smooth, then replace the bearings and the grease. Unfortunately if the inner races are pitted or worn, it's time for new hubs. That's why it's crucial to keep on top of the adjustment.

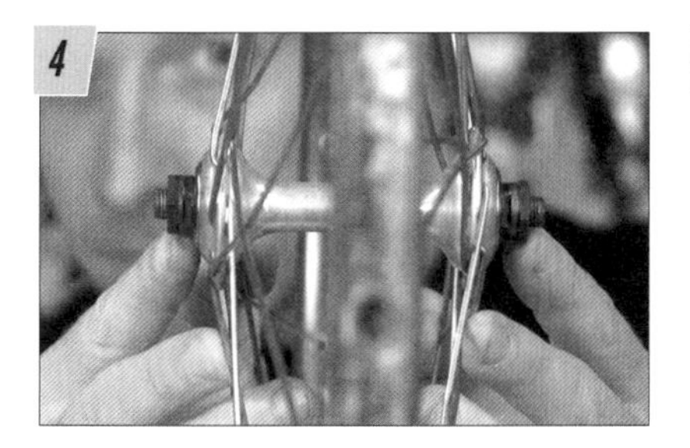

Before starting to adjust the bearings check the axle is central. There should be the same amount projecting from each side of the hub. However, previous adjustments can make them drift to one side or another over time, so rebalance accordingly.

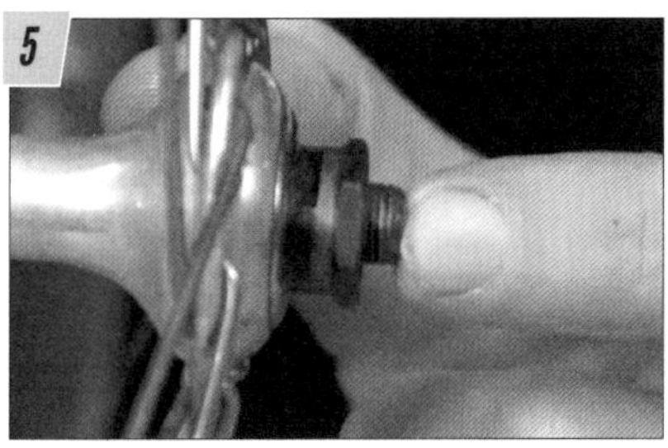

Once everything is clean and balanced it's time for the fine adjustment. Start by lightly greasing the axle threads so everything moves easily. Then tighten the cone into the hub with your fingers until there's no wobble in the axle, but it's still spinning smoothly.

TOP TIP

The key to success is patience and making the smallest possible tweaks until the cone preload is perfect. Don't be too stubborn to take a coffee break and regroup if it becomes more about swearing than bearings though.

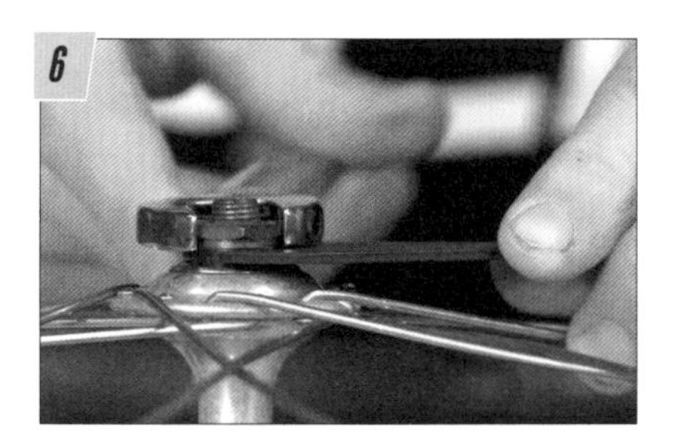

Hold the cone in place with the spanner and finger tighten the locknut into place against it. Check again for wobble or tightness and adjust if necessary. Now use an adjustable spanner or second cone wrench to nip the lockring tight against the cone.

TOP TIP

If you find the cone always moves easier than the locknut when trying to tighten them together, try slightly over-tightening the cone so that it 'backs off' to the correct adjustment against the locknut. Alternatively, hold the locknut on the far side of the wheel so that you're tightening against that rather than potentially loosening the cone.

If you're lucky or some kind of bearing whisperer, the hub will be smooth and wobble-free first time. However, for most of us there now follows a process of repeated tiny adjustments between too stiff and too loose. You'll get there eventually and it's a really satisfying feeling when you do.

Ride Faster For Free
Find out how over on page 232

ESSENTIAL REPAIRS

HOW TO SERVICE YOUR FREEHUB

Your freehub can get gunged up with lube and road muck over time. Here's how to extract it from your wheel and get it running as good as new

DIFFICULTY 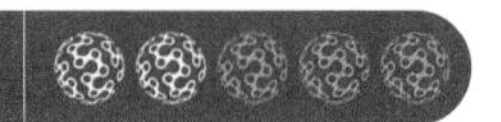

TIME	20 - 30 Minutes
TOOLS	• Allen keys • Cone spanners • Degreaser • Dry lube • Cleaning rags
WHEN	• The engagement from your freehub feels sluggish

TECH EXPLAINED

How A Freehub Works

The freehub body is the part of your rear wheel on which the cassette sits. Inside the hub are a number of small sprung levers (known as pawls) encircled by a much larger number of teeth. The freehub is designed so that when you freewheel, the pawls and teeth click past each other rather than engage, but when you pedal, the pawls lock onto the teeth and propel your bike forward. After many hours of riding in foul weather, dirt and grime can enter the freehub and gunge up the spring mechanism so that the pawls are slow to move and engage with the teeth, or in extreme scenarios, don't engage at all. Servicing your freehub after a hard winter of riding is a good idea to keep it in good condition.

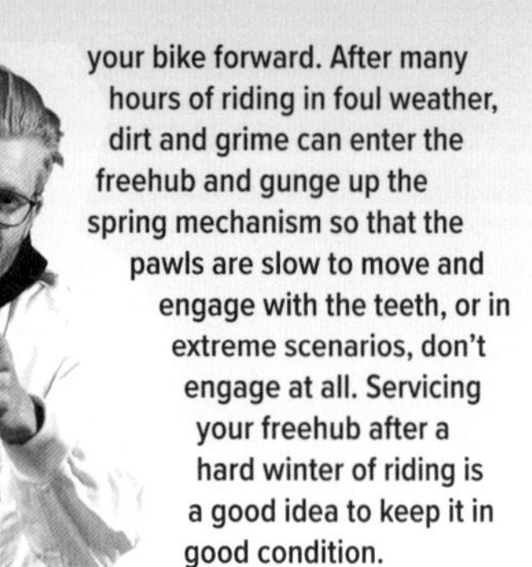

"After many hours of riding in foul weather, dirt and grime can enter the freehub and gunge up the spring mechanism"

WATCH THE VIDEO

Free show-how and know-how

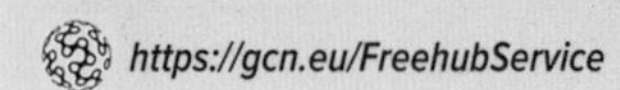

TOP TIP

In addition to servicing your freehub, you may need to change it to a different type if you're switching to a new drivetrain. For example, SRAM's 12-speed and some of their newer 11-speed cassettes use an XDR freehub rather than the standard Shimano HG type. Before going down this route though, you'd better check that your existing rear wheel is compatible with your intended new freehub.

1

Remove your rear wheel from your bike and then take the cassette off the wheel – see page 70 for our step-by-step guide on how to do that.

Service Your Wheel Bearings
Head over to page 166

There are a few different ways to remove a freehub from a wheel. Here we'll look at the three most common. Some freehubs are kept in place by the wheel being held in the dropouts and can be simply pulled off when the wheel is free from the bike.

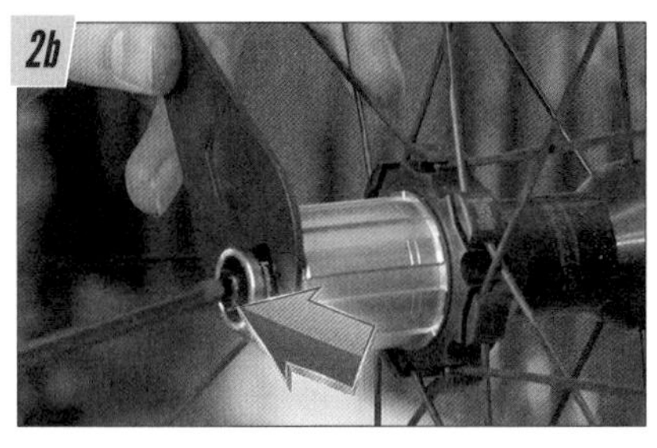

Other wheel brands use a locknut to hold the freehub in place. To take it off, hold the locknut with a cone spanner and then turn the axle with an Allen key. Once the nut is removed the freehub will pull straight off.

Another common method of removing the freehub requires holding an Allen key in the non-drive side of the axle and then using another Allen key to unscrew a locknut from the drive side.

Most systems have the pawls on the freehub body itself and the teeth on the inside of the wheel hub. However, on some wheels the pawls and teeth are the other way around.

Whatever set-up you have, take care not to dislodge the pawls and springs when removing the freehub from the wheel.

Depending on your freehub, you may be able to remove the pawls and springs to clean them individually, but it's often easier and less fiddly to spray them with degreaser and gently wipe them down in place.

Once clean, don't be tempted to use regular grease to re-lube your freehub as it's far too viscous and sticky. While specialist freehub greases are available if you want to use them, dry chain lube does the job too.

Simply put a few drops of dry lube on each pawl and spring, then you're ready to carefully reassemble your rear wheel.

SECTION 5

FRAME & FORKS

Arguably the most important components of any bike and the ones the get the least attention. Here we also have advice on headsets, bottom brackets, internal cabling and much more

TOP TIPS

KEEP YOUR BIKE LOOKING LIKE NEW

How to protect your bike from getting scratched, rubbed and chipped to help it stay in showroom condition for longer

STONE CHIPS

Particularly if you're a gravel rider or you regularly ride rough roads, the underneath of your downtube and the rear of your seat tube are two places that are really susceptible to stone chips. To keep them at bay, applying some long strips of helicopter tape will provide a protective barrier.

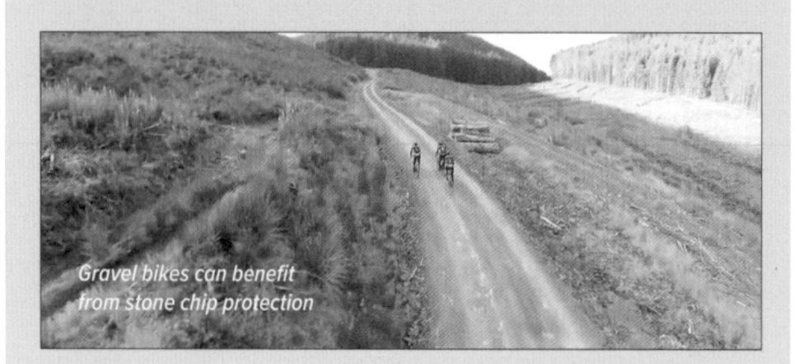

Gravel bikes can benefit from stone chip protection

HEEL RUB

Scuffed crank arms is a particular problem for those who ride with their toes angled away from the bike. No amount of protective tape is going to protect your cranks from scuffing, but you could move your cleats further towards the inside of the shoe to give your heels a bit more clearance and stop them rubbing. Consult a bike fitter before doing this though as this may over-stress your knees.

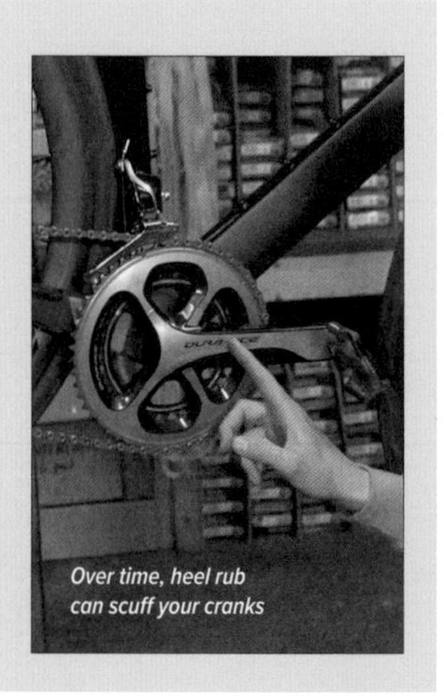

Over time, heel rub can scuff your cranks

CABLE RUB

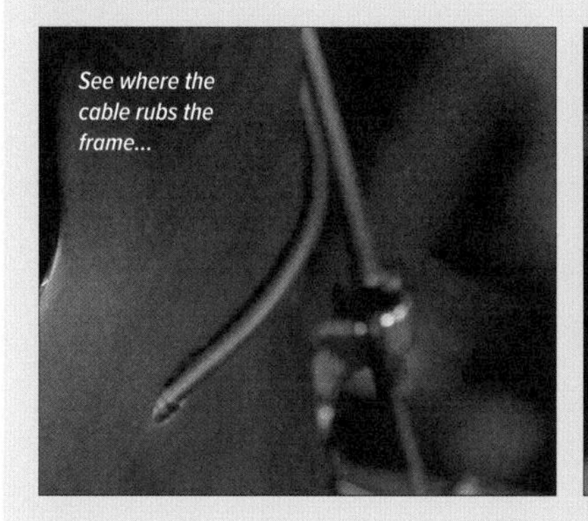
See where the cable rubs the frame...

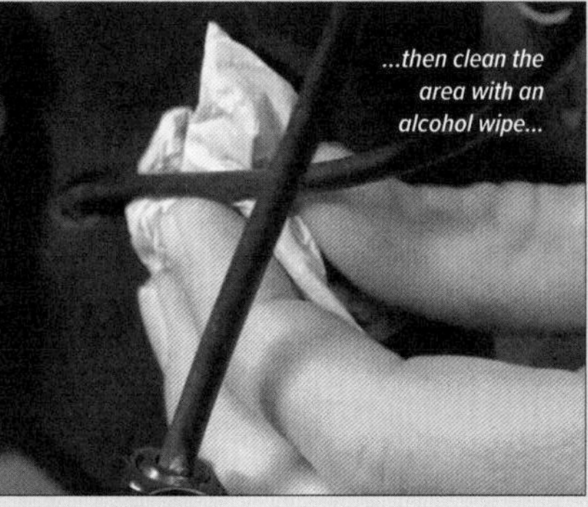
...then clean the area with an alcohol wipe...

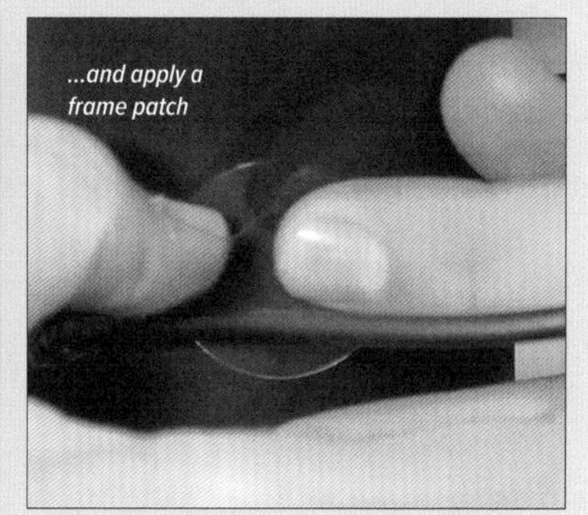
...and apply a frame patch

Cables that rub against your frame are a common problem around the head tube, but it can also happen down on the chainstays. Fortunately though, it's an easy problem to fix. To see where your cables are likely to rub, turn the handlebars back and forth and note any areas where the cables come in contact with your frame.

There are two methods for protecting your frame. The first is to apply protective clear plastic stick-on patches to any affected areas. Ensure the section you're going to apply your patch to is totally free of grease and grime, by using an alcohol wipe before applying your patch. While you can buy pre-made patches, a cheaper and more customisable alternative is to buy a sheet of helicopter tape and cut out your own.

The other option is buy some rubber cable protectors to slide onto your cables where they are likely to make contact with your frame. Being softer than the cables, the protectors won't chafe your paintwork. While they look neater than clear patches, they can work their way off out of position as you ride.

Chainstays can take a real beating from chain slap

Protecting your chainstay will also quieten your ride

TOP TIP

When leaning your bike up against the wall or something similar, put the rear tyre in contact with the wall (as opposed to your handlebars or saddle). This makes the bike more stable and you're less likely to get scuffs on your bar tape or the edges of your saddle.

BATTERED CHAINSTAYS

Your chainstays are an area that can take a hammering on rough roads, as the chain is likely to bounce around, hit your stays and chip the paint. They can also get damaged when you remove the rear wheel to transport your bike in a car or a bike bag, as the chain can end up rubbing on against the paintwork.

Often bikes will come supplied with a stick-on chainstay protector, or you can buy and apply them yourself. A cheaper solution is to neatly apply a strip to two of electrical tape along the chainstays, though you'll probably need to replace it regularly. There is a third and more heavy duty option which is standard on mountain bikes, but less common on road bikes, and that is to fit a neoprene protector that wraps around the lower chainstay.

For The Ultimate Cleaning Regime
Fast forward to page 214

PROBLEMS SOLVED

INTERNAL CABLING ROUTING HACKS

Fitting a cable into an internally routed frame can be fiddly and frustrating. Here are a few different methods that will make it far easier

Bikes with internally routed cables look great as their sleek lines are not cluttered up with brake and gear cables. However, the flipside of cables that run inside your frame is that they're much tricker to replace. While some frames and components have internal cable guides that make the job of changing your hoses or cables much easier, many others do not. Here we're going to look at a few different ways in which you can make installing new internal cables or hoses a much easier job.

ALWAYS USE A NEW CABLE

You can reuse cable if it's in good condition

If you're replacing a standard inner cable, always use a fresh new one. If you try reusing an old cable, however good the condition, it's likely that while threading the cable through the inside of a frame or handlebar it will rub up against the inside wall causing it to fray. New cables are usually soldered very finely on the end to prevent them from fraying. If you must use an old cable though, you could try giving it a fresh trim and then add a dab of super glue to try and seal the ends together before you start the threading process.

GRABBING TOOL METHOD

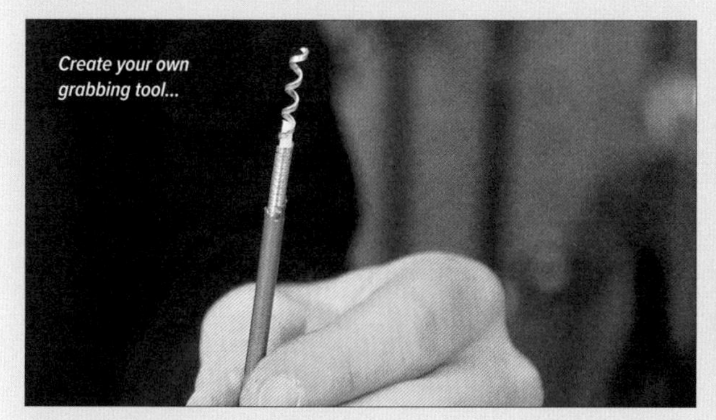
Create your own grabbing tool...

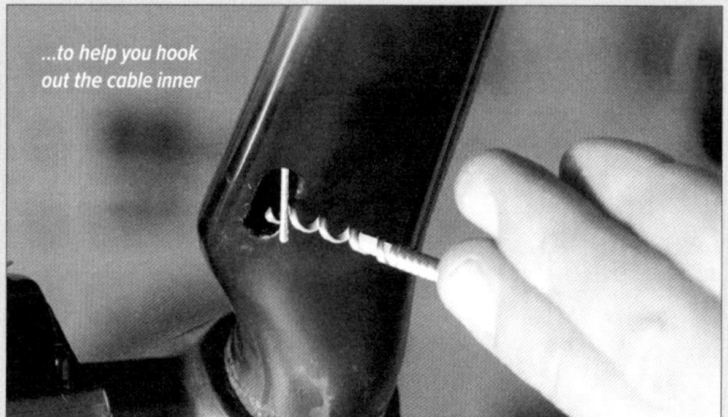
...to help you hook out the cable inner

When you need to run an outer cable through a new frame or set of bars, run an inner cable through the frame first, then once that's successfully in place, you can just run the outer along it and use it as a guide. However, the chances of successfully pushing the new inner through the entry hole and then wriggling it around so that it emerges from the exit hole are very slim. Shining a torch up inside the frame through the bottom bracket, head tube or another cable entry point will make it easier to see where your new cable has got to.

But even if you can see it, persuading the tip to emerge through the exit point is still far from easy.

Here's where a homemade grabbing tool can come in handy. Take an old brake cable outer, cut off 15cm or so, then strip away 5 or 6cm of the plastic sheathing away. Take a pair of pliers and pull hard on the stripped end, so that it pulls apart to resemble a tiny corkscrew. Once you can see your new inner cable is near the exit hole, you can insert your tool inside and use the corkscrew section to grab onto it and gently pull it out through the hole.

GARDEN WIRE METHOD

Alternatively, you could try putting the outer cable through to start with and keep your fingers crossed, but you're very unlikely to get the cable to emerge from your frame. This is when a piece of thin wire can come in handy, something like some garden wire is ideal. Insert it at the point at which you want the cable to exit your frame and try and poke it into the open end of your cable outer. This can be a bit tricky, but once you push it in there, you should have no problem pulling the cable outer free.

Thin wire can be useful to help lever out cable outers

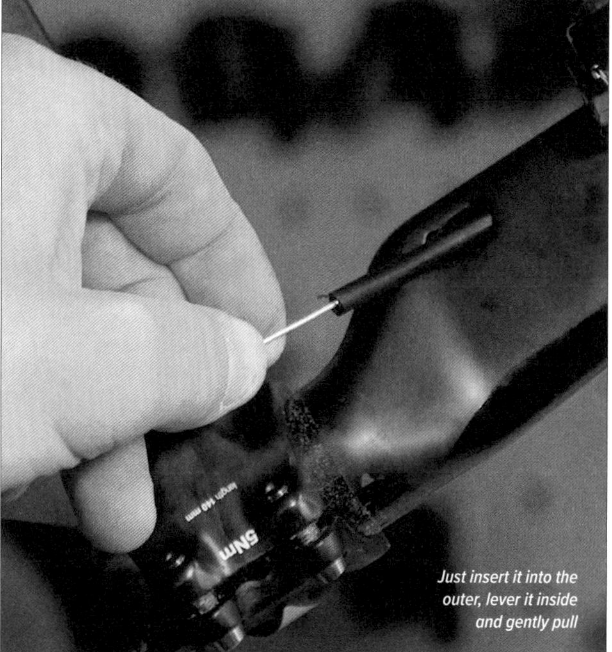

Just insert it into the outer, lever it inside and gently pull

INTERNAL CABLING ROUTING HACKS

CABLE SHEATHING METHOD

Thread a cable sheath over the in-situ cable

You can then remove the old inner, replace it, and then remove the sheath

If you're replacing existing inner or outer cables, probably the easiest method of doing so involves using some cable sheathing that you should be able to get from your local bike shop. It comes in two different thicknesses – for gear and brake inner cables. Brake cables are slightly thicker, so you may as well get the sheathing that fits them as you can also use it for gear cables.

Once you've got your hands on a length of sheathing, unclamp the inner cable from your brake or derailleur, remove the outer if necessary, but leave the inner cable threaded through your frame. If you have any fraying strands on your inner cable, trim it well above the frayed section with cable cutters, then start threading your cable sheathing over the inner and into your frame. It should slide all the way along your inner cable and emerge near your brake or shifter. You can then remove the old inner cable ensuring that both ends of your cable sheath remain outside of the frame. With the sheath in place you should easily be able to thread your new inner along it (threading the inner through the lever section of outer cable first if replacing brake cables). Once done, remove the sheath and thread on your cable outer – if required.

This technique works for both internal brake and gear cables

Need To Set Up Cable Disc Brakes?
See page 136 for a full walkthrough

MAGNET METHOD

Using a magnet of the kind that you might find on an old-school bike computer sensor grafted onto an old spoke, you should be able to draw an inner cable down your frame tube and out of the hole at the other end. Depending on the size of the hole and then you may still have to pull it out using something like the improvised grabbing tool we showed back on page 177. Gravity is also your friend here, so position your frame so that the cable is dropping down vertically. As well as repurposing old magnets as guides, you can also buy dedicated kits that do the same thing. Depending on which kit you buy, some come with have a threaded metal end which allows you to harness magnetic power when threading a hydraulic brake hose through a frame too.

You can use a magnet to draw an inner cable through the frame

Remember to make gravity work for you – as well as magnetism

VACUUM CLEANER METHOD

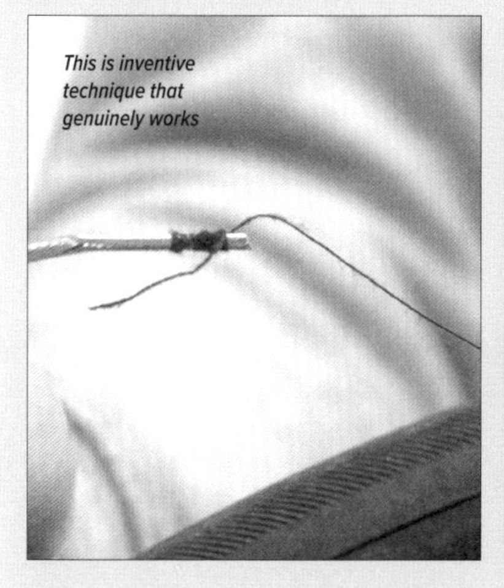
This is inventive technique that genuinely works

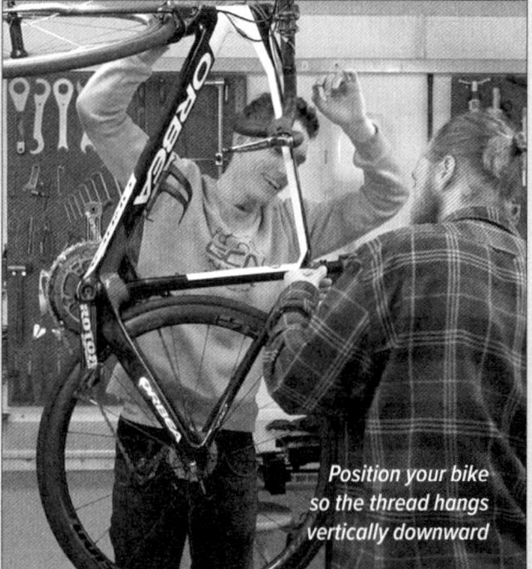

Position your bike so the thread hangs vertically downward

Put the vacuum cleaner over the exit and turn it on!

Possibly even more inventive than using a magnet to draw your cable through your frame is the thread and vacuum cleaner method. Take a length of cotton sewing thread and tie off one end onto your handlebar. Position your bike so that the thread is running vertically down, then insert the free end into the cable hole in your frame near the head tube and dangle as much thread as you can into the frame. Then, ideally using a friend to help you, take your vacuum cleaner and with the nozzle over the cable exit hole in your frame, suck the thread though the frame and out of the desired hole. Once you've got the thread running through your frame, untie the end near your handlebars, tightly tie it around the end of the inner cable then carefully pull it though your frame. You might need one of the tools mentioned earlier to guide your inner out of the frame.

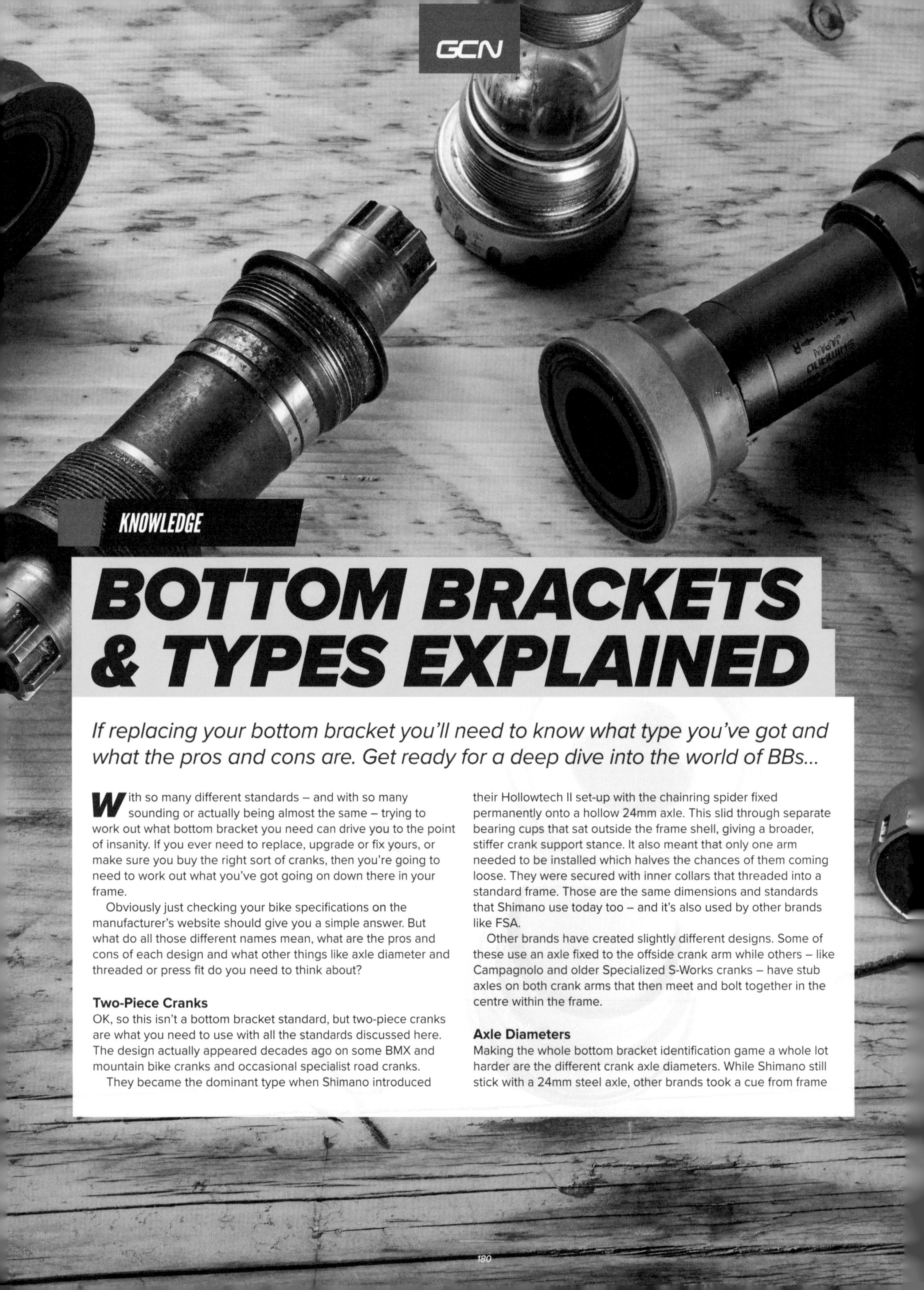

BOTTOM BRACKETS & TYPES EXPLAINED

If replacing your bottom bracket you'll need to know what type you've got and what the pros and cons are. Get ready for a deep dive into the world of BBs...

With so many different standards – and with so many sounding or actually being almost the same – trying to work out what bottom bracket you need can drive you to the point of insanity. If you ever need to replace, upgrade or fix yours, or make sure you buy the right sort of cranks, then you're going to need to work out what you've got going on down there in your frame.

Obviously just checking your bike specifications on the manufacturer's website should give you a simple answer. But what do all those different names mean, what are the pros and cons of each design and what other things like axle diameter and threaded or press fit do you need to think about?

Two-Piece Cranks

OK, so this isn't a bottom bracket standard, but two-piece cranks are what you need to use with all the standards discussed here. The design actually appeared decades ago on some BMX and mountain bike cranks and occasional specialist road cranks.

They became the dominant type when Shimano introduced their Hollowtech II set-up with the chainring spider fixed permanently onto a hollow 24mm axle. This slid through separate bearing cups that sat outside the frame shell, giving a broader, stiffer crank support stance. It also meant that only one arm needed to be installed which halves the chances of them coming loose. They were secured with inner collars that threaded into a standard frame. Those are the same dimensions and standards that Shimano use today too – and it's also used by other brands like FSA.

Other brands have created slightly different designs. Some of these use an axle fixed to the offside crank arm while others – like Campagnolo and older Specialized S-Works cranks – have stub axles on both crank arms that then meet and bolt together in the centre within the frame.

Axle Diameters

Making the whole bottom bracket identification game a whole lot harder are the different crank axle diameters. While Shimano still stick with a 24mm steel axle, other brands took a cue from frame

Screw Fit Or Press Fit?

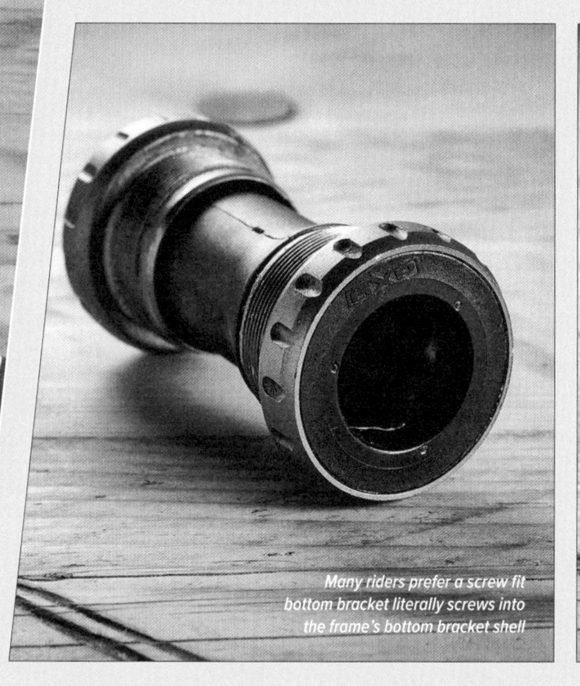

Many riders prefer a screw fit bottom bracket literally screws into the frame's bottom bracket shell

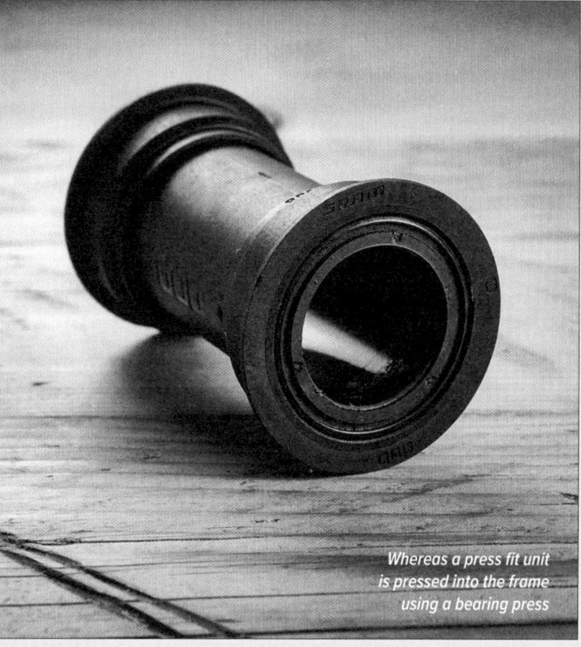

Whereas a press fit unit is pressed into the frame using a bearing press

While screw-in (aka threaded) bottom brackets have been the dominant standard for over a century, there have always been various press/push-fit bottom bracket designs around too. It really kicked off on road bikes when manufacturers wanted to save the weight of metal thread inserts on carbon frames. Press fit bearings also let them make the bottom bracket area wider and with a bigger hole in it, so it was a bigger, stiffer structure at a lower weight.

Being able to slap a bottom bracket straight into the frame rather than threading in two separate cups is also much quicker from a manufacturing point of view. Press fit bearings are more awkward to fit correctly into a frame though and misalignment can cause excess drag and bearing wear. The bearing cups can also come loose in the frame over time which can permanently damage the frame.

designers and used a bigger tube to create a stiffer axle at a lower weight. Obviously different crank axle diameters need different sized bearings and bottom brackets too. Sometimes those numbers form the basis for the name of the bottom bracket, BB30 for example. That's when things are relatively simple, but some designs (SRAM GXP – 22/24mm, Praxis – 28/30mm) use a stepped axle that's a different diameter on each side. Campagnolo Ultra-Torque and Power-Torque axles use a unique 25mm axle. Finally, SRAM DUB is a 28.99mm oversized alloy axle standard that's just too small to work with 30mm bearings.

As well as axle diameter you need to know which length of crank axle will work with your BB/bike frame. That's because BB30 and PF30 designs (and other press fit 68mm wide derivatives) need a specific short axle BB/PF30 crankset.

Is your head hurting yet? Well, it's only going to get worse...

"That's because BB30 and PF30 designs (and other press fit 68mm wide derivatives) need a specific short axle BB/PF30 crankset. Is your head hurting yet? Well it's only going to get worse..."

▶▶ BOTTOM BRACKETS & TYPES EXPLAINED

THE BB BUFFET

Square Taper

We'll start off with the square taper bottom bracket because that's the oldest standard you still might find on some cheaper or retro bikes. The name comes from the ends of the axle which have four 'flat' surfaces which slightly taper towards the end of the axle. (They're often actually fractionally convex to give a better expansion fit, but that's getting really geeky and 'fractionally convex, four-faced tapered bottom bracket' never caught on as a name.)

These work with matching square socket cranks which are tightened into place using a central flanged bolt that threads into each side of the axle. That drags the cranks up the taper until they lock solid into place.

The bearings themselves can either be separate cup and cone/loose bearing set ups on older bikes. These can be adjusted yourself if you're brave and you'll be able to tell if you've got one by the locking collar on the outside of the screw-in cups. Most square taper bottom brackets are a cartridge design with fully sealed bearings and axle in one self-contained unit. This is screwed into the bottom bracket shell and then a supporting collar screwed into the other side of the frame to lock everything into place.

PROS

- *Simple*
- *Good ones spin beautifully*
- *Still available in the back of beyond*
- *Some have serviceable bearings*

CONS

- *Very heavy*
- *Flexy*
- *Creaky*
- *Often come loose*

Isis/Octalink

Square taper was replaced for a while by two different larger diameter axle bottom bracket types.

Shimano had Octalink which used an oversized, hollow, 8-splined (raised locating ribs) axle. You then bolted matching Octalink cranks onto it in the same way as a square taper set-up. Isis was essentially the same larger diameter ribbed set-up but with thinner splines and had a reputation for less reliable bearings. Both used cartridge bottom brackets that fitted into a conventional threaded frame shell.

PROS

- *Lighter than square taper*
- *Stiffer than square taper*
- *Really smooth spin when working*

CONS

- *Heavier than external bearing set-ups*
- *Not as stiff as external bearing set-ups*
- *Short bearing life on ISIS*
- *Potential loosening issues*

BB30

BB30 was originally a Cannondale/FSA collaboration but they made it open source so anyone could use it. It does away with any threads in the frame as, instead, the large diameter bearings get pressed directly into cups in the frame and are then secured with circlips. It's built for larger 30mm diameter alloy axles which are also stiffer and lighter. The frames can be made lighter and potentially stiffer too because they don't need any threads. It still uses a 68mm wide bottom bracket shell with a 37mm shell diameter. BB30 does rely on tighter manufacturing tolerances to stop creaking and loosening. BB30A and BB30-83 Ai are Cannondale-only derivatives with an asymmetric offset.

PROS
- *Very light and stiff*
- *Big bearings*

CONS
- *Easy to damage frame*
- *Very easy to misalign*
- *Only works with short 30mm axles*
- *Needs a bearing press to fit*

PF30

PF30 is similar to BB30 except that the bearings are in softer nylon cups which press into the frame instead of the bearings fitting directly. The softness of the cups means the frame doesn't have to be as accurately made and reduces the chance of the frame being damaged. It still uses a 68mm wide bottom bracket shell, but with a 42mm internal shell diameter. The soft cups also self-align to some degree so they spin smoother than a badly installed BB30 set-up.

PROS
- *Light and stiff*
- *Large bearing size*
- *Easier to fit than BB30*

CONS
- *Easy to misalign*
- *Only works with short 30mm axles*
- *Needs a bearing press to fit*

BB86/BB92

Another soft cup, press fit system but with an 86.5mm frame shell width rather than 68mm. BB92 is a Shimano designed version of essentially the same system as BB86, but with a 92mm shell width. You can get BB86 bottom bracket bearings to fit most axle sizes so make sure you specify the right one for your cranks. BB86/BB92 are generally only available to fit 24mm axles – so primarily Shimano and FSA.

PROS
- *Light, wide and stiff*
- *Easier to fit than BB30*

CONS
- *Easy to misalign*
- *Only fits smaller diameter cranks*
- *Needs a bearing press to fit*

▸▸ BOTTOM BRACKETS & TYPES EXPLAINED

THE BB BUFFET CONTINUED

OSBB

OSBB is what Specialized call all their press fit BBs. However, this can range from early plastic cup versions with a very narrow 61mm width, to 68mm wide versions, which fit into alloy frames (or alloy sleeves in carbon frames) and are essentially just BB30 standard.

PROS

- *Light and stiff*
- *Large bearing size*

CONS

- *Easy to misalign*
- *Early ones are trouble*
- *Only works with short 30mm axles*
- *Needs a bearing press to fit*

BB90

BB90 was a 90mm wide bottom bracket shell design used by Trek to make the frame as wide and stiff as possible. It uses a slightly slacker bearing fit than BB30 which made it more likely to both creak and damage the direct fit into the frame. Trek released a V2 bearing option which was 0.1mm larger to reduce creak/ movement in stretched BBs, but now most Trek bikes are being built around the T47 standard.

PROS

- *Very stiff frame*
- *Large bearing size*

CONS

- *Easy to misalign*
- *Can stretch frame*
- *Small diameter axles only*

BBright

This is a Cervelo designed system using press fit cups with an 11mm wider 79mm width to work with asymmetric frames. It's designed to work best with full length 30mm axles but adaptors are available for most other crank axle sizes. It comes in direct-fit versions which are 42mm internal diameter and circlip secured like BB30, or soft cup PF30 style versions.

PROS

- *Very stiff frame*
- *Large bearing size*

CONS

- *Easy to misalign*
- *Needs a bearing press to fit*

BB65

A unique design from Look which uses a 90mm wide, 65mm diameter bottom bracket shell that only works with their own 50mm axle Zed one piece cranks.

PROS

- *Very stiff and light frame and crank*
- *Huge bearing size*

CONS

- *Currently Look only*

BB386 Evo

BB386 Evo is a FSA system using a PF30 style design but with an 86.5mm shell width for extra stiffness. It's designed to work best with full length 30mm axles, but adaptors are available for most other crank axle sizes.

PROS

- *Very stiff frame*
- *Large bearing size*

CONS

- *Easy to misalign*
- *Needs a bearing press to fit*

ThreadFit82.5

A Colnago design which uses large alloy inserts threaded into an 86mm wide carbon frame shell to create a more accurate and replaceable mount for BB86 cups.

PROS

- *Very stiff frame*
- *Large bearing size*
- *Replaceable inserts*

CONS

- *Currently Colnago only*
- *Needs a bearing press to fit*

T47

T47 is an attempt by premium custom builder Argonaut Bicycles, and bearing gurus Chris King and White Industries to create a reliable, universal fit bottom bracket standard. It uses a 46mm inner diameter shell the same as PF30/BB86/BB92, but with threads for external cups. It's proved popular with custom steel, alloy and titanium frame builders who can use a bigger diameter shell that works better with bigger frame tubes and wider chainstay spacing. Trek have also started using it on some bikes too.

PROS

- *Stiff wider frame potential*
- *Large bearing size*
- *Accurate threaded alignment*

CONS

- *Limited frame/bike options*
- *Why isn't it called T46?*
- *Needs a specific fit tool*

Need To Change Your Bottom Bracket?
See page 186 for how to get it right

SET-UP SECRETS

HOW TO FIT A THREADED BB

Threaded bottom brackets (BBs) are much easier to work on than their press fit cousins. Here's how to extract and install them

DIFFICULTY 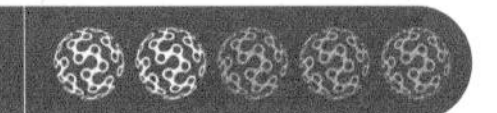

TIME	30 - 50 Minutes
TOOLS	• Allen keys • Crank tool • Bottom bracket tool
WHEN	• Your bottom bracket is noisy or feels rough

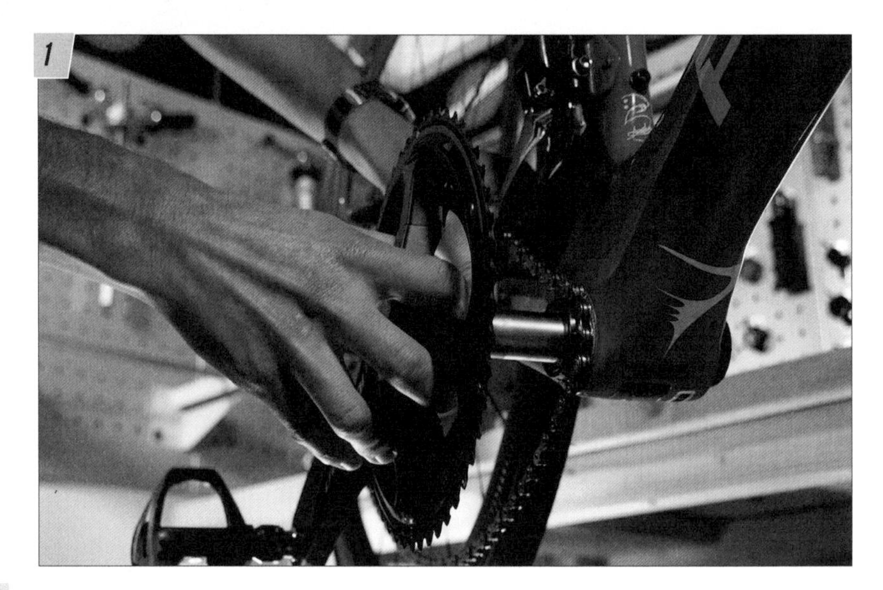

Before you can work on your bottom bracket, you'll first need to remove your cranks. For a step by step breakdown on how to do that, head over to page 84.

Fit your tool to the bottom bracket shell and make sure it is sitting nice and square on the shell. If you don't have the tool fitted correctly, you run the risk of stripping the notches off the cup, which makes your job a whole lot harder.

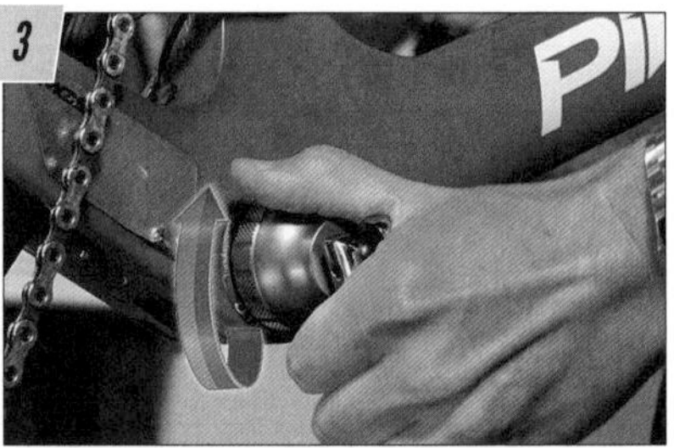

Apply pressure in the appropriate direction to loosen the bottom bracket. Anti-clockwise for the drive side and clockwise for the non-drive side. If it was installed without grease, or overtightened previously, you might find you have to give it a bit of force to loosen the threads.

WATCH THE VIDEO

Free show-how and know-how

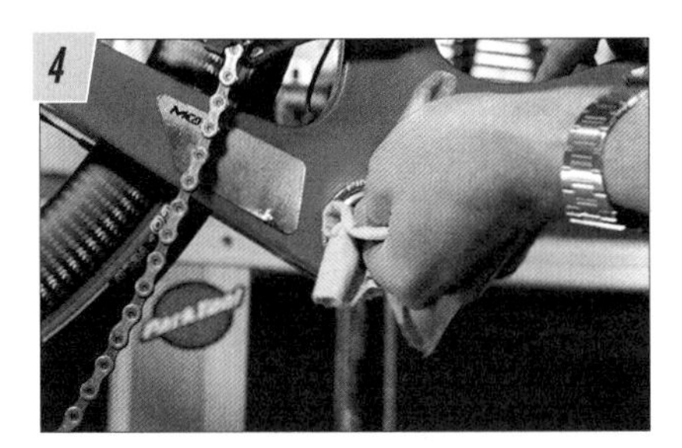
4

With the bottom bracket now removed, you can take a look at the threads inside the frame. Using an old rag, give them a proper clean and make sure they're clear of any old grease and grit that's found its way inside.

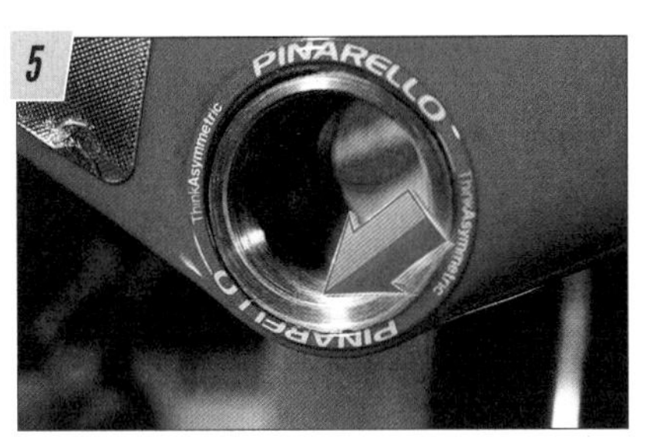
5

Make sure the threads in the frame are in good condition. If you've ever cross-threaded your bottom bracket, you might find some of the threads a bit chewed up and may need to look at getting them re-tapped. This is probably a job for your local bike shop.

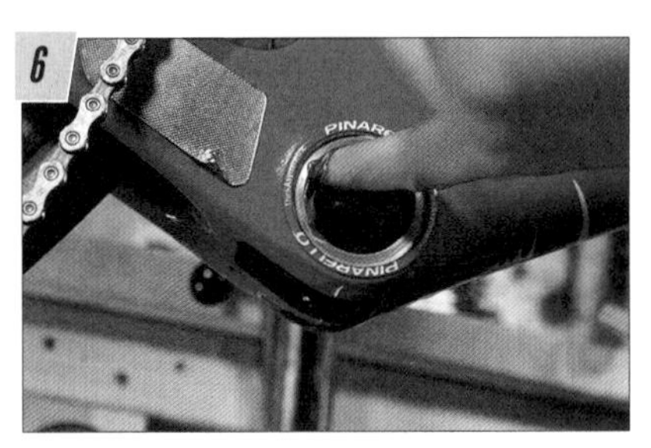
6

Assuming that everything looks good, apply a thin layer of grease to the bottom bracket shell inside the frame.

7

Now to reinstall the bottom bracket, but first apply some grease to its threads. Don't worry too much if there's a lot of excess on there, it'll work it's way out as you install the bottom bracket and you can clean it up later.

8

Nearly all threaded bottom brackets will be labelled as left and right specific – so check that you're installing the correct half of the bottom bracket to the correct side of the frame.

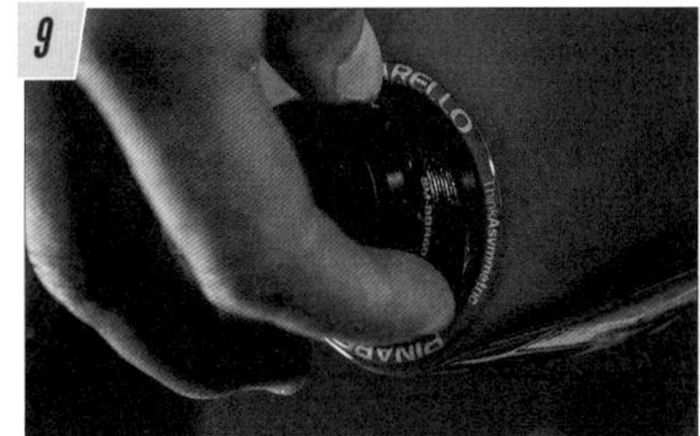
9

Offer the bottom bracket up to the frame and line up the threads. Start to screw it in by hand. If you feel any resistance as you're hand-tightening the bottom bracket, you may have cross-threaded it. If so, unscrew it, check, and start again.

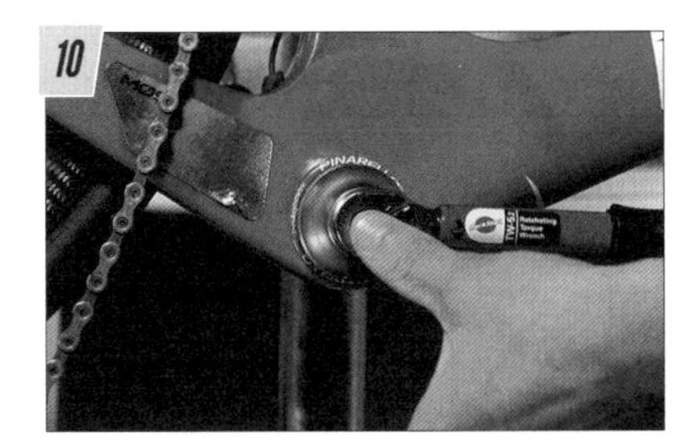
10

As the bottom bracket works its way into the frame fit the tool (in the same way you did when removing it) and continue to tighten it up.

11

Bottom brackets have quite a high torque rating of around 35-45Nm, and you might not have a large enough torque wrench to accommodate this. This is much less of a problem than small bolts with very low torque ratings, so just give the bottom bracket a fair bit of force so it's done up nice and tight.

12

Repeat the re-fitting process on the opposite side of the bottom bracket shell, then reattach your cranks (see page 84 again) and you're ready to ride.

Running A Press Fit Bottom Bracket?
Turn the page for how service them

SET-UP SECRETS

HOW TO REMOVE & INSTALL A PRESS FIT BB

If there's resistance or a lot of noise coming from your bottom bracket it's time to change it. Here we show how to remove and fit the press fit version

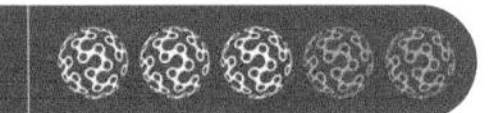

TIME 30 - 60 Minutes

TOOLS
- Crank extractor
- Allen key set
- Press fit BB bearing tool
- Bearing press
- Hammer
- Grease

WHEN
- Your bottom bracket is noisy or not running smoothly

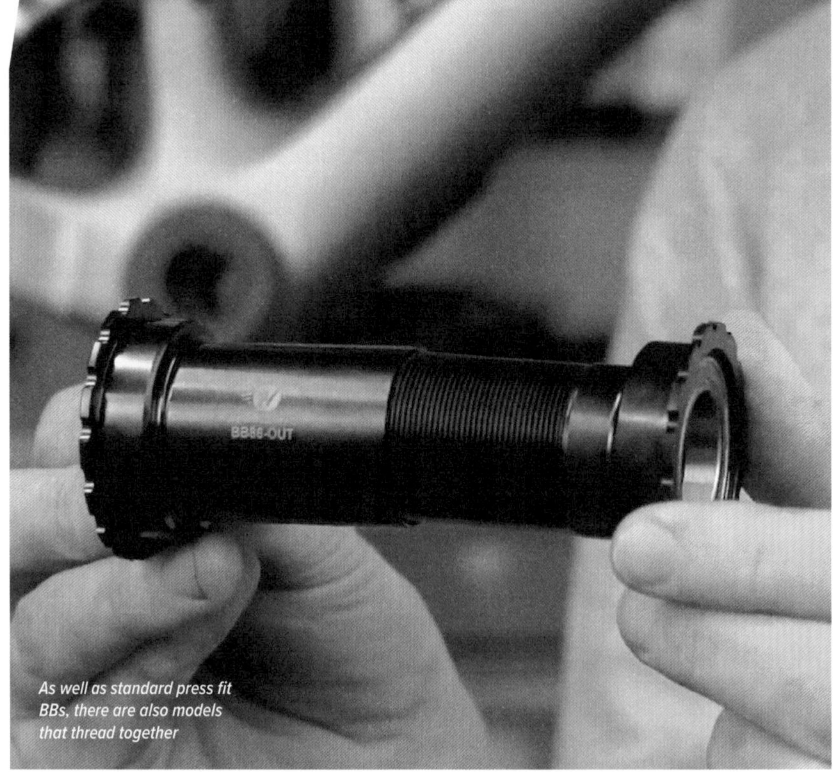

As well as standard press fit BBs, there are also models that thread together

The bottom bracket (BB) is one of the hardest working components on a bike and one that also takes a hell of a lot of abuse. Sitting in the lowest point of your frame, they will end up bearing the brunt of any water that enters via your seat tube, head tube or anywhere else. They are also close to the road and get hit by wheel spray, so your BB will always end up with a face full of whatever you happen to be riding though. They are also the focal point for every watt you crank out, so it's no wonder they wear out from time to time.

Fitting a new bottom bracket might seem like a fairly challenging procedure, but with the right tools it's far less daunting than you might imagine. Carefully follow each step in our guide and you'll soon be replacing that creaky old BB for a silky smooth new one.

BOTTOM BRACKETS EXPLAINED

So what exactly is a press fit bottom bracket? Essentially, it's a set of bearings

Other BB variations include bearings that just press into the frame shell

that are housed within a pair of aluminium or plastic cups, which are then pushed inside of a frame's bottom bracket shell

The main alternative to the press fit bottom bracket is the more traditional threaded version, which as the name suggests, threads into the bottom bracket shell using a dedicated spanner which fits on to the notches on the external face of the bottom bracket. Their screw-on nature makes threaded BBs easier to remove and refit, but press fit bottom brackets are much more common these days. See page 180 for more on both types.

Other variants include bottom brackets consisting of a pair of simple bearings which are pushed into each side of the frame by hand and have clips to secure them in place. There are also press fit versions that thread together inside the bottom bracket shell to help to prevent any potential creaking, such as the ones made by Wheels Manufacturing.

TECH EXPLAINED

Buying A New Bottom Bracket

If you've already shopped for a replacement bottom bracket you'll be aware of the vast amount of different types that are out there. The best way to be sure you get the correct BB for your bike is to check the manufacturer's website, or closely inspect the one that's already fitted. You should see the size and standard stamped on the outside of one of the cups. You don't need to get the exact same model as the bottom bracket that you're replacing (you may wish to upgrade to something like a Chris King model for example), but if you do choose something different, ensure it is compatible with your crankset.

BEFORE YOU START

There are some specialist removal and fitting tools you'll need that are vital to this job...

To remove most types of press fit bottom bracket, you'll need a dedicated tool with splayed end that looks like a long, thin, metal shuttlecock.

However, if you have a BB30 type bottom bracket, the tool you'll need has a flat 'T' shaped head (see step 2b). Both types of tool are used in a very similar way.

To fit your new bottom bracket, you'll need a bearing press along with installation cups that will snugly fit inside your bottom bracket when sized correctly.

HOW TO REMOVE AND INSTALL A PRESS FIT BOTTOM BRACKET

TOP TIP

Before you start the process of removing your bottom bracket, it's a good idea to be 100 per cent sure it is the BB that's making the creaks and groans. Check your headset and saddle rails first as they are also prime candidates for unwanted noise. See page 244 for more on silencing a noisy bike.

You'll need to remove the cranks before you start on the bottom bracket (see page 84 for a full breakdown on how to do this). Keep an eye out for any spacers or washers that sit in between the cranks and the bottom bracket itself as you'll need to refit them in the correct order later on.

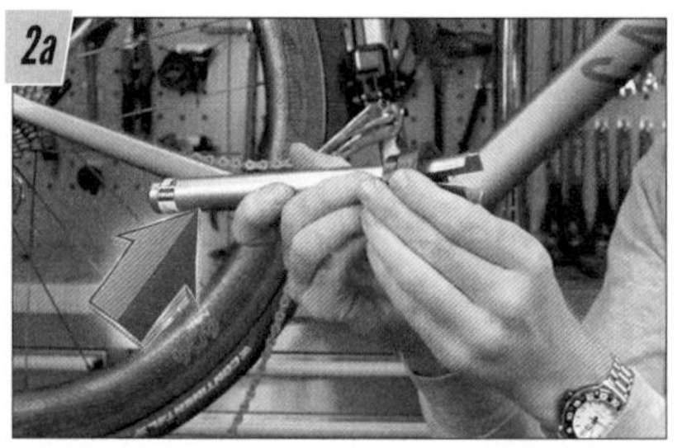

It's important to use a dedicated bottom bracket removal tool to extract your old bottom bracket. Ensure to check that the tool you're using is the correct one for your bottom bracket standard.

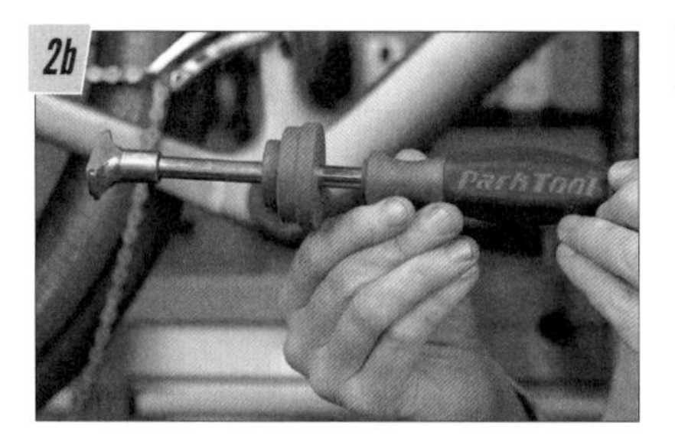

If you have a press fit 30 (PF30) style of bottom bracket, you'll need a different type of extraction tool (pictured). While it looks quite different, you use it in much the same way as the regular tool.

Thread the blunt end of your bottom bracket removal tool through the axle hole until the sprung ends open up into position and you hear a satisfying click.

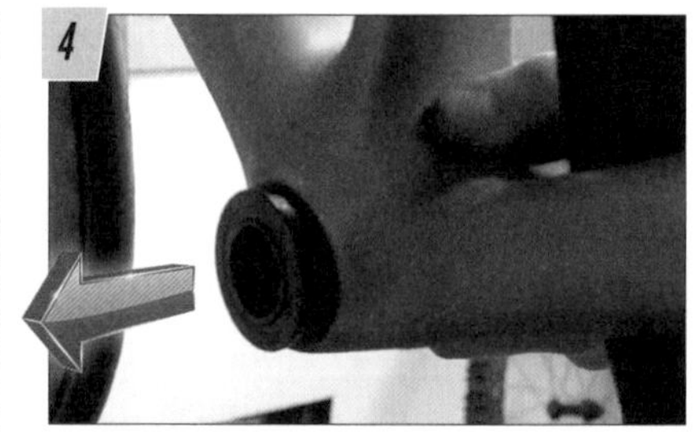

Using your hammer, give the protruding blunt end of the tool a few sharp blows to start removing the cup from the bottom bracket shell itself. Take care around anything that could get damaged though, as the bottom bracket can fire out when you finally get it free.

You may have a removable sleeve inside your bottom bracket shell. If so, now is a good time to pick it out – you'll likely have a new one with your replacement bottom bracket.

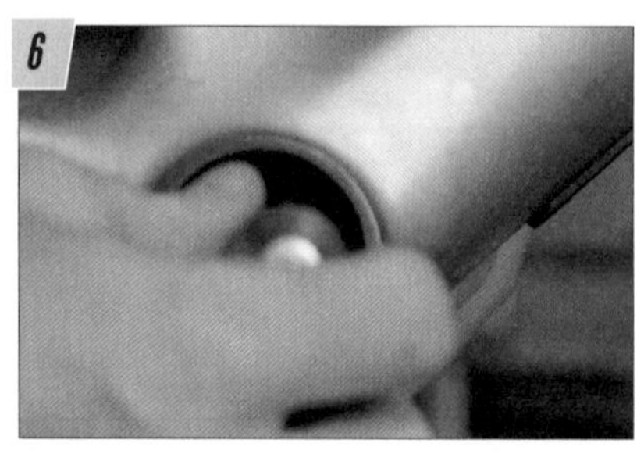

Remove the tool and repeat the last step to tap out the opposite side of your bottom bracket.

TOP TIP

Some old hands will tell you that you can remove your bottom bracket by bashing it out with a hammer and a screwdriver. While this can be done, you may distort your bottom bracket shell in the process which could lead to having to shell out for a new frame. Don't risk it and always use the correct tools.

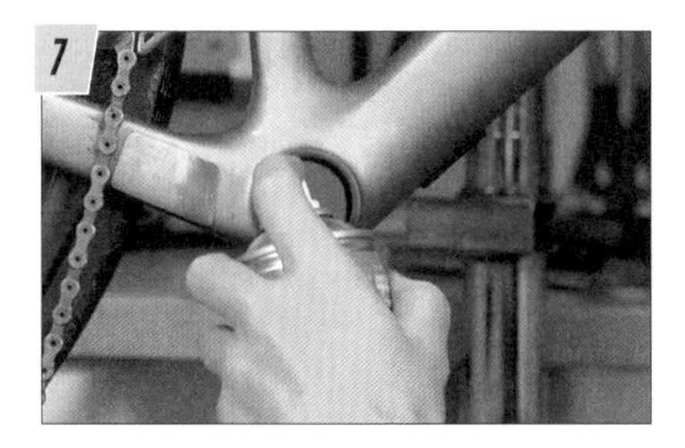

Before fitting your new bottom bracket, it's a good idea to give the frame shell a good clean out as all kinds of dirt and debris can find their way in over time. Use some degreaser and some cloth to get it really clean.

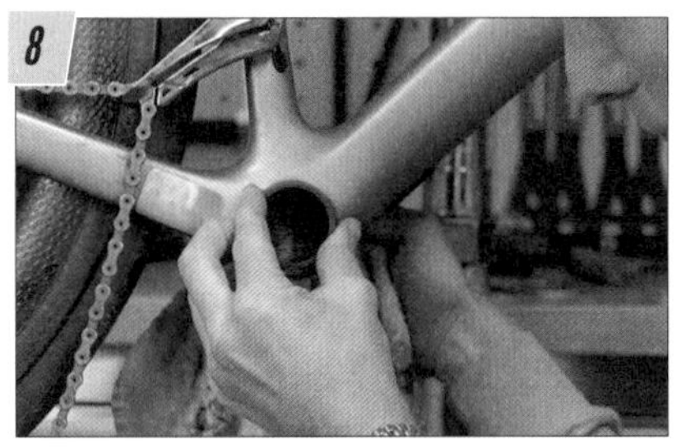

If you have an aluminium-lined bottom bracket shell, using some grease will make fitting easier and reduce the likelihood of creaks. However, if you've got yourself a carbon-lined shell, then the general consensus is not to use grease at all as it may adversely affect the carbon.

To really guard against any future creaks, consider applying some adhesive primer and press fit retaining compound, allowing them to dry before fitting the bottom bracket. The compound will take up some of the tolerance and differences between the two components to keep creaks at bay.

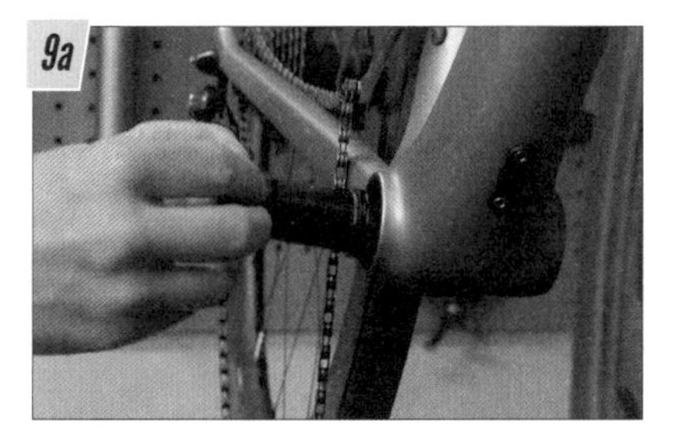

Now it's time to start pressing the bottom bracket cups into the shell and most mechanics install both sides at the same time.

It's ultra-important to use the correct size drifts for your bottom bracket with your press, as you could end up distorting your bottom bracket shell with an incompatible size.

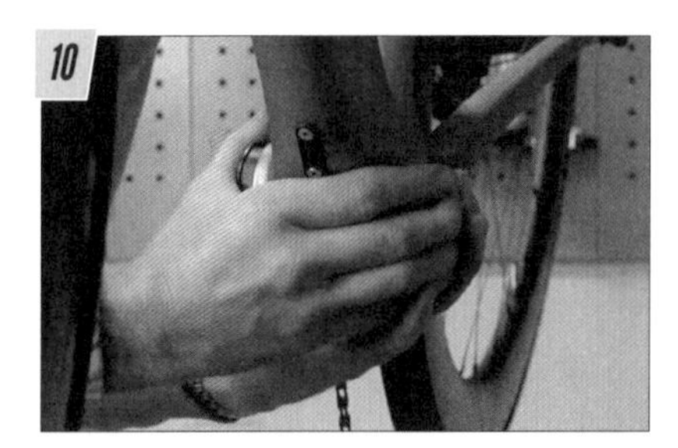

You should be able to get them just gently started by hand, making sure they're not going in lopsided at all, before introducing your bearing press and the drifts.

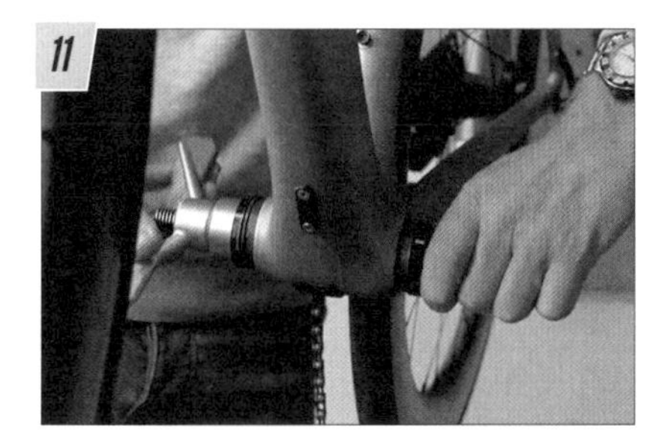

Insert and begin to tighten the bearing press ensuring that the cups are actually going into the shell and there are pushing in dead straight. If they start to look lopsided, remove them and restart the fitting process.

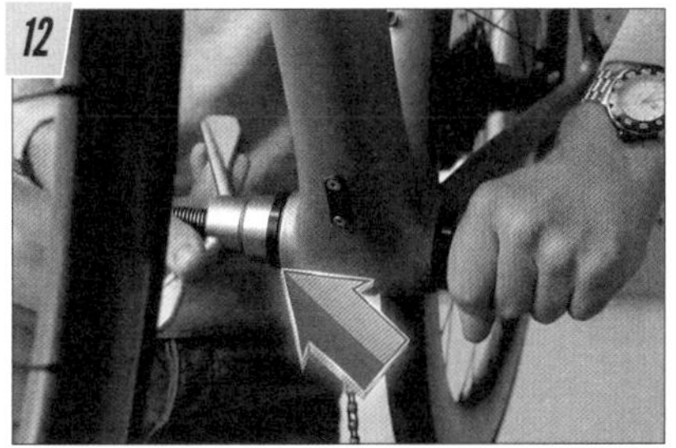

Keep going with the bearing press until the bearing cups are flush up against the bottom bracket shell. Take care not to overtighten them as this could damage your bottom bracket.

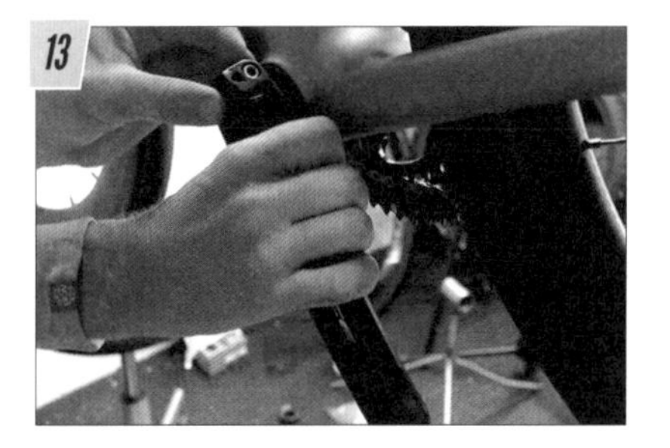

Finally, clean off any excess grease, refit your chainset, ensuring to correctly place any spacers etc that came off with it, then you're ready to ride.

Want A Sparkling Clean Drivetrain?
Then head over to page 220

SET-UP SECRETS

HOW TO REMOVE & INSTALL A HEADSET

If the steering on your road bike starts to feel rough, you may need to change part or all of the headset. Here's how it's done

DIFFICULTY

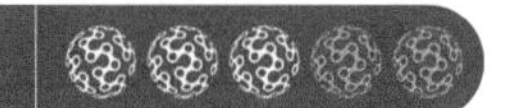

TIME 30 - 60 Minutes

TOOLS
- 4 and 5mm Allen keys
- Torque wrench
- Rubber mallet
- Cleaning rags
- Teflon grease

WHEN
- Your headset needs stripping down or replacing

Your headset should be free from judder and allow the bars to move smoothly

Your headset performs two roles on your bike. It holds your forks in place inside the head tube and it also gives you super-smooth steering. However, it is open to all sorts of abuse while you're riding as it has to deal with every single bump you hit in the road and all the water spray from your tyres which can work its way inside its bearings. It's a good idea to quickly check your headset as described opposite before every ride and give it clean and re-grease your headset every six to nine months – or after a prolonged period of regular riding in wet weather.

HOW TO CHECK YOUR HEADSET

It's easy to see if your headset needs attention, just rock your bike back and forth with the front brake on. If there's any movement through your forks then your headset needs adjusting. However, if it feels rough and gritty when you turn the bars with the front wheel lifted off the ground, you'll need to investigate the problem further. A clean and a new coat of grease may be all that is required, but it could be time to replace the bearings or even possibly the whole headset.

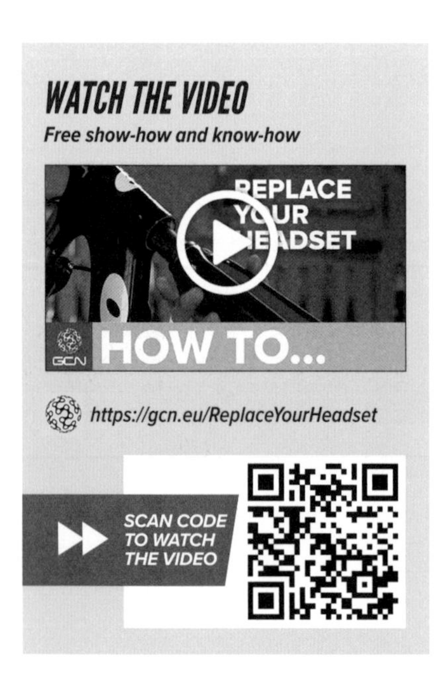

TECH EXPLAINED

Threaded & Threadless Headsets

There are two types of headset – threaded and threadless. Threaded headsets are typically only found on retro bikes these days, as most modern bikes have threadless headsets that clamp onto the fork steerer tube and are much simpler and easier to adjust. It's easy to tell if you're running a threaded headset, as you'll have a large nut sitting on top of the headset and you'll also be running an old fashioned quill type stem.

"Modern bikes have threadless headsets that clamp onto the fork steerer tube and are much simpler"

First, remove the front wheel. If you've got rim brakes, you'll need to undo the release mechanism on the front brake to open up the calliper. Then undo the quick-release or bolt-through axle and you can drop the front wheel from your bike. See page 40 if you're unsure how to do this.

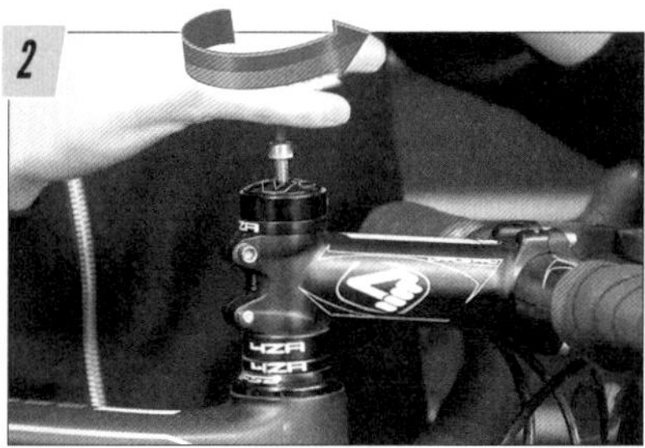

Next, use an Allen key to loosen the tensioning bolt from your stem's top cap, then completely remove them both along with any headset spacers that may be sitting above the stem.

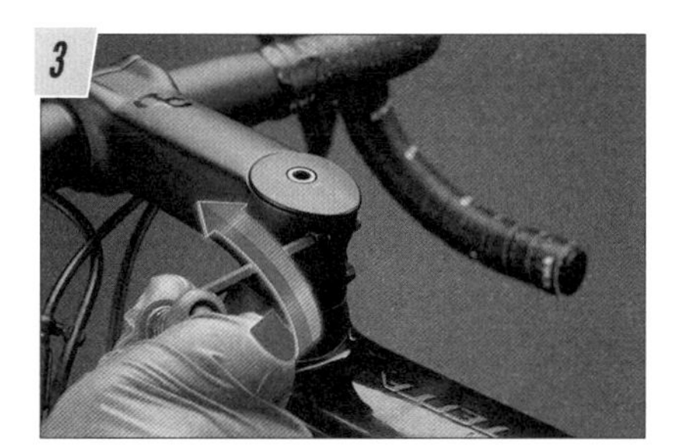

Loosen the stem bolts where it clamps on to the fork steerer. Release each one a little at a time to avoid over-stressing them.

Remove the stem and handlebars from the steerer tube. Even with the loosened bolts, the stem is likely to still be tight, so you'll probably have to work it from side to side to free it from the fork. Hold onto the forks as you don't want them to hit the floor if the stem suddenly comes free.

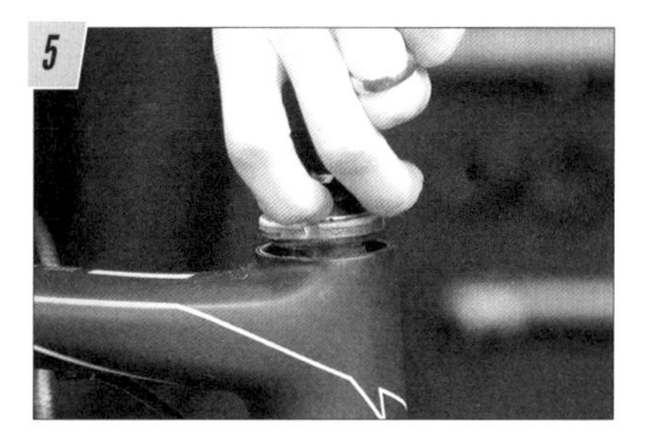

Take off any remaining spacers and the headset bearing cover – keep an eye out for any washers that might be sitting below it.

HOW TO REMOVE & INSTALL A HEADSET

Remove the compression ring that sits below the headset cover. If it's tough to get it free, tap the fork steerer with your rubber mallet to release it. Once again, ensure to hold on to the fork so that it doesn't hit the floor when the compression ring is released.

Remove the fork completely (you might want to unbolt the brake calliper here) and you can now see if you've got a modern cartridge bearing, or older type free bearings which sit in a metal cage. Be very careful with the free bearings as it's easy for them to drop onto the floor and disappear forever.

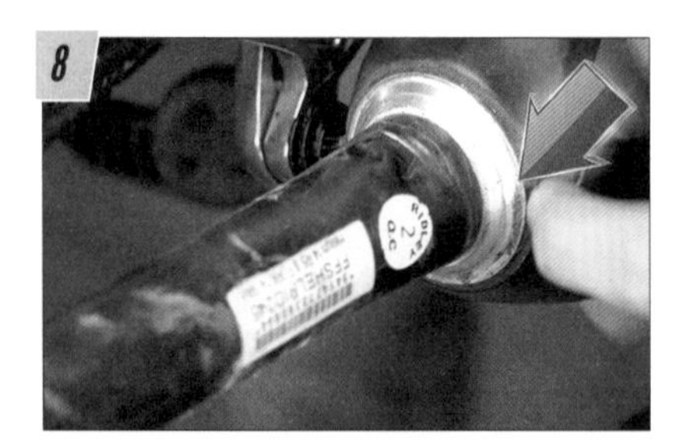

Completely remove the lower bearing and thoroughly clean off any old grease and grime. Clean up the crown race and the fork's steerer tube too.

TOP TIP

If you're struggling to remove your headset bearings from the frame by hand, you can gently prise them free with a flat-bladed screwdriver. Work around the bearings a little at a time and you'll be able to get them free without damaging your bearing or bearing cup.

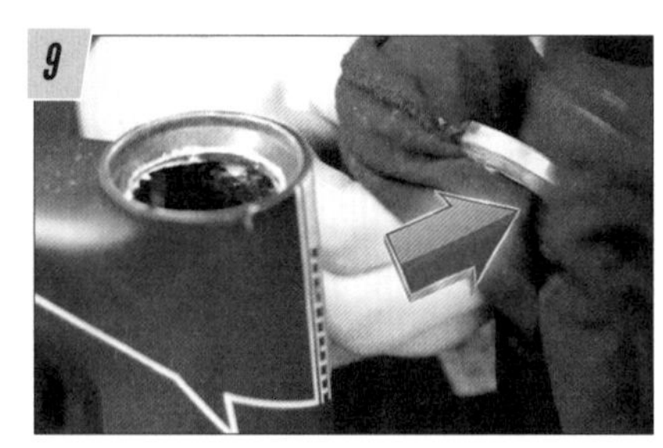

Remove the upper headset bearing and give that a good clean with your rag too.

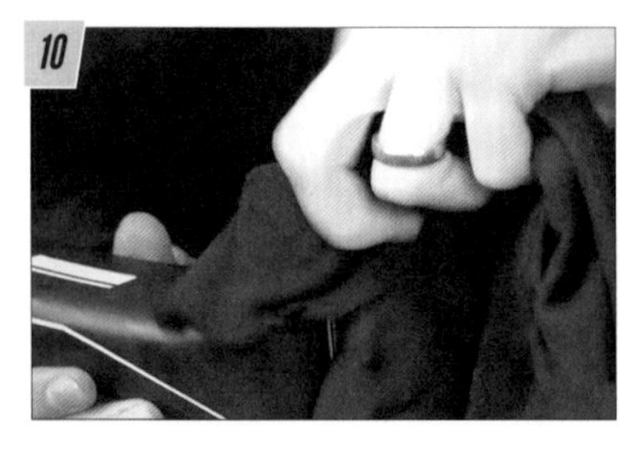

Thoroughly wipe away grime and old grease from inside the frame's steerer tube with your rag.

If either cartridge bearing is visibly rusted or has unwanted movement, you'll likely need to replace it – though you may be able to prise open the bearing, clean then re-grease the internals. The serial code printed on the outside of the bearing will allow you to find a direct replacement.

Check the crown race that sits at the bottom of your fork's steerer tube for any scoring or damage. It needs to be smooth for the bearings to run correctly on top of it. If there's any damage at all, you'll need to replace it.

If your crown race has a split in it, you'll be able to pull it off by hand or gently prise it free with a flat screwdriver. If not, you will need a crown race puller to get it off, which are expensive. Your best bet is to buy a new crown race then head to your local bike shop and ask them to switch them over.

TECH EXPLAINED

Head Tubes & Headsets

The head tubes on most modern frames are tapered, being wider at the bottom and narrower at the top. One of the advantages that tapered head tubes give is to allow for a bigger lower bearing in your headset which will better handle the forces absorbed from the road while riding. Head tubes also come in different diameters, which means there's a huge range of different sized headset bearings out there.

"A bigger lower bearing in your headset will better handle the forces absorbed from the road while riding"

INSTALLING YOUR HEADSET

Before reassembly, liberally coat the top and bottom races of your frame with plenty of grease to keep everything running smoothly. Be sure to smear some grease over each new bearing too.

Fit the upper bearing inside the frame ensuring it is the correct way up. The rounded edges should face down on the upper bearing and upwards on the lower bearing. Slide the lower bearing onto the crown race and carefully replace the fork.

Refit the compression ring, then the bearing cover and any spacers that sat underneath the stem. Next, refit the stem along with any spacers that were stacked on top of it. Don't tighten the stem bolts just yet.

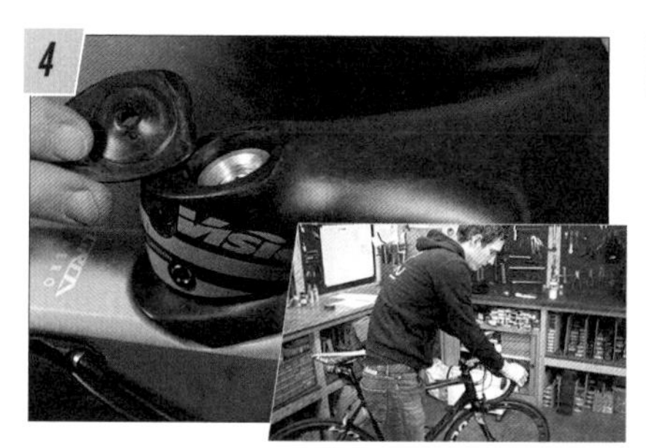

Look down inside your stem and check that there is a 5mm or so gap between the top of the fork's steerer tube and the top of your stem. If there's no gap, you won't be able to tension the headset properly. If not, check your spacers and add an extra one if required.

Refit the top cap and stem bolt. Then use the stem bolt to take up any play in the fork – it's easiest to do this with the bike on the floor. Take care not to over-tighten though, if the steering has any resistance or you can feel the individual bearings moving, you've gone too far.

Line up your bars – it's helpful to sight them along the top tube, then tighten up the stem bolts to the manufacturer's torque specifications.

For More Details On Stem Set-Up
Turn to page 202

ESSENTIAL REPAIRS

HOW TO SERVICE YOUR HEADSET

Your headset is on the frontline when it comes to getting battered by the elements, so it's important to regularly check it, clean it and apply new grease

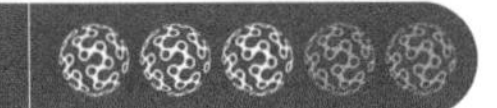

TIME 15 - 30 Minutes

TOOLS
- *4 and 5mm Allen keys*
- *Torque wrench*
- *Rubber mallet*
- *Cleaning rags*
- *Teflon grease*

WHEN
- *You've been regularly riding in wet conditions*

Undo the quick-release or bolt-though axle to drop out your front wheel and put it out of the way. You may need to also undo the release on the front brake to allow the tyre through. See page 40 if you're unsure of how to do this.

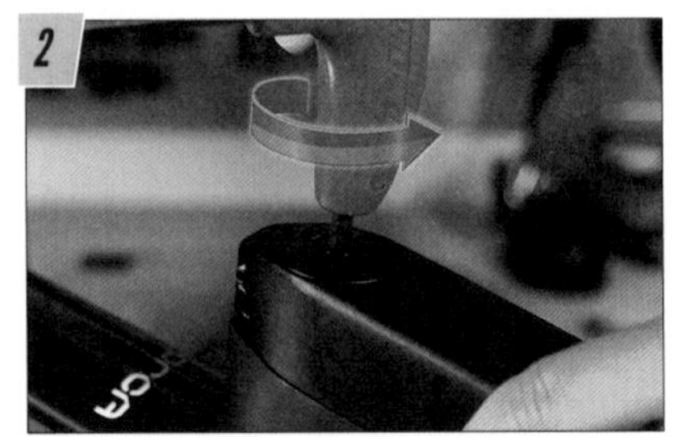

Undo the tensioning bolt in your headset's top cap and remove them both along with any headset spacers that may be sitting on top of the stem.

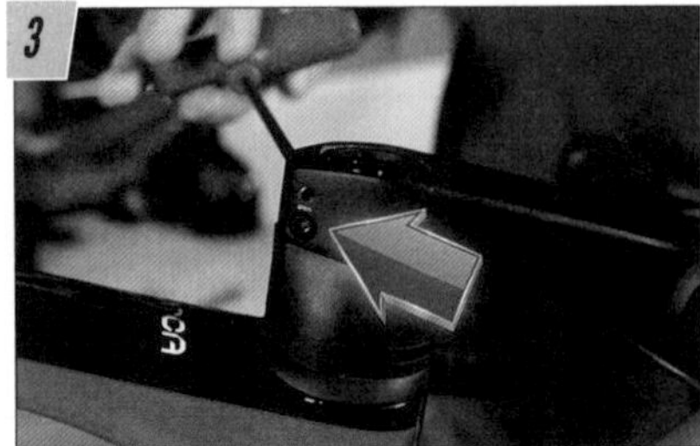

Undo the stem bolts where the stem clamps on to the fork steerer. Undo each one a little at a time to avoid over-stressing them.

WATCH THE VIDEO

Free show-how and know-how

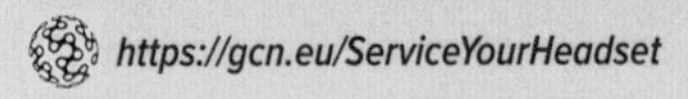

You should then be able to remove the stem from the steerer tube, if it's really tight, wiggle the fork from side to side to work it free. Take care to hold on to the forks though as you don't want them to hit the floor when the stem comes free. Take off any remaining spacers and the headset bearing cover.

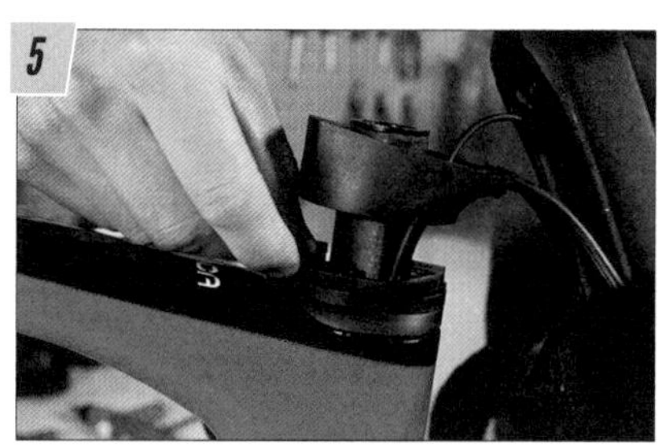

Remove the compression ring that sits below the headset cover. If you're struggling to get it free, give the fork steerer a little tap with a rubber mallet to release it. Take care to hold on to the fork though as you don't want it to hit the floor when the compression ring comes free.

Drop the fork out completely and you'll now be able to see if you've got a modern cartridge bearing, or on older bikes you might have free bearings which sit in a metal cage. Take great care if you have the free bearing type as it's easy for them to drop out and never be seen again.

Remove the lower bearing and clean any remaining grease off it and the crown race which will still be sitting on your fork. The lower headset bearing which is the part of the headset that has to endure the worst of any wet weather as it's constantly being hit with wheel spray.

Remove the bearing from the top of the headset and give that a good clean with an old rag too. Then clean any gunk, grit or old grease from inside the frame's steerer tube with your cleaning rag.

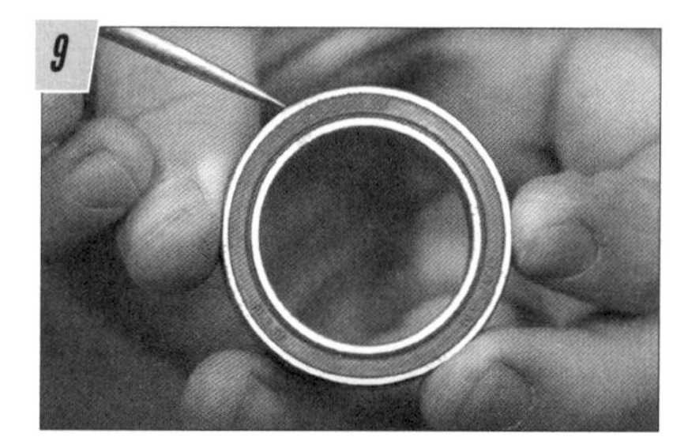

If either bearing is rusted or the bearings themselves have any flat spots, you'll need to replace them. If you do need to change your cartridge bearing, you'll find a serial code printed on the outside of the bearing which will allow you to find a direct replacement.

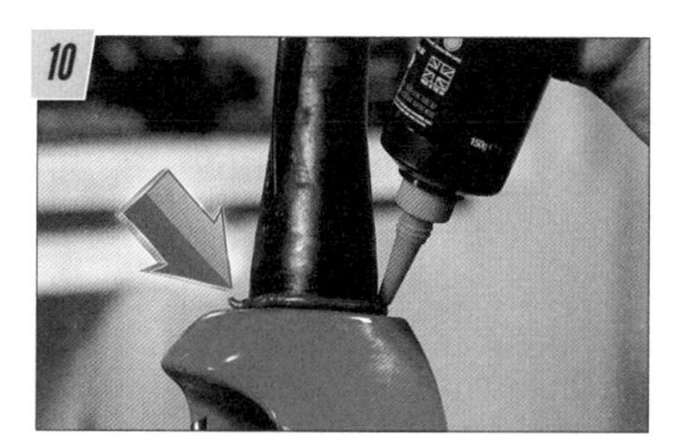

Before reassembly, liberally coat the top and bottom races of your frame with grease. Smear some grease over each bearing too. Fit the upper bearing ensuring you orientate it the correct way up. Then slide the lower bearing onto the fork race and insert the steerer back through the frame.

Secure the fork in place by sliding on the compression ring, followed by the bearing cover and any spacers that sat below the stem. Next, slide the stem back on along with any spacers that sat on top of it. Do not tighten the stem bolts yet.

Replace the bolt and top cap, being sure not to over-tighten the bolt. You want it tight enough to remove any play, but not so tight that you feel any resistance or the individual bearings themselves. Align your bars and tighten the stem bolts to the fork steerer, then reattach your wheel.

Want To Get Rid Of Annoying Noises?
Turn to page 244 for a silent running bike

SECTION 6

CONTROLS & CONTACT POINTS

Here you'll discover how to custom-tune your cockpit, get the perfect pedal set-up and lots more

SET-UP SECRETS

HOW TO WRAP BAR TAPE

Fitting new bar tape can seem daunting, but it needn't be. Here's how to do it the easy way

DIFFICULTY 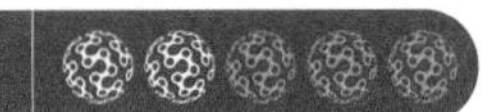

TIME 15 - 30 Minutes

TOOLS
- Bar tape
- Electrical tape
- Scissors

WHEN
- Your tape needs replacing or you're fitting new bars

1

Before getting started with your new bar tape, your bars need to be super-clean, which means getting rid of all traces of the old tape and any sticky sections left by glue from old electrical tape.

2a

Use the electrical tape to ensure your cables are firmly taped to your handlebars. It's important that they're held tightly in place because any flex will reduce the performance of your brakes and gears.

2b

Tape the cables at the midpoint of the flat section of your bars and also in the corner where the cables leave the brake housing. It's worth putting some extra tape in the corners to make sure the cables are really secure here.

WATCH THE VIDEO

Free show-how and know-how

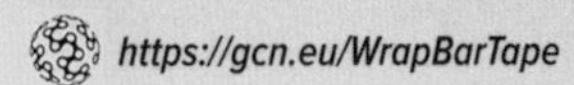
https://gcn.eu/WrapBarTape

SCAN CODE TO WATCH THE VIDEO

To Adjust Your Brake Levers
Head over to p110

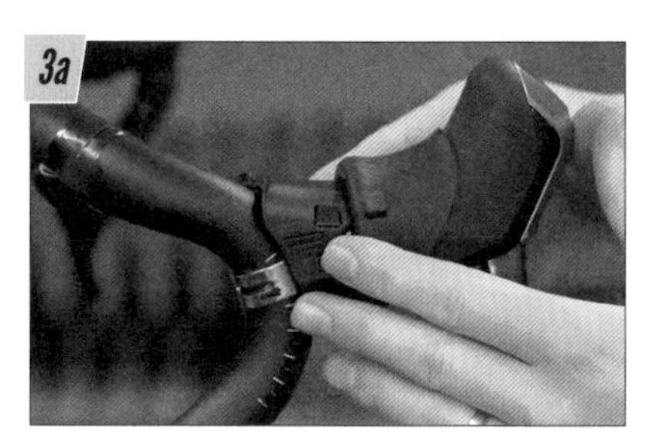

Roll back your brake hoods, then start at the end of your handlebar and keep in mind the two golden rules – tape firmly and tape evenly.

Begin taping with a full complete turn that has about half the width of the bar tape sticking off the end of the handlebar. This will enable you to tuck the overlapping tape inside the bar and hold it in place with your bar plug later on in the process.

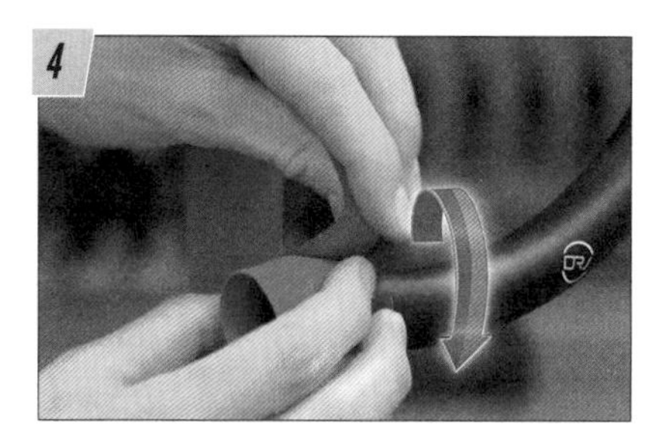

Tape from the inside of the handlebar to the outside. So that means on the right-hand side you're taping in clockwise direction and on the left-hand side of the bars you're taping in an anti-clockwise direction.

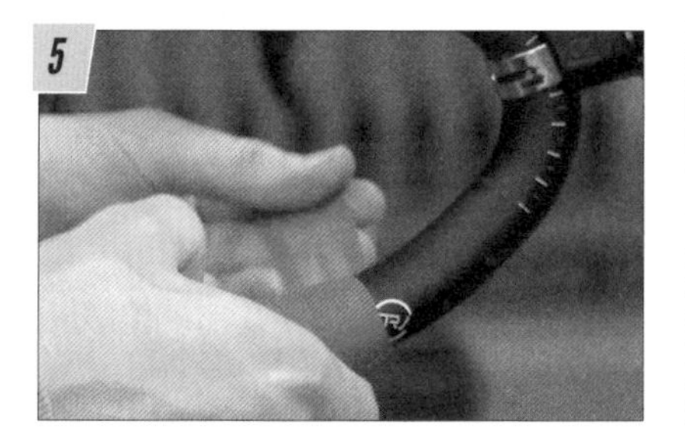

As you're winding the tape along the bar, overlap it each time by about a quarter to a third of the width of the tape. The bigger your overlap, the thicker the tape job will be when you finish it off.

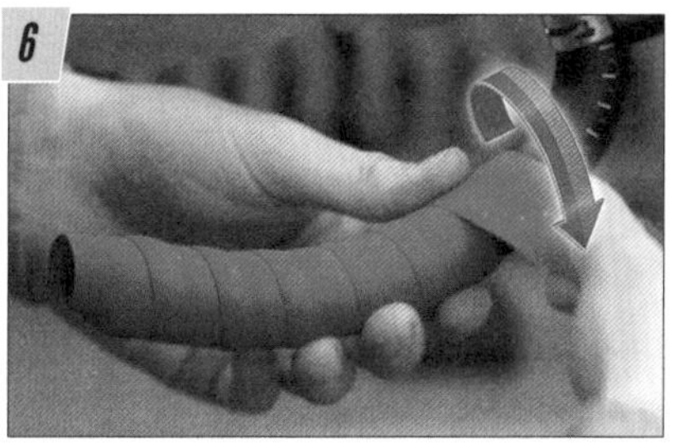

As you get to the corners of the handlebar, you're going to need to overlap more on the inside and then slightly less on the outside to work it through the turns. Keep the tape tight at all times, but avoid pulling it so hard that it gets distorted.

TOP TIP

If the tape you're using has a sticky strip on the back, it's helpful to expose a large section of the sticky bit every so often. Make sure to tear off the backing tape when you do, so that it doesn't get wrapped around itself and get in your way while you're taping.

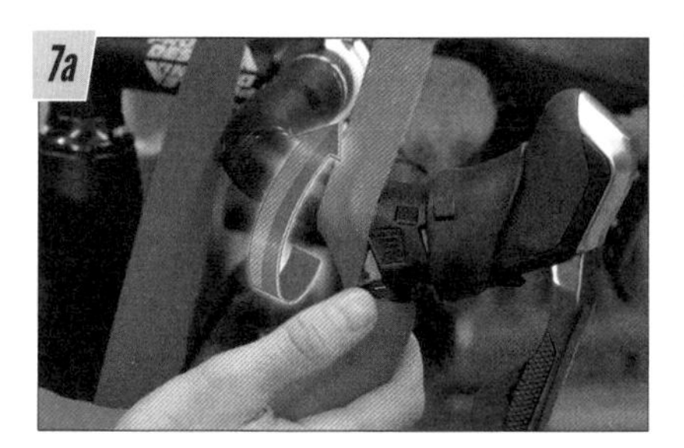

When you reach the levers, the aim is to get a good covering of tape so that when the hoods are rolled back in place there are no gaps at all. Use a figure-of-eight motion that begins right up to close to the bottom of the lever then goes up and over the top of the lever and down the other side.

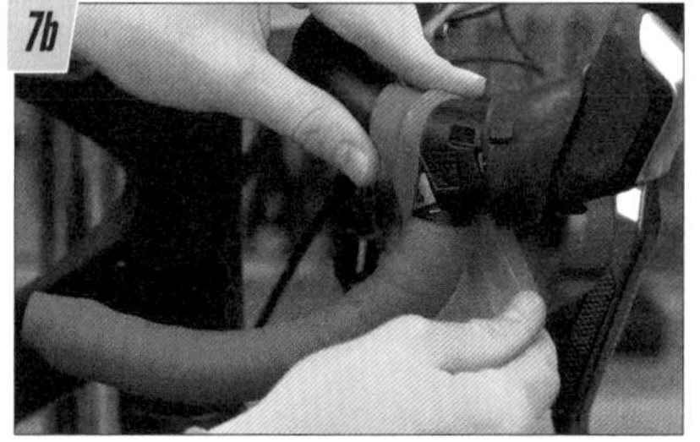

Now run the tape so it goes back in front of the lever and then over the top of the bar and so you can now carry on taping as before. If your figure-of-eight wrap has gone well, there will be no gaps around the hoods and you'll be wrapping from the front of the bar to the back.

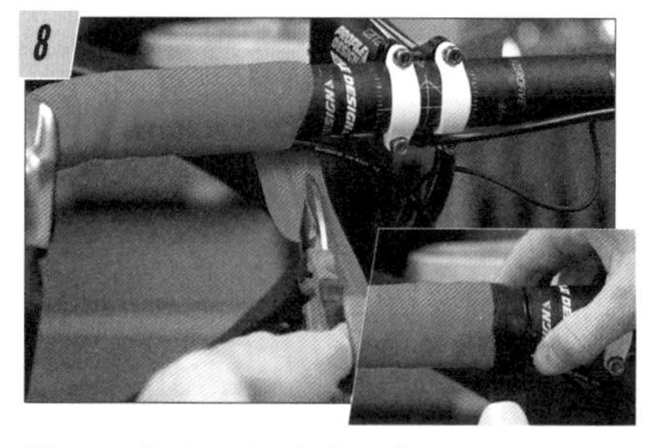

When you've taped up to the point you want, which is generally about 3 or 4cm from the stem, make a long diagonal cut into the tape, so it ends up square to the bar. Then wrap it a couple of rounds of electrical tape to secure it in place. Finish by inserting the bar plug in the end of the bar.

HOW TO CHANGE YOUR STEM

If you want to upgrade to a fancier one or are making some adjustments to the reach of your bike, here's how to simply and easily fit a new stem

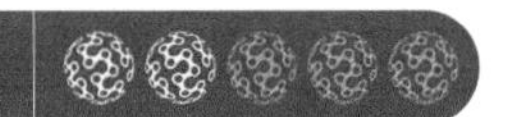

TIME	15 - 30 Minutes
TOOLS	• Allen/Torx keys • Torque wrench • Cleaning rags
WHEN	• You want to upgrade you stem or adjust the reach of your bike

WATCH THE VIDEO

Free show-how and know-how

For Lots More On Headsets
Head over to p192

CHECK THE HEADSET

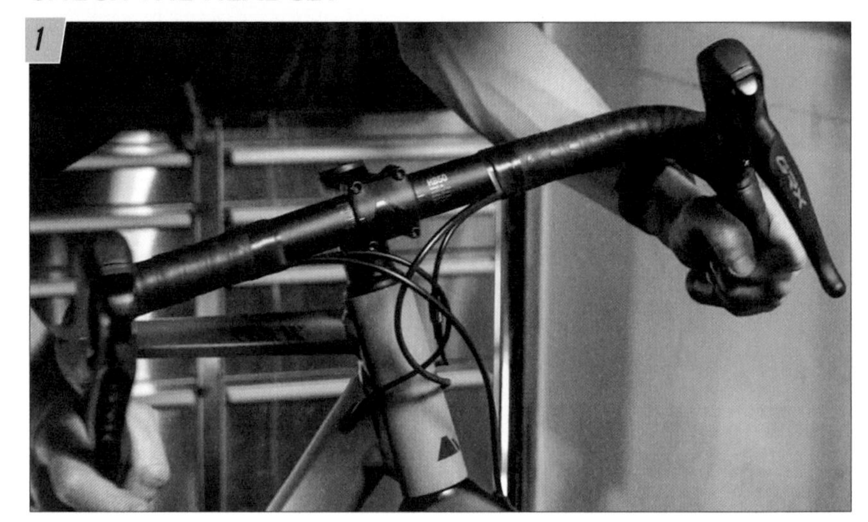

With your bike on the ground, check your headset to see how it feels, then apply the front to see if it feels loose when you rock the bike forward. If your bearings feel rough or there is knocking, as you'll be removing the stem, this is also a good time to service your headset. See page 196 for how to do that.

REMOVE THE BARS

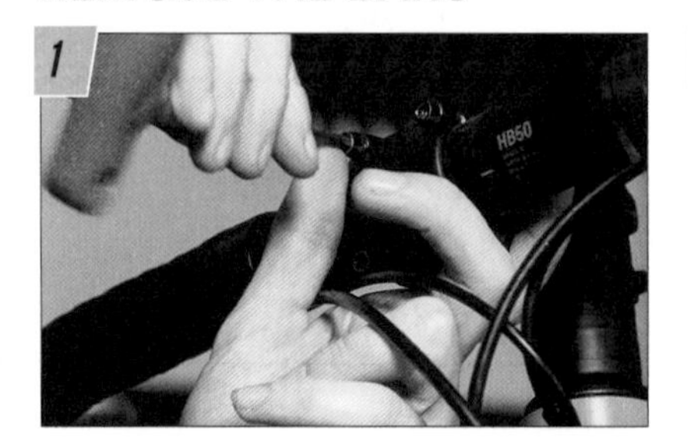

To remove the faceplate on your stem, take either your Torx or Allen key and start undoing each of the bolts a little before moving on to the next. Do not completely undo a single bolt at a time as you will put a lot of pressure on its opposite number.

With the faceplate and bolts removed, gently rest your bars on your wheel, taking care not to over-stress any of the gear and brake cables.

REMOVE THE STEM

Before removing the stem you'll need to stop the fork dropping onto the floor without the stem in place to secure it. Work with your bike on the floor, or if you want to use a workstand, tie the fork to the frame with an old inner tube.

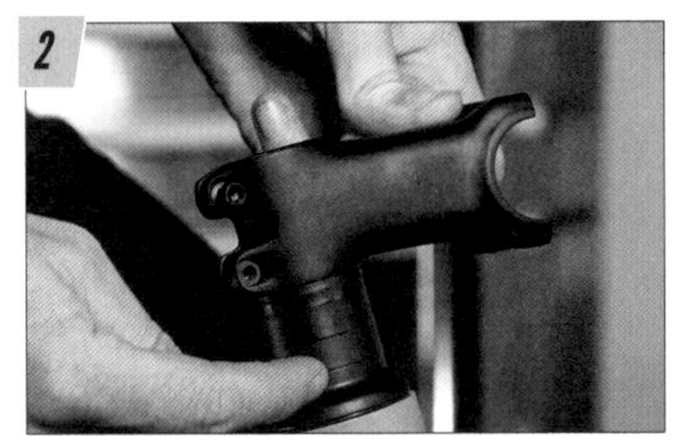

Start by removing the top cap from the stem, then undo the stem bolts that clamp the stem onto the fork's steerer tube. With the bolts loose you can now wriggle the stem up and off the steerer tube. Ensure to note the position of all the spacers.

TOP TIP

Never grease the fork steerer or your stem as this could cause the steerer to slip beneath the stem at some point and obviously you don't want that. If you've got a carbon stem and a carbon fork, you could apply some carbon assembly paste (fibre grip) to help the surfaces really hold together.

FIT YOUR NEW STEM

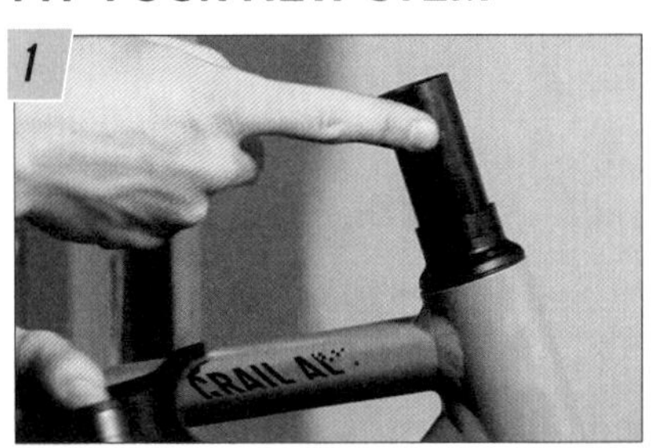

Before fitting your new stem, give the fork steerer tube a good clean as dirt and grime may well have built up under the spacers and stem over time.

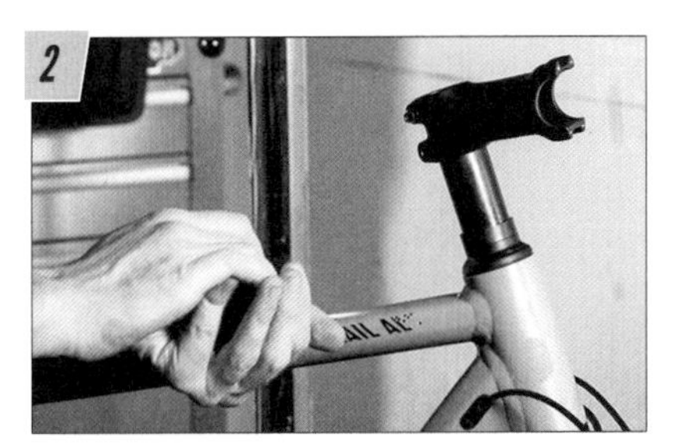

Check you're running your stem the correct way up before you start to fit it – though some more flexible riders like to run inverted stems for a super-low riding position. Also check that the stack height of your new stem is the same as your old one and adjust your spacers accordingly if not.

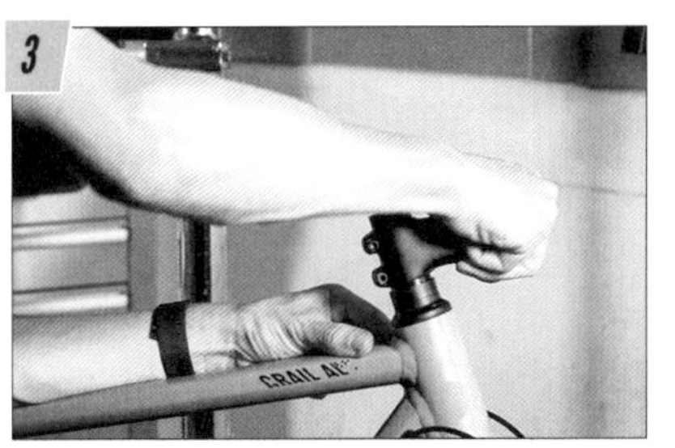

Ensure the bolts on your new stem are loose enough so that it can slide freely onto the steerer tube. Once the stem is on, you can slightly nip the bolts up if you wish, but do not tighten them at this stage.

Put the top cap back in place and install the bolt, though this only needs to be finger tight at this point. Reinstall your handlebars ensuring you tighten the stem's faceplate bolts a little at a time and use the manufacturer's torque settings.

ADJUSTING THE HEADSET

It's important to properly set the headset's compression with the top cap bolt before tightening the stem bolts. Your don't want it to feel loose or overtight, as either one will effect the handling and damage your components (see page 196 for more).

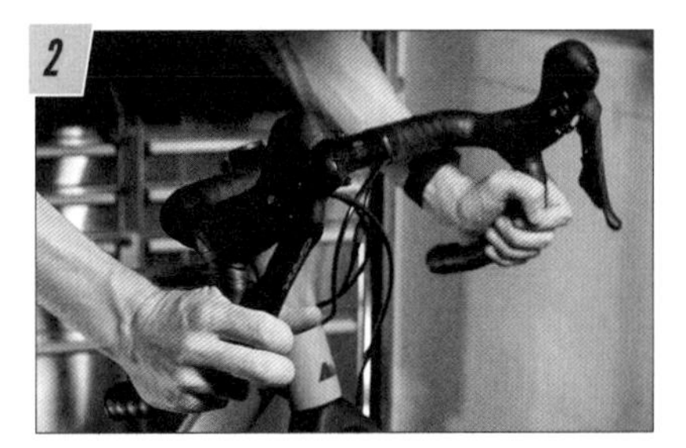

Tighten the top cap bolt a quarter turn at a time. Squeeze the brakes and check for movement, keep going until there's none. Lift the front wheel and see if you can feel the bearings moving. If so, release the tension until they feel totally smooth.

SET-UP SECRETS

HOW TO CHANGE YOUR HANDLEBARS

If you want to upgrade your bars or perhaps you need to replace them after a crash, here's how to do it

DIFFICULTY 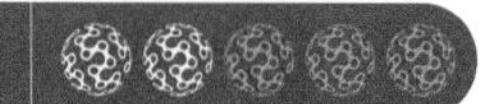

TIME 10 - 20 Minutes

TOOLS
- *Allen/Torx keys*
- *Torque wrench*
- *Tape measure*
- *Electrical tape*
- *Bar tape*
- *Handlebars*
- *Grease*

WHEN
- *Upgrading or replacing your bars*

1

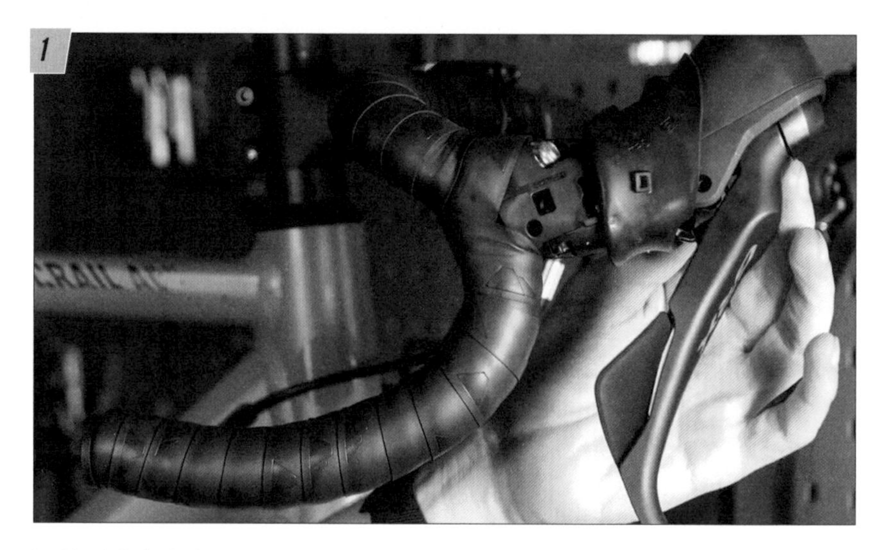

Peel back the brake hoods then remove the bar tape. If you're able to remove the tape without tearing it, you should be able to refit it if you like.

WATCH THE VIDEO

Free show-how and know-how

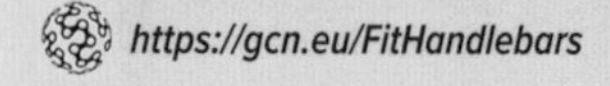

https://gcn.eu/FitHandlebars

2a

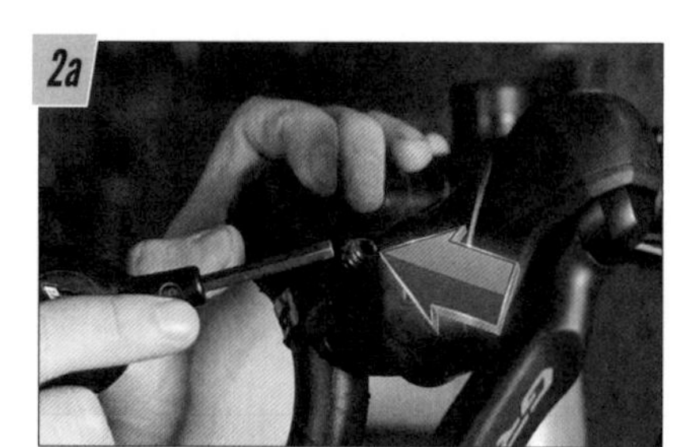

Loosen the clamp bolt that holds the brakes and shifters to the bars – this is usually a 5mm Allen key bolt. You can either completely undo the clamps from the shifter, then slide the clamp off, or leave it on and slide them both off together, though this is more likely to scratch your bars.

2b

If you've got internally routed bars and cable pull brakes and gears, you'll have to release the cables from the derailleurs and callipers and remove the inner cables before you can completely remove the bars from the bike. See page 114 for more on removing cables.

Setting Up Cable Rim Brakes?
You'll find instructions on p122

If you've got internally routed bars with hydraulic disc brakes, then things get a little more complicated as you'll need to undo the hydraulic hoses. Head over the page 140 for more info on how to do that.

REMOVE THE BARS

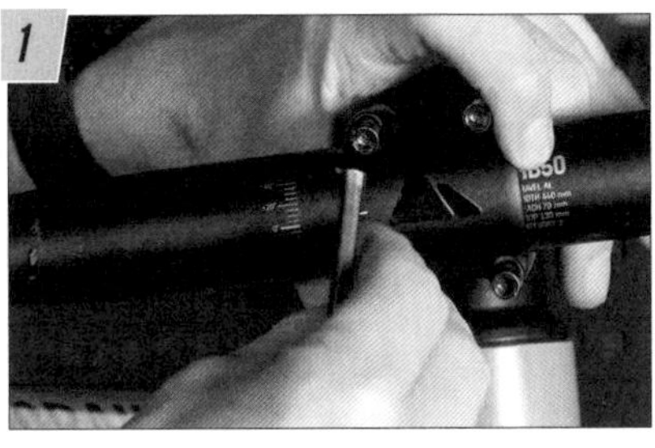

Begin to undo the stem plate bolts. The best thing to do is to loosen a little at a time and work your way around all four bolts until they are loose. Completely undoing one at a time is bad practice as it can cause undue stress on the remaining bolts.

FIT THE NEW BARS

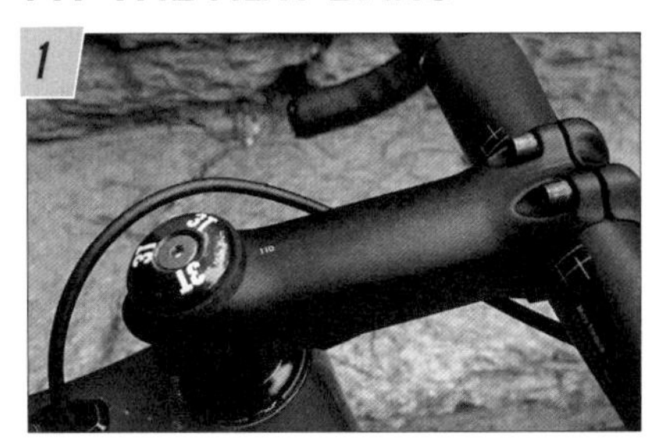

If you're fitting carbon bars, unless the bars already have a roughened section on the area where it will be clamped in the stem, it's a good idea to apply a little fibre grip here. Too much can damage the carbon though, so use it sparingly.

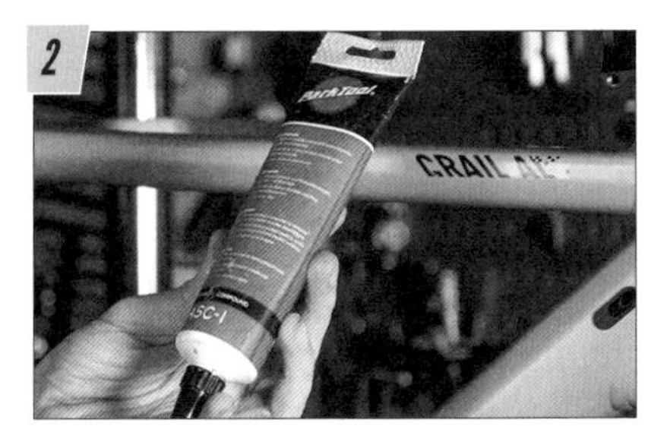

Whatever bars you use, it's a good idea to apply some grease or anti-seize to the bolts on the stem's faceplate. Do not grease the bars themselves though as they will likely end up slipping in the stem while you ride and could be very dangerous.

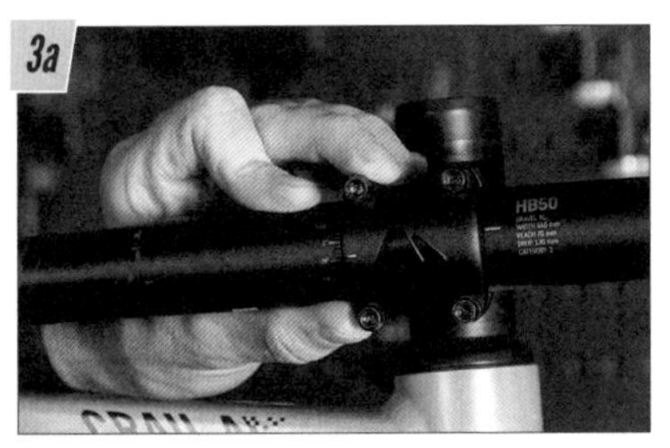

Reattach the face plate to the stem with your new bars in place. On most handlebars you'll find graduations and markings around the area which is clamped to the stem. Use these to get your handlebar centred, but don't worry too much about getting the angle right at this stage.

In a similar way to how you removed the stem bolts, be sure to tighten them a little at a time in sequence, rather than cranking each one fully tight and moving on to the next. Use your torque wrench to finish tightening them as required.

TOP TIP

If the torque setting on your stem says 6Nm, but it's 5Nm on your bars, always go with the lower number as you run the risk of damaging the weaker component or causing it to fail further down the line.

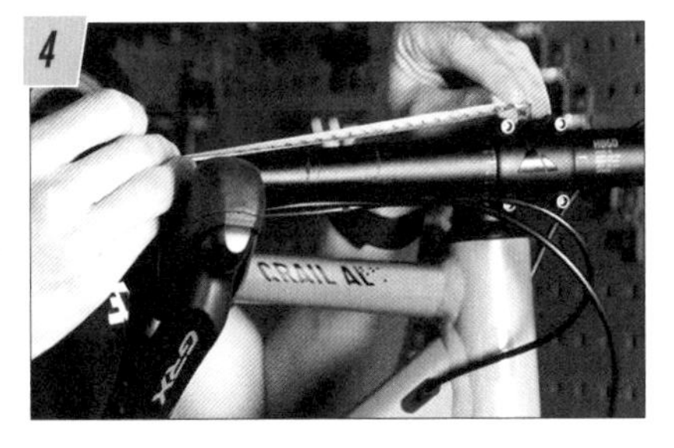

With the bars in place, you can refit your levers and shifters. Ensure to adjust them into the right position before tightening up the clamp bolt. Use your tape measure to help get them evenly spaced. For more info on positioning them, see page 110.

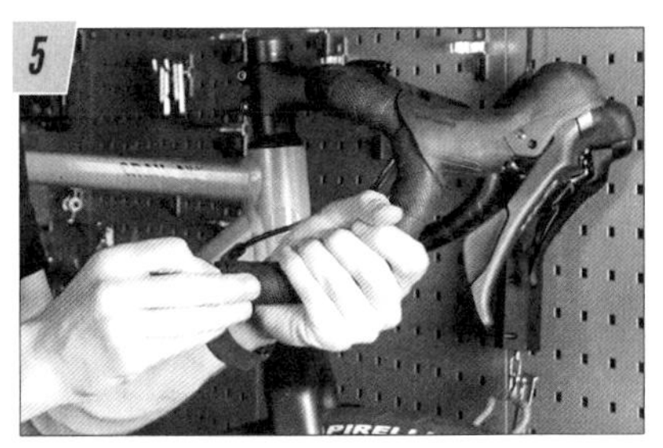

Now you can re-wrap your bar tape and fold your hoods back down. For a full guide on fitting bar tape, head back to page 200.

SET-UP SECRETS

HOW TO SET UP CLIP-IN PEDAL CLEATS

If you're new to clip-in pedals, here's how to set your cleats up. For more seasoned clip-in riders, we'll show you how to transfer your cleats to new shoes

DIFFICULTY 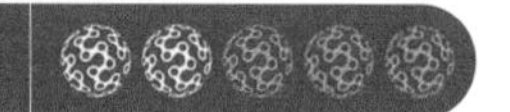

TIME 20 - 30 Minutes

TOOLS
- *Tape measure*
- *Allen keys*
- *Phillips screwdriver*
- *Grease*
- *Pencil*
- *A4 size paper*
- *Masking tape*

WHEN
- *Setting up new shoes and cleats*

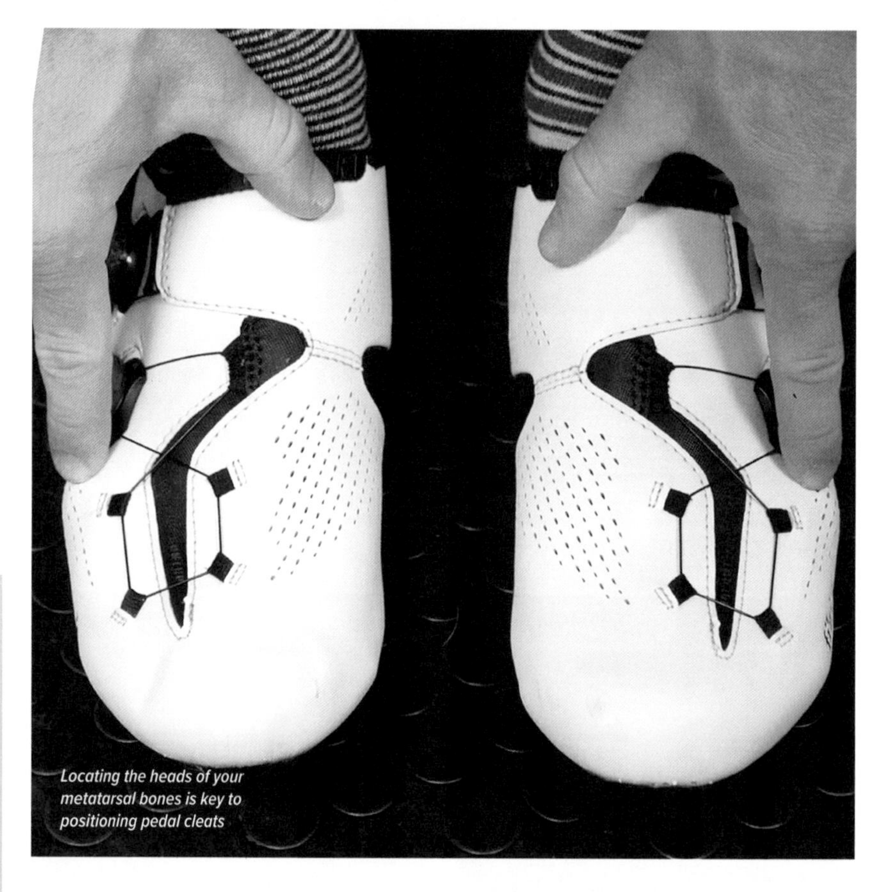

Locating the heads of your metatarsal bones is key to positioning pedal cleats

WATCH THE VIDEO

Free show-how and know-how

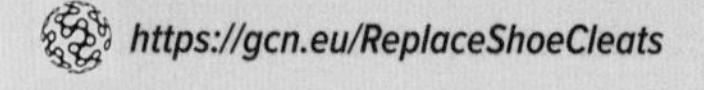

https://gcn.eu/ReplaceShoeCleats

If you're serious about road bike riding, using clip-in pedals is a must. The power and efficiency benefits you'll get are huge, plus you'll also look like you mean business. Correctly setting up cleats for the first time isn't easy though, similarly, transferring an existing cleat set-up to new shoes can be a fiddly affair too. Here we show you the best way to take on both of these procedures without hours of painful trial and error.

FITTING CLEATS FOR THE FIRST TIME

If you're using cleated shoes for the first time, it can be difficult to know how to best position the cleats, but it's something you need to get right as setting them in an incorrect position is likely to give you knee pain while riding.

To begin with, loosely attach the cleats to your shoes – adding a dab of grease on each bolt. Position the cleat in the middle of each bolt head. To get an idea of the natural position of your feet, sit on a table or tall chair and let your feet dangle below you. Most people's heels will hang slightly inwards, so and adjust your cleats to try to replicate the angles of your feet.

Stick a strip of masking tape on the widest point of each side of your shoe and put them on. Once on, feel for the bone in the widest part of your foot (the metatarsal bone) and put a pencil mark on each side of the tape to indicate exactly where that is.

With your bike on a turbo trainer or leaning up against a wall, mount your bike and clip into your pedals. You want the marks on the masking tape to line up with the front edge of your pedal axle – this will likely take a few attempts to get in the right position.

Ideally, you should be using free-float rather than fixed cleats (see our first Top Tip). You want your cleat positioned so you have roughly the same amount of float (lateral movement) inwards and outwards when your shoe is clipped into the pedal. Once you're happy with the position of your cleats, tighten the cleat bolts to the manufacturer's recommended torque setting and take your new shoes for a short test ride.

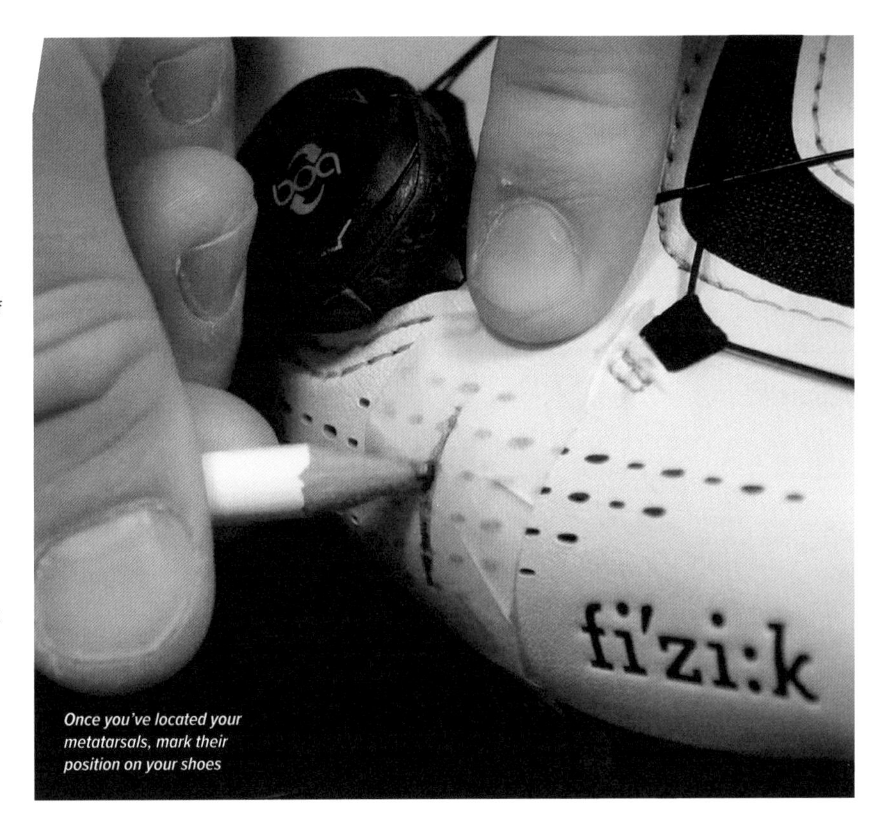

Once you've located your metatarsals, mark their position on your shoes

"To get an idea of the natural position of your feet, sit on a table or tall chair and let your feet dangle below you"

REPLACING CLEATS

If you need to replace broken or worn out cleats on an existing pair of cycling shoes, simply draw around the existing cleats before you remove them from your shoes, then ensure the new cleats match up to the marked position.

FITTING TO NEW SHOES

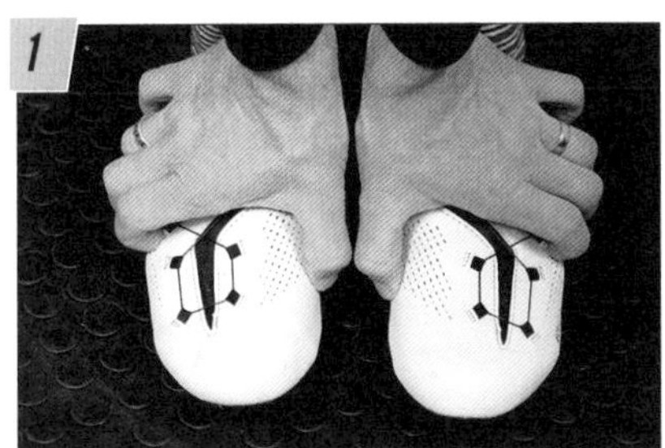

Put your old shoes on and locate the ball of your foot, this is just at the head of your metatarsal bones – aka the sticky out bits on either side near the base of your toes.

TOP TIP

Most pedal manufacturers offer their cleats in fixed and free-float varieties. Free-float means that that cleat will give you more movement on the pedal before your cleat starts to disengage from it. This allows your feet to be in a more natural position which can help avoid injury. If you're new to riding with cleats and clip-in pedals, free-float cleats are a great idea.

HOW TO SET UP CLIP-IN PEDAL CLEATS

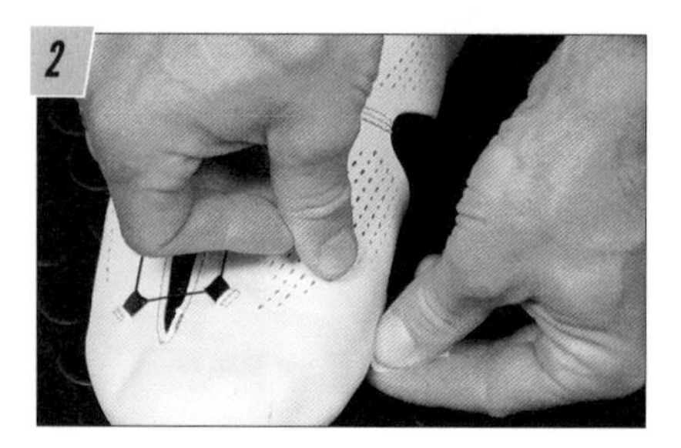

Place some masking tape onto your shoes over the points at which your metatarsal bones sit.

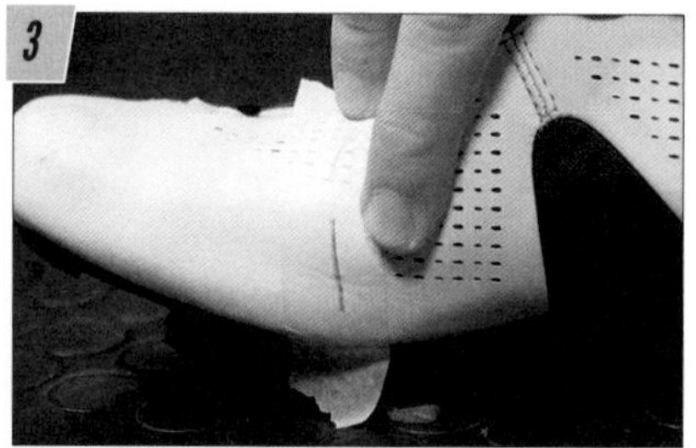

Draw a nice clear line on the masking tape to indicate the widest point of each metatarsal bone. You should now have four lines at 90 degrees to the ground.

TECH EXPLAINED

Mountain Bike Cleats & Pedals

You may have noticed cycling shoes that have two cleat bolt holes in rather than three, these are designed to work with MTB cleats and pedals. Mountain bike riders tend to clip and unclip more often than road cyclists given the rough and varied terrain they ride. Some road riders prefer the ease of SPD cleats and pedals – which also have the added bonus of allowing you to clip into either side of the pedal face.

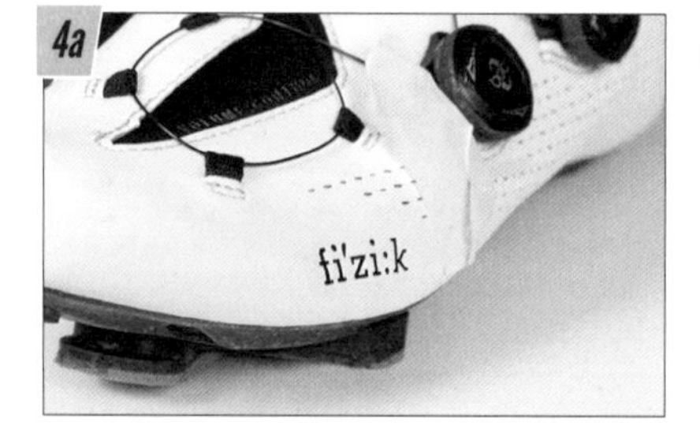

With the pencil line markers in place, it's time to measure the difference from them to the centre point of the pedal axle and the cleat. To do this you'll need two sheets of paper, your pencil and tape measure.

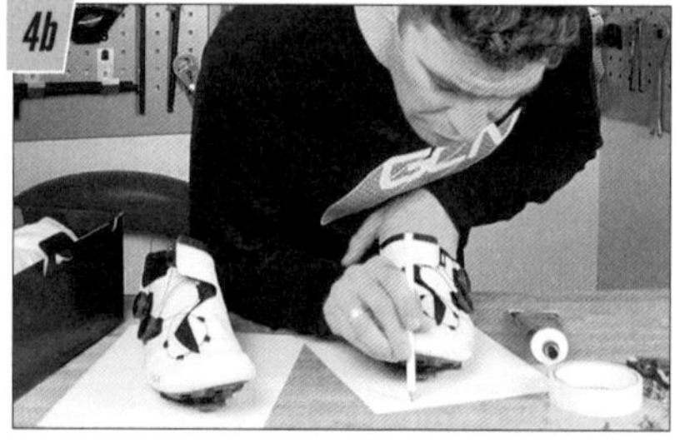

Remove your shoes and place each one on a piece of paper and push it down into so it creates an indentation on the paper's surface. Add pencil marks at the heel, edges of the cleat and tip of each shoe too.

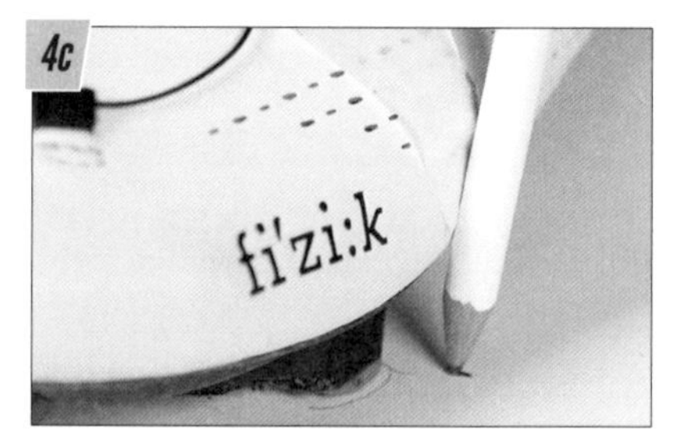

Without moving the shoe, carefully follow the pencil lines on each shoe to mark on the paper where your metatarsal bones would be.

If you have custom insoles, don't forget to take them out of your old shoes and slip them into your new pair.

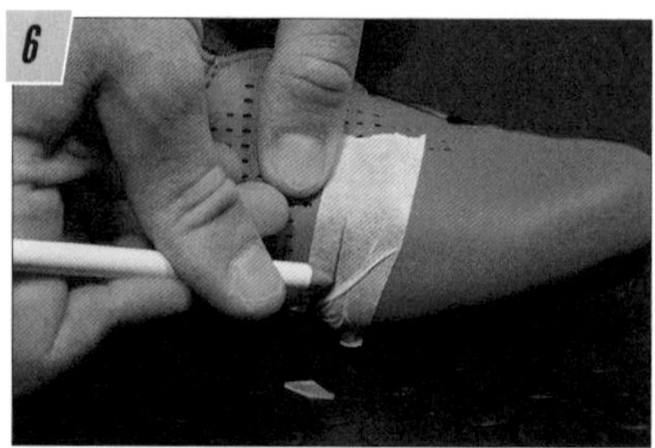

Put on your new shoes and with the masking tape and pencil, mark the centre of your metatarsal bones in the same way as you did with your old shoes.

Next, remove your shoes and, adding a small amount of grease to each cleat bolt, loosely attach the cleats onto the bottom of your new shoes.

For Essential Pre-Ride Checks
Head on over to p60

TOP TIP

If you're not keen on getting grease anywhere near your shiny new shoes and thinking of bolting your cleats on grease-free, you are likely to regret the decision later. When the time comes to remove the cleats, given all the water and muck that gets onto your shoes, the cleat bolts are likely to be seized in place and it may take drastic surgery to remove them – see page 226 for more on that.

Now is the time to get out your tape measure to ensure you're attaching the cleat in exactly the right place by measuring the distance from the front of the cleat to the toe and the back of it to the heel and comparing those distances with the marks you made on the paper.

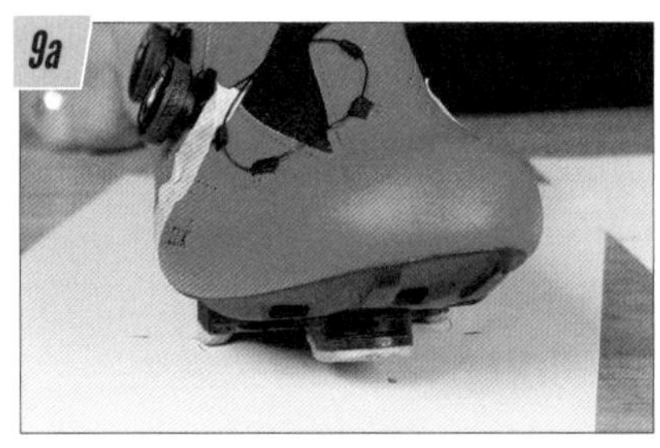

Put your new shoes on the pieces of paper and ensure you're getting the angle of each cleat spot on. If your new shoes have a different shape than your old pair, line up all the marks as best you can.

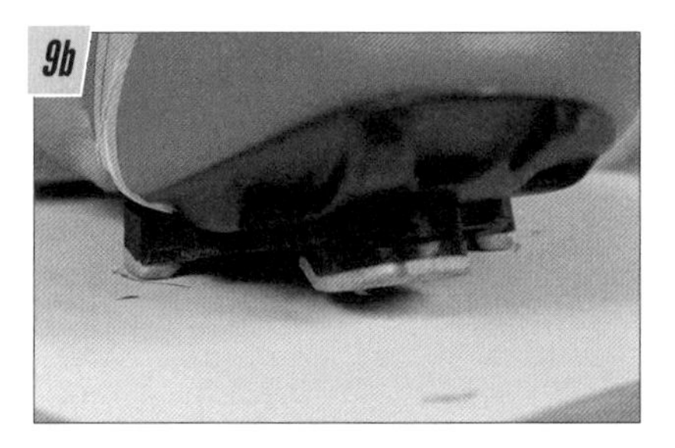

If you are really struggling to get your markers to line up, start by putting the cleat into its indentation that you made in the paper and then adjust the shoe around the cleat.

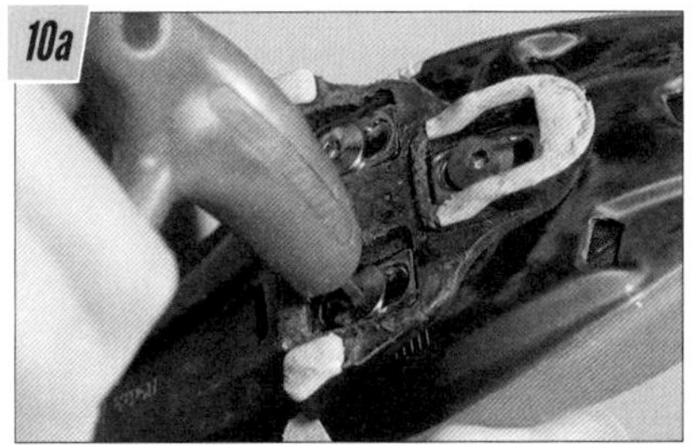

If the position of each cleat looks good, you can now tighten your cleats onto the bottom of your new shoes.

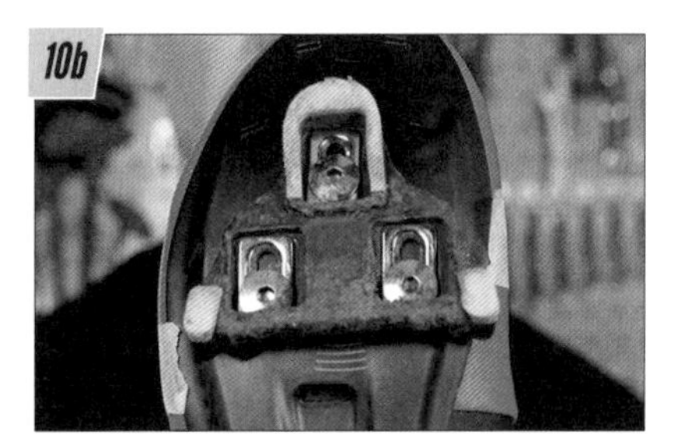

Tighten them up to around 90 per cent so you can clip into your pedals without your cleats moving, then test them out their position on a turbo trainer or by leaning up against the wall.

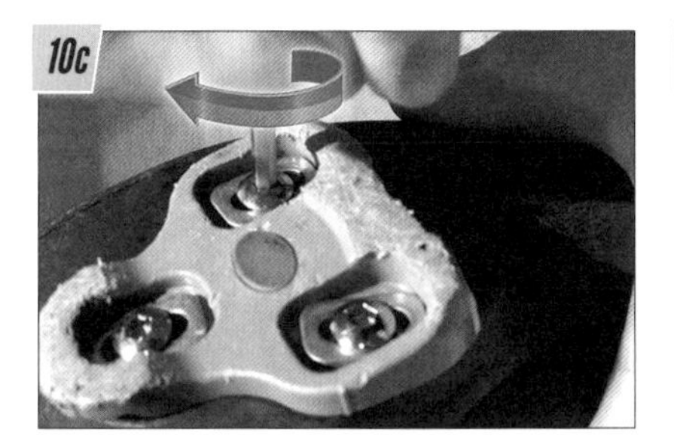

Once you're happy with the cleat position on the pedal, tighten them to the manufacturer's recommended setting using a torque wrench.

Now you're ready to give your shoes a full test ride. Keep it fairly short and easy though as you don't want to give yourself any leg joint pain should your cleats need further adjustment.

TECH EXPLAINED

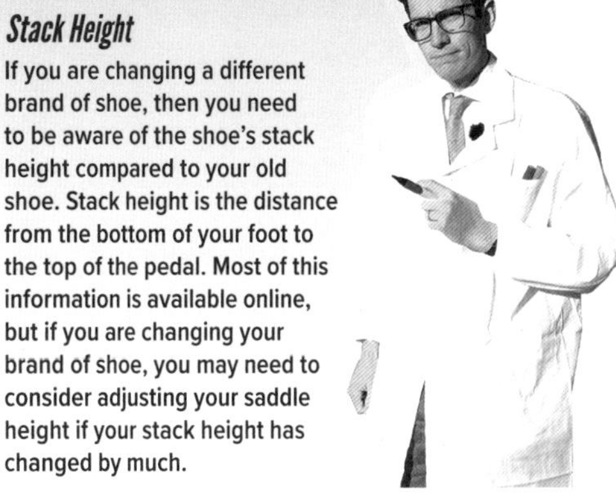

Stack Height

If you are changing a different brand of shoe, then you need to be aware of the shoe's stack height compared to your old shoe. Stack height is the distance from the bottom of your foot to the top of the pedal. Most of this information is available online, but if you are changing your brand of shoe, you may need to consider adjusting your saddle height if your stack height has changed by much.

ESSENTIAL REPAIRS

HOW TO SERVICE YOUR PEDALS

If you look after them properly, a good set of pedals can last for many many years and basic servicing is a really easy job

DIFFICULTY 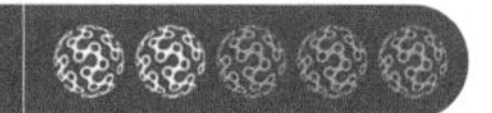

TIME 10 - 30 Minutes

TOOLS
- *6 or 8mm Allen key*
- *Bench vice (not essential)*
- *Shimano 105, R550 and R540: Shimano TL-PD40 tool*
- *Shimano Dura Ace or Ultegra: 17mm spanner*
- *Shimano bearings: 7 and 10mm spanners*
- *Look: collar tool*
- *Grease gun or syringe*
- *Lubricating grease*
- *Phillips screwdriver*
- *Dry lube (for cleats)*

WHEN
- *Your pedals aren't spinning smoothly*

WATCH THE VIDEO

Free show-how and know-how

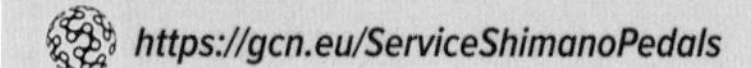
https://gcn.eu/ServiceShimanoPedals

For Advice On Removing Pedals
Turn back to p44

First things first – clean your pedals. As a matter of fact, anytime you're doing any maintenance or taking a bike to a shop you should ensure your bike or part is clean.

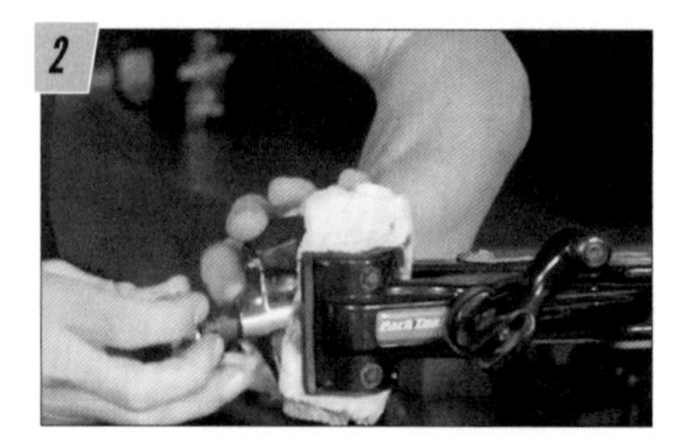

With your pedals all cleaned up, remove them from the cranks using the 6 or 8mm Allen key in the back of the axle. If you have a bench vice, wrap the pedal in the rag so it doesn't scratch and clamp it gently but securely into the vice. Otherwise just hold it in your hand.

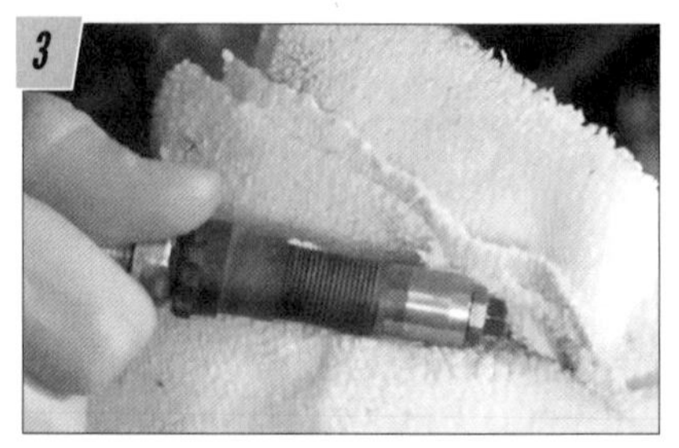

Now, you just need to remove the pedal axle. Simply affix your 17mm spanner or Shimano tool to the lockring and undo. The right-hand pedal will have a reverse thread, so this will loosen clockwise. With the axle out of the pedal, give it a wipe down and set it to the side.

If you need to replace your bearings, now is the time to do that. Otherwise, just service your existing ones. Use the appropriate spanner or removal tool to loosen the axle collar. Be aware that left and right-hand pedals unscrew in different directions (otherwise they might unscrew while you were pedalling).

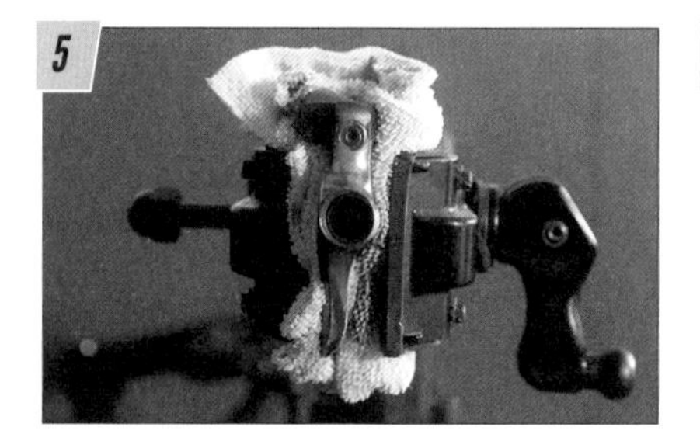

Look pedals use cartridge bearings so it's just a case of cleaning old grease from inside of the pedal and off the axle and bearings. Shimano bearings have two sets of 'cup and cone' bearings which you can adjust with a 7mm and 10mm spanner. See page 168 for more on this bearing type.

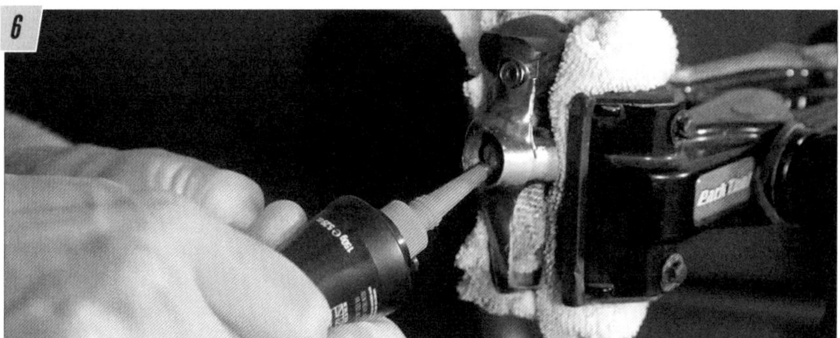

Once the pedal and axle are clean, inject a generous amount of grease into the pedal and screw the axle back in. If you struggle to tighten the collar, you've put too much grease in, so take a bit out and try again until it works. Check the pedal turns smoothly and doesn't wobble, then re-fit to your bike.

SPEEDPLAY PEDALS

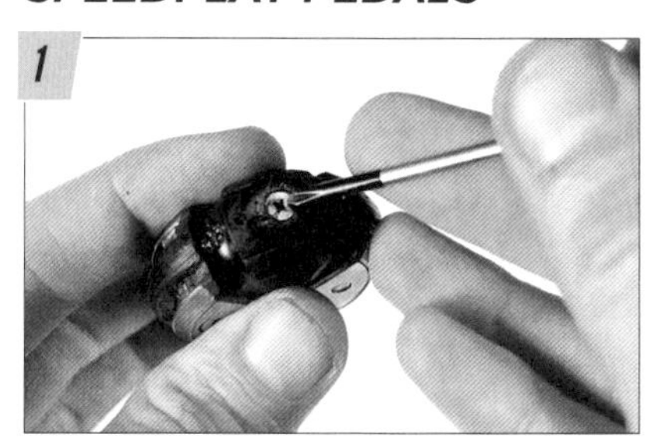

Speedplay pedals are designed so that you can just pump fresh grease in rather than stripping them down to service them. Clean the pedals as usual and then use a Phillips head screwdriver to undo the small grease port screw on the end.

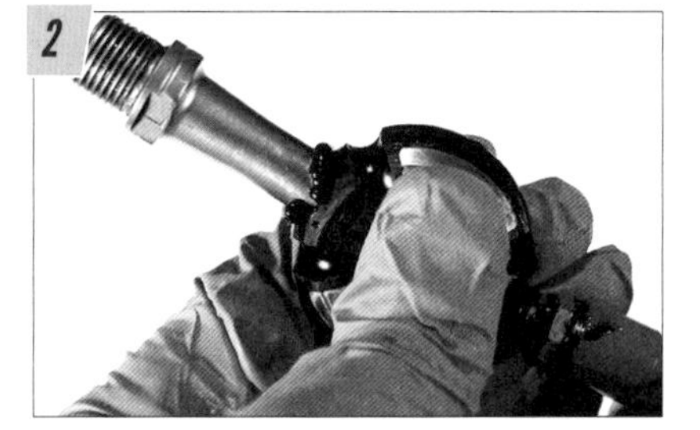

Pump in the fresh grease until it pushes all the dirty grease out of the inside edge of the axle and only fresh grease is squeezing out. Screw the grease port cover back in and wipe down the whole pedal and re-install it.

Because the spring and release mechanism is actually in the shoe cleats on the Speedplay system you need to clean and lube them too. Once you've cleaned them (an old toothbrush works well), make sure you use a dry lube that doesn't attract dirt.

SECTION 7

BIKE CARE & CLEANING

Regularly cleaning and lubricating your bike will help ensure your components work effectively and last as long as possible. Follow the advice here and you can't go wrong

BEGINNER BASICS

HOW TO CLEAN YOUR BIKE

Keeping your bike clean will ensure it stays in top condition and help you spot any potential problems before they become an issue out on the road

DIFFICULTY 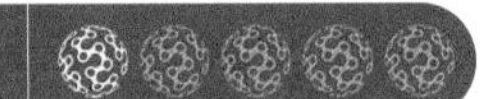

TIME 30 - 40 Minutes

TOOLS
- Workshop stand
- Hot water
- Hosepipe
- Bucket
- Sponges
- Dummy hub
- Rags
- Microfibre cloth
- Stiff bristled brushes
- Bottle brush
- Flathead screwdriver
- Car or bike wash
- Degreaser

WHEN
- After a dirty ride

A deep clean is a good way to remove stubborn dirt in those hard to reach places

Unless you like to always keep your bike in showroom condition, you can usually get away with a quick wipe down after the majority of your rides. It's still a good idea to do the thorough cleaning routine we're going to show you here on a fairly regular basis though, as dirt and grime can work it's way into your components over time which can dramatically shorten their lifespan. It's also well worth doing before a race or a sportive to ensure your bike is functioning properly and sort any potential issues before they become more serious problems or affect you during your event.

WHERE TO WASH

In this walkthrough, we're assuming that you have access to some kind of outdoor space to wash your bike, but if you don't,

WATCH THE VIDEO

Free show-how and know-how

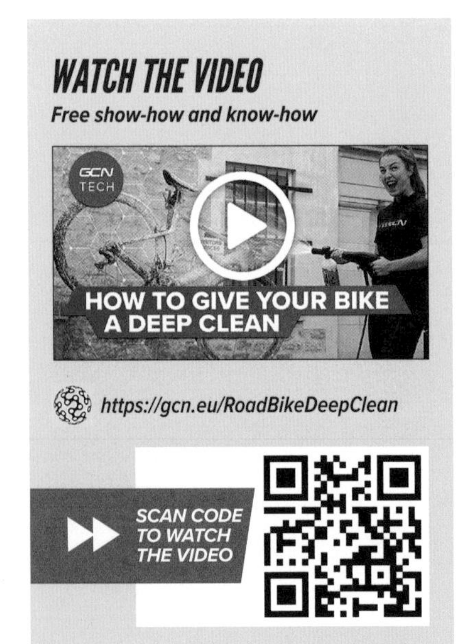

https://gcn.eu/RoadBikeDeepClean

SCAN CODE TO WATCH THE VIDEO

one option is to stick your bike in your bath to wash it. When doing that, ensure to put the dirtiest (usually the rear) end of the bike lower than the rest of it, so that you don't get that dirt over the rest of the bike as you clean. Also ensure you move anything such as towels, soap and shampoo bottles out of the way before you get started!

Alternatively, you could use a jet wash at a petrol station, but ensure to use the lightest jet of water you can (e.g. a rinse setting), or stand well back while hosing down, as the powerful blast can force water into your bearings and wash out the grease that protects them.

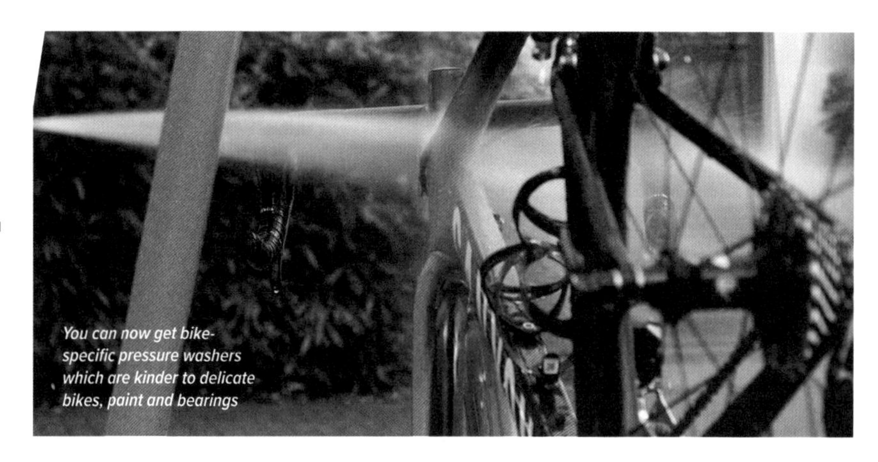

You can now get bike-specific pressure washers which are kinder to delicate bikes, paint and bearings

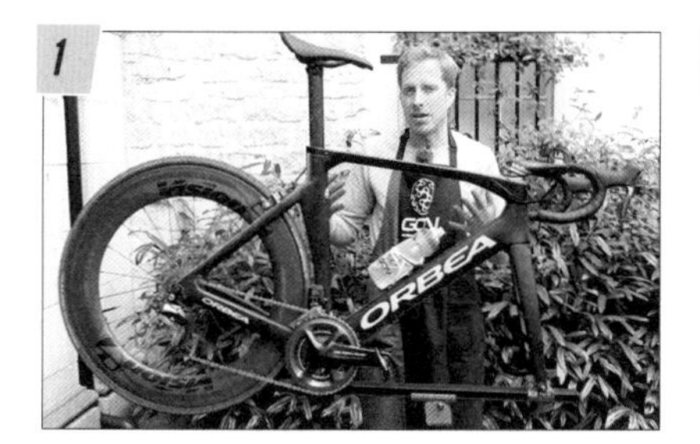

Sticking your bike in a workshop stand (if you've got one) makes life a lot easier when it comes to cleaning. If you don't have a stand, resist the urge to clean your bike upside down as it is not great for your saddle, bar tape or brake hoods.

Before you start, ensure you remove any accessories such as pumps, water bottles, etc from your bike as they will only get in the way.

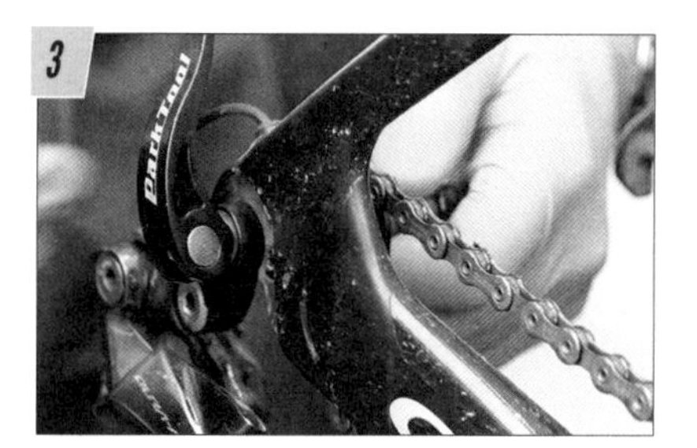

Remove the wheels and insert your dummy hub into the rear dropouts to keep your chain in position and away from the paintwork. If you don't have one, you'll probably find it easier to leave your back wheel in place until you've cleaned your drivetrain.

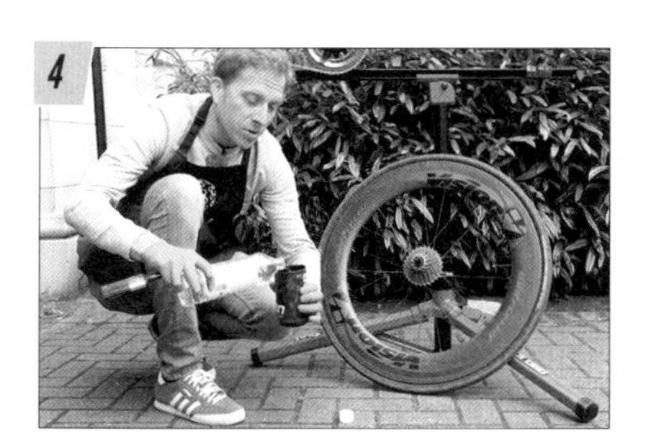

Before your bike gets wet, decant some degreaser into a pot, half an old water bottle works particularly well, then use a fairly stiff brush to liberally paint the degreaser onto the cassette taking care not to get any in your wheel bearings.

TOP TIP

Before painting with degreaser, take a flathead screwdriver and use it to scrape off all the gunk off that builds up on your derailleur's jockey wheels. Removing the worst of that oily gunge first will allow the degreaser to really get to work.

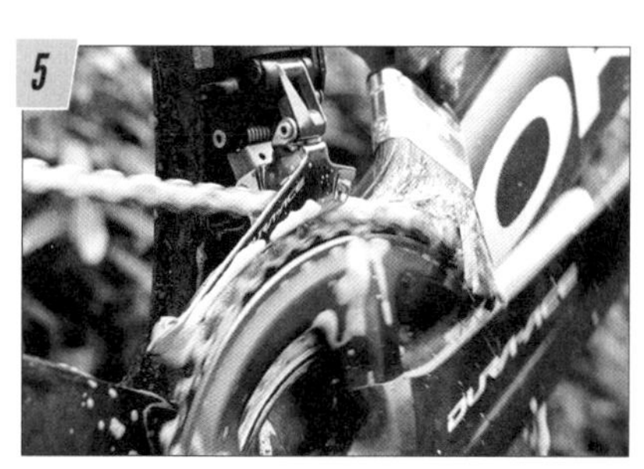

Once done, sparingly paint some degreaser onto jockey wheels, then last but not least, coat the chain and chainrings with degreaser and leave it to fully get to work on those components.

HOW TO CLEAN YOUR BIKE

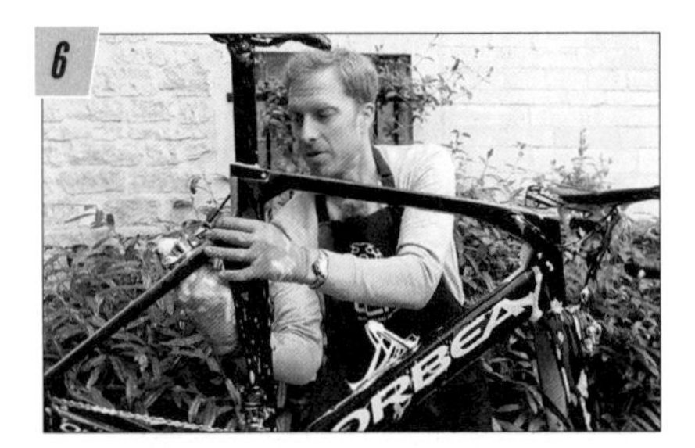

Get a bucket of hot water and bike wash, then start washing everything down with a clean sponge. If your bike is particularly dirty, it's a good idea to first hose off the worst of the mud to prevent potentially scratching your paintwork.

TOP TIP

Should you have any stubborn, oily patches on your paint that you can't get off with soap and water, a spray from a can of water disperser, an old rag and a fair bit of elbow grease should help to get rid of it. This is particularly useful on matt paintwork which tends to hold onto greasy marks a little bit more than glossy paint.

When you get to your drivetrain, swap your clean sponge for an older one as this is one of the greasiest, dirtiest areas. It's a good idea to have your chain on your big chainring as this makes it easier to clean the outside of the chain.

If you've wiped down your chain and it's still looking dirty, give it another coat of degreaser, leave it to soak in then wipe it down again.

Now turn your attention to the derailleur and the chainrings. Using a small, stiff brush allows you to really get inside the derailleur cage and between the chainrings.

Clean inside your forks and chainstays. Having the wheels out allows you to really clean the brake callipers. Check your pads for wear while you're doing this.

Give the wheels and tyres a really good clean, paying particular attention to braking surfaces on your rims – if you have conventional brakes. Don't forget the spokes and hub outers, using a bottle brush here makes life much easier.

TOP TIP

To ensure your cassette is totally free from built-up oil, grease and bits of debris, remove it from the wheel (turn to page 70 for advice on how to do that) and scrub each sprocket individually with degreaser and a stiff brush.

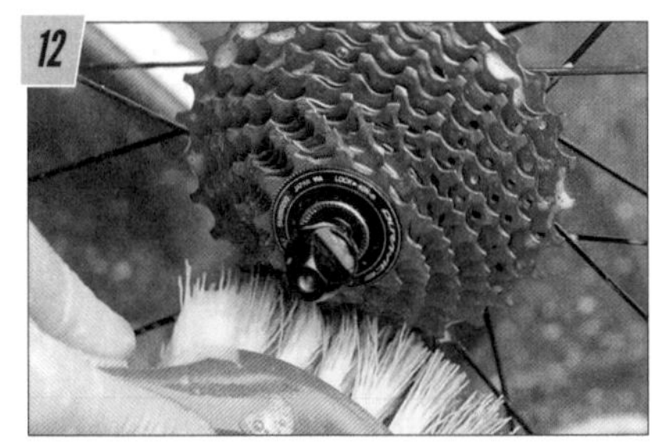

A nail brush does a good job of cleaning your cassette. Make sure you use the free hub body to your benefit as it doesn't spin backwards. Once you've cleaned a section, rotate it forwards a little bit and simply keep repeating that process. You can also use a rag to clean between the sprockets.

Hose or sponge down your bike with clean water, ensuring to thoroughly rinse the areas where you've used degreaser, as any left on your components will break down your lubes.

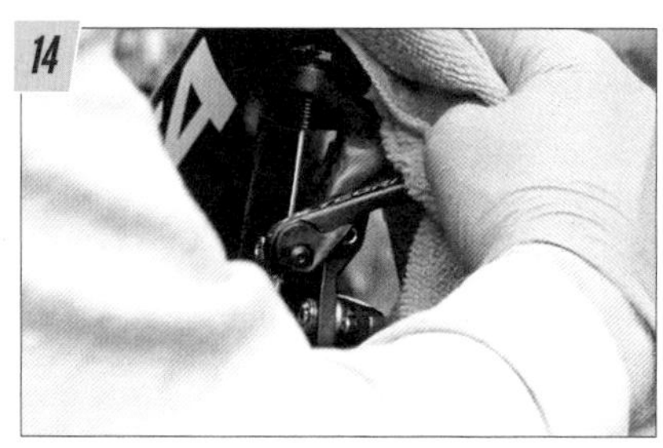

Dry off your frame and forks with the microfibre cloth, paying particular attention to mounts or any other bolts with the potential for rust. Then use an old rag to thoroughly dry off your chain.

TOP TIP

If you want to take your cleaning regime to the next level, applying some car or bike-specific polish will not only give your bike an extra level of sheen, but it will also help shrug off dirt and keep your paintwork looking good for longer. If you have a matt paint job there are polishes with a matt finish too.

TOP TIP

If you've got white bar tape, you'll know that it's tough, if not impossible, to get it back to the pure white it was when new. Soap and water doesn't have much of an effect, but we've found that toothpaste and a stiff brush do a much better job. You also get the bonus of a minty fresh smell! See page 218 for more bar tape cleaning tips.

Now that everything is clean, take the opportunity to inspect your bike for any issues that might cause problems while riding.

Check your tyres for bits of glass or thorns that may be stuck into them and remove them with a flat screwdriver. Seal any small holes you discover with glue from a puncture repair kit, though if you find any large holes, it's time for a new tyre. See page 152 for how to change a tyre.

With the wheels out, check your brake pads as they can get little shards of metal stuck in them if you've got alloy rims. Checking the pads is also really important if you're running carbon rims, as any bits of grit or other debris in your pads can damage those expensive wheels. See page 118.

Now to lube your chain. Fit your rear wheel if you don't have a dummy hub, then use the lube (wet or dry) best suited to the conditions you ride in and carefully apply to your links. Once you've worked all the way round, give the cranks a few spins, leave to fully penetrate and use a rag to wipe up any excess.

TOP TIP

If you have a cabled (non-electric) derailleurs or cable-pull brakes, carefully turn your bike upside down and run a drop or two of lubricant onto the inner cables and allow it to just run down and work its way into the outers. This will help keep your shifting and braking running smoother for longer.

Want To Weatherproof Your Bike?
Then head over to page 240

HOW TO CLEAN YOUR BAR TAPE

Want super-clean bar tape? Here are three different methods for getting the grime off

DIFFICULTY 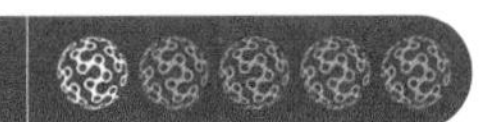

TIME	10 - 30 Minutes
TOOLS	• Soap and water • Sponge • Toothpaste • Stiff brush • Bike-specific cleaner • Bucket • Clean rags
WHEN	• Your bar tape starts to look grubby

SOAP AND WATER

1

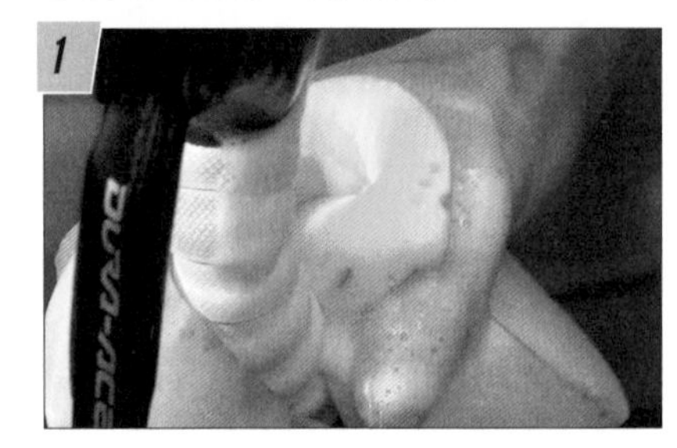

Get some general household soap, washing up liquid for example, and add a squirt of it to a big, warm bucket of water.

2

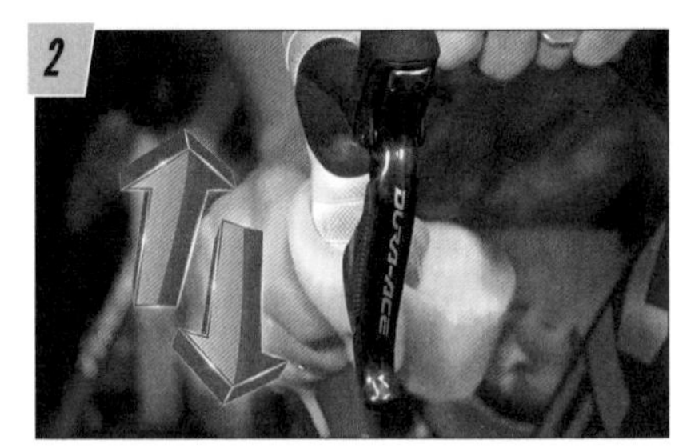

Use your sponge to thoroughly rub down the bar tape with the soapy water, pay particular attention to the tape around the hoods and on the drops as it tends to be used the most often.

> *"Pay particular attention to the tape around the hoods and on the drops"*

3

Gripping the bar with the sponge, turn it in the direction in which the tape is wound as you don't want to risk loosening the tape while cleaning.

4

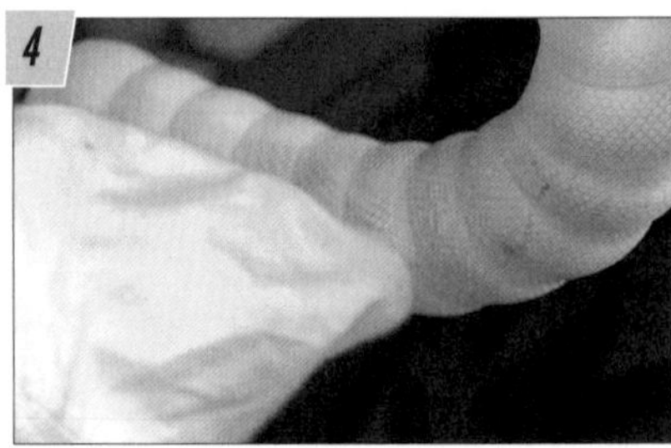

Once you've got as much grime off the tape as possible, dry it off with your clean rags.

WATCH THE VIDEO

Free show-how and know-how

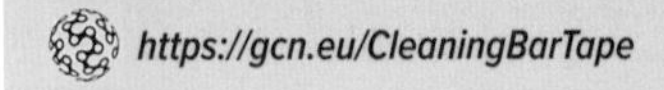

https://gcn.eu/CleaningBarTape

Want To Change Your Bar Tape?
See page 200 for full instructions

TOOTHPASTE AND BRUSH

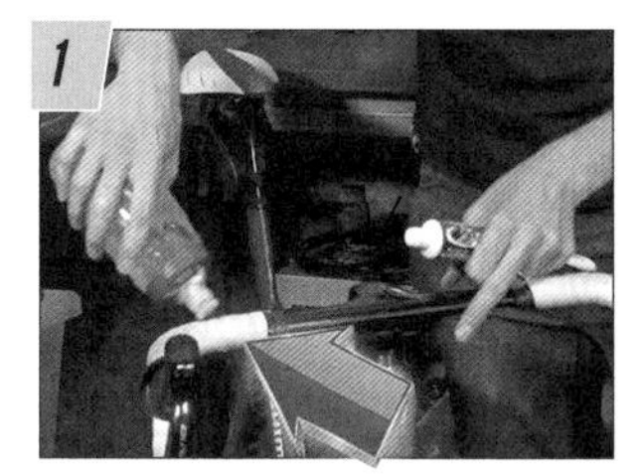

Before you start, wet the bar tape to help activate the cleaning products in the toothpaste. We've gone traditional here with a toothbrush, but a nail brush or something similar may well help you to clean a bit faster.

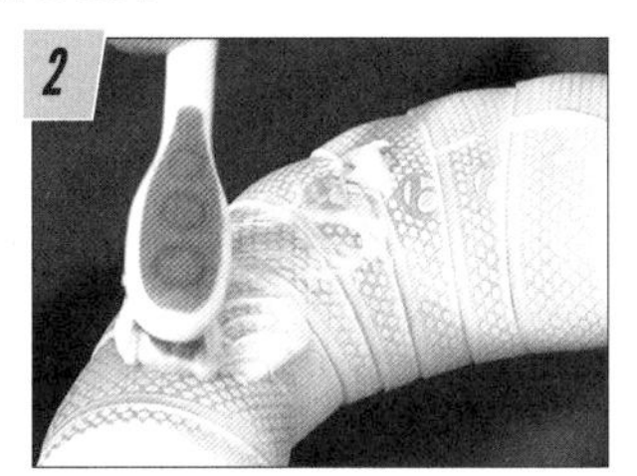

Apply some toothpaste to the handlebar tape and start to scrub it in. Pay close attention to the areas of the bar that you use the most often.

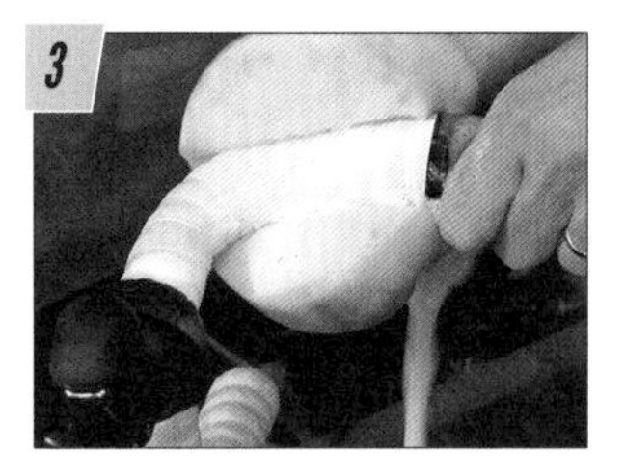

Rinse off with clean water and depending on how dirty your tape was to start with, you may well want to give it another scrub with the toothpaste and brush.

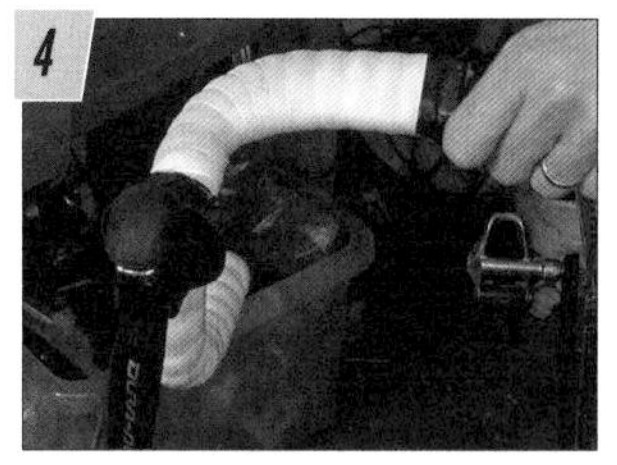

Dry everything off with your rags, then step back and admire your minty-fresh handlebars.

BIKE-SPECIFIC CLEANER

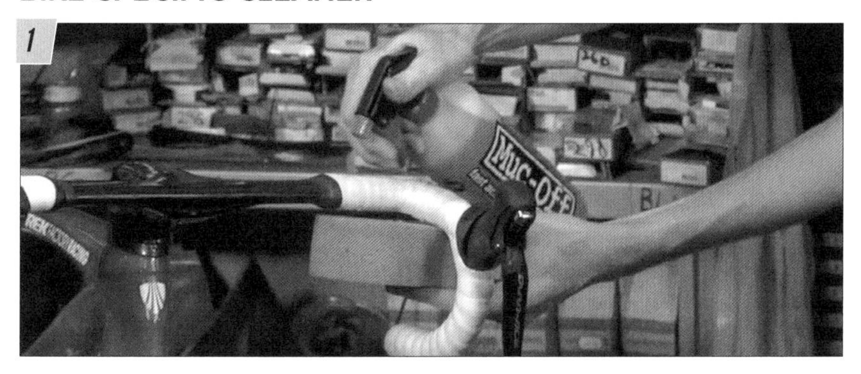

Apply the cleaner to your bar tape. If it comes in a spray bottle, take care not to get any on your drivetrain as you don't want it to attack your nicely lubricated parts.

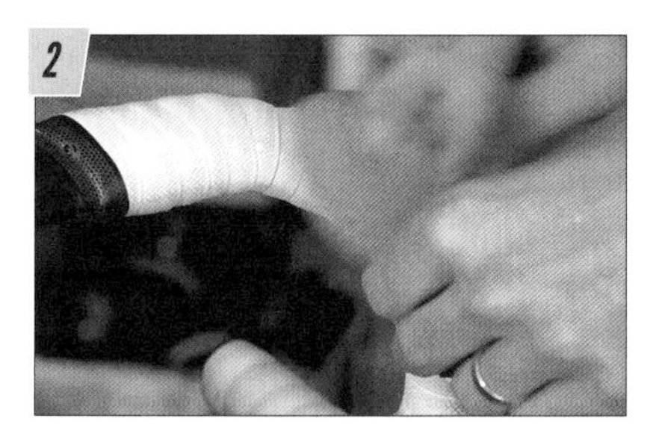

Give the spray a minute or two to attack the dirt, then use your sponge and plenty of elbow grease to really get into those dirty nooks and crannies on the bars.

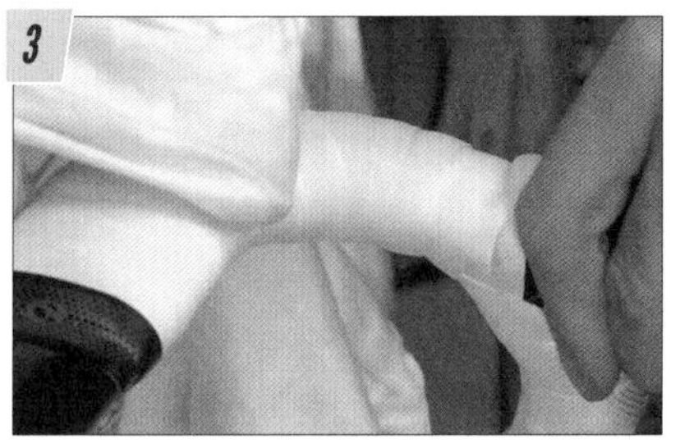

Rinse the cleaner off, then then dry then bar tape with your rags.

TOP TIP

White bar tape looks great when new, but quickly gets grubby – particularly after a few mid-ride mechanical stops. The only way to keep it looking good is to clean it after every ride which can be a chore. Of course, an option that is less high maintenance – though arguably doesn't look as cool, is to fit black bar tape.

TOP TIPS

HOW TO DEEP-CLEAN YOUR DRIVETRAIN

If you want a showroom sparkling drivetrain, you're going to have to remove it from your bike and clean the parts individually. Here's how to do it

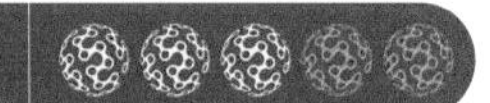

DIFFICULTY

TIME 60 - 120 Minutes

TOOLS
- *Chain tool or master link tool*
- *Stiff brushes*
- *Plastic container*
- *Degreaser*
- *Cleaning rags*
- *Disposable gloves*
- *Chain lube*
- *Grease*

WHEN
- *You want to remove every trace of grime from your drivetrain*

WATCH THE VIDEO

Free show-how and know-how

https://gcn.eu/DrivetrainDeepClean

SCAN CODE TO WATCH THE VIDEO

1

Before you start on the drivetrain, give the rest of your bike a thorough wash first. Then remove the rear wheel, break your chain with your chain tool (see page 68) or master link tool (if your chain has a master link fitted) and remove the chain from your bike.

2

Now that your chain is free, place it in your plastic container – ideally using one that is big enough to take your chainrings later on. Then pour in enough degreaser to completely cover the chain.

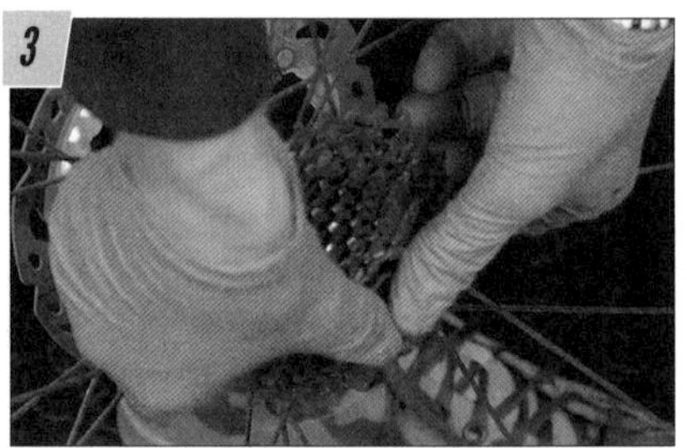

3

While the degreaser is working on the chain, it's time to remove the cassette from the wheel – see page 70 for more detail on how to do that.

Next, take your stiff brushes and start to work on scrubbing your chain clean. Keep it in the bath of degreaser while you do and really work at cleaning the rollers and pins of each individual link. Once you've got it as clean as possible, rinse with water and dry it off with your rags.

Stick your cassette or individual sprockets in to soak in the degreaser. Once they've had a few minutes in there, scrub each part individually (a toothbrush is handy here), then rinse, dry and put to one side.

Use your Allen keys to remove the jockey wheels from the rear derailleur and clean them with your cloths. If they feel rough when you spin them on your fingers, try taking the bearing covers off and re-greasing them, or buy some replacements. See page 76 for more on jockey wheels.

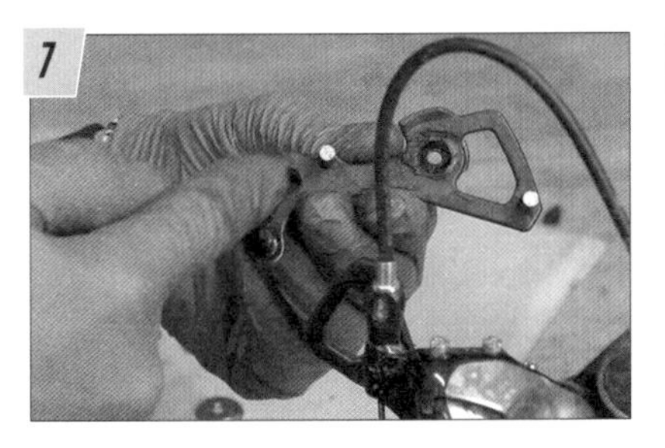

It's also worth cleaning inside the derailleur cage as dirt, grime and old chain oil can build up in there.

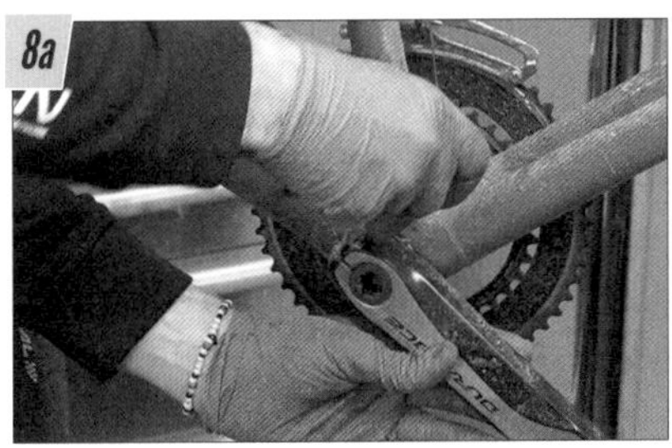

The only way to thoroughly clean your chainrings to take them off the bike which means removing the crankset. Head over to page 84 for a full description on how to do that.

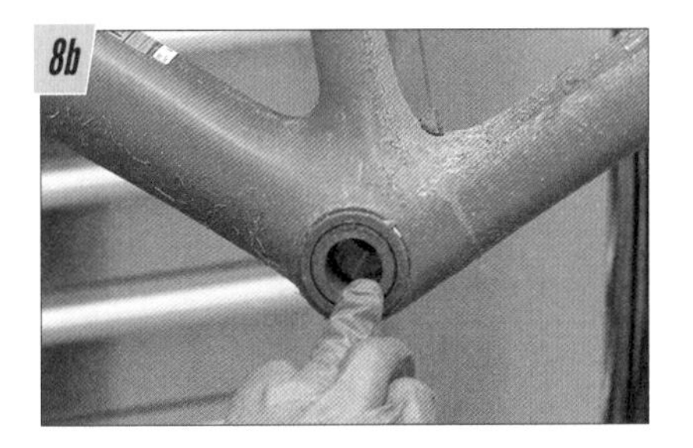

Removing your cranks will also allow you to check your bottom bracket, if it's feeling rough you'll likely need to replace it, though a clean and re-grease may well buy you some more time. See page 180 for lots more on bottom brackets.

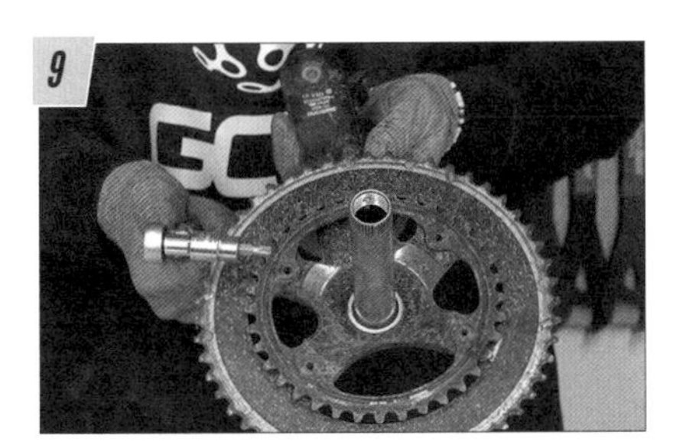

With your cranks off the bike, it's time to unbolt the chainrings from the spider on the crank arm. Depending on which type you have you'll either need Torx or Allen keys, or possibly a chainring nut spanner. Head over to page 74 for more details.

Once removed, soak the chainrings in your degreaser for at least five minutes, then scrub them in the same way you did with the cassette sprockets. Clean the cranks themselves with a rag dipped in degreaser.

Now that all your drivetrain components are completely clean, it's time to reassemble all of them back on the bike. Take your time, ensure you orientate everything correctly, re-grease as required and carefully lube your chain.

To Properly Lube Your Chain

Turn over to the next page

BEGINNER BASICS

HOW TO LUBE YOUR CHAIN

Keeping your chain properly lubed will help your gear shifts and stop your drivetrain components from wearing out prematurely

DIFFICULTY 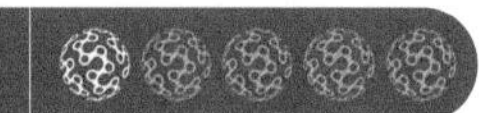

TIME 5 - 10 Minutes

TOOLS
- *Chain lube*
- *Cloth*

WHEN
- *After washing your bike or when your chain is not running smoothly*

CHOOSE YOUR LUBE

1

The lube most of us will be familiar with is wet lube. It's called wet because its oils don't dry on your chain, they stay wet. It's best used in poor weather conditions as it won't easily get washed away, but being wet and oily, it can attract more dirt and grime than other lubes.

> *"There are a host of specialist chain lubricants out there, such as race day lubes which minimise chain friction"*

2

For better weather conditions, there is dry lube. While it is wet when you apply it, this lube dries off to leave a film-like coating across the chain links and the rollers. It doesn't attract as much dirt as wet lube, but it can get washed off far more easily.

3

As well as those two, there are a host of other specialist chain lubricants out there, such as race day lubes which minimise chain friction, but must be reapplied far more frequently than standard lubes.

WATCH THE VIDEO

Free show-how and know-how

Want Perfect Shifting?
Find out how over on page 64

APPLYING BOTTLE LUBES

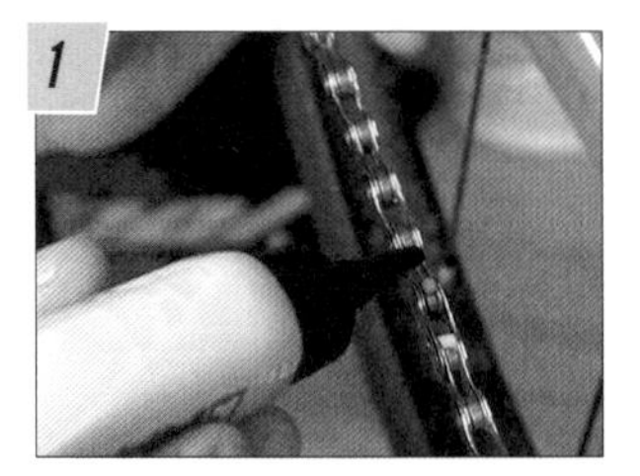

Start with as clean a drivetrain as possible (see page 220 for more on that), then locate your joining pin or master link on the chain (to give you a point of reference) and move it to the bottom run of the chain.

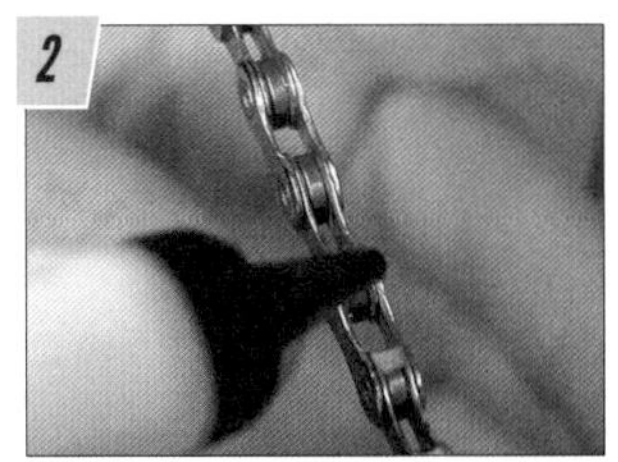

Shake the bottle, then starting at your master link, apply a drop of lube to each individual roller on the chain slowly turning the cranks as you go.

When you're back at the master link, let the lube soak into the chain for 30 seconds or so, then pedal the chain for another 30 seconds which will help distribute the lube to all the chain's moving parts.

COFFEE BREAK

Okay, maybe two or three coffee breaks as you want to leave that chain alone for at least an hour or so. Once back with your bike, take your rag and run it over the chain while turning the cranks to remove any excess lube from the outside of the chain – it serves no purpose there and will just attract dirt. Now, you're ready to ride.

APPLYING SPRAY LUBES

Ensuring your drivetrain is clean and dry before you begin, locate your joining pin or master link and turn the cranks so it sits in the bottom run of your chain.

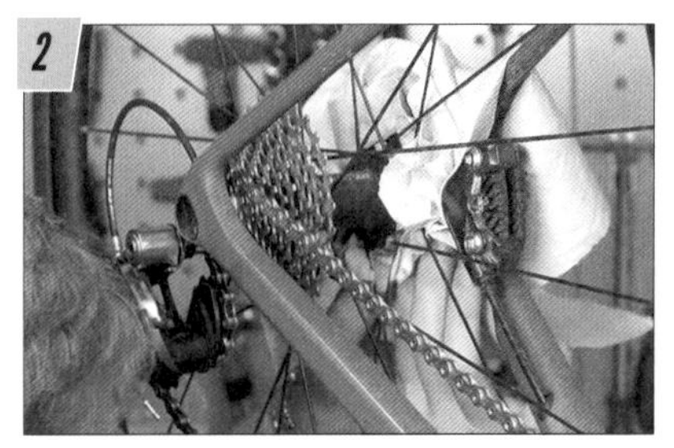

If you've got disc brakes, cover the rotors with a clean cloth to stop any accidental contamination while spraying your lube.

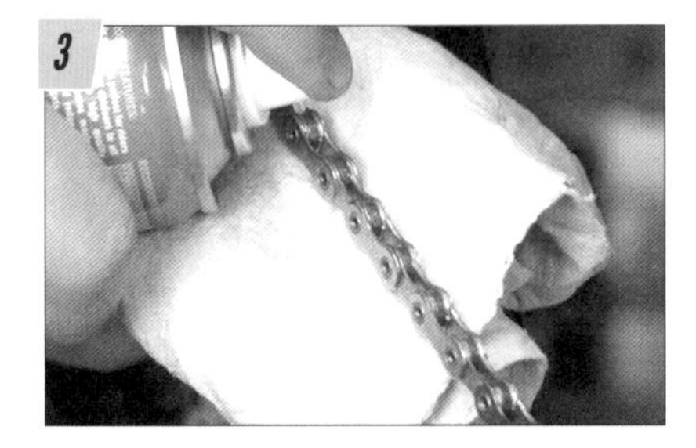

After giving your can of chosen lube a good shake, spray a small amount onto each individual roller at a time, while holding a rag beneath the chain to soak up any excess spray.

As you're using both hands at once, having a friend to slowly turn the cranks for you makes this process easier. Once you get to your master link, you've done a full rotation and the chain is completely lubed.

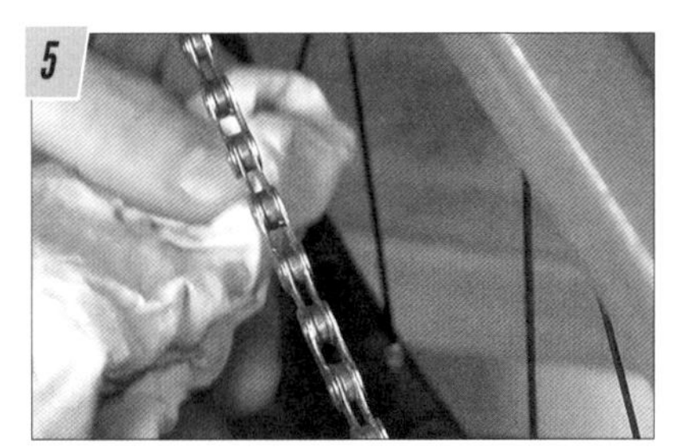

Once the lubing is done, the process is exactly the same as with bottled lube. Give it 30 seconds then spin the cranks for 30 seconds. Wait an hour then wipe off any excess and you're good to go.

SECTION 8

HACKS & KNOW-HOW

Presenting maintenance techniques that while may not be strictly by the book, are guaranteed to save you time, effort and cash

12 ESSENTIAL WORKSHOP & MAINTENANCE HACKS

Presenting our selection of prime tips and hacks designed to save effort, money and aggravation

SQUEAK-FREE CLEAN

Regularly and thoroughly wash your bike

OK, this is more good practice than an actual hack, but keeping your bike as clean as possible will help it to work well for longer, saving you the time and money you'd otherwise spend to put things right. Head over to page 214 for a full breakdown on how to thoroughly clean your bike. If you're short of time, however, you can get away with just focussing on keeping your drivetrain and brake surfaces free from grime, as accumulated dirt in either of these areas will dramatically shorten the life of these expensive components.

02

HOTEL ROOM RAID

Stop contamination with a shower cap

Protecting your disc brake rotors when using a degreaser on your drivetrain is a very good idea. Any contamination of the rotors will make them squeal as well as giving you less effective braking. While covering up your rotors with a clean cloth does a pretty good job, putting a shower cap over them will do a far better one as the plastic surface will shrug off any degreaser and the elastic trim will secure the cap in place.

TAPE IT UP

Use clear tape to guard against chafing

Accessories such as saddle bags, bar bags and frame bags can constantly rub against your frame as you ride, damaging your paint and even your frame material in extreme cases. This can also happen in places where your cables rub against the frame, usually around the head tube as you steer. This gets worse in wet, dirty conditions as well as the moisture and grime can get in between the two surfaces that are rubbing together and accelerate the process. A simple solution to prevent this unwanted scenario is to protect your frame with some clear tape, such as helicopter tape which comes in large sheets or on a roll. Cut the tape to your desired shape, stick it to your clean frame and, hey presto, no more wear on your frame.

03

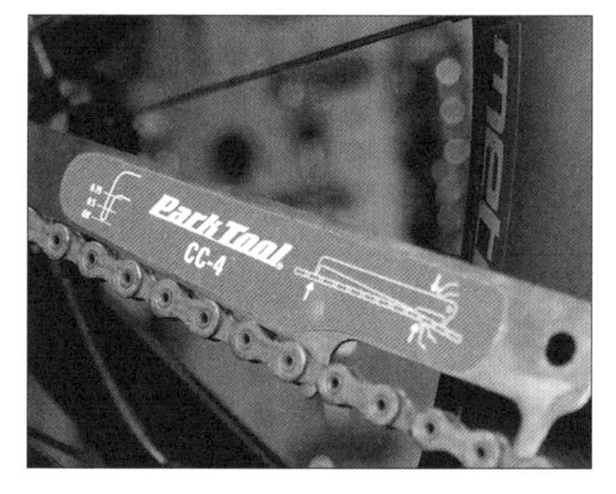

CHECK FOR WEAR

Replace worn chains and bearings before they damage other parts

04

It's a good idea to regularly check your bike for any parts that might be starting to wear out. Worn parts could have an adverse effect on other components – as well as affecting your bike's performance. A worn chain will accelerate the wear on your more expensive cassette, meaning you'll eventually need to replace them both. Using a chain checker will let you know when to fit a new chain before it starts to damage your cassette.

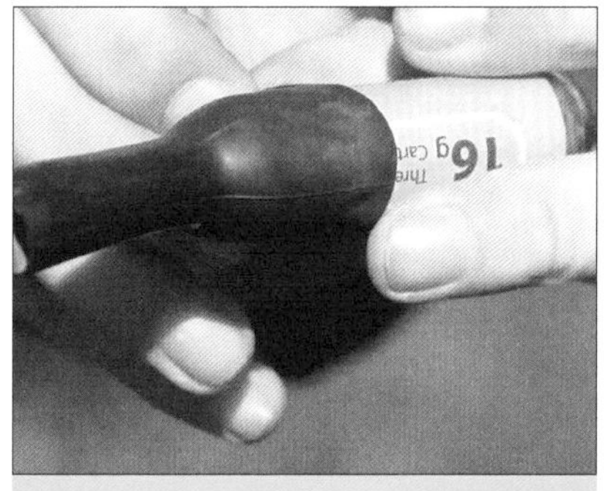

REPAIR & REUSE

There's still life left in those damaged tubes

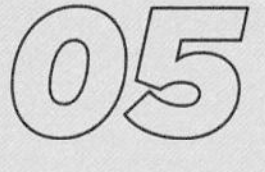

Inner tubes are a great example of something that people seem to have forgotten can be easily repaired. It's easier than ever using the self-adhesive patches that are available these days. If you'd rather fit a fresh tube by the roadside, repair your punctured one when you get home and use it as a spare. Old tubes have all kinds of other uses, such as CO_2 cartridge covers, securing clamped accessories and much more.

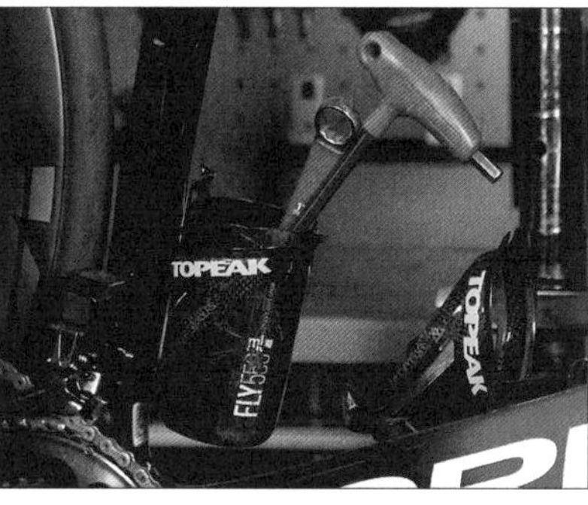

DON'T BIN THAT BIDON

Turn your bottle into a handy tool holder

If you've got an old water bottle that's no longer fit to drink from, don't lob it in the recycling box just yet. Simply cut it down by a few inches with some sharp scissors, then place it in your bottle cage when you're working on your bike. You've now got a really handy pot for keeping small tools such as Allen keys, etc within easy reach while you work.

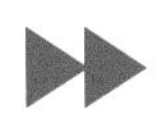

12 ESSENTIAL WORKSHOP & MAINTENANCE HACKS

REMOVE A SEIZED BOLT

A stuck bolt means hassle, here's three ways to shift them

07

A seized Allen bolt with a rounded out the head from failed removal attempts is no laughing matter. Fortunately there are a few techniques that should help get it free. Before any further attempts to remove it, try spraying the offending bolt with a liberal amount of penetrating oil and leaving it to work its way in – preferably overnight. If your bolt head is not too severely rounded out, try holding a wide rubber band over the head of your Allen key before inserting it into the bolt head. The rubber band should fill the rounded out gaps and hopefully provide enough grip to remove the bolt.

08 OK, it's time to get a bit more brutal with your seized bolt and ram in a Torx key to use it's six-pointed star shape to get some extra purchase. You're going to need to increase the size of the Torx key relative to the Allen key, so if you've got a 3mm Allen bolt, you'd need to use a T-20 key which is slightly bigger. To get your Torx key to fit in place you'll need to whack it into the bolt head with a rubber hammer, then you should have enough grip to finally turn the bolt. Bear in mind that taking a hammer to your Torx key risks damaging the key, so take it as easy as you can.

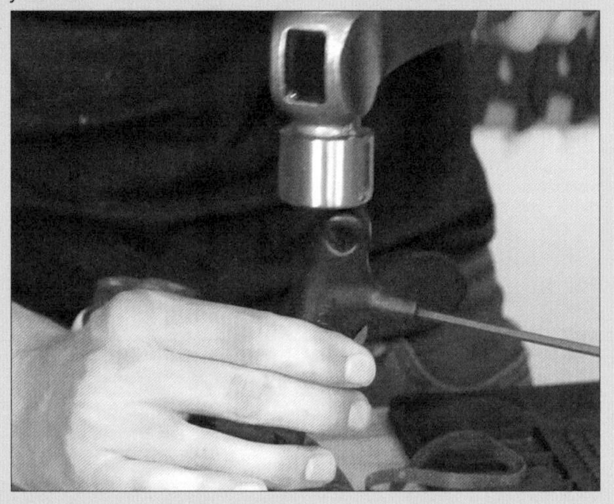

09 CHECK YOUR TYRES

Remove glass and flints before you ride

It's a good idea before or after a ride to just check your tyres for any little flints or shards of glass that have got stuck in them, then get some tweezers or a small screwdriver and carefully pry them out. If left in place they can work their way deeper into the tyre causing you an unnecessary puncture. Also, check your tyres for wear as you definitely don't want a blow out mid-way through a ride. Some tyres actually have wear holes to indicate when they need to be replaced.

For More On Cleats & Shoes
Head over to page 206

TAPE FROM THE TOP

How to get super-neat looking bars

10

Rather than wrapping your bar tape starting at the end of the drops and finishing on the tops, try wrapping it the other way and start on the tops first. Doing it this way means you don't need to use any electrical tape, because you can just wrap the bar tape under itself to secure it in place. Make sure that you wrap it very tightly all the way along, and then finish it at the drop with the normal bar bung method. You'll then end up with a really nice clean look.

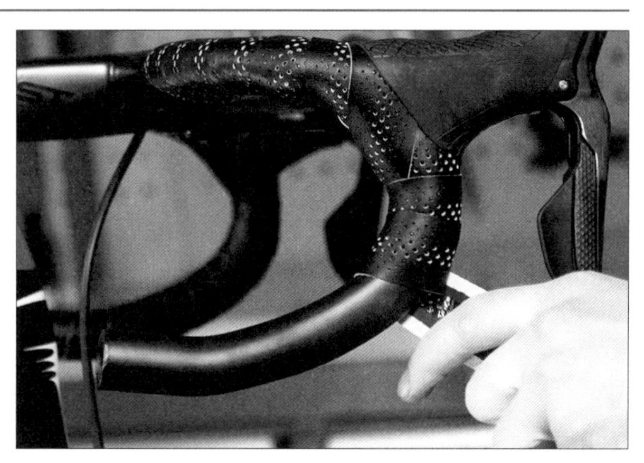

FIX FRAYED CABLE ENDS

Solder your inners to extend their life

11

If you've lost a cable end ferrule and your cable has become frayed, it can be very difficult to put one back on. Without a ferrule in place, the cable can continue to just get more and more frayed until you have to replace it. If your brake cable is relatively new and generally in good condition, there is a solution. Using a soldering iron and some flux or solder, you can tidy up the end of frayed cables and prevent any more fraying. To do it, hold a soldering iron onto the end of the cable and just heat it up, and then apply some of the solder to the frayed end.

POLISHED PERFECTION

Buff up your bike to keep the crud away

Don't underestimate giving the frame and forks of your bike a good polish every now and then after you've washed it. The polish won't just make your bike look cleaner and shinier, it will help it shrug off dirt and also protect it from corrosive chemicals such as road salt – as they'll be less able to stick to the polished areas as you ride through them.

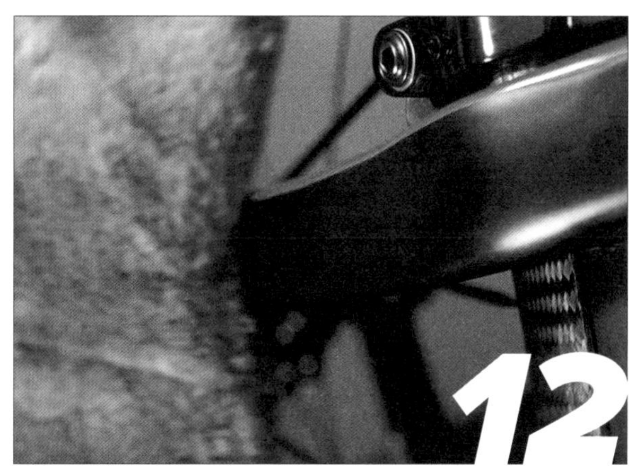

SET-UP SECRETS

HOW TO PUNCTURE PROOF YOUR BIKE

If going tubeless really isn't for you, here are five hacks that will result in far fewer punctures on your road bike

INJECT TUBELESS SEALANT

Protect your tubes with latex liquid

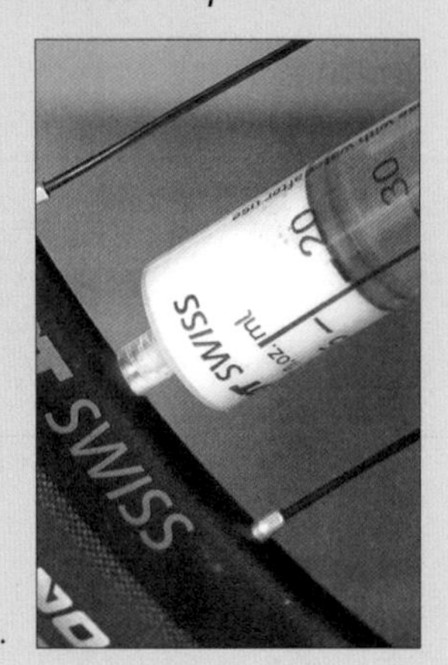

Just because you're not running road tubeless doesn't mean that you can't get the puncture-proofing benefits of latex sealant. All you've got to do is remove the valve core from your inner tube, which is the threaded bit that sits just below the locknut of the valve, then inject 40ml of sealant inside the tube. Many sealant bottles come with a clear tube to make it a lot easier to do this. Once you've squirted in the sealant, replace your core, inflate your tyre and off you go.

RUN FLINT CATCHERS

Guard against flats the old-school way

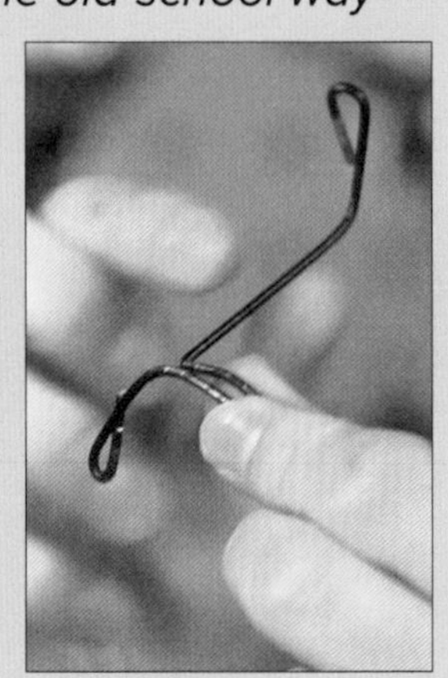

While flint catchers may have gone the way of the dodo many years ago, if you suffer from a lot of sharp object related punctures, then you may be interested in bringing them back from the dead. They work by bolting on to your brake calipers so that a section of wire sits just above the tyre. Then should any sharp objects get picked up, they will get brushed off before they've had the chance to work their way through the carcass of the tyre and into your inner tube.

Decided To Go Tubeless?
Find out how to do it on page 156

DOUBLE UP YOUR TYRES

Line your tyres with old ones for twice as much puncture protection

Rather than throwing your old worn out tyres in the bin, you could try turning them into a protective liners for your new tyres. Cut off the bead with a pair of scissors and then line the inside of your new tyre with your old one. Most potential punctures are unlikely to make it through two tyres. However, this will likely make your bike feel sluggish and slow, so is not something to do on your regular bike. It's best suited to a town or touring bike, where riding rapidly is less of a concern.

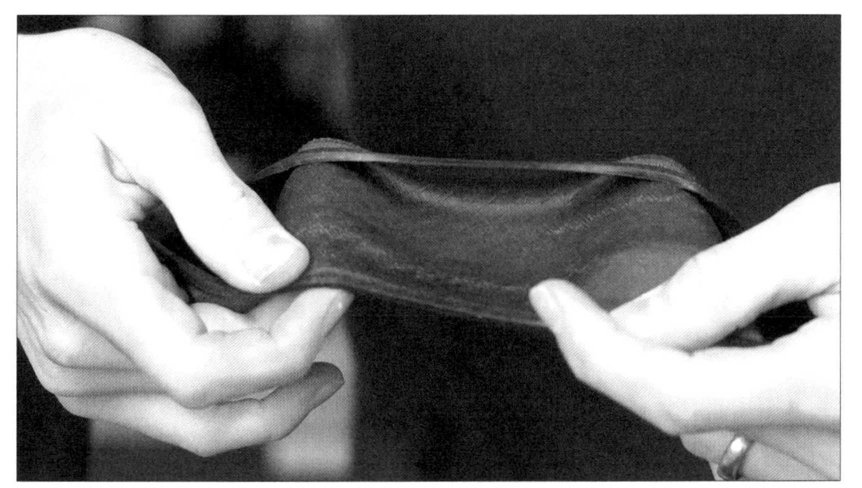

FIT HEAVY DUTY TYRES

Switch to tougher tyres for fewer flats

Technically, a hack isn't a hack if you've got to spend actual money on it, but considering that we all have to replace our tyres from time to time, we're going with it. If you switch from your usual tyre to one that is a little bit tougher, it's going to be much more impervious to penetration from sharp objects. With most manufacturers selling heavier duty versions of their regular tyres, there's a decent amount of choice out there.

USE THICKER RIM TAPE

Guard against the enemies inside your rim

It's not just sharp objects from the outside of the tyre that can cause punctures, but particularly on older wheels, you might find that you're getting them from the rim bed itself. Sharp edges can push through worn rim tape and end up protruding through, with chief culprits being the valve hole and the spoke holes. To prevent this from happening, you could run an extra layer of rim tape, or fit some extra thick rim tape to give better protection.

HOW TO RIDE FASTER FOR FREE

10 ways to give yourself a speed boost that (mostly) won't cost you a penny

GET LOWER

1 Beginners tend to ride on the hoods as opposed to the drops or in an aero hoods position. However, because you generate far less drag in these less comfortable positions, they will make a big difference to your speed – even if you can only maintain them for short periods. The aero hoods position tends to be the fastest because your forearm is parallel to the airflow and can be over 30w faster than riding on the tops. When you go down to the drops more of your forearm is exposed, so it's a little bit slower than an aero hoods position, but it can be more maintainable. As a general rule, the lower you can get your torso angle, the faster you go.

Getting your low will help you get more aero

RE-PACK THE RAIN CAPE

If you put a rain cape on and then ride with it open or half unzipped once the wet weather has passed, you're creating far more drag than you would be with it fully zipped up or if you weren't wearing it at all. Riding with a rain cape packed away in a rear jersey pocket or stuffed up the back of your jersey creates very little additional drag, so take it off and stuff it in there when the rain stops for some easy speed gains.

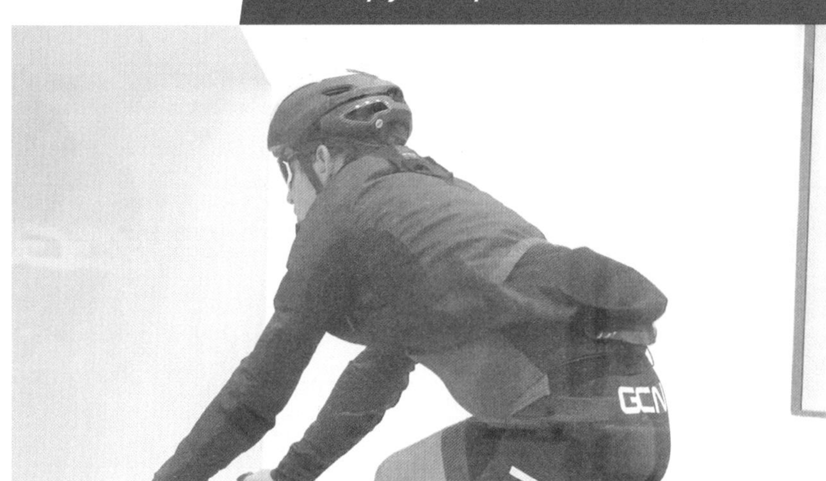

Keep your cape stowed when not in use

RACE DAY GAINS

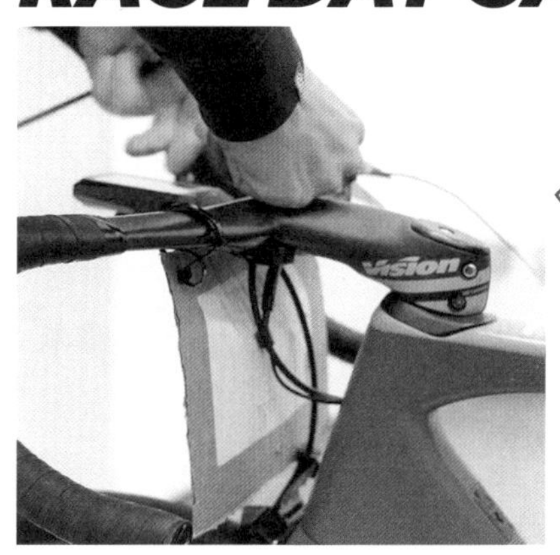

3 If you're riding an event, you're going to have to attach a race number to your bike and pin one to the back of your jersey. Zip-tying the race plate to your bars will add a fair amount of drag to your bike, so cunningly wrap it around your head tube instead where it will have a negligible effect. Similarly, if you pin your race number on your jersey in all four corners, but position the lower pins slightly closer together to make a kind of fin shape, this will actually increase the aerodynamic shape of your back and make you go ever so slightly faster.

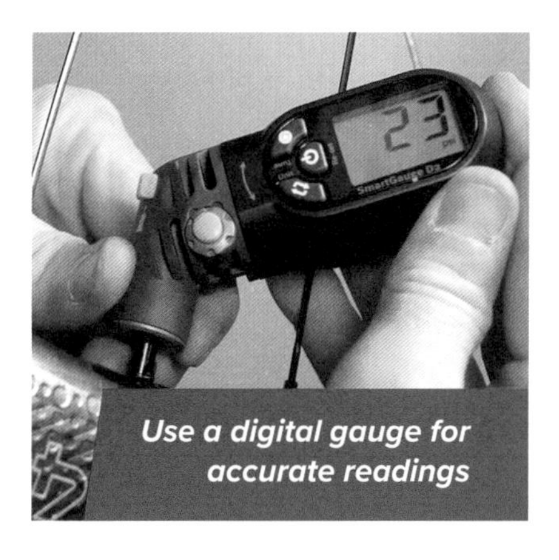

Use a digital gauge for accurate readings

Wrap your race number around your head tube

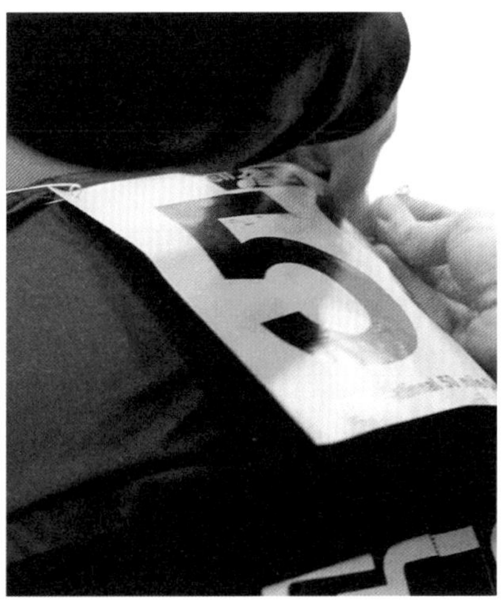

TYRE PRESSURES

4 Different tyre pressures totally transform the feel and comfort level of your bike. However, you can actually get some speed for free by playing around with your tyre pressures. In the past, most of us rode with our tyre pressures pumped up to the maximum and got bounced around from every little bit of rough surface on the road. Nowadays, we know that slightly lower pressures that better suit the road surface and your weight can actually improve your speed. So go ahead and experiment to see what works best for you.

HOW TO RIDE FASTER FOR FREE

TIDY UP YOUR CABLES

Long floppy cables increase your drag which will make you slower. To minimise this negative effect, get rid of any excess cable length. But before you start chopping, make sure that you can still operate your brakes and gears and can still turn your handlebars properly. If you've got additional cabling from an electronic group set, think about joining the electronic wire to the rear brake cable as this will help decrease your drag too.

5

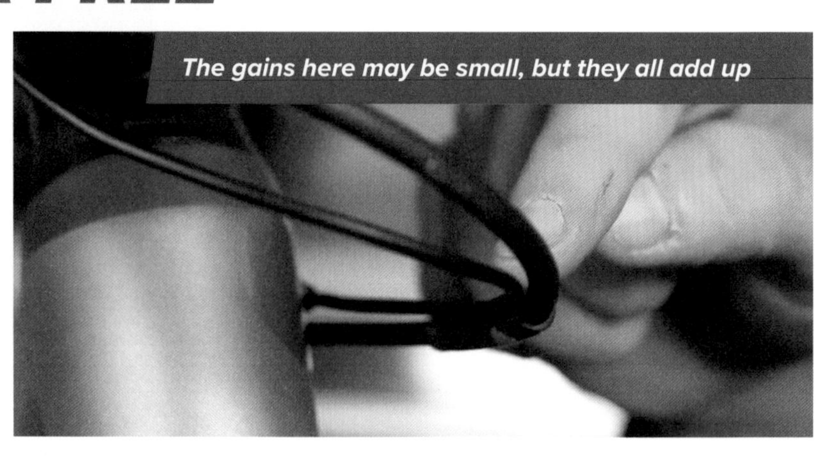
The gains here may be small, but they all add up

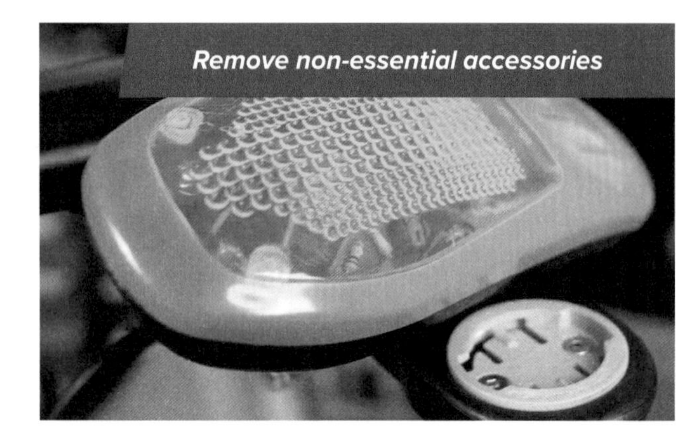
Remove non-essential accessories

GET RID OF THE CLUTTER

6

Riding with all kinds of paraphernalia attached to your bike makes it heavier and less aerodynamic. So unless you really have to take your lights, frame pump, saddlebag, frame bag, bike lock and more on every ride, try and take only what you need and declutter your bike as much as possible. If you're looking to set a new PB on your local climb, you could even go as far as removing your bottles, then put them back on your bike once you've nailed it.

CLEANER IS FASTER

A clean bike is a happy bike and a happy bike is a faster bike. But why exactly? Well, being free from dirt will mean that all your components can work properly – especially your drivetrain as all of your gears are going to be working perfectly (providing you've set them up properly of course), which will help you ride faster. You'll also get a psychological boost because you're going to be happier riding that super-clean bike. Whether you choose to go high-tech, ultrasonic chain cleaning or good old fashioned soap and water, it will make a difference. Go ahead, clean that bike – it will go faster, but don't forget to lube the chain properly too.

7

What's not to love about an ultra-clean bike?

For A Showroom Clean Bike
Turn back to page 214

REMOVE YOUR BEARING SEALS

8

OK, this may be a very extreme measure, but bearing seals can increase the friction when the bearing tries to turn. This is especially true on contact seal type bearings where the rubber on the seal touches the inner ring of the bearing. Removing the seals from your bearings will make them more efficient, but it will considerably shorten their lifespan because the seal protects the bearings from water, dirt and grime. We would only recommend doing this if you were going for some kind of record at an indoor velodrome, because it would be bone dry and there would be far less dirt around that could get pulled into your bearings.

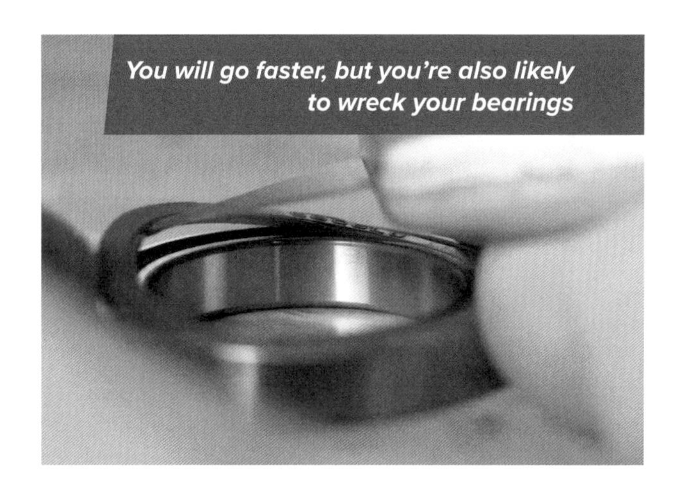

You will go faster, but you're also likely to wreck your bearings

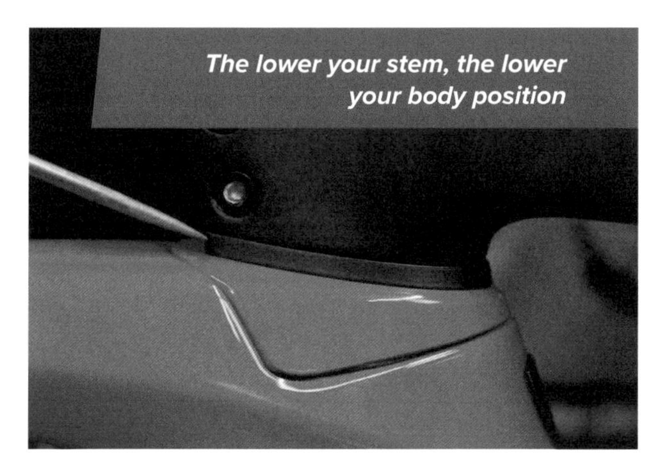

The lower your stem, the lower your body position

SLAM YOUR STEM

9

Lowering your stem is a sure fire way to get a little bit of extra speed and could save you up to 10w. It works by lowering your upper body and reducing drag in the same way that getting into a more aero riding position does. While it's tempting to immediately cut down your steerer tube and slam your stem to gain as big an aero advantage as possible, you will still need to have a comfortable body position available to you, as you'll otherwise find it difficult to ride your bike for long periods. We'd suggest only reducing the height of your stem by 5mm at a time. This will allow you to get used to a lower position and see if you'd like to drop your stem height still further. You will of course need some 3 or 5mm spacers to do this, so you may need to swap out a thicker spacer for some thin ones first.

CROSS-CHAINING

Not only does cross-chaining look really bad, but it's also inefficient and will shorten the life of your chain. If you're running your chain from the big ring to the big sprocket on your cassette, the chain will be forced into an extreme angle which increases friction and puts more stress on its pins and rollers. Likewise, if you're in the small ring and smallest sprocket you're going to have the same problem. The best angle to run your chain at is the smallest one possible, so it can run smoothly and efficiently as you pedal. Switching to a bigger chainring than the standard 53 or 54 tooth versions will help keep your chain running in the middle of your cassette. Many time trialists have been running a 60t front ring in recent years, so something that size would help give you a nice straight chain line.

Bigger rings mean better chain lines

PROBLEMS SOLVED

MAKE YOUR BIKE MORE COMFORTABLE

Setting up your bike to give you the perfect riding position can be a case of trial and error – here are eight things you need to consider

SORT YOUR SADDLE HEIGHT

Too low or too high will make riding harder

1 It's very common to see riders with the wrong saddle height and is a sure-fire way of making your riding very uncomfortable. Rotating your hips more than they need to can cause injury to your knees. Regardless of whether you've had a bike fit or not, it's pretty easy to set up your saddle height if you follow these simple steps.

Sit on your bike, unclip, and place your heel in the middle of the pedal axle when it's at its lowest point and the crank is in line with the seat tube. Your hips shouldn't have to rock to reach the pedal, but your leg should be completely straight. This will allow a slight bend at your knee when you clip in.

Once you've sorted your saddle height, getting a professional bike fit is still a great idea, as it will take into account all the unique characteristics of your body.

PROPER CLEAT SET-UP

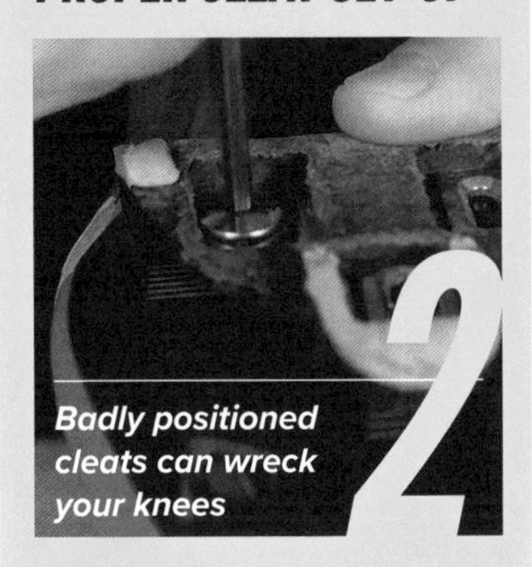

Badly positioned cleats can wreck your knees

Using cleats and cycling-specific shoes have many benefits, as they will improve your transfer of power as well as your pedal stroke efficiency. Cleats are the only fixed interface between you and the bike, so getting them in the right position is vital. Not only will it keep you comfortable and ensure you're efficient as possible, but it will also help avoid injury. Getting their position exactly right may take a lot of fiddling, but it is definitely worth spending time on. Putting your bike in a static trainer is a big help in setting your cleats up. For more info on getting the perfect cleat position, turn to page 206.

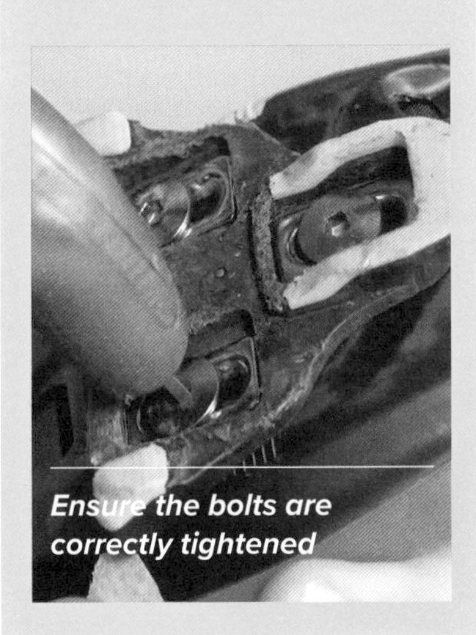

Ensure the bolts are correctly tightened

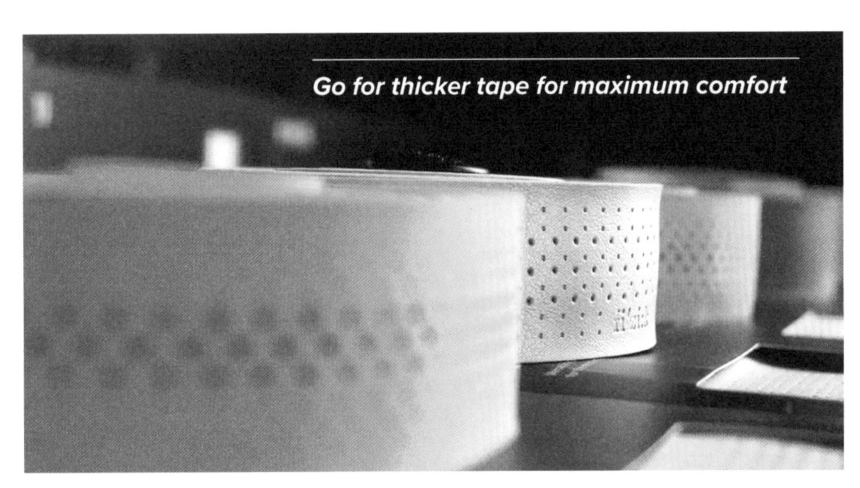

Go for thicker tape for maximum comfort

DOUBLE-WRAP YOUR BARS

3

Have you ever had sore, achy hands from riding? Well, double-wrapping your bar tape could solve that problem. A lot of the pros will run double-wrapped bar tape during the Classics when they're riding over those extremely bumpy cobbles. However, double-wrapped bars are also the choice of many pros all year round. You could do this by buying two lots of standard bar tape and taping one on top to the other, but there are also specific bar tapes which are much thicker – see page 200 for the easiest way to apply bar tape. Don't forget that there are multiple hand positions you can adopt on your drop bars. Make the most of these and move your hands around to keep the blood moving.

Lower pressures can be faster

PERFECT TYRE PRESSURES

4

Getting the right tyre pressure is easy, right? You just pump up the tyres to the recommended range on the sidewall and off you go. But as your tyres have to do a lot of different roles, it's not quite that simple. They need to give you grip and control, but also smooth out rough roads. They have to be tough enough not to puncture, but light and thin enough to roll well. All these different factors are affected by the pressure, the construction and the tyre design. There's no one-size-fits-all tyre pressure as it will always be unique to you. Try riding the same route on different pressures, as long as they're not too low or too high, and see how each one feels to find the pressure that suits you best.

MAKE YOUR BIKE MORE COMFORTABLE

5 CHANGE YOUR SADDLE

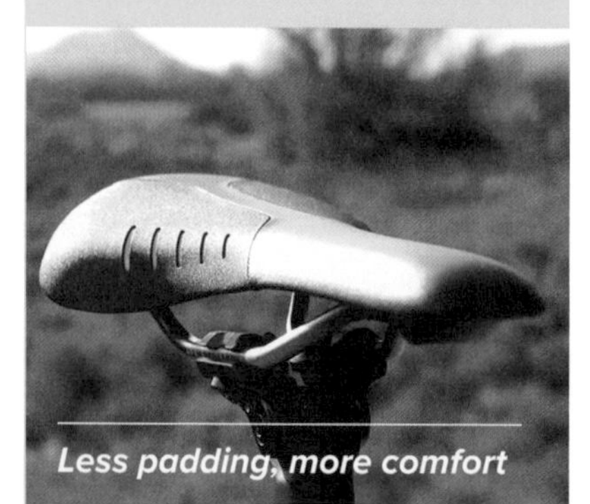
Less padding, more comfort

If you wear bib shorts with a padded chamois, avoid matching them up with a highly padded or gel saddle. Too much padding in both areas won't mean more comfort, but more friction between your sit-bones and your saddle. This will actually result in increased discomfort particularly over long rides.

6 CHAMOIS CREAM

Chamois cream isn't for everyone, but it's definitely worth giving it a go to see if it works for you. If you've not encountered it before, it's a cream designed to help eliminate friction between your saddle and your clothing and is applied directly to your skin where it comes in contact with the saddle. It often contains antibacterial elements to guard against getting infections on chafed skin. Most pro cyclists ride multiple times a day, every day, so using products like chamois cream is essential for them to avoid issues such as saddle sores that can sometimes lead to time off the bike.

Be a friend to your rear end

Want To Fit New Bar Tape?
Head over to page 200

SADDLE POSITION & STEM CHOICE

If you're fully stretched out, fit a shorter stem

7 We've already looked at setting your saddle height, but what can be more important from the comfort perspective is the distance from the tip of the saddle to your handlebars. If too long it puts undue pressure on your lower back, neck and shoulders as they all have to rotate to accommodate the extra length as you pedal. To remedy this, change your stem for a shorter one which will move your handlebars further back and allow you to relax your upper body. However, you might not need a new stem if you've got any spacers on top of your current one, as you can run them beneath the stem and that'll raise your handlebars.

LARGER TYRES

Lower pressures will give a plusher ride

9

As a general rule, lowering your tyre pressures is the key to a smoother ride. You will need to increase the size of your tyres if you drop the pressure too far though, as a small tyre with low pressure is a recipe for impact punctures. If you're running 85psi in a 25c tyre and switch to a 28c tyre, then you could drop to 70psi which would give you a plusher feel. Before ordering some bigger tyres though, you'd better check that you have enough clearance on your frame and forks to accommodate them. Finally, if you are able to swap your tyres out for larger ones, more expensive tyres with more supple casings usually do a better job of dampening road buzz.

CHANGE YOUR BARS 8

Try a smaller or bigger handlebar

The size of the handlebars on your bike is often overlooked as a way of adjusting your riding position when in actual fact it can radically alter it. Compact bars can have a reach of 70mm and a drop of 122mm, while more standard bars can have a reach of 80mm and a drop of 148mm – the difference between them in terms of riding position can be huge. If you've got small hands and struggle to reach the brake levers when you're on the drops, then switching to a compact bar will be a big help. Similarly, if you've got poor low back flexibility, the shorter drop distance of a compact bar is going to allow you to ride on the drops more easily. Though, if you've got really large hands or you're a rider who's taller than most, then larger bars will allow you to have more variation in your riding position which will improve your level of comfort.

PROBLEMS SOLVED

HOW TO WEATHER-PROOF YOUR BIKE

If you're riding in all weathers, here's our guide to keeping your bike working and performing well in nasty conditions

CHANGE YOUR TYRES

Fit winter rubber for extra grip and protection

When the weather takes a turn for the worse, punctures are more likely. Not only do you have potholes that are often hidden from view by being filled with water, but there's more debris on the road as rainwater washes all the flints and thorns out of the gutters. This makes switching to a winter tyre in foul weather an excellent idea. With their tougher rubber compounds (some also have a puncture-resistant belt), you are far less likely to get a flat. It's also worth considering going for a wider tyre in bad weather as this will give you more grip on slippery road surfaces. Wider tyres may be a bit slower due to their increased rolling resistance, but it's a worthwhile trade-off for making punctures and crashes less likely.

Protect your drivetrain with the right lubrication

USE A WET LUBE

For a weather-proof drivetrain you need to use a wet lube. Dry lube washes off very quickly at the first sign of rain, so clearly won't do the job. Wet lube flicking off your chain can make your bike a little bit dirtier and it will attract more dirt to your drivetrain than a dry lube, but crucially it goes on protecting your chain even during sustained rain and road spray. Take care not to let dirty lube build up on your drivetrain though, as it will turn into a cutting paste that will wear down your components much faster. Degrease and apply fresh lube as often as possible to prevent this from happening.

GO FOR MARINE GREASE

To give your bearings maximum protection from the elements, the lubricant of choice is marine grease. Being thick and viscous it stays in one pace and it's also resistant to salt and corrosion. The downside is that your bearings won't spin so freely as marine grease is so thick and it's also less widely available than regular grease. If you can't get hold of any, then a fresh application of a multi-purpose grease will still do the job.

It may slow you down, but it will keep the elements at bay

FIT SOME MUDGUARDS

Fit deep mudguards front and rear for maximum protection

Mudguards may not be everyone's cup of tea, but if you're riding in foul weather, they will help keep your bike in good condition for longer. They work by containing all the road spray inside the mudguard which stops it from getting all over your bike and into your greased bearings. Getting water into these areas will start washing that grease out, resulting in dry bearings that will eventually go rusty and need replacing. Mudguards also help keep you and your bike cleaner by capturing much of the dirt that flies up off the road. If you're going to go down the mudguard route, it's best to go for as much wheel coverage as possible, though this will depend on how much clearance you have on your frame and whether you have dedicated mudguard fixings. There are loads of options available whether your bike has mudguard fixings or not though, with some models that attach directly to the fork and the seat stays.

HOW TO WEATHER-PROOF YOUR BIKE

Run lights to see and be seen

LIGHT IT UP

Bad weather means poor visibility, so a weatherproof bike should have a set of lights. USB rechargeable ones tend to be better sealed and so have more protection from the elements. They are also a little bit more economical to run and definitely better for the environment. You also won't find yourself scrabbling around at the worst possible time looking for some new batteries either – so long as you've remembered to charge them that is.

LUBE YOUR CABLES

While dry fitting brake and gear cables will give you the fastest and smoothest shifting. In bad conditions, there is nothing to stop water getting pulled inside the cable housing where it will remain and corrode your delicate cables. To make your cables far more weatherproof, remove your inner cables and coat them with grease. Alternatively, you could upgrade to a sealed cable system where the ferrules have rubber seals that are really effective at keeping water and grit from entering your cables.

Add a drop of lube to your inner cables

CLEAN YOUR BRAKES & RIMS

Keep your braking surfaces clean

Riding in the wet can cause accelerated damage to your rims as the brake track will wear down far more rapidly when braking on wet, grimy roads. As a result, it's really important to give your wheels and brake pads a good clean after wet and mucky rides. Remove your wheels to better clean the insides of your brake pads and also inspect them for any embedded dirt, flints or metal shards which will scrape your rims and cause even more damage. While disc brakes perform better and require less maintenance in bad conditions, you should still wipe down your discs with a disc brake cleaner and clean your pads so they last as long as possible. Whether you run rim or disc brakes, it's also well worth keeping an eye on how quickly your pads are wearing as they can erode at an alarming rate on wet and dirty roads. Rim brake users should also consider swapping to wet weather brake pads as they give much better braking performance in foul weather.

For Internal Cabling Hacks
Flip back to page 176

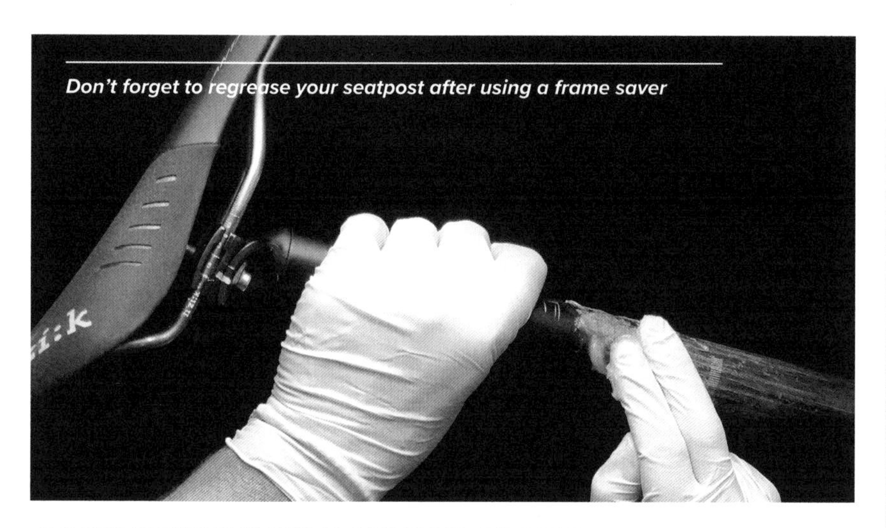

Don't forget to regrease your seatpost after using a frame saver

PROTECT THE INSIDE OF YOUR FRAME

Unless you have a full carbon frame, which won't corrode anyway, it's a really good idea as well to treat the non moving parts on your bike with an anti-corrosive spray. There are lots of different branded ones around and they are usually called 'frame savers'. To treat your bike, remove your seat post and then spray the product inside to coat all the tubes with the anti-corrosive spray. When you replace your seat post, ensure to give it a good coating of grease.

Use a hydrophobic sealant on the outside of your frame

PROTECT THE OUTSIDE OF YOUR FRAME

While polishing your frame will help your bike shrug off a lot of the muck that will undoubtedly get splattered all over it in dodgy weather, for next level protection you could give it a coating of hydrophobic sealant. Designed for use on car bodywork, these coatings are designed to actively repel muck and water, and last for up to three months. To apply the sealant, simply spray or rub it on to your frame and forks, but remove your wheels and cover your braking surfaces to avoid getting any sealant on them.

KEEP IT ULTRA CLEAN

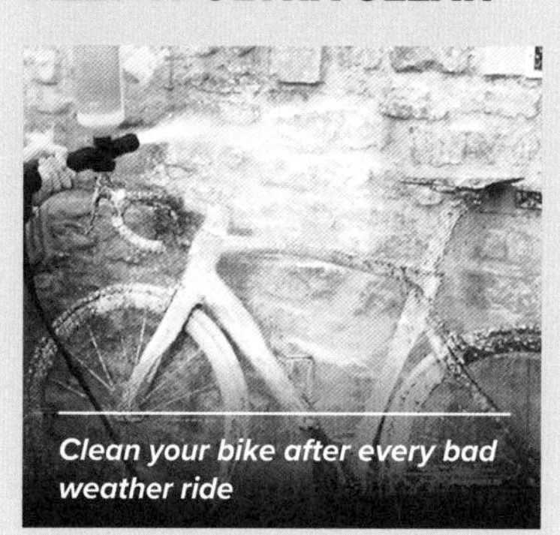
Clean your bike after every bad weather ride

We've already touched on it a few times in this chapter, but it's worth pointing out again, that keeping your bike clean when riding in bad weather is even more important than cleaning it during the drier months. Dirty, wet components will wear out far faster than clean, wet components as the wet muck will form into a paste that eats away at your drivetrain, rims, bearings and any other moving parts. As you'll be using heavier lubes in bad weather, it's important to use a really good degreaser to clean your components with. Also ensure to really rinse off your bike after washing as there may well be road salts on it that will also cause accelerated corrosion.

A clean drivetrain is particularly vital

PROBLEMS SOLVED

HOW TO SILENCE A NOISY BIKE

A noisy bike is an annoying bike. Creaks, grinds, rattles or squeals can be enough to drive you properly bonkers over time – particularly during long, gruelling rides. Not only that, noisy bike owners struggle to find riding partners as no-one else wants to spend hours listening to someone else's bike making a racket either.

But where are these dreaded sounds coming from? Well, the search could be quite a lengthy one, but fortunately a small(ish) group of suspects are responsible for the majority of bike noises. Here we'll look at each potentially troublesome area in turn and how you can silence them all for good.

DRIVETRAIN & PEDALS

With plenty of moving parts, your drivetrain and pedals are prone to making all kinds of annoying noises.

If you've got grinding noises that occur while pedalling, the chances are that your drivetrain is the culprit. While your gear shifting may well be fine, if your indexing is slightly out or one of your derailleurs needs a little adjustment, then they are likely to produce excess noise.

Fine-tune your gear indexing in a workstand and check that the jockey wheels of your derailleur properly line up with your highest and lowest sprockets on your cassette (see page 64 for full details on those procedures).

Clicking sounds that happen as the cranks turn are usually blamed on the bottom bracket, which in truth is often the case particularly if it's of the press fit variety (see 180 for more on BBs). However, before going down that fairly time-consuming path, it's worth checking a few other potential culprits first.

Examine your pedals to make sure they are tightened to the correct torque on the cranks and also they've got some grease on the threads too. If there's unwanted movement of the pedal body on the axle, your pedal will need servicing, so head over to page 210 for how to do that.

Another source of noise can be loose or over-tight chainring bolts, so check they are done up to the manufacturer's settings with your torque wrench.

The band on your front derailleur can also be the cause of creaks, so try adjusting its tension. Similarly, if the bolt that holds your rear derailleur to the hanger is dry, it can cause creaks too. Dry quick-release, bolt-on axles and the bolts that attach rim brakes to your frame or forks can all make clicking sounds that may appear to be drivetrain related.

Finally, it's worth checking to see if the noise is coming from your cleats. Ride clipped-in with one leg at a time to test each cleat and adjust the bolts if necessary.

Check your pedals are torqued up properly

If all else fails, remove and re-grease your BB

Get your indexing perfectly dialled in

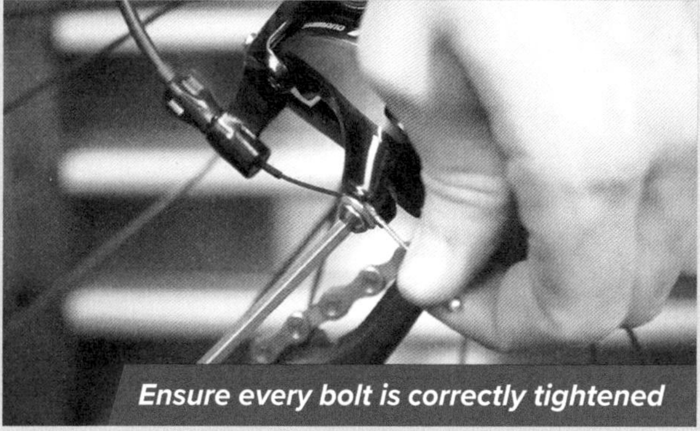

Ensure every bolt is correctly tightened

HOW TO SILENCE A NOISY BIKE

SEATPOST & SADDLE

A creaking saddle or seatpost is one of the easier noises to identify, not least because they can be very loud.

Creaks or clicks from the saddle or seatpost area are easy to spot as they of course only happen when you're putting pressure through them by sitting down. In the case of a saddle, often the culprits are the rails creaking against the saddle clamp, so check that the clamp is done up to the correct torque. If this hasn't solved your problem, it's worth running a little copper paste on the rails, though if you have a carbon-railed saddle use carbon paste instead.

Similarly, check that the seatpost clamp is correctly torqued and use grease on the length of seatpost that sits within the frame if you have a metal frame and seatpost – this will guard against it seizing up too. If you're running a carbon frame and/or post, use carbon paste rather than grease.

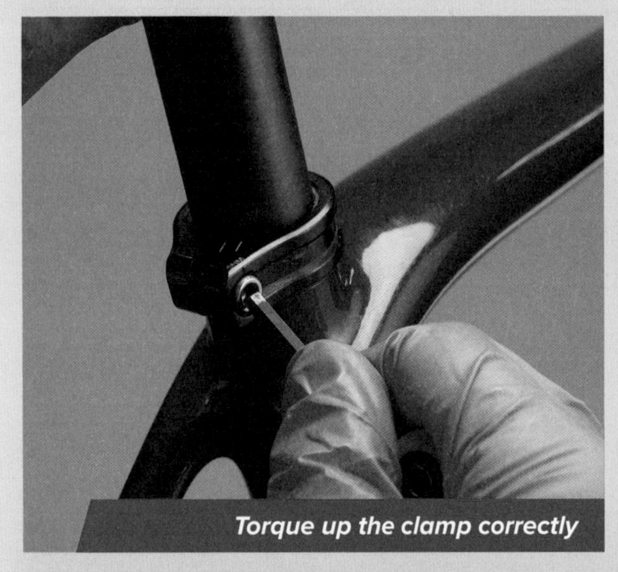

Torque up the clamp correctly

Add some carbon paste to your saddle rails

Check the saddle clamp is tightened evenly

TOP TIP

If torqued incorrectly, particularly without any grease or anti-seize, any bolt on your bike could be a source of the dreaded mystery creak. So if you're scratching your head as to where that noise is coming from, it's well worth greasing and properly torquing every bolt on your bike – unless they are specifically designed to be run dry. As a bonus, you'll also know that everything is correctly tightened up too.

BARS, STEM & HEADSET

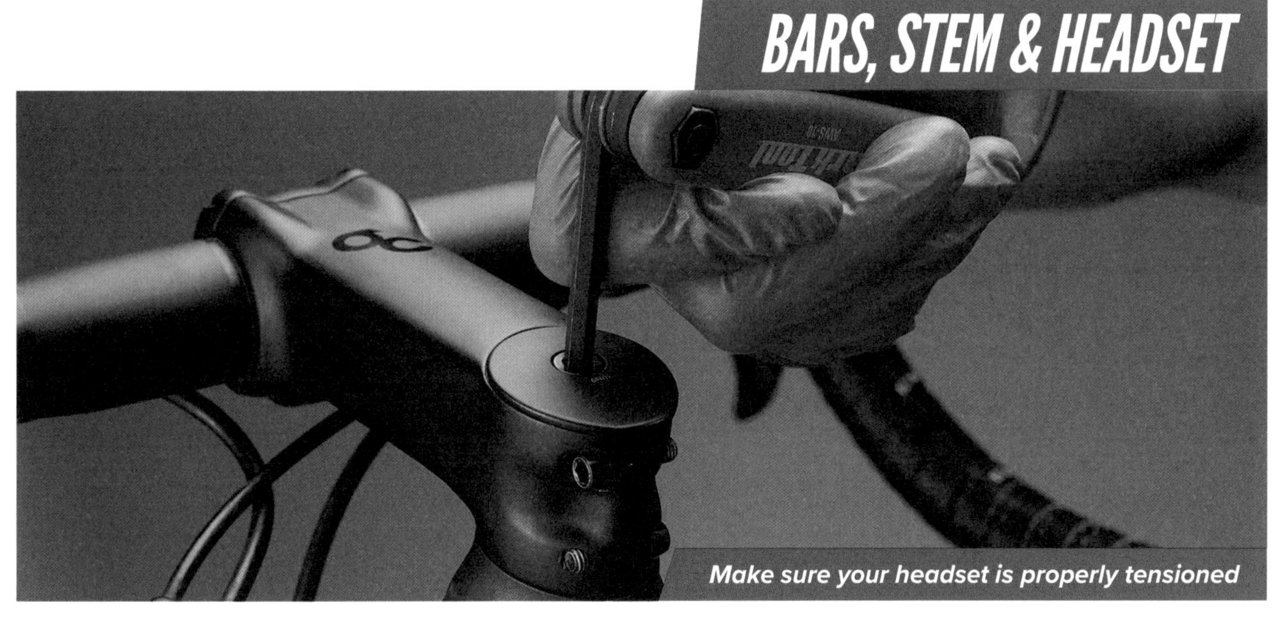
Make sure your headset is properly tensioned

You're likely to notice creaks or clicks from your cockpit when climbing or sprinting as this puts extra pressure through these components.

First, check your stem bolts and your brake lever clamp bolts are done up to the correct torque settings specified by the manufacturer. To get to your lever clamp bolts, roll back your brake hoods and you'll see them below. Don't forget to put grease or anti-seize on the bolts of metal stems. You could also use some fibre grip on the clamped section of bar in the stem (even if you have metal components) to reduce any chance of slippage, and check that the stem face plate has the same gap at the top and the bottom.

It's easy to check if your headset is overtightened or is in need of service, just lift the front wheel and slowly turn the bars left and right. If everything is OK, it should all feel nice and smooth, but if it feels stiff or you can feel the bearings moving, you'll need to loosen the stem cap bolt or give your headset a service. If it feels too loose or has any play, you'll need to tighten it. See page 192 for how to sort any of these issues out.

If your cockpit is still creaking and your handlebars have taken a whack at some point, you may well have a crack on your handlebars – even if they are aluminium. The only way to know for sure is to remove your bar tape. If there's a crack, however small, don't ride your bike as the bars could fail when out on the road. Unfortunately, you will need to replace them.

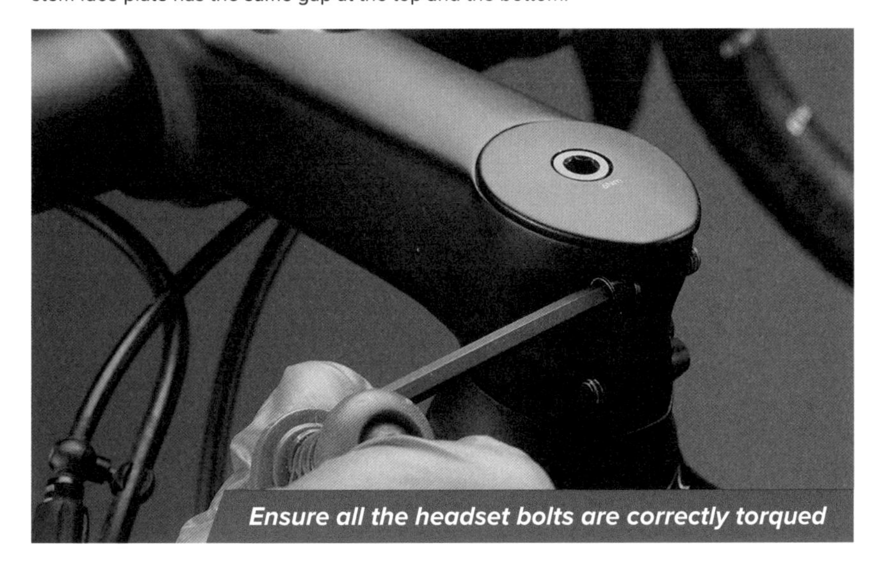
Ensure all the headset bolts are correctly torqued

"Check your stem bolts and brake lever clamps are done up to the correct torque settings specified by the manufacturer"

HOW TO SILENCE A NOISY BIKE

BRAKES

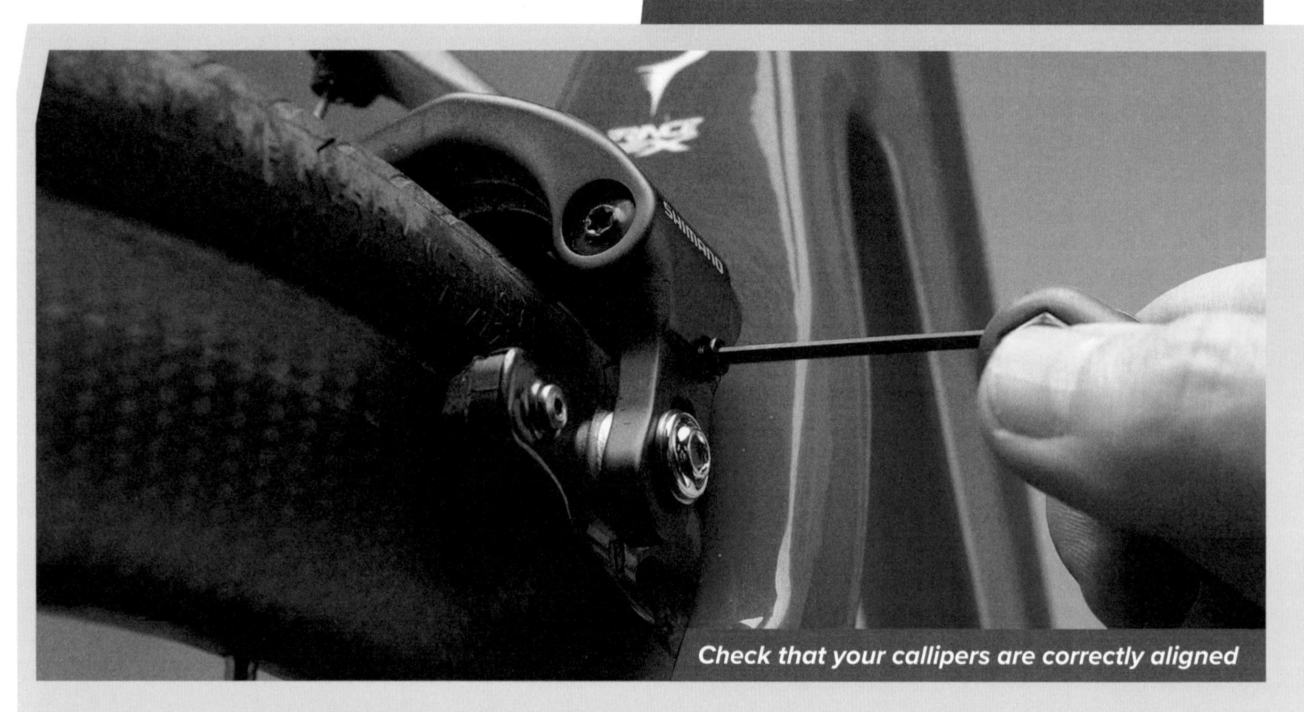
Check that your callipers are correctly aligned

As well as being deafening, a screeching brake is a less efficient brake. Here's how to sort them out

"The good news is that you can cure your noisy brakes with some thorough cleaning"

Your brakes are open to all kinds of contamination from any road dirt and grime that gets thrown up when riding, to over-sprays of lubricants and polishes when applied to other parts of your bike. The end result of all this contamination is a less efficient braking system and a deafening squeal whenever you grab the levers.

Clean Them Up

The good news is that you can cure your noisy brakes with some thorough cleaning and this applies to both rim and disc varieties. First, take a look at your brake pads. Are they covered in a powdery-like, dark substance, or maybe they look slightly glazed and shiny? If that is the case, get yourself some isopropyl alcohol, apply it to a nice, clean cloth and simply rub it over the surfaces of your pads to try and get rid of any of that contamination.

If that didn't do the trick, get some emery paper, or some very fine sandpaper, and carefully rub off that glossy appearance, so the surface of your pads has more of a matte finish to it. You can do this on rim brakes with only the wheel removed, but if you're working on disc brakes, you should take the pads from the callipers to do this (see page 130). Rim brake users also need to make sure their braking surfaces are as clean as possible. Use a sponge and some hot soapy water, or even your isopropyl alcohol and a cloth, and thoroughly clean the braking surface of your wheels with a firm amount of pressure.

Even if they look fairly clean, you'll be amazed at how much dirt you can shift. Try to lift out all that braking dust and road grime to try and make them look as shiny as possible, this will massively improve the efficiency of your brakes as well as making them far less likely to squeal.

If you're running disc brakes, you can clean up your rotors with hot soapy water or some disc brake cleaner. Ensure not to touch the rotor surfaces with your bare hands as the natural oils in your skin can contaminate them all over again.

Want To Fit New Rim Brakes?
Turn back to page 122

BRAKES

Check Your Pads

If your pads and braking surfaces are thoroughly clean, but you're still getting noise, it could be that your pads are past their best and are the cause for the noise. Inspect them closely. If you've got rim brakes, check you've still got at least a few millimeters of rubber compound left on them. Some pads have wear indicators or grooves in the surface. Once those grooves disappear, it's time for some fresh pads.

With disc brake pads, if they've got less than a millimetre of compound left on there, it's time to replace them (see page 130). When buying new pads, organic compounds are usually quieter than metallic (aka sintered) versions, however, they don't tend to last as long.

Toeing-In Rim Brake Pads

To minimise the likelihood of brake squeal, rim brake pads need to be toed-in. This means ensuring the first two-thirds of the pad touch the rim a fraction before that last third. The easiest way to toe-in your pads is to take a thin piece of card (e.g. a business card) and hold it between the pad and rim covering the rear third of the pad. Then pull and hold your brake lever, loosen off then retighten the pad retaining bolt.

Right Pads For Your Wheels?

Finally, if you're running rim brakes, make sure you've got the correct brake pads fitted, i.e. pads designed for carbon rims or designed for aluminium rims, as the braking compounds are very different. If you're running aluminium-specific brake pads on carbon rims, you're likely to get loud screams, poor braking performance and, ultimately, premature wear of the braking surfaces on your expensive carbon wheelset.

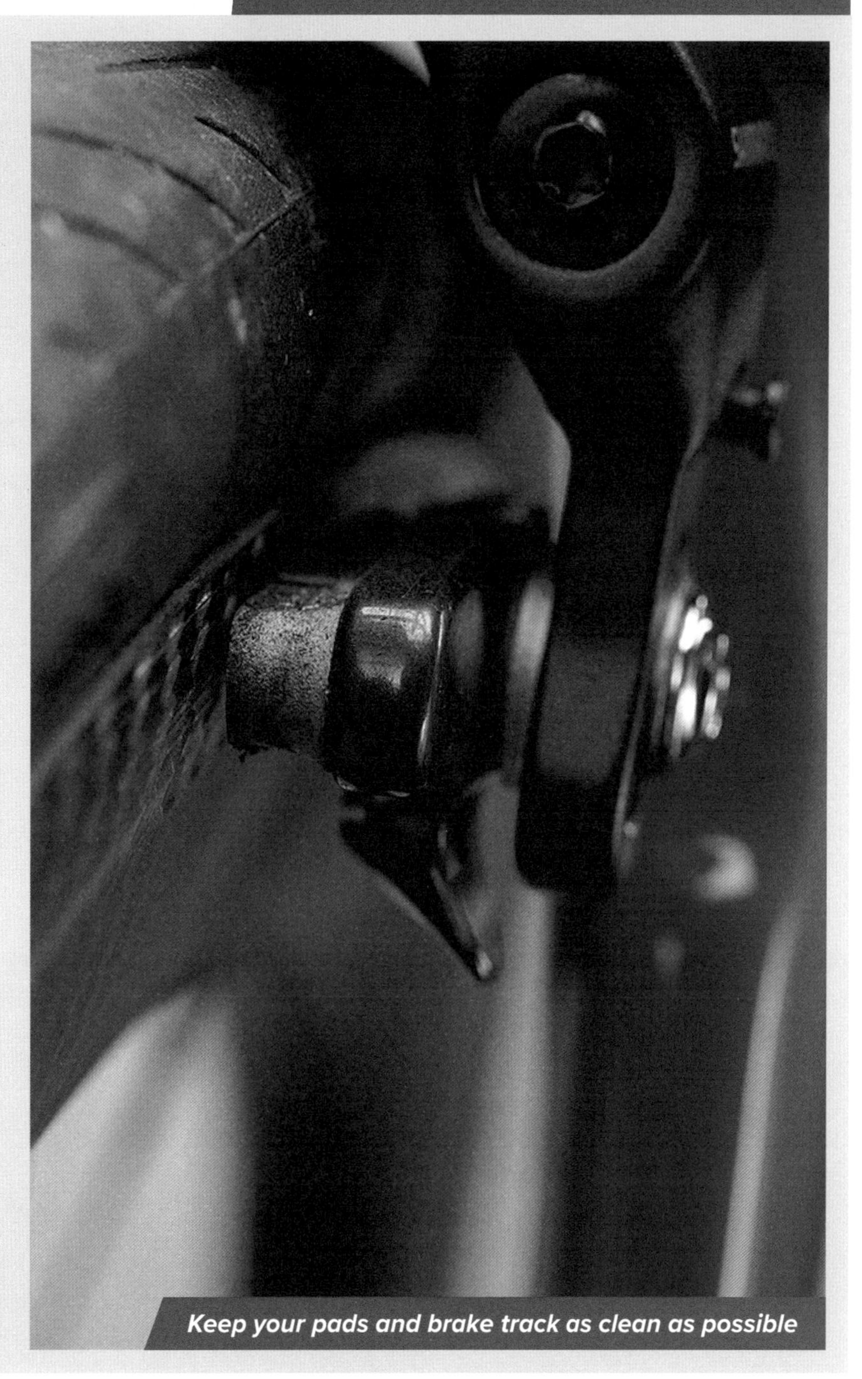

Keep your pads and brake track as clean as possible

PROBLEMS SOLVED

ESSENTIAL ROADSIDE HACKS & FIXES

However well you prepare, things can still go wrong with your bike on a ride. Here's how to solve the most common problems

TOOLS

- *Multitool with all the Allen key and screwdriver heads you need for the components of your bike*
- *Chain-tool*
- *Connecting chainlink that matches your chain (10, 11 or 12-speed, etc)*
- *Pump*
- *Patch kit and spare inner tube*
- *Tyre plugs and tool if you're running tubeless*
- *Tyre levers*
- *Spoke key*
- *Nitrile gloves to keep your hands clean*
- *Small torch if you're riding at night*
- *Adhesive tape*
- *Zip-ties*

We've all been there out on a nice ride enjoying ourselves and next thing you get a mechanical out of nowhere and you're sat there twiddling your thumbs not knowing how to fix it. Most of us won't have a team car with a mechanic ready to jump out and fix the problem either, so here are the essential skills you need to know to get you going again.

A Safe Place To Fix Your Bike

Whatever the issue and however long it's likely to take to fix it, get yourself and your bike to a safe place to work. It may be a quiet back road when you get to work, but a car or lorry might come charging round the bend and if you've got your bike upside down in bits then that's going to be a big problem. Even gravel roads have farm and forestry traffic and you can guarantee they'll appear at the worst possible moment.

In other words, make sure you find a gateway or lay-by well off the road, or at least get yourself onto the verge. If you're working on grass though that adds an extra issue of losing bits, so try and find a clear patch for your wild workshop.

> **"Make sure you find a gateway or lay-by well off the road, or at least get yourself onto the verge"**

DROPPED CHAIN

The chain falling off the chainrings when shifting is a very common problem. Sometimes you can scoop it back on while you're still rolling by shifting the other way and pedalling very slowly and carefully. If you don't want to risk scuffing your frame or cranks though, stop safely as soon as possible.

(1) Start by shifting into the ring nearest the chain. So the inside ring if the chain has fallen off the inside, or the outer ring if it's gone over the top. Feel underneath the bike for the chain. Grab it just back from the chainset and pull it back onto the chainring you've shifted into. **(2)** Wrap it as far round the chainring as you can. **(3)** Carefully turn the pedals backwards so the replaced chain section goes back through the front derailleur cage and the chain is completely back in place on the ring. Pedal forward to check everything is working fine and you're good to go.

If the chain has come off at the rear then it's a similar process but you might find it's really well jammed between the cassette and spokes or the cassette and frame. If the former, you'll have to try and pull it out carefully – wiggling it sideways when pulling can help to free it. If the chain is jammed between cogs and frame then its best to try and remove the wheel to reduce the chance of frame damage.

Once the chain is back on, check the gear hanger is correctly aligned – as if not, it may have caused the shifting issue. Even if it looks fine, avoid shifting into the top or bottom cog until you can adjust the derailleur limiting screws and stop it from happening again.

1

2

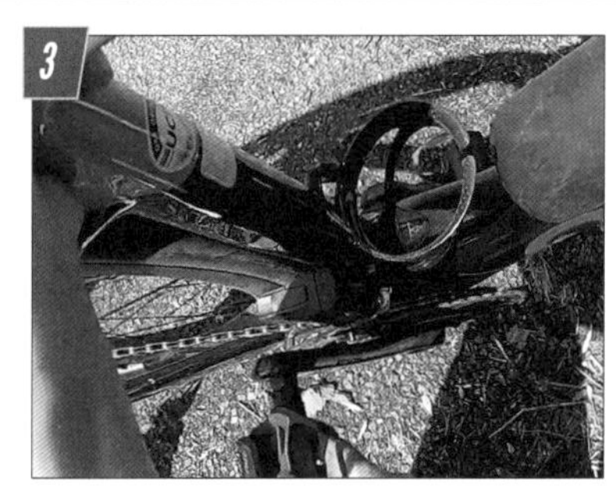
3

SNAPPED SPOKE

A single snapped spoke is unlikely to cause a wheel collapse, but the biggest potential issue is the spoke getting jammed in something and locking the wheel up. Find the spoke and try and remove it by pushing it though at the hub end and unscrewing it from the nipple on the rim. If you need to take off a 6-bolt rotor to remove the spoke that shouldn't be an issue – presuming you have the right tools. However, if you can't get it out because there's a cassette or centrelock rotor in the way, you'll need to try and secure it safely. If you've been smart and bought tape or zip-ties with you, now is the time to feel very smug. If not, take the snapped spoke and hook or gently twist it round one of the neighbouring spokes. It doesn't matter if it rattles a bit, but make sure it doesn't spring back out again when you spin the wheel. While spinning the wheel, check that it's still true too. Also check the other spokes in the wheel to see if any of them are loose or damaged. If the wheel needs truing or you need to tighten spokes then refer to our wheel truing guide on page 164. If it's still running straight though, take the shortest and safest route home avoiding any rough roads.

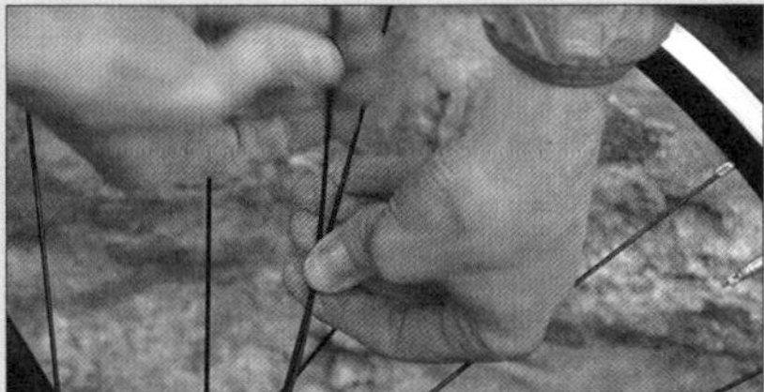

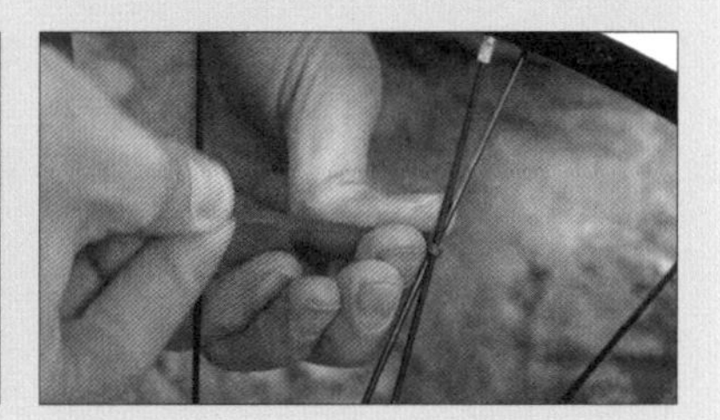

ESSENTIAL ROADSIDE HACKS & FIXES

BAR DROOP

Over time, things can work loose on your bike, so we recommend giving it a check over making sure everything is tight at least once a month. **(1)** Should your bars slip while riding after hitting a pothole, **(2)** they will need fixing before going any further as they're likely to slip again. This is a really easy fix if you or a riding buddy has a multi-tool, but if not, head to a local bike shop and ask if you can borrow their Allen keys.

(3) Loosen the stem front bolts a little, **(4)** then get your handlebars back into the right position. **(5)** Tighten each bolt back up, **(6)** but don't go crazy and overtighten them. Check they are secure by standing in front of the bike with your hands on the hoods and putting a little downward pressure on the bars. **(7)** Increase the pressure until you're giving them a proper shunt and if they're still staying put, then it's safe to ride.

1

2

3

4

5

6

7

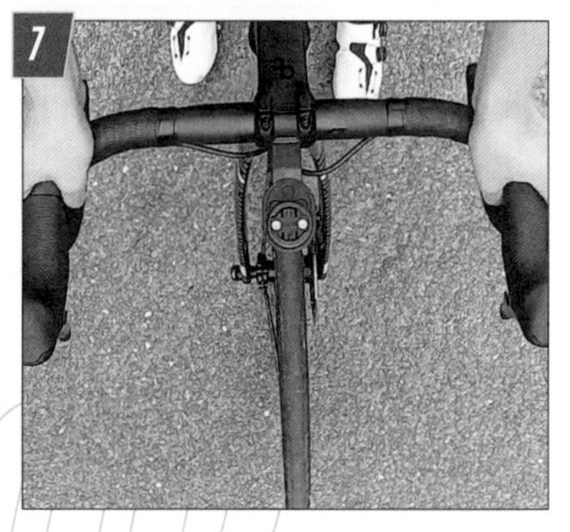

BAR DROOP

BRAKE RUB

If your brakes start rubbing while out on the road, while there are a few potential causes, most are easy to put right. First, check that the wheel is correctly sitting in the dropouts. **(1)** Open the quick-release skewer and press the wheel firmly into the dropouts. Close the skewer and give the wheel a spin to see if that's done the trick. If not and you're running disc brakes, check the rotor is straight. If there's no obvious wobble, **(2)** check for loose rotor mounting bolts, or the lockring on centrelock versions. Next, check to see where it's actually rubbing by looking down either side of the rim or rotor as you slowly spin the wheel. If the wheel is buckled there's not much you can do here, but if brake calliper has moved out of position, on a disc brake, loosen the calliper mounting bolts, **(3)** then retighten them while pulling the lever. On a rim brake, **(4)** check the calliper is properly aligned on the fork or stays and adjust the mounting bolt or **(5)** centring screw. If the problem is caused by disc brake brake pads not pulling back properly, remove the wheel and try to **(6)** carefully push them back into the callipers. If one of your rim brake pads looks out of position. **(7)** Squeeze and hold the calliper on both sides so that the pad is sitting near the rim, then loosen and re-position the pad so it will **(8)** hit the rim's braking track when the lever is pulled.

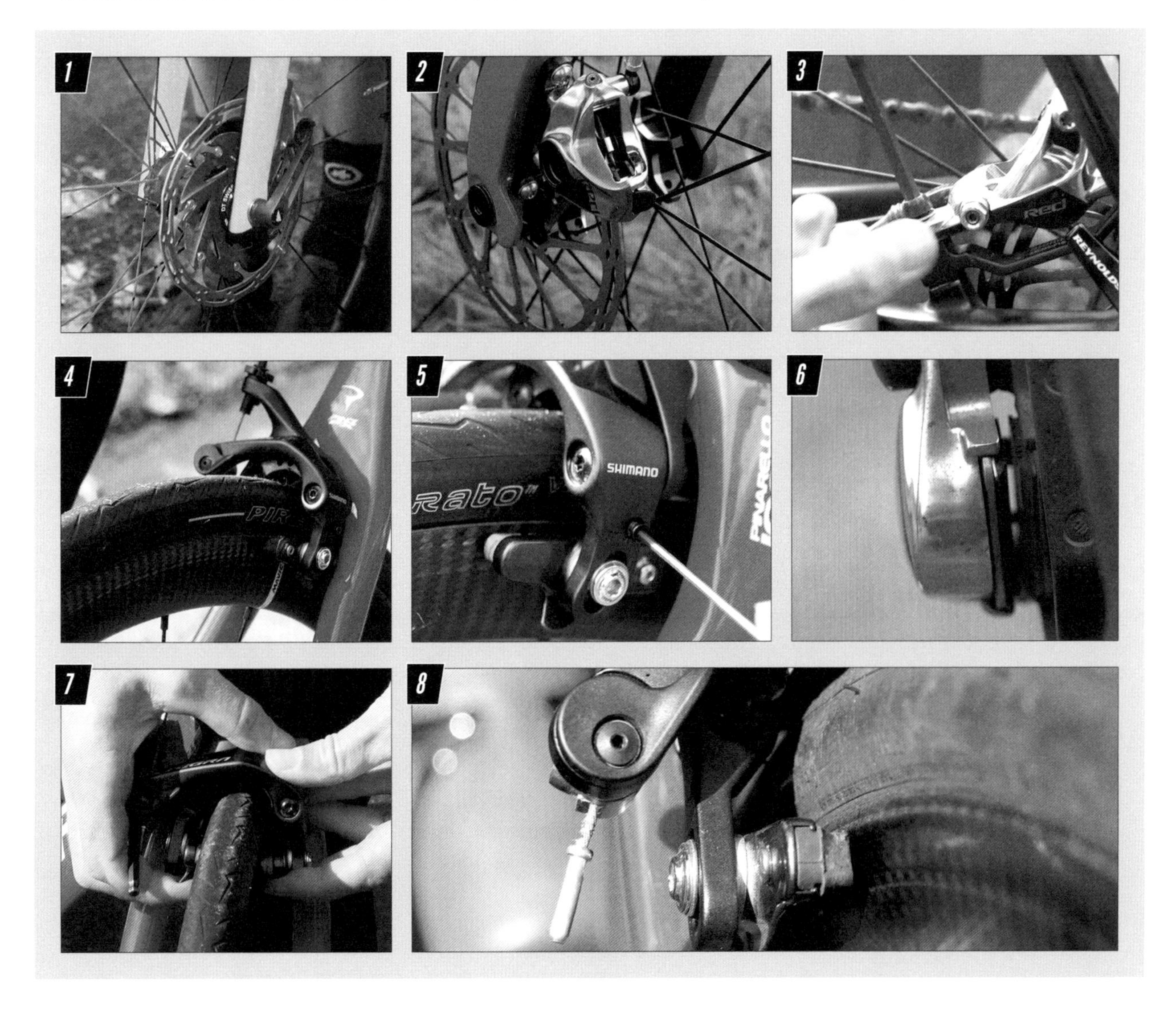

FIXING A CHAIN WITH A MASTER LINK

(1) Should you snap your chain while out riding you're unlikely to have a serious problem as long as you have **(2)** a chain tool and a master link. You'll normally have an undamaged inner link at one end and a broken outer on the other. A master link allows you to make a quick repair, but first you'll need to remove the broken outer link with your chain tool. **(3)** Use the tool to push out the rivet on the broken outer so you have **(4)** two inner ends.

(5) Feed the chain carefully back through the derailleurs making sure it runs correctly around the jockey wheels and tabs on the rear. You want to end up with the two chain ends meeting on the lower chain run, midway between the chainrings and the cassette.

A handy bit of kit to carry is **(6)** an old bit of spoke bent at both ends. Use this to hold the two ends of the chain together when fitting your master link. Ensuring you **(7)** orientate the link the right way up, **(8)** insert the pins into each end of the chain and push each one through the opposing side of the link. **(9)** Now you need to properly seat the pins. Standing on the pedals with the brakes on will pull them into place. Spin the cranks slowly to check the chain runs OK. If you've had to remove more than one link be careful using the big chainring and big sprocket as the chain might now be too short.

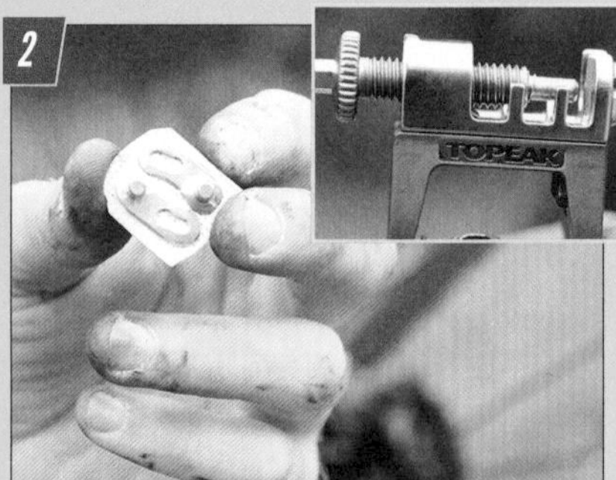

FIXING A CHAIN WITH A MASTER LINK

Want To Fit A New Chain?
Head over to page 68

4
5
6
7
8
9

FIXING A ROADSIDE PUNCTURE

There's nothing more deflating than the sound of air escaping from an inner tube when you're riding along. So let's have a look at how to repair a punctured inner tube at the side of the road.

(1) Remove the punctured wheel from the bike (see page 40 if you're unsure about this). With the wheel out you want to try and put the bike somewhere where it won't get damaged.

(2) Use your tyre levers to carefully unhook one side of the tyre. This is easier if you fully deflate the tube and pull the bead into the middle of the rim first. Once you have one side completely off, pull out the inner tube. Whether you're repairing that tube or just sticking a fresh one in for speed, check the inside of the tyre for anything that might have caused the puncture and remove it. Take care though, as if it's a bit of glass or a thorn, you could well cut your finger.

If you're repairing the inner tube, re-inflate it slightly, then **(3)** rotate it tube near your face as listen for any hissing and try to feel the escaping air on your cheek.

1

2

3

Once you've found the hole, use the sandpaper in your repair kit to roughen the area around the puncture to help the repair patch stick. If you're using a traditional patch, then dab rubber solution around the hole over a bigger area than the patch and wait for it to dry. **(4)** Apply the patch and hold it in place until it's secure. If you're using a self-adhesive patch, put it straight onto the tube, making sure that the offending hole is in the central most part of the patch. Apply pressure to the patch for about a minute so that it sticks as well as possible.

Put a small amount of air into the inner tube. Not enough to stretch the patch and risk it peeling open, just enough to give it a little bit of shape so it's less likely to get trapped when you put it back in the tyre. One final check to do before reinserting the inner tube is to carefully run your fingers around inside of the tyre just in case you missed the cause of the puncture the first time, or there's another sharp stuck in there.

Push the valve through the wheel's rim hole and then push the inner tube into the tyre all the way round. Fit the open side of the tyre back onto the rim – starting opposite the valve and working your way back to it. **(5)** Be careful not to trap the tube between the tyre and the rim or you may well cause another puncture.

Carefully inflate the tube to around 40 or 50psi pressure, then have a look to make sure it is properly seated onto the rim. **(6)** An easy way to do that is to check the sidewall. It should look the same all the way around, just above the braking surface or edge of the rim. If it's not, you can wrestle it into position with your thumbs or just deflate, relocate and go again. Fully inflate the tyre and check again for any escaping air. If all looks and sounds good, then refit the wheel, give it a spin to double-check everything is OK and carry on with your ride.

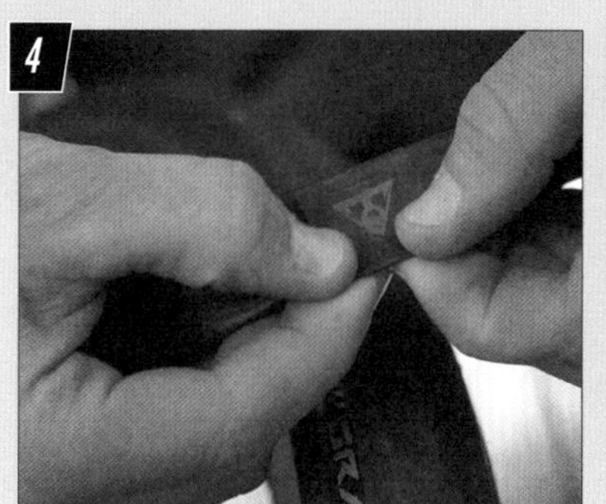
4

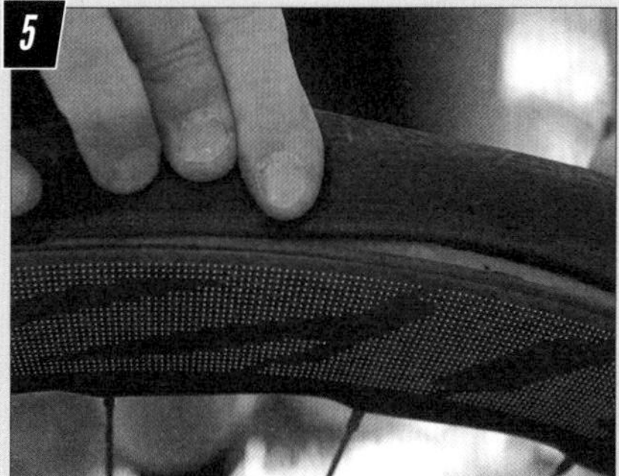
5

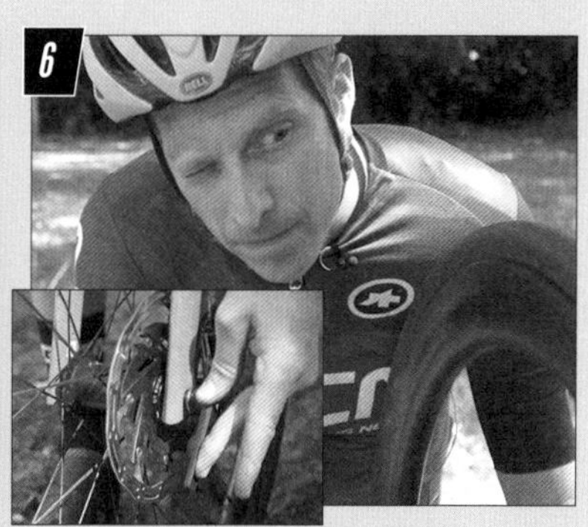
6

FIXING A ROADSIDE PUNCTURE

GCN
GLOBAL CYCLING NETWORK